MW00629198

SUETONIUS

I

31

SUETONIUS

WITH AN ENGLISH TRANSLATION BY
J. C. ROLFE, Ph.D.

PROFESSOR OF THE LATIN LANGUAGE AND LITERATURE
IN THE UNIVERSITY OF PENNSYLVANIA

IN TWO VOLUMES

I

CAMBRIDGE, MASSACHUSETTS
HARVARD UNIVERSITY PRESS
LONDON
WILLIAM HEINEMANN LTD
MCMLXXIX

British ISBN 0 434 99031 0
American ISBN 0-674-99035-8

First printed 1913
Reprinted 1920, 1924, 1930, 1944
Revised and Reprinted 1951
Reprinted 1960, 1964, 1970, 1979

Printed in Great Britain

PREFACE

THE translation of the *Lives of the Caesars* is based upon the text of Maximilian Ihm, Leipzig, 1907 (*editio minor*, 1908) with some slight changes in punctuation, capitalisation, and orthography, to conform more nearly with English and American usage. Where Ihm does not offer a readable text, conjectures have been admitted and mentioned in the footnotes, and in a few other cases a different reading from his has been adopted.

The aim has been a translation, rather than the easier task of a paraphrase. The version of Philemon Holland (London, 1606) cannot be surpassed in style and spirit, and it is more accurate than any other English translation. An attempt has been made to compete with it in the only possible way, namely in greater fidelity to a better text than was available in his day, and in a nearer approach to the manner of Suetonius. The text and interpretation of Suetonius offer many difficulties, all of which have received careful consideration; but it is hardly to be hoped that the results have been satisfactory in all cases.

PREFACE

I am indebted for many valuable suggestions to the excellent German translation of Adolf Stahr, Stuttgart, 1857, in the new edition published at Munich in 1912.

To the *Lives of the Caesars* have been added those extracts from the *Lives of Illustrious Men* which afford a continuous text and are generally regarded as authentic. See the Prefatory Note to Part II.

A complete Index to the whole work will be found at the end of Volume II.

JOHN C. ROLFE.

PHILADELPHIA, *April*, 1913.

CONTENTS

		PAGE
PREFACE	. . . .	V
THE LIFE AND WORKS OF SUETONIUS	. . . .	ix
THE LIVES OF THE CAESARS	. . . .	xv
GENERAL CHARACTERISTICS	. . . .	xvii
THE MANUSCRIPTS	. . . .	xxi
BIBLIOGRAPHICAL NOTE	. . . .	xxvii
SIGLA	. . . .	xxxi
BOOK I.—THE DEIFIED JULIUS	. . . .	1
BOOK II.—THE DEIFIED AUGUSTUS	. . . .	121
BOOK III.—TIBERIUS	. . . .	289
BOOK IV.—GAIUS CALIGULA	. . . .	403
STEMMA OF THE JULIO-CLAUDIAN EMPERORS	. . .	498

THE LIFE AND WORKS OF SUETONIUS

GAIUS SUETONIUS TRANQUILLUS is one of the numerous Roman writers who give us little information about themselves. He only tells us [1] that he was the son of Suetonius Laetus, a Roman knight, who took part in the battle of Betriacum as tribune of the thirteenth legion; for four other casual allusions [2] add nothing of importance, although they are of assistance in conjecturing the date of his birth, which Mommsen [3] assigns to the year 77 A.D., Macé [4] with somewhat greater probability to 69. The rest of our information is derived from the *Letters* of the Younger Pliny and from a single allusion in Spartianus, who in the time of Diocletian wrote a biography of Hadrian.

His birthplace is unknown, and it is possible that he was one of the few Roman writers who were born in the city of Rome.[5] The date of his death is also uncertain. Our last reference to him is in 121, but

---

[1] *Otho*, x. 1.
[2] *Calig.* xix. 3; *Nero*, lvii. 2; *Dom.* xii. 2; *Gr.* iv.
[3] *Hermes*, iii. p. 43.   [4] *Essai sur Suétone*, pp. 35 ff.
[5] There is no prominent writer of whom this can be asserted positively; it seems probable in the case of Caesar and Lucretius; for Suetonius see Macé, *Essai*, p. 33 f.

the number and extent of his works, and the implication in one of Pliny's Letters [1] that he was slow to publish, suggest that he must have lived to a good old age, perhaps including a part of the reign of Antoninus Pius. From Pliny we learn that he practised at the bar, [2] although it was apparently only for a short time. That he was a schoolmaster, which is asserted by Macé and others, seems to lack evidence. [3] He took no part in political life, and although he secured a military tribuneship through Pliny's good offices, he soon had it transferred to a relative. [4] He received from Trajan the *ius trium liberorum*, [5] but this was not justified by the number of his offspring. Apparently he had no children, but there is no evidence that his marriage was unhappy as well as unfruitful, [6] as some assert. That he received the privilege from an emperor so reluctant to grant it to those who could not legally lay claim to it, is perhaps evidence of his high character. In his letter to Trajan Pliny refers to Suetonius as *contubernalis*, which indicates an intimate friendship and an approximately equal age. The latter is not inconsistent with Pliny's language in *Epist.* 3. 8. 1, [7] since his position was so much higher than that of Suetonius, and it is in accord with *Epist.* 9. 34, where Pliny consults his friend as to the advisability of reading his verses in public.

The letters of Pliny which refer to Suetonius cover approximately the period from 96 to 112.

---

[1] 5. 10.   [2] *Epist.* 1. 18.
[3] *Scholasticis dominis*, in Pliny, *Epist.* 1. 24. 4, means "scholars turned landowners."   [4] Pliny, *Epist.* 3. 8.
[5] Pliny, *Epist.* 10. 94 and 95.
[6] *parum felix*, Pliny, *Epist.* 10. 94. 2.
[7] *reverentia quam mihi praestas.*

THE LIFE AND WORKS OF SUETONIUS

From Spartianus [1] we learn that he held the position of secretary [2] to Hadrian, probably during the period when his friend and patron Gaius Septicius Clarus was a prefect of the praetorian guard (119 to 121). It was doubtless at this time that Suetonius gave Hadrian the little statuette of Augustus, referred to in *Aug.* vii. 1. Spartianus tells us that both Suetonius and Septicius were discharged by Hadrian, "quod apud Sabinam uxorem *iniussu eius* familiarius tunc se egerant quam reverentia domus aulicae postulabat." While this statement is far from clear or definite, the words *iniussu eius* suggest some violation of court etiquette, rather than any more serious misconduct. From this time on we lose sight of Suetonius, and it seems probable that he lived in retirement and devoted himself to literary work.

The references to his works are considerably more numerous. A catalogue of them is preserved by Suidas,[3] to which additions have been made from other sources. He was a man of scholarly tastes and habits, and according to the fashion of his later years, when the greater part of the work appears to have been done, apparently wrote in Greek as well as in Latin. His writings were in the fields of history (biography), antiquities, natural history and grammar, and may be listed as follows :—

I.—BIOGRAPHICAL AND HISTORICAL.

1. The Lives of the Caesars.
2. On Illustrious Men (in the field of literature).
3. On Famous Courtesans.
4. On the Kings.

[1] *Vit. Hadr.* 11. 3.
[2] *Ab epistulis*, referred to by Spartianus by the later title of *magister epistularum.*   [3] *s.v.* Τράγκυλλος.

THE LIFE AND WORKS OF SUETONIUS

II.—Antiquities.

1. On Rome (*Roma*).
      (*a*) Manners and Customs.
      (*b*) The Roman Year.
      (*c*) The Roman Festivals.
      (*d*) Clothing.
2. The Games of the Greeks.
3. On Public Offices.
4. On Cicero's *De Re Publica*.

III.—Natural History (*Pratum*).

1. On Mankind (On Bodily Defects).
2. On the Reckoning of Time.
3. On Nature.

IV.—Grammatical.

1. On Terms of Abuse in Greek.
2. Grammatical Questions (*De Rebus Variis*).
3. On the Critical Marks used in Books.[1]

Of all these the only work which has come down to us entire, or nearly so, is the *Lives of the Caesars*, published in 120. It includes the biographies of twelve "Caesars," from Julius to Domitian, and except for some inconsiderable lacunae, lacks only the first few chapters of the life of Julius. From a reference of Johannes Lydus,[2] of the sixth century, it appears that he used a codex with the dedication

[1] Schanz, *Gesch. d. röm. Litteratur*, in Müller's *Handbuch d. klass. Altertumswissenschaft*, viii. 3, pp. 53 f. Various arrangements of these eighteen titles are made by different scholars; see for example Macé, *Essai*, p. 355, and the editions of Suetonius.   [2] *De Magistr.* 2. 6, p. 102 Fuss.

to Septicius Clarus, and hence presumably with the missing portion of the *Julius*. This must therefore have been lost between the sixth century and the early part of the ninth century (see p. xxi). Preud'-homme [1] believes that he has demonstrated the existence of a complete manuscript of the fifth century, written in capitals.

Besides the *Lives of the Caesars* we have considerable fragments of the *Lives of Illustrious Men*, of which those which are generally regarded as authentic and offer a continuous text of any length are given in Part II. [2]

The voluminous publications of Suetonius gave him lasting fame and were used as sources by later writers in various fields. In this way a great number of detached passages from his lost works and from the missing portions of the *De Viris Illustribus* have been preserved, in the form of more or less literal excerpts. The historical writers, such as Eutropius, Aurelius Victor, and Orosius drew on him freely, and so frequently reproduce his exact language as to be of occasional help in the criticism of his text.

He exercised a great influence on the form of historical writing, which took a biographical turn for some centuries. He found imitators and successors in Marius Maximus (165-230), whose works have perished, and in the writers of the Augustan History (*Scriptores Historiae Augustae*), whose biographies have come down to us, while Tacitus did not find a follower until the time of Ammianus Marcellinus (330-400). His influence extended to the Christian writers and

---

[1] *Mémoires couronnés et autres mémoires publiées par l'Académie royale de Belgique*, lxiii. pp. 84–88.

[2] See Schanz, *l.c.* p. 47, and the Prefatory Note to Part II.

is seen in the form of the *Life of Ambrosius* by his secretary Paulinus, and even to the Middle Ages, when Einhardus wrote a *Life of Charles the Great* on the model of Suetonius, perhaps using the manuscript which is the archetype of those that have come down to us (see p. xxi).

His other works were no less esteemed as authorities. Tertullian in his *De Spectaculis* made use of Suetonius's work of a similar title, and we find his influence in Censorinus, Solinus, Macrobius, in the scholiasts on Germanicus, Horace, and Juvenal, in the commentator Servius, and especially in Isidore, who has preserved many fragments of the lost works of Suetonius.

PART I

THE LIVES OF THE CAESARS

THE LIVES OF THE CAESARS

General Characteristics

The biographies of Suetonius are interesting both for their contents and as a form of literature. Strictly speaking they are neither history nor biography. Great historical events, such as Caesar's campaigns in Gaul, are dismissed in a brief chapter, or with a casual allusion, like the defeat of Varus. The acts of the senate and people, and the edicts of the emperors, receive fuller attention, but are wholly subordinate to the personal element. On the other hand no ideal life is presented, to inspire imitation and point a moral, and no attempt is made to trace the development of character as influenced by heredity, education, and environment. The *Lives*, as Leo has shown,[1] are of the " grammatical " type,[2] and they furnish material for biographies in the true sense of the word, giving the thoughtful reader abundant opportunity for the reflexions and deductions which the writer has omitted.

[1] *Die griechisch-römischen Biographie*, Leipzig, 1901.
[2] These were originally designed as introductions to works of literature, and their material was drawn in a great measure from those works themselves ; but they were afterwards extended to men eminent in other fields. For fuller details on this and other points I may refer to my paper " Suetonius and his Biographies" in the *Proc. of the Amer. Philosophical Soc.*, lii. pp. 206 ff.

Suetonius was rather a student and a searcher of records than an observer or inquirer, and his interests lay in the past rather than in the present. The *Lives* become shorter as he approaches his own time, when the written sources were fewer and the opportunities for obtaining personal information greater. He had at his disposal a great amount of material in the form of histories and memoirs which are now lost; he had access either directly or indirectly through his colleague *Ab studiis*, to the imperial archives while he was Hadrian's secretary; and his intimacy with Pliny must have made him familiar with senatorial records and opinions. Occasionally he made use of hearsay evidence[1] and of personal observation.[2] That he seems to have made little use of inscriptions[3] is doubtless due in large measure to his possession of other material which is not available to-day.

On the rare occasions when he gives us an insight into his method of handling his sources, as in *Calig.* viii, it seems clear that he examined conflicting statements with care and intelligence, whenever he thought it necessary to do so; but the plan of his work does not often call for such an investigation. Although he aims to be strictly impartial, scrupulously recounting the virtues and vices of the emperors in separate lists,[4] he seems as a rule to pay little regard to the source from which his information comes, and rarely makes any personal comment.[5]

[1] *Calig.* xix. 3.   [2] *Nero*, lvii. 2; *Dom.* xii. 2.
[3] See Dennison, *Amer. Jour. of Arch.*, sec. series, ii. pp. 26 ff.
[4] See *Aug.* ix., lxi.; *Tib.* lxi. 2.; *Cal.* xxii. 1.; *Nero*, xix. 3.   [5] See, however, *Tib.* xxi. 2; *Tit.* i.

This apparent impartiality does not give us a fair and unbiassed estimate of the emperors. To be convinced of this we have only to imagine a biography of some prominent man of our own day, made up of praise and blame drawn indiscriminately from the organs of his own party and of the opposition, and presented without comment. Just as such a method would yield a considerable number of absolute falsehoods, so many of the statements of Suetonius must be rejected for one reason or another.

He is often, perhaps generally, regarded as a scandal-monger and a man of prurient mind, but neither of these charges seems justified. The details which give rise to the latter are relatively few in number and are presented with the same judicial coldness which characterises his work in general; while the so-called scandal-mongery is in reality a feature of the development of realism [1] in the writing of the early Empire and of the prevailing interest in the personality and private life of prominent men.

The style of Suetonius is rather that of the scholar and investigator than of the man of letters. It is plain and concise, with no attempt at fine writing or rhetorical embellishment, and has been well characterised as "businesslike." His brevity is rarely obscure, and when it is, the obscurity is generally the result of our imperfect knowledge. At times his conciseness yields sentences worthy of Tacitus, but these, like his intensely dramatic passages, are due rather to the subject matter than to any departure from his usual style. He has the grammarian's feeling

[1] See H. T. Peck, *Julius and Augustus*, Introduction, pp. v ff.

for language, and his words are always well chosen and effective. While at times the catalogues of crimes and of petty personal details are somewhat monotonous, the *Lives* as a whole are of absorbing interest, and give us a wealth of anecdotes, witticisms, and curious information of great variety.

THE MANUSCRIPTS

Two critical editions of the *Lives of the Caesars* have appeared within the past few years, those of M. Ihm, Leipzig, 1907, and of L. Preud'homme, Groningen, 1906, each based on a painstaking and independent study of the manuscripts. These show remarkably few deviations from the work of Roth (1858) and from each other. The text therefore may be regarded as practically settled, at least until the independent value of the fifteenth century codices has been demonstrated. (See p. xxv.)

It is generally agreed that all our existing manuscripts are derived from one at Fulda, written in rustic capitals (Ihm) or uncials (Preud'homme). This seems to have been the only one in existence at the time, and it is known to us from a letter of Servatus Lupus, abbot of Ferrières, of the year 884. This codex and a copy of it in minuscules, which was sent to Servatus Lupus at his request, are now lost; but the latter was extensively copied, and the number of manuscripts at present existing is very large. The Fulda codex (Ω, Ihm ; P, Preud'homme [1]) lacked the beginning of the *Life of Julius Caesar* and had other lesser lacunae and numerous errors, but seems to have been free from interpolation. The copies how-

[1] Ω is used by Preud'homme to designate the manuscript mentioned on p. xiii.

ever were extensively emended, so that by the twelfth century the text was in bad condition.

The manuscripts used by Ihm, with the sigla which he employs, are the following; the sigla of Preud'homme are given in parentheses:

M (A). The *codex Memmianus* of the ninth century. Our oldest and best manuscript, either a copy of the one sent to Servatus Lupus or closely related to it, apparently free from interpolations, though not without errors and lacunae. None of our other manuscripts is derived from it. It contains corrections made by another hand, not later than the twelfth century (M^2).

This codex came originally from the monastery of St. Martin of Tours, was later in the possession of Henri de Mesmes, and is now in the National Library in Paris. It is commonly called Memmianus, from de Mesmes, but was formerly called Turonensis; its present designation is Codex Parisinus, 6115, formerly 5984.

G (C). The *codex Gudianus* of the eleventh century, now at Wölffenbuttel (Gudianus, 268). Closely related to M and derived from a similar original, but inferior to it. It has numerous corrections, made in part by the scribe (M^2) and in part in the fifteenth century (M^3).

V (B). The *codex Vaticanus*, 1904, of the eleventh century, a little younger than G but more trustworthy. It frequently agrees with M, and is of almost equal value; but it comes to an end at *Calig.* iii, *detecta sua re*. It was used by Lipsius in 1574. It contains glosses of the same general character as M^2.

Preud'homme regards his D (Parisinus, 5804), of

the fourteenth century, as in the same class with the above; Ihm, who assigns it to the fifteenth century, rates it much less highly.

The other important manuscripts fall into two classes, each represented by a large number of examples. The first class is represented by the following:

L (a). The *codex Laurentianus*, 68. 7, of the twelfth century, in the Mediccan Library at Florence, the *Mediceus Tertius* of Oudendorp. It also contains Caesar, *De Bello Gallico*, and has corrections by an earlier (L²) and a later hand (L³).

P (b). The *codex Parisinus*, 5801, of the twelfth century, with corrections from a manuscript of the second class (P²), according to Ihm.

O (c). The *codex Laurentianus*, 66. 39, of the twelfth century, in the Medicean Library at Florence. Has corrections similar to those in P (O²).

S (f). The *codex Montepessulanus*, 117, of the twelfth century, at Montpelier. Corrected in the same manner as P and O.

T. The *codex Berolinensis*, Lat. 337, of the fourteenth century, formerly *Hulsianus* or *Hagianus*. Frequently agrees with V and L. Corrected by a hand of about the same date as the original scribe.

From the agreement of L, P, O, S, and T, the readings of their archetype are recovered, a lost manuscript from the same original as V, but inferior to V, designated by X (X'). The agreement of X and V gives the readings of X', a lost codex of the class of M and V.

The second class contains more errors and interpolations than the first. It is represented by a very

THE MANUSCRIPTS

large number of manuscripts, of which Ihm uses the following:

Π (β). The *codex Parisinus*, 6116, of the twelfth century, corrected from a manuscript of the variety represented by R.

Q (γ). The *codex Parisinus*, 5802, of the twelfth century, corrected in the fifteenth.

R (a). The *codex Regius* of the twelfth century, in the British Museum (15. C. iii), and rated high by Bentley. It comes to an end with *Dom.* xiv, *non alias magis*, but seems to have been complete in the sixteenth century.

The agreement of these codices gives the readings of their archetype (Y), a lost codex of about the same date as X, but inferior to it; and since P, O, S, and T were corrected from a manuscript of this class, their agreement with Y gives the readings of another lost manuscript Y'.

Besides the manuscripts of the whole work we have two collections of selections, which have some critical value. The earliest of these was made by Heiric of Auxerre between 871 and 876 and based on Lupus's copy of the codex Fuldensis. It is of considerable value, but has suffered from emendation; H (Y). A fuller epitome of the thirteenth century, of comparatively little value, is preserved in codex Parisinus, 17903, formerly Notre-Dame, 188; N.

Ihm and Preud'homme are in substantial agreement in their classification of the manuscripts. The latter divides them into two classes, X and Z, the first including M, V, X, G, δ, and H (or in his nomenclature, A, B, X', C, D, and Y); the second, R, Π, Q, and Suessionensis, 119 (in his nomenclature, a, β, γ, ε).

The only important difference of opinion is as to

the independent value of the fifteenth-century manuscripts, which frequently offer good readings not found in the earlier codices. Roth came to the conclusion that these were mere conjectures, without value in determining the readings of the archetype, and the careful and independent investigations of Ihm and Preud'homme led them to the same opinion. The contrary view is held by some scholars,[1] but cannot be regarded as sufficiently established.

[1] See especially C. L. Smith and A. A. Howard, *Harvard Studies in Class. Phil.*, xii. pp. 54 ff. and 261 ff.

BIBLIOGRAPHICAL NOTE

THE earliest editions are two published in Rome in 1470, one in July by Johannes Campanus, and the other in December by Johannes Aleriensis; these were immediately followed by a Venetian edition of 1471, and all three are regarded as *editiones principes*. Among other early editions are those of Beroaldus, Bologna, 1493 and 1506, the latter with a valuable commentary; Erasmus, Basle, 1518; R. Stephanus (Robert Étienne), Paris, 1543; and Casaubon, Geneva, 1595 and Paris, 1610.

Down to 1820 more than forty editions were issued, including some second editions, among them those of Gronovius, Leyden, 1698; Burman, Amsterdam, 1736, with the full commentary of a number of his predecessors and selections from those of others; Ernesti, Leipzig, 1748 and 1775; Oudendorp, Leyden, 1751; Baumgarten-Crusius, Leipzig, 1816, with a commentary and very full indices (*Clavis Suetoniana*). This is still the standard annotated edition. It was issued with some additions by C. B. Hase at Paris in 1828. Bentley planned an edition which was never finished, but his material is preserved in the British Museum.

In later times the editions have been few in number. That of C. L. Roth, Leipzig, 1858, was

the standard text until the appearance of those of Ihm and Preud'homme.

The *Lives of the Caesars* still lacks a commentary in English and a full and satisfactory one in any language. There are annotated editions of separate lives by H. T. Peck, *Julius and Augustus*, New York, 1893²; E. S. Shuckburgh, *Augustus*, Cambridge, 1896; and J. B. Pike, *Tiberius, Caligula, Claudius and Nero*, Boston, 1903; to these may be added H. Smilda, *Claudius*, Groningen, 1896, and C. Hofstee, *Galba, Otho and Vitellius*, Groningen, 1898.

The *Caesars* have been translated into English by Philemon Holland, London, 1606; John Clarke, London, 1732, with the Latin text; and by Alexander Thomson, London, 1796. A revision of Thomson's translation was made by T. Forester, and published in the Bohn Library (London) without a date.

Of books and monographs dealing with Suetonius the following may be mentioned : A. Macé, *Essai sur Suétone*, Paris, 1900 ; Fr. Leo, *Die griechisch-römischen Biographie*, Leipzig, 1901 ; L. Preud'homme, *Première, deuxième, troisième étude sur l'histoire du texte de Suétone de vita Caesarum*, Bulletins de l'Académie royale de Belgique, 1902 and 1904 ; Ihm, *Hermes*, 36, 37 and 40 ; H. R. Thimm, *De usu atque elocutione C. Suet. Tranq.*, Regimonti, 1867 ; P. Bagge, *De elocutione C. Suet. Tranq.*, Upsala, 1875 ; I. W. Freund, *De Suetonii usu atque genere dicendi*, Breslau, 1901 ; W. Dennison, " The Epigraphic Sources of Suetonius," *Amer. Jour. of Archæology*, Second Series, II., pp. 26 ff.; L. Damasso, *La Grammatica di C. Suet. Tranq.*, Turin, 1906 ; C. L. Smith, *Harvard Studies in Class. Phil.*, xii. pp. 54 ff ; A. A. Howard, *idem*, vii, 210 ff., x. pp. 23 ff., and xii. pp. 261 ff.; J. C. Rolfe, " Suetonius

and his Biographies," *Proc. Amer. Philosophical Soc.* lii, pp. 206 ff.

The reader may be reminded of S. Baring-Gould's *Tragedy of the Caesars*, London, 1902 ; Sienkiewicz's *Quo Vadis* ; Gardthausen's *Augustus und seine Zeit*, Leipzig, 1891; Shuckburgh's *Augustus*, London, 1903; and of other general and special works dealing with the period.

Editor's Note (1979): The following items may now be added:

(A) Editions
 Life of Julius, H. E. Butler–M. Cary, 1927
 Life of Augustus, M. Adams, 1939
 Lives of Galba-Domitian, G. W. Mooney, 1930
 Life of Vespasian, A. W. Braithwaite, 1927
 De Poetis, A. Rostagni, 1944

(B) Index Verborum, A. A. Howard and C. N. Jackson, repr. 1963

(C) D. R. Stuart, *Epochs of Greek and Roman Biography*, 1928
 W. Steidle, *Sueton und die antike Biographie*, 1963

G.P.G.

SIGLA

Ω = the archetype of our existing codices, restored by the agreement of X' and Y'.

M = Codex Memmianus.

G = Codex Gudianus.

X' = the archetype of V and X.

    V = Codex Vaticanus.

    X = the archetype of
        L = Codex Laurentianus, 68.7.
        P = Codex Parisinus, 5801.
        O = Codex Laurentianus, 66.39.
        S = Codex Montepessulanus.
        T = Codex Berolinensis.

Y = the archetype of
        Π = Codex Parisinus, 6116.
        Q = Codex Parisinus, 5802.
        R = Codex Regius.

Y' = the agreement of Y with S and T, usually accompanied by that of P^2 and O (O^2).

ς = all the codices not included in the above list.

THE
LIVES OF THE CAESARS

BOOK I

THE DEIFIED JULIUS

DE VITA CAESARUM

LIBER I

DIVVS IVLIVS

*　*　*　*　*　*　*　*1

I. Annum agens sextum decimum patrem amisit;
sequentibusque consulibus flamen Dialis destinatus
dimissa Cossutia, quae familia equestri sed admodum dives praetextato desponsata fuerat, Corneliam Cinnae quater consulis filiam duxit uxorem,
ex qua illi mox Iulia nata est; neque ut re-
pudiaret compelli a dictatore Sulla ullo modo
2 potuit. Quare et sacerdotio et uxoris dote et gen-
tilicis hereditatibus multatus diversarum partium
habebatur, ut etiam discedere e medio et quamquam morbo quartanae adgravante prope per singulas noctes commutare latebras cogeretur seque
ab inquisitoribus pecunia redimeret, donec per virgines Vestales perque Mamercum Aemilium et Aure-
lium Cottam propinquos et adfines suos veniam
3 impetravit. Satis constat Sullam, cum deprecantibus

[1] *See p.* xxi.

[a] 85/84 B.C., according to the chronology of Suetonius,
which makes the year of Caesar's birth 100 B.C. The argu-
ments in favour of 102 are however very strong.
[b] By Marius and Cinna, consuls in 86; see Vell. 2. 43. 1.

THE LIVES OF THE CAESARS

BOOK I

THE DEIFIED JULIUS

*   *   *   *   *   *   *   *

I. In the course of his sixteenth year [a] he lost his father. In the next consulate, having previously been nominated priest of Jupiter,[b] he broke his engagement with Cossutia, a lady of only equestrian rank, but very wealthy, who had been betrothed to him before he assumed the gown of manhood, and married Cornelia, daughter of that Cinna who was four times consul, by whom he afterwards had a daughter Julia; and the dictator Sulla could by no means force him to put away his wife. Therefore besides being punished by the loss of his priesthood, his wife's dowry, and his family inheritances, Caesar was held to be one of the opposite party. He was accordingly forced to go into hiding, and though suffering from a severe attack of quartan ague, to change from one covert to another almost every night, and save himself from Sulla's detectives by bribes. But at last, through the good offices of the Vestal virgins and of his near kinsmen, Mamercus Aemilius and Aurelius Cotta, he obtained forgiveness. Everyone knows that when Sulla had long

3

amicissimis et ornatissimis viris aliquamdiu denegasset atque illi pertinaciter contenderent, expugnatum tandem proclamasse sive divinitus sive aliqua coniectura : vincerent ac sibi haberent, dum modo scirent eum, quem incolumem tanto opere cuperent, quandoque optimatium partibus, quas secum simul defendissent, exitio futurum ; nam Caesari multos Marios inesse.

II. Stipendia prima in Asia fecit Marci Thermi praetoris contubernio ; a quo ad accersendam classem in Bithyniam missus desedit apud Nicomeden, non sine rumore prostratae regi pudicitiae ; quem rumorem auxit intra paucos rursus dies repetita Bithynia per causam exigendae pecuniae, quae deberetur cuidam libertino clienti suo. Reliqua militia secundiore fama fuit et a Thermo in expugnatione Mytilenarum corona civica donatus est.

III. Meruit et sub Servilio Isaurico in Cilicia, sed brevi tempore. Nam Sullae morte comperta, simul spe novae dissensionis, quae per Marcum Lepidum movebatur, Romam propere redit. Et Lepidi quidem societate, quamquam magnis condicionibus invitaretur, abstinuit, cum ingenio eius diffisus tum occasione, quam minorem opinione offenderat.

IV. Ceterum composita seditione civili Cornelium Dolabellam consularem et triumphalem repetun-

---

^a A chaplet of oak leaves, given for saving the life of a fellow-citizen, the Victoria Cross of antiquity.

held out against the most devoted and eminent men of his party who interceded for Caesar, and they obstinately persisted, he at last gave way and cried, either by divine inspiration or a shrewd forecast: "Have your way and take him; only bear in mind that the man you are so eager to save will one day deal the death blow to the cause of the aristocracy, which you have joined with me in upholding; for in this Caesar there is more than one Marius."

II. He served his first campaign in Asia on the 81 B.C. personal staff of Marcus Thermus, governor of the province. Being sent by Thermus to Bithynia, to fetch a fleet, he dawdled so long at the court of Nicomedes that he was suspected of improper relations with the king; and he lent colour to this scandal by going back to Bithynia a few days after his return, with the alleged purpose of collecting a debt for a freedman, one of his dependents. During 30 B.C. the rest of the campaign he enjoyed a better reputation, and at the storming of Mytilene Thermus awarded him the civic crown.[a]

III. He served too under Servilius Isauricus in Cilicia, but only for a short time; for learning of the death of Sulla, and at the same time hoping to profit 78 B.C. by a counter revolution which Marcus Lepidus was setting on foot, he hurriedly returned to Rome. But he did not make common cause with Lepidus, although he was offered highly favourable terms, through lack of confidence both in that leader's capacity and in the outlook, which he found less promising than he had expected.

IV. Then, after the civil disturbance had been quieted, he brought a charge of extortion against Cornelius Dolabella, an ex-consul who had been 77 B.C.

darum postulavit; absolutoque Rhodum secedere statuit, et ad declinandam invidiam et ut per otium ac requiem Apollonio Moloni clarissimo tunc dicendi magistro operam daret. Huc dum hibernis iam mensibus traicit, circa Pharmacussam insulam a praedonibus captus est mansitque apud eos non sine summa indignatione prope quadraginta dies cum uno

2 medico et cubiculariis duobus. Nam comites servosque ceteros initio statim ad expediendas pecunias, quibus redimeretur, dimiserat. Numeratis deinde quinquaginta talentis expositus in litore non distulit quin e vestigio classe deducta persequeretur abeuntis ac redactos in potestatem supplicio, quod saepe illis minatus inter iocum fuerat, adficeret. Vastante regiones proximas Mithridate, ne desidere in discrimine sociorum videretur, ab Rhodo, quo pertenderat, transiit in Asiam auxiliisque contractis et praefecto regis provincia expulso nutantis ac dubias civitates retinuit in fide.

V. Tribunatu militum, qui primus Romam reverso per suffragia populi honor optigit, actores restituendae tribuniciae potestatis, cuius vim Sulla deminuerat, enixissime iuvit. L. etiam Cinnae uxoris fratri, et qui cum eo civili discordia Lepidum secuti post

---

[a] See chap. lxxiv. 1.

honoured with a triumph. On the acquittal of
Dolabella Caesar determined to withdraw to Rhodes,
to escape from the ill-will which he had incurred,
and at the same time to rest and have leisure to
study under Apollonius Molo, the most eminent 74 b.c.
teacher of oratory of that time. While crossing to
Rhodes, after the winter season had already begun,
he was taken by pirates near the island of Pharmacussa
and remained in their custody for nearly forty days
in a state of intense vexation, attended only by a
single physician and two body-servants; for he had
sent off his travelling companions and the rest of
his attendants at the outset, to raise money for his
ransom. Once he was set on shore on payment of
fifty talents, he did not delay then and there to
launch a fleet and pursue the departing pirates, and
the moment they were in his power to inflict on
them the punishment which he had often threatened
when joking with them.[a] He then proceeded to
Rhodes, but as Mithridates was devastating the
neighbouring regions, he crossed over into Asia, to
avoid the appearance of inaction when the allies of
the Roman people were in danger. There he levied
a band of auxiliaries and drove the king's prefect
from the province, thus holding the wavering and
irresolute states to their allegiance.

V. While serving as military tribune, the first
office which was conferred on him by vote of the
people after his return to Rome, he ardently
supported the leaders in the attempt to re-establish
the authority of the tribunes of the commons, the
extent of which Sulla had curtailed. Furthermore, 70 b.c.
through a bill proposed by one Plotius, he effected
the recall of his wife's brother Lucius Cinna, as well

7

necem consulis ad Sertorium confugerant, reditum in civitatem rogatione Plotia confecit habuitque et ipse super ea re contionem.

VI. Quaestor Iuliam amitam uxoremque Corneliam defunctas laudavit e more pro rostris. Et in amitae quidem laudatione de eius ac patris sui utraque origine sic refert :

" Amitae meae Iuliae maternum genus ab regibus ortum, paternum cum diis inmortalibus coniunctum est. Nam ab Anco Marcio sunt Marcii Reges, quo nomine fuit mater ; a Venere Iulii, cuius gentis familia est nostra. Est ergo in genere et sanctitas regum, qui plurimum inter homines pollent, et caerimonia deorum, quorum ipsi in potestate sunt reges."

2   In Corneliae autem locum Pompeiam duxit Quinti Pompei filiam, L. Sullae neptem ; cum qua deinde divortium fecit adulteratam opinatus a Publio Clodio, quem inter publicas caerimonias penetrasse ad eam muliebri veste tam constans fama erat, ut senatus quaestionem de pollutis sacris decreverit.

VII. Quaestori ulterior Hispania obvenit ; ubi cum mandatu praetoris iure dicundo conventus circumiret Gadisque venisset, animadversa apud Herculis templum Magni Alexandri imagine ingemuit et quasi pertaesus ignaviam suam, quod nihil dum a se

---

[a] The festival of Bona Dea, from which all men were excluded.

as of the others who had taken part with Lepidus in his revolution and after the consul's death had fled to Sertorius; and he personally spoke in favour of the measure.

VI. When quaestor, he pronounced the customary orations from the rostra in praise of his aunt Julia and his wife Cornelia, who had both died. And in the eulogy of his aunt he spoke in the following terms of her paternal and maternal ancestry and that of his own father: "The family of my aunt Julia is descended by her mother from the kings, and on her father's side is akin to the immortal Gods; for the Marcii Reges (her mother's family name) go back to Ancus Marcius, and the Julii, the family of which ours is a branch, to Venus. Our stock therefore has at once the sanctity of kings, whose power is supreme among mortal men, and the claim to reverence which attaches to the Gods, who hold sway over kings themselves." 67 B.C.

In place of Cornelia he took to wife Pompeia, daughter of Quintus Pompeius and granddaughter of Lucius Sulla. But he afterward divorced her, suspecting her of adultery with Publius Clodius; and in fact the report that Clodius had gained access to her in woman's garb during a public religious ceremony [a] was so persistent, that the senate decreed that the pollution of the sacred rites be judicially investigated. 62 B.C.

VII. As quaestor it fell to his lot to serve in Farther Spain. When he was there, while making the circuit of the assize-towns, to hold court under commission from the praetor, he came to Gades, and noticing a statue of Alexander the Great in the temple of Hercules, he heaved a sigh, and as if out of patience with his own

memorabile actum esset in aetate, qua iam Alexander
orbem terrarum subegisset, missionem continuo
efflagitavit ad captandas quam primum maiorum
2 rerum occasiones in urbe. Etiam confusum eum
somnio proximae noctis—nam visus erat per quietem
stuprum matri intulisse—coniectores ad amplissimam
spem incitaverunt arbitrium terrarum orbis portendi
interpretantes, quando mater, quam subiectam sibi
vidisset, non alia esset quam terra, quae omnium
parens haberetur.

VIII. Decedens ergo ante tempus colonias Latinas
de petenda civitate agitantes adiit, et ad audendum
aliquid concitasset, nisi consules conscriptas in
Ciliciam legiones paulisper ob id ipsum retinuissent.

IX. Nec eo setius maiora mox in urbe molitus est ;
siquidem ante paucos dies quam aedilitatem iniret,
venit in suspicionem conspirasse cum Marco Crasso
consulari, item Publio Sulla et L. Autronio post
designationem consulatus ambitus condemnatis, ut
principio anni senatum adorirentur, et trucidatis quos
placitum esset, dictaturam Crassus invaderet, ipse ab
eo magister equitum diceretur constitutaque ad arbitrium re publica Sullae et Autronio consulatus resti-
2 tueretur. Meminerunt huius coniurationis Tanusius

---

^a The towns beyond the river Po, such as Verona, Comum,
and Cremona, wished to obtain the rights of citizenship,
which had been given to many of the Italian towns at the
close of the Social War (89–88 B.C.).

incapacity in having as yet done nothing noteworthy at a time of life when Alexander had already brought the world to his feet, he straightway asked for his discharge, to grasp the first opportunity for greater enterprises at Rome. Furthermore, when he was dismayed by a dream the following night (for he thought that he had offered violence to his mother) the soothsayers inspired him with high hopes by their interpretation, which was : that he was destined to rule the world, since the mother whom he had seen in his power was none other than the earth, which is regarded as the common parent of all mankind.

VIII. Departing therefore before his term was over, he went to the Latin colonies which were in a state of unrest and meditating a demand for citizenship[a]; and he might have spurred them on to some rash act, had not the consuls, in anticipation of that very danger, detained there for a time the legions which had been enrolled for service in Cilicia.

IX. For all that he presently made a more daring attempt at Rome ; for a few days before he entered upon his aedileship he was suspected of having made a conspiracy with Marcus Crassus, an ex-consul, and likewise with Publius Sulla and Lucius Autronius, who, after their election to the consulship, had been found guilty of corrupt practices. The design was 65 B.C. to set upon the senate at the opening of the year and put to the sword as many as they thought good ; then Crassus was to usurp the dictatorship, naming Caesar as his master of horse, and when they had organized the state according to their pleasure, the consulship was to be restored to Sulla and Autronius. This plot is mentioned by Tanusius Geminus in his

11

Geminus in historia, Marcus Bibulus in edictis, C.
Curio pater in orationibus. De hac significare videtur
et Cicero in quadam ad Axium epistula referens
Caesarem in consulatu confirmasse regnum, de quo
aedilis cogitarat. Tanusius adicit Crassum paenitentia
vel metu diem caedi destinatum non obisse et idcirco
ne Caesarem quidem signum, quod ab eo dari con-
venerat, dedisse; convenisse autem Curio ait, ut
3 togam de umero deiceret. Idem Curio sed et M.
Actorius Naso auctores sunt conspirasse eum etiam
cum Gnaeo Pisone adulescente, cui ob suspicionem
urbanae coniurationis provincia Hispania ultro extra
ordinem data sit; pactumque ut simul foris ille, ipse
Romae ad res novas consurgerent, per Ambranos[1] et
Transpadanos; destitutum utriusque consilium morte
Pisonis.

X. Aedilis praeter Comitium ac Forum basilicasque
etiam Capitolium ornavit porticibus ad tempus
extructis, in quibus abundante rerum copia pars
apparatus exponeretur. Venationes autem ludosque
et cum collega et separatim edidit, quo factum est,
ut communium quoque inpensarum solus gratiam
caperet nec dissimularet collega eius Marcus Bibulus,
evenisse sibi quod Polluci; ut enim geminis fratri-
bus aedes in Foro constituta tantum Castoris vocaretur, ita suam Caesarisque munificentiam unius

---

[1] Ambranos] Lambranos, *Sabellicus*; Ambrones, *Beroaldus*;
Ambarros, *Urlichs*; Arvernos, *Mommsen*; Campanos, *Madvig*.

---

[a] *Forum ornare* was the technical term for the display
there by the aediles of the material to be used in their
public shows.

History, by Marcus Bibulus in his edicts, and by
Gaius Curio the elder in his speeches. Cicero too
seems to hint at it in a letter to Axius, where he
says that Caesar in his consulship established the despotism which he had had in mind when he was aedile.
Tanusius adds that Crassus, either conscience-stricken
or moved by fear, did not appear on the day appointed for the massacre, and that therefore Caesar
did not give the signal which it had been agreed
that he should give ; and Curio says that the arrangement was that Caesar should let his toga fall from
his shoulder. Not only Curio, but Marcus Actorius
Naso as well declare that Caesar made another plot
with Gnaeus Piso, a young man to whom the province of Spain had been assigned unasked and out of
the regular order, because he was suspected of
political intrigues at Rome ; that they agreed to rise
in revolt at the same time, Piso abroad and Caesar
at Rome, aided by the Ambrani and the peoples
beyond the Po ; but that Piso's death brought both
their designs to naught.

X. When aedile, Caesar decorated *a* not only the 65 B.C.
Comitium and the Forum with its adjacent basilicas,
but the Capitol as well, building temporary colonnades for the display of a part of his material. He
exhibited combats with wild beasts and stage-
plays too, both with his colleague and independently.
The result was that Caesar alone took all the credit
even for what they spent in common, and his
colleague Marcus Bibulus openly said that his was
the fate of Pollux: "For," said he, "just as the
temple erected in the Forum to the twin brethren,
bears only the name of Castor, so the joint liberality
of Caesar and myself is credited to Caesar alone."

2 Caesaris dici. Adiecit insuper Caesar etiam gladiatorium munus, sed aliquanto paucioribus quam
destinaverat paribus; nam cum multiplici undique
familia conparata inimicos exterruisset, cautum est de
numero gladiatorum, quo ne maiorem cuiquam
habere Romae liceret.

XI. Conciliato populi favore temptavit per partem
tribunorum, ut sibi Aegyptus provincia plebiscito
daretur, nanctus extraordinarii imperii occasionem,
quod Alexandrini regem suum socium atque amicum
a senatu appellatum expulerant resque vulgo impro-
babatur. Nec obtinuit adversante optimatium fac-
tione; quorum auctoritatem ut quibus posset modis
in vicem deminueret, tropaea Gai Mari de Iugurtha
deque Cimbris atque Teutonis olim a Sulla disiecta
restituit, atque in exercenda de sicariis quaestione eos
quoque sicariorum numero habuit, qui proscriptione ob
relata civium Romanorum capita pecunias ex aerario
acceperant, quamquam exceptos Corneliis legibus.

XII. Subornavit etiam qui Gaio Rabirio perduellionis diem diceret, quo praecipuo adiutore aliquot
ante annos Luci Saturnini seditiosum tribunatum
senatus coercuerat, ac sorte iudex in reum ductus

ᵃ As *iudex quaestionis*, an office held by Caesar between the
aedileship and the praetorship.

ᵇ As *iudex perduellionis*, or *duumvir perduellionis*, one of a
commission of two men appointed to try cases of high treason.
Of these one was selected by lot (*sorte ductus*) to conduct the
trial, if one were necessary, and pass sentence. An appeal
was allowed and the duumvir then brought the case before the
comitia centuriata (in the regal period before the *comitia
curiata*). See Livy 1. 26. 5 ff.; Cic. *Rab.* 4.

Caesar gave a gladiatorial show besides, but with somewhat fewer pairs of combatants than he had purposed; for the huge band which he assembled from all quarters so terrified his opponents, that a bill was passed limiting the number of gladiators which anyone· was to be allowed to keep in the city.

XI. Having won the goodwill of the masses, Caesar made an attempt through some of the tribunes to have the charge of Egypt given him by a decree of the commons, seizing the opportunity to ask for so irregular an appointment because the citizens of Alexandria had deposed their king, who had been named by the senate an ally and friend of the Roman people, and their action was generally condemned. He failed however because of the opposition of the aristocratic party; wishing therefore to impair their prestige in every way he could, he restored the trophies commemorating the victories of Gaius Marius over Jugurtha and over the Cimbri and Teutoni, which Sulla had long since demolished. Furthermore in conducting prosecutions for murder,[a] he included in the number of murderers even those who had received moneys from the public treasury during the proscriptions for bringing in the heads of Roman citizens, although they were expressly exempted by the Cornelian laws.

XII. He also bribed a man to bring a charge of high treason against Gaius Rabirius, who some years before had rendered conspicuous service to the senate in repressing the seditious designs of the tribune Lucius Saturninus; and when he had been selected by lot to sentence the accused,[b] he did so with such eagerness, that when Rabirius appealed to

tam cupide condemnavit, ut ad populum provocanti
nihil aeque ac iudicis acerbitas profuerit.

XIII. Deposita provinciae spe pontificatum maximum petit non sine profusissima largitione; in qua
reputans magnitudinem aeris alieni, cum mane ad
comitia descenderet, praedixisse matri osculanti fertur
domum se nisi pontificem non reversurum. Atque
ita potentissimos duos competitores multumque et
aetate et dignitate antecedentes superavit, ut plura
ipse in eorum tribubus suffragia quam uterque in
omnibus tulerit.

XIV. Praetor creatus, detecta coniuratione Catilinae senatuque universo in socios facinoris ultimam
statuente poenam, solus municipatim dividendos
custodiendosque publicatis bonis censuit. Quin et
tantum metum iniecit asperiora suadentibus, identidem ostentans quanta eos in posterum a plebe
Romana maneret invidia, ut Decimum Silanum
consulem designatum non piguerit sententiam suam,
quia mutare turpe erat, interpretatione lenire, velut
2 gravius atque ipse sensisset exceptam. Obtinuisset
adeo transductis iam ad se pluribus et in his
Cicerone consulis fratre, nisi labantem ordinem
confirmasset M. Catonis oratio. Ac ne sic quidem
impedire rem destitit, quoad manus equitum Roman-

ᵃ As governor of Egypt; see chap. xi.

the people, nothing was so much in his favour as the bitter hostility of his judge.

XIII. After giving up hope of the special commission,[a] he announced his candidacy for the office of pontifex maximus, resorting to the most lavish bribery. Thinking on the enormous debt which he had thus contracted, he is said to have declared to his mother on the morning of the election, as she kissed him when he was starting for the polls, that he would never return except as pontifex. And in fact he so decisively defeated two very strong competitors (for they were greatly his superiors in age and rank), that he polled more votes in their tribes than were cast for both of them in all the tribes.

XIV. When the conspiracy of Catiline was detected, and all the rest of the senate favoured inflicting the extreme penalty on those implicated in the plot, Caesar, who was now praetor elect, alone proposed that their goods be confiscated and that they be imprisoned each in a separate town. Nay, 63 B C more, he inspired such fear in those who favoured severer measures, by picturing the hatred which the Roman commons would feel for them for all future time, that Decimus Silanus, consul elect, was not ashamed to give a milder interpretation to his proposal (since it would have been humiliating to change it) alleging that it had been understood in a harsher sense than he intended. Caesar would have prevailed too, for a number had already gone over to him, including Cicero, the consul's brother, had not the address of Marcus Cato kept the wavering senate in line. Yet not even then did he cease to delay the proceedings, but only when an armed

orum, quae armata praesidii causa circumstabat,
inmoderatius perseveranti necem comminata est,
etiam strictos gladios usque eo intentans, ut sedentem una proximi deseruerint, vix pauci complexu
togaque obiecta protexerint. Tunc plane deterritus
non modo cessit, sed et in reliquum anni tempus
curia abstinuit.

XV. Primo praeturae die Quintum Catulum de
refectione Capitoli ad disquisitionem populi vocavit
rogatione promulgata, qua curationem eam in alium
transferebat; verum impar optimatium conspirationi,
quos relicto statim novorum consulum officio fre-
quentes obstinatosque ad resistendum concucurrisse
cernebat, hanc quidem actionem deposuit.

XVI. Ceterum Caecilio Metello tribuno plebis
turbulentissimas leges adversus collegarum intercessionem ferenti auctorem propugnatoremque se
pertinacissime praestitit, donec ambo administratione
rei publicae decreto patrum submoverentur. Ac
nihilo minus permanere in magistratu et ius dicere
ausus, ut comperit paratos, qui vi ac per arma pro-
hiberent, dimissis lictoribus abiectaque praetexta
domum clam refugit pro condicione temporum
2 quieturus. Multitudinem quoque biduo post sponte
et ultro confluentem operamque sibi in adserenda

---

[b] When the consuls went to the Capitol to offer sacrifice at
the commencement of their term of office (on January 1),
their friends escorted them to the temple and back to their
homes. Caesar took advantage of the absence of the aristocrats for his attack on Catulus.

troop of Roman knights that stood on guard about
the place threatened him with death as he persisted
in his headstrong opposition. They even drew their
swords and made such passes at him that his friends
who sat next him forsook him, while a few had much
ado to shield him in their embrace or with their
robes. Then, in evident fear, he not only yielded the
point, but for the rest of the year kept aloof from
the House.

XV. On the first day of his praetorship he called 62 ᴮ.ᴄ.
upon Quintus Catulus to render an account to the
people touching the restoration of the Capitol,
proposing a bill for turning over the commission to
another.ᵃ But he withdrew the measure, since he
could not cope with the united opposition of the
aristocrats, seeing that they had at once dropped
their attendance on the newly elected consuls ᵇ and
hastily gathered in throngs, resolved on an obstinate
resistance.

XVI. Nevertheless, when Caecilius Metellus,
tribune of the commons, brought forward some bills
of a highly seditious nature in spite of the veto of
his colleagues, Caesar abetted him and espoused his
cause in the stubbornest fashion, until at last both
were suspended from the exercise of their public
functions by a decree of the senate. Yet in spite of
this Caesar had the audacity to continue in office and
to hold court; but when he learned that some were
ready to stop him by force of arms, he dismissed his
lictors, laid aside his robe of office, and slipped off
privily to his house, intending to remain in retirement because of the state of the times. Indeed,
when the populace on the following day flocked to
him quite of their own accord, and with riotous

dignitate tumultuosius pollicentem conpescuit. Quod cum praeter opinionem evenisset, senatus ob eundem coetum festinato coactus gratias ei per primores viros egit accitumque in curiam et amplissimis verbis conlaudatum in integrum restituit inducto priore decreto.

XVII. Recidit rursus in discrimen aliud inter socios Catilinae nominatus et apud Novium Nigrum quaestorem [1] a Lucio Vettio indice et in senatu a Quinto Curio, cui, quod primus consilia coniuratorum detexerat, constituta erant publice praemia. Curius e Catilina se cognovisse dicebat, Vettius etiam 2 chirographum eius Catilinae datum pollicebatur. Id vero Caesar nullo modo tolerandum existimans, cum inplorato Ciceronis testimonio quaedam se de coniuratione ultro ad eum detulisse docuisset, ne Curio praemia darentur effecit; Vettium pignoribus captis et direpta supellectile male mulcatum ac pro rostris in contione paene discerptum coniecit in carcerem; eodem Novium quaestorem, quod compellari apud se maiorem potestatem passus esset.

XVIII. Ex praetura ulteriorem sortitus Hispaniam retinentes creditores interventu sponsorum removit ac neque more neque iure, ante quam provinciae

---

[1] quaestorem, Ω.

[a] Novius seems to have been *quaesitor*, a special commissioner appointed to conduct the investigation (*quaestio*) of the Catilinarian conspiracy; perhaps we should read *quaesitorem.*

demonstrations offered him their aid in recovering his position, he held them in check. Since this action of his was wholly unexpected, the senate, which had been hurriedly convoked to take action about that very gathering, publicly thanked him through its leading men; then summoning him to the House and lauding him in the strongest terms, they rescinded their former decree and restored him to his rank.

XVII. He again fell into danger by being named among the accomplices of Catiline, both before the commissioner[a] Novius Niger by an informer called Lucius Vettius and in the senate by Quintus Curius, who had been voted a sum of money from the public funds as the first to disclose the plans of the conspirators. Curius alleged that his information came directly from Catiline, while Vettius actually offered to produce a letter to Catiline in Caesar's handwriting. But Caesar, thinking that such an indignity could in no wise be endured, showed by appealing to Cicero's testimony that he had of his own accord reported to the consul certain details of the plot, and thus prevented Curius from getting the reward. As for Vettius, after his bond was declared forfeit and his goods seized, he was roughly handled by the populace assembled before the rostra, and all but torn to pieces. Caesar then put him in prison, and Novius the commissioner went there too, for allowing an official of superior rank to be arraigned before his tribunal.

XVIII. Being allotted the province of Farther Spain after his praetorship, Caesar got rid of his creditors, who tried to detain him, by means of sureties and contrary both to precedent and law was

61 B.C.

21

ornarentur,[1] profectus est : incertum metune iudicii,
quod privato parabatur, an quo maturius sociis
inplorantibus subveniret ; pacataque provincia pari
festinatione, non expectato successore ad triumphum

2 simul consulatumque decessit. Sed cum edictis iam
comitiis ratio eius haberi non posset nisi privatus
introisset urbem, et ambienti ut legibus solveretur
multi contra dicerent, coactus est triumphum, ne
consulatu excluderetur, dimittere.

XIX. E duobus consulatus competitoribus, Lucio
Lucceio Marcoque Bibulo, Lucceium sibi adiunxit,
pactus ut is, quoniam inferior gratia esset pecunia-
que polleret, nummos de suo communi nomine per
centurias pronuntiaret. Qua cognita re optimates,
quos metus ceperat nihil non ausurum eum in summo
magistratu concordi et consentiente collega, auctores
Bibulo fuerunt tantundem pollicendi, ac plerique
pecunias contulerunt, ne Catone quidem abnuente
eam largitionem e re publica fieri.

2 Igitur cum Bibulo consul creatur. Eandem ob
causam opera ab optimatibus data est, ut provinciae
futuris consulibus minimi negotii, id est silvae callesque,[2] decernerentur. Qua maxime iniuria instinctus

---

[1] ornarentur, *Lambinus* ; ordinarentur, Ω.
[2] id est. . . . callesque, *del. Willems, Le Sénat de la ré-
publique romaine*, ii. 576, N. 5.

---

[a] That is, without waiting for the decrees of the senate
which formally confirmed the appointments of the new
governors, and provided them with funds and equipment.

[b] If *silvae callesque* should stand in the text, it is used in a
different sense from *calles* in Tac. *Ann.* 4. 27. It seems to
designate provinces where the duties of the governor would
be confined to guarding the mountain-pastures and keeping
the woods free from brigands. The senate would not run the
risk of letting Caesar secure a province involving the command of an army. Cf. note on **xxiv.** 1.

on his way before the provinces were provided for [a];
possibly through fear of a private impeachment or
perhaps to respond more promptly to the entreaties
of our allies for help. After restoring order in his
province, he made off with equal haste, and without
waiting for the arrival of his successor, to sue at the
same time for a triumph and the consulship. But
inasmuch as the day for the elections had already
been announced and no account could be taken of
Caesar's candidacy unless he entered the city as a
private citizen, and since his intrigues to gain
exemption from the laws met with general protest,
he was forced to forgo the triumph, to avoid losing
the consulship.

XIX. Of the two other candidates for this office, 6) ▲◀
Lucius Lucceius and Marcus Bibulus, Caesar joined
forces with the former, making a bargain with him
that since Lucceius had less influence but more funds,
he should in their common name promise largess to
the electors from his own pocket. When this
became known, the aristocracy authorized Bibulus to
promise the same amount, being seized with fear that
Caesar would stick at nothing when he became chief
magistrate, if he had a colleague who was heart and
soul with him. Many of them contributed to the
fund, and even Cato did not deny that bribery under
such circumstances was for the good of the commonwealth.

So Caesar was chosen consul with Bibulus. With
the same motives the aristocracy took care that provinces of the smallest importance should be assigned
to the newly elected consuls ; that is, mere woods and
pastures.[b] Thereupon Caesar, especially incensed by
this slight, by every possible attention courted the

omnibus officiis Gnaeum Pompeium adsectatus est offensum patribus, quod Mithridate rege victo cunctantius confirmarentur acta sua ; Pompeioque Marcum Crassum reconciliavit veterem inimicum ex consulatu, quem summa discordia simul gesserant ; ac societatem cum utroque iniit, ne quid ageretur in re publica, quod displicuisset ulli e tribus.

XX. Inito honore primus omnium instituit, ut tam senatus quam populi diurna acta confierent et publicarentur. Antiquum etiam rettulit morem, ut quo mense fasces non haberet, accensus ante eum iret, lictores pone sequerentur. Lege autem agraria promulgata obnuntiantem collegam armis Foro expulit ac postero die in senatu conquestum nec quoquam reperto, qui super tali consternatione referre aut censere aliquid auderet, qualia multa saepe in levioribus turbis decreta erant, in eam coegit desperationem, ut, quoad potestate abiret, domo abditus nihil aliud quam per edicta obnuntiaret.

2   Unus ex eo tempore omnia in re publica et ad arbitrium administravit, ut nonnulli urbanorum, cum quid per iocum testandi gratia signarent, non Caesare et Bibulo, sed Iulio et Caesare consulibus actum

---

^a Business could be interrupted or postponed at Rome by the announcement of an augur or a magistrate that he had seen a flash of lightning or some other adverse sign ; sometimes an opponent merely announced that he would '' watch the skies '' for such omens.

^b Torrentius put *per iocum* after *signarent*, but such jesting would not be tolerated in actual legal documents.

goodwill of Gnaeus Pompeius, who was at odds with the senate because of its tardiness in ratifying his acts after his victory over king Mithridates. He also patched up a peace between Pompeius and Marcus Crassus, who had been enemies since their consulship, which had been one of constant wrangling. Then he made a compact with both of them, that no step should be taken in public affairs which did not suit any one of the three. 60 B.C.

XX. Caesar's very first enactment after becoming consul was, that the proceedings both of the senate and of the people should day by day be compiled and published. He also revived a by-gone custom, that during the months when he did not have the fasces an orderly should walk before him, while the lictors followed him. He brought forward an agrarian law too, and when his colleague announced adverse omens,[a] he resorted to arms and drove him from the Forum; and when next day Bibulus made complaint in the senate and no one could be found who ventured to make a motion, or even to express an opinion about so high-handed a proceeding (although decrees had often been passed touching less serious breaches of the peace), Caesar's conduct drove him to such a pitch of desperation, that from that time until the end of his term he did not leave his house, but merely issued proclamations announcing adverse omens.

From that time on Caesar managed all the affairs of state alone and after his own pleasure; so that sundry witty fellows, pretending by way of jest to sign and seal testamentary documents,[b] wrote " Done in the consulship of Julius and Caesar," instead of " Bibulus and Caesar," writing down

scriberent bis[1] eundem praeponentes nomine atque
cognomine, utque vulgo mox ferrentur hi versus :

Non Bibulo quiddam nuper sed Caesare factum est ;
Nam Bibulo fieri consule nil memini.

3 Campum Stellatem maioribus consecratum agrumque
Campanum ad subsidia rei publicae vectigalem
relictum divisit extra sortem ad[2] viginti milibus
civium, quibus terni pluresve liberi essent. Publicanos remissionem petentis tertia mercedum parte
relevavit ac, ne in locatione novorum vectigalium
inmoderatius licerentur, propalam monuit. Cetera
item, quae cuique libuissent, dilargitus est contra
dicente nullo ac, si conaretur quis, absterrito.

4 Marcum Catonem interpellantem extrahi curia per
lictorem ducique in carcerem iussit. Lucio Lucullo
liberius resistenti tantum calumniarum metum iniecit,
ut ad genua ultro sibi accideret. Cicerone in iudicio
quodam deplorante temporum statum Publium Clodium inimicum eius, frustra iam pridem a patribus
ad plebem transire nitentem, eodem die horaque
5 nona transduxit. Postremo in universos diversae
factionis indicem induxit[3] praemiis, ut se de infer-

---

[1] bis. . . cognomine, *regarded as a gloss by Lipsius and others.*
[2] ad, *Casaubon;* ac, Ω.
[3] indicem, *omitted in* Ω ; induxit, *Stephanus* ; inductum, Ω.

---

[a] Through a special commission of twenty men.
[b] By making a speech of several hours' duration ; Gell.
4. 10. 8. The senate arose in a body and escorted Cato to
prison, and Caesar was forced to release him.
[c] For his conduct during the war with Mithridates.
[d] That is, after the close of the business day, an indication
of the haste with which the adoption was rushed through.

the same man twice, by name and by surname.
Presently too the following verses were on everyone's lips :—

" In Caesar's year, not Bibulus', an act took place of
    late ;
  For naught do I remember done in Bibulus'
    consulate."

The plain called Stellas, which had been devoted
to public uses by the men of by-gone days, and the
Campanian territory, which had been reserved to
pay revenues for the aid of the government, he
divided without casting lots[a] among twenty thousand
citizens who had three or more children each. When
the publicans asked for relief, he freed them from
a third part of their obligation, and openly warned
them in contracting for taxes in the future not to bid
too recklessly. He freely granted everything else that
anyone took it into his head to ask, either without
opposition or by intimidating anyone who tried to
object. Marcus Cato, who tried to delay proceedings,[b]
was dragged from the House by a lictor at Caesar's
command and taken off to prison. When Lucius
Lucullus was somewhat too outspoken in his opposition, he filled him with such fear of malicious
prosecution,[c] that Lucullus actually fell on his knees
before him. Because Cicero, while pleading in court,
deplored the state of the times, Caesar transferred the
orator's enemy Publius Clodius that very same day
from the patricians to the plebeians, a thing for 59 B.C.
which Clodius had for a long time been vainly
striving ; and that too at the ninth hour.[d] Finally
taking action against all the opposition in a body,
he bribed an informer to declare that he had been

27

enda Pompeio nece sollicitatum a quibusdam pro-
fiteretur productusque pro rostris auctores ex con-
pacto nominaret ; sed uno atque altero frustra nec
sine suspicione fraudis nominatis desperans tam
praecipitis consilii eventum intercepisse veneno
indicem creditur.

XXI. Sub idem tempus Calpurniam L. Pisonis
filiam successuri sibi in consulatu duxit uxorem
suamque, Iuliam, Gnaeo Pompeio conlocavit re-
pudiato priore sponso Servilio Caepione, cuius vel
praecipua opera paulo ante Bibulum inpugnaverat.
Ac post novam adfinitatem Pompeium primum rogare
sententiam coepit, cum Crassum soleret essetque
consuetudo, ut quem ordinem interrogandi sententias
consul Kal. Ianuariis instituisset, eum toto anno
conservaret.

XXII. Socero igitur generoque suffragantibus ex
omni provinciarum copia Gallias potissimum elegit,
†cuius[1] emolumento et oportunitate idonea sit materia
triumphorum.   Et initio quidem Galliam Cisalpinam
Illyrico adiecto lege Vatinia accepit ; mox per
senatum Comatam quoque, veritis patribus ne, si ipsi
2 negassent, populus et hanc daret. Quo gaudio
elatus non temperavit, quin paucos post dies
frequenti curia iactaret, invitis et gementibŭs adversariis adeptum se quae concupisset, proinde ex eo

---

[1] cuius] quae et, *Bentley;* quae sibi, *Kiessling. Of the
various emendations of the passage* cuius . . . triumphorum
none is convincing. The general sense is, however, clear.

egged on by certain men to murder Pompey, and
to come out upon the rostra and name the guilty
parties according to a prearranged plot. But when
the informer had named one or two to no purpose
and not without suspicion of double-dealing, Caesar,
hopeless of the success of his over-hasty attempt,
is supposed to have had him taken off by poison.

XXI. At about the same time he took to wife
Calpurnia, daughter of Lucius Piso, who was to
succeed him in the consulship, and affianced his own
daughter Julia to Gnaeus Pompeius, breaking a
previous engagement with Servilius Caepio, although
the latter had shortly before rendered him conspicuous service in his contest with Bibulus. And
after this new alliance he began to call upon Pompey
first to give his opinion in the senate, although it
had been his habit to begin with Crassus, and it was
the rule for the consul in calling for opinions to
continue throughout the year the order which he had
established on the Kalends of January.

XXII. Backed therefore by his father-in-law and
son-in-law, out of all the numerous provinces he
made the Gauls his choice, as the most likely to
enrich him and furnish suitable material for
triumphs. At first, it is true, by the bill of Vatinius
he received only Cisalpine Gaul with the addition of
Illyricum; but presently he was assigned Gallia Comata
as well by the senate, since the members feared
that even if they should refuse it, the people would
give him this also. Transported with joy at this
success, he could not keep from boasting a few days
later before a crowded house, that having gained
his heart's desire to the grief and lamentation of his
opponents, he would therefore from that time mount

insultaturum omnium capitibus ; ac negante quodam
per contumeliam facile hoc ulli feminae fore, responderit [1] quasi adludens : in Suria quoque regnasse
Sameramin magnamque Asiae partem Amazonas
tenuisse quondam.

XXIII.   Functus consulatu Gaio Memmio Lucioque Domitio praetoribus de superioris anni actis
referentibus cognitionem senatui detulit ; nec illo
suscipiente triduoque per inritas altercationes
absumpto in provinciam abiit.   Et statim quaestor
eius in praeiudicium aliquot criminibus arreptus est.
Mox et ipse a Lucio Antistio tr. pl. postulatus
appellato demum collegio optinuit, cum rei publicae
2 causa abesset, reus ne fieret.   Ad securitatem ergo
posteri temporis in magno negotio habuit obligare
semper annuos magistratus et e petitoribus non alios
adiuvare aut ad honorem pati pervenire, quam qui
sibi recepissent propugnaturos absentiam suam ;
cuius pacti non dubitavit a quibusdam ius iurandum
atque etiam syngrapham exigere.

XXIV. Sed cum Lucius Domitius consulatus
candidatus palam minaretur consulem se effecturum
quod praetor nequisset adempturumque ei exercitus,
Crassum Pompeiumque in urbem provinciae suae
Lucam extractos conpulit, ut detrudendi Domitii

---

[1] responderit, *all the mss., except ρ and some other late
codices, which have* respondit ; responderet, ϛ (*Torrentius*).

ᵃ Used in a double sense, the second unmentionable.

on their heads; [a] and when someone insultingly
remarked that that would be no easy matter for any
woman, he replied in the same vein that Semiramis
too had been queen in Syria and the Amazons in
days of old had held sway over a great part of
Asia.

XXIII. When at the close of his consulship the
praetors Gaius Memmius and Lucius Domitius moved
an inquiry into his conduct during the previous year,
Caesar laid the matter before the senate; and when
they failed to take it up, and three days had been
wasted in fruitless wrangling, went off to his
province. Whereupon his quaestor was at once
arraigned on several counts, as a preliminary to his
own impeachment. Presently he himself too was
prosecuted by Lucius Antistius, tribune of the
commons, and it was only by appealing to the
whole college that he contrived not to be brought
to trial, on the ground that he was absent on
public service. Then to secure himself for
the future, he took great pains always to put the
magistrates for the year under personal obligation,
and not to aid any candidates or suffer any to be
elected, save such as guaranteed to defend him in
his absence. And he did not hesitate in some cases
to exact an oath to keep this pledge or even a
written contract.

XXIV. When however Lucius Domitius, candi- 55 B.C.
date for the consulship, openly threatened to effect
as consul what he had been unable to do as praetor,
and to take his armies from him, Caesar compelled
Pompeius and Crassus to come to Luca, a city in his
province, where he prevailed on them to stand for
a second consulship, to defeat Domitius; and he also

causa consulatum alterum peterent, perfecitque per[1] utrumque, ut in quinquennium sibi imperium prorogaretur. 2 Qua fiducia ad legiones, quas a re publica acceperat, alias privato sumptu addidit, unam etiam ex Transalpinis conscriptam, vocabulo quoque Gallico—Alauda enim appellabatur—, quam disciplina cultuque Romano institutam et ornatam postea universam civitate donavit. 3 Nec deinde ulla belli occasione, ne[2] iniusti quidem ac periculosi abstinuit, tam foederatis quam infestis ac feris gentibus ultro lacessitis, adeo ut senatus quondam legatos ad explorandum statum Galliarum mittendos decreverit ac nonnulli dedendum eum hostibus censuerint. Sed prospere cedentibus[3] rebus et saepius et plurium quam quisquam umquam dierum supplicationes impetravit.

XXV. Gessit autem novem annis, quibus in imperio fuit, haec fere. Omnem Galliam, quae saltu Pyrenaeo Alpibusque et monte Cebenna, fluminibus Rheno ac Rhodano continetur patetque circuitu ad bis et tricies centum milia passuum, praeter socias ac bene meritas civitates, in provinciae formam redegit, eique |C̄C̄C̄C̄|[4] in singulos annos stipendii nomine in- 2 posuit. Germanos, qui trans Rhenum incolunt, primus Romanorum ponte fabricato adgressus maximis adfecit cladibus; adgressus est et Britannos

---

[1] per *added by Roth.*   [2] ne *added by Erasmus.*
[3] cedentibus, ς ; decedentibus, Ω.
[4] *The number is preserved only in V ; Eutropius,* 6.17, *has* quadringenties.

---

[a] A Celtic word meaning a crested lark (Plin. *N.H.* 11. 37) which was the device on the helmets of the legion.

[b] Roman measure ; about 3106 English miles, taking the Roman foot (296 mm.) as 0·97 English.

[c] For this and similar sums see Index, s.v. *sestertius.*

succeeded through their influence in having his term as governor of Gaul made five years longer. Encouraged by this, he added to the legions which he had received from the state others at his own cost, one actually composed of men of Transalpine Gaul and bearing a Gallic name too (for it was called Alauda[a]), which he trained in the Roman tactics and equipped with Roman arms; and later on he gave every man of it citizenship. After that he did not let slip any pretext for war, however unjust and dangerous it might be, picking quarrels as well with allied, as with hostile and barbarous nations; so that once the senate decreed that a commission be sent to inquire into the condition of the Gallic provinces, and some even recommended that Caesar be handed over to the enemy. But as his enterprises prospered, thanksgivings were appointed in his honour oftener and for longer periods than for anyone before his time.

XXV. During the nine years of his command 58/49 this is in substance what he did. All that part of B.C. Gaul which is bounded by the Pyrenees, the Alps and the Cévennes, and by the Rhine and Rhone rivers, a circuit of some 3,200[b] miles, with the exception of some allied states which had rendered him good service, he reduced to the form of a province; and imposed upon it a yearly tribute of 40,000,000 sesterces.[c] He was the first Roman to build a bridge and attack the Germans beyond the Rhine; and he inflicted heavy losses upon them. He invaded the Britons too, a people unknown before,

ignotos antea superatisque pecunias et obsides
imperavit; per tot successus ter nec amplius
adversum casum expertus; in Britannia classe vi
tempestatis prope absumpta et in Gallia ad
Gergoviam legione fusa et in Germanorum finibus
Titurio et Aurunculeio legatis per insidias caesis.

XXVI. Eodem temporis spatio matrem primo,
deinde filiam, nec multo post nepotem amisit. Inter
quae, consternata Publi Clodi caede re publica, cum
senatus unum consulem nominatimque Gnaeum
Pompeium fieri censuisset, egit cum tribunis plebis
collegam se Pompeio destinantibus, id potius ad
populum ferrent, ut absenti sibi, quandoque imperii
tempus expleri coepisset, petitio secundi consulatus
daretur, ne ea causa maturius et inperfecto adhuc
bello decederet. Quod ut adeptus est, altiora iam
meditans et spei plenus nullum largitionis aut officiorum in quemquam genus publice privatimque omisit.
Forum de manubiis incohavit, cuius area super
sestertium milies constitit. Munus populo epulumque
pronuntiavit in filiae memoriam, quod ante eum
nemo. Quorum ut quam maxima [1] expectatio esset,
ea quae ad epulum pertinerent, quamvis macellariis

2

---

[1] maxima, *G. ; the other mss. have* maxime.

vanquished them, and exacted moneys and hostages. Amid all these successes he met with adverse fortune but three times in all: in Britain, where his fleet narrowly escaped destruction in a violent storm; in Gaul, when one of his legions was routed at Gergovia; and on the borders of Germany, when his lieutenants Titurius and Aurunculeius were ambushed and slain.

XXVI. Within this same space of time he lost first his mother, then his daughter, and soon afterwards his grandchild. Meanwhile, as the community was aghast at the murder of Publius Clodius, the senate had voted that only one consul should be chosen, and expressly named Gnaeus Pompeius. When the tribunes planned to make him Pompey's colleague, Caesar urged them rather to propose to the people that he be permitted to stand for a second consulship without coming to Rome, when the term of his governorship drew near its end, to prevent his being forced for the sake of the office to leave his province prematurely and without finishing the war. On the granting of this, aiming still higher and flushed with hope, he neglected nothing in the way of lavish expenditure or of favours to anyone, either in his public capacity or privately. He began a forum with the proceeds of his spoils, the ground for which cost more than a hundred million sesterces. He announced a combat of gladiators and a feast for the people in memory of his daughter, a thing quite without precedent. To raise the expectation of these events to the highest possible pitch, he had the material for the banquet prepared in part by his own household, although he had let contracts to the

3 ablocata, etiam domesticatim apparabat. Gladiatores
notos, sicubi infestis spectatoribus dimicarent, vi ra-
piendos reservandosque mandabat. Tirones neque
in ludo neque per lanistas, sed in domibus per
equites Romanos atque etiam per senatores armorum
peritos erudiebat, precibus enitens, quod epistulis
eius ostenditur, ut disciplinam singulorum susciperent
ipsique dictata exercentibus darent. Legionibus
stipendium in perpetuum duplicavit. Frumentum,
quotiens copia esset, etiam sine modo mensuraque
praebuit ac singula interdum mancipia e praeda [1]
viritim dedit.

XXVII. Ad retinendam autem Pompei neces-
situdinem ac voluntatem Octaviam sororis suae
neptem, quae Gaio Marcello nupta erat, condicionem
ei detulit sibique filiam eius in matrimonium petit
Fausto Sullae destinatam. Omnibus vero circa eum
atque etiam parte magna senatus gratuito aut levi
faenore obstrictis, ex reliquo quoque ordinum genere
vel invitatos vel sponte ad se commeantis uberrimo
congiario prosequebatur,[2] libertos insuper servulosque
cuiusque, prout domino patronove gratus qui [3] esset.
2 Iam [4] reorum aut obaeratorum aut prodigae iuventutis
subsidium unicum ac promptissimum erat, nisi quos
gravior criminum vel inopiae luxuriaeve vis urgeret,
quam ut subveniri posset a se; his plane palam
bello civili opus esse dicebat.

[1] " *Ex praeda* quidam," *Casaubon*—" quidam " *being
apparently Ursinus*; et praedia, Ω.
[2] prosequebatur, *L²T⸲*; persequebatur, Ω.
[3] quis, *mss. except M¹* (quivis, *G.*).
[4] Iam, *⸲*; tam, *MGX'*; tum, *Υ*.

[a] When ordinarily they would be put to death.

markets as well. He gave orders too that whenever famous gladiators fought without winning the favour of the people,[a] they should be rescued by force and kept for him. He had the novices trained, not in a gladiatorial school by professionals, but in private houses by Roman knights and even by senators who were skilled in arms, earnestly beseeching them, as is shown by his own letters, to give the recruits individual attention and personally direct their exercises. He doubled the pay of the legions for all time. Whenever grain was plentiful, he distributed it to them without stint or measure, and now and then gave each man a slave from among the captives.

XXVII. Moreover, to retain his relationship and friendship with Pompey, Caesar offered him his sister's granddaughter Octavia in marriage, although she was already the wife of Gaius Marcellus, and asked for the hand of Pompey's daughter, who was promised to Faustus Sulla. When he had put all Pompey's friends under obligation, as well as the great part of the senate, through loans made without interest or at a low rate, he lavished gifts on men of all other classes, both those whom he invited to accept his bounty and those who applied to him unasked, including even freedmen and slaves who were special favourites of their masters or patrons. In short, he was the sole and ever ready help of all who were in legal difficulties or in debt and of young spendthrifts, excepting only those whose burden of guilt or of poverty was so heavy, or who were so given up to riotous living, that even he could not save them; and to these he declared in the plainest terms that what they needed was a civil war.

XXVIII. Nec minore studio reges atque provincias
per terrarum orbem adliciebat, aliis captivorum milia
dono offerens, aliis citra senatus populique auctoritatem, quo vellent et quotiens vellent, auxilia submit-
tens, superque Italiae Galliarumque et Hispaniarum,
Asiae quoque et Graeciae potentissimas urbes praeci-
2 puis operibus exornans ; donec, attonitis iam omnibus
et quorsum illa tenderent reputantibus, Marcus Claudius Marcellus consul, edicto praefatus, de summa se re
publica acturum, rettulit ad senatum, ut ei succedere-
tur ante tempus, quoniam bello confecto pax esset ac
dimitti deberet victor exercitus ; et ne absentis ratio
comitiis haberetur, quando nec plebiscito Pompeius
3 postea abrogasset.   Acciderat autem, ut is legem de
iure magistratuum ferens eo capite, quo petitione
honorum absentis submovebat, ne Caesarem quidem
exciperet per oblivionem, ac mox lege iam in aes
incisa et in aerarium condita corrigeret errorem. Nec
contentus Marcellus provincias Caesari et privilegium
eripere, rettulit etiam, ut colonis, quos rogatione
Vatinia Novum Comum deduxisset, civitas adimeretur,
quod per ambitionem et ultra praescriptum data
esset.

---

^a That is, in correcting the bill after it had been passed
and filed, as explained in the following sentence.

XXVIII. He took no less pains to win the devotion of princes and provinces all over the world, offering prisoners to some by the thousand as a gift, and sending auxiliary troops to the aid of others whenever they wished, and as often as they wished, without the sanction of the senate or people, besides adorning the principal cities of Asia and Greece with magnificent public works, as well as those of Italy and the provinces of Gaul and Spain. At last, when all were thunder-struck at his actions and wondered what their purpose could be, the consul Marcus Claudius Marcellus, after first **51 b.c.** making proclamation that he purposed to bring before the senate a matter of the highest public moment, proposed that a successor to Caesar be appointed before the end of his term, on the ground that the war was ended, peace was established, and the victorious army ought to be disbanded ; also that no account be taken of Caesar at the elections, unless he were present, since Pompey's subsequent action[a] had not annulled the decree of the people. And it was true that when Pompey proposed a bill touching the privileges of officials, in the clause where he debarred absentees from candidacy for office he forgot to make a special exception in Caesar's case, and did not correct the oversight until the law had been inscribed on a tablet of bronze and deposited in the treasury. Not content with depriving Caesar of his provinces and his privilege, Marcellus also moved that the colonists whom Caesar had settled in Novum Comum by the bill of Vatinius should lose their citizenship, on the ground that it had been given from political motives and was not authorized by the law.

XXIX. Commotus his Caesar ac iudicans, quod
saepe ex eo auditum ferunt, difficilius se principem
civitatis a primo ordine in secundum quam ex
secundo in novissimum detrudi, summa ope restitit,
partim per intercessores tribunos, partim per Servium
Sulpicium alterum consulem.   Insequenti quoque
anno Gaio Marcello, qui fratri patrueli suo Marco in
consulatu successerat, eadem temptante collegam
eius Aemilium Paulum Gaiumque Curionem vio-
lentissimum tribunorum ingenti mercede defensores
2 paravit.   Sed cum obstinatius omnia agi videret et
designatos etiam consules e parte diversa, senatum
litteris deprecatus est, ne sibi beneficium populi
adimeretur, aut ut ceteri quoque imperatores ab
exercitibus discederent ; confisus, ut putant, facilius
se, simul atque libuisset, veteranos convocaturum
quam Pompeium novos milites.   Cum adversariis
autem pepigit, ut dimissis octo legionibus Transalpi-
naque Gallia duae sibi legiones et Cisalpina provincia
vel etiam una legio cum Illyrico concederetur, quoad
consul fieret.

XXX. Verum neque senatu interveniente et adversariis negantibus ullam se de re publica facturos
pactionem, transiit in citeriorem Galliam, conventi
busque peractis Ravennae substitit, bello vindica-
turus si quid de tribunis plebis intercedentibus pro
se gravius a senatu constitutum esset.
2   Et praetextum quidem illi civilium armorum hoc

ᵃ When the senate passed a decree that Caesar should disband
his army before a given date, the tribunes Mark Antony and
Quintus Cassius exercised their privilege and vetoed it (Caesar,
B.C. 1. 2. 6–7); not only did the senate disregard the veto, but
the tribunes were obliged to seek safety in flight (id. 1. 5. 1–2).

XXIX. Greatly troubled by these measures, and thinking, as they say he was often heard to remark, that now that he was the leading man of the state, it was harder to push him down from the first place to the second than it would be from the second to the lowest, Caesar stoutly resisted Marcellus, partly through vetoes of the tribunes and partly through the other consul, Servius Sulpicius. When next year Gaius Marcellus, who had succeeded his cousin Marcus as consul, tried the same thing, Caesar by a heavy bribe secured the support of the other consul, Aemilius Paulus, and of Gaius Curio, the most reckless of the tribunes. But seeing that everything was being pushed most persistently, and that even the consuls elect were among the opposition, he sent a written appeal to the senate, not to take from him the privilege which the people had granted, or else to compel the others in command of armies to resign also; feeling sure, it was thought, that he could more readily muster his veterans as soon as he wished, than Pompey his newly levied troops. He further proposed a compromise to his opponents, that after giving up eight legions and Transalpine Gaul, he be allowed to keep two legions and Cisalpine Gaul, or at least one legion and Illyricum, until he was elected consul.

XXX. But when the senate declined to interfere, and his opponents declared that they would accept no compromise in a matter affecting the public welfare, he crossed to Hither Gaul, and after holding all the assizes, halted at Ravenna, intending to resort to war if the senate took any drastic action against the tribunes of the commons who interposed vetoes in his behalf.[a] Now this was his excuse

41

fuit; causas autem alias fuisse opinantur. Gnaeus
Pompeius ita dictitabat, quod neque opera consum-
mare, quae instituerat, neque populi expectationem,
quam de adventu sui[1] fecerat, privatis opibus explere

3 posset, turbare omnia ac permiscere voluisse. Alii
timuisse dicunt, ne eorum, quae primo consulatu
adversus auspicia legesque et intercessiones gessisset,
rationem reddere cogeretur; cum M. Cato identidem
nec sine iure iurando denuntiaret delaturum se
nomen eius, simul ac primum exercitum dimisisset;
cumque vulgo fore praedicarent, ut si privatus redis-
set, Milonis exemplo circumpositis armatis causam

4 apud iudices diceret. Quod probabilius facit Asinius
Pollio, Pharsalica acie caesos profligatosque adver-
sarios prospicientem haec eum ad verbum dixisse
referens : " Hoc voluerunt; tantis rebus gestis Gaius
Caesar condemnatus essem, nisi ab exercitu auxilium

5 petissem." Quidam putant captum imperii consuetudine pensitatisque suis et inimicorum viribus
usum occasione rapiendae dominationis, quam aetate
prima concupisset. Quod existimasse videbatur et
Cicero scribens de Officiis tertio libro semper
Caesarem in ore habuisse [2] Euripidis versus, quos sic
ipse convertit :

> " Nam si violandum est ius, regnandi [3] gratia
> violandum est; aliis rebus pietatem colas."

---

[1] sui, *MGX'*; suo, *Υ*.
[2] *after* habuisse *the mss. have the gloss,* est in Phoenissis :
εἴπερ γὰρ ἀδικεῖν χρή, τυραννίδος πέρι κάλλιστον ἀδίκημα· τὰ δ'
ἄλλα εὐσεβεῖν χρεών. 		[3] regnandi, *supplied by* ς.

---

[a] 3. 82. 		[b] *Phoenissae*, 524 f. 		[c] Way.

for the civil war, but it is believed that he had other motives. Gnaeus Pompeius used to declare that since Caesar's own means were not sufficient to complete the works which he had planned, nor to do all that he had led the people to expect on his return, he desired a state of general unrest and turmoil. Others say that he dreaded the necessity of rendering an account for what he had done in his first consulship contrary to the auspices and the laws, and regardless of vetoes ; for Marcus Cato often declared, and took oath too, that he would impeach Caesar the moment he had disbanded his army. It was openly said too that if he was out of office on his return, he would be obliged, like Milo, to make his defence in a court hedged about by armed men. The latter opinion is the more credible one in view of the assertion of Asinius Pollio, that when Caesar at the battle of Pharsalus saw his enemies slain or in flight, he said, word for word : " They would have it so. Even I, Gaius Caesar, after so many great deeds, should have been found guilty, if I had not turned to my army for help." Some think that habit had given him a love of power, and that weighing the strength of his adversaries against his own, he grasped the opportunity of usurping the despotism which had been his heart's desire from early youth. Cicero too was seemingly of this opinion, when he wrote in the third book of his *De Officiis* [a] that Caesar ever had upon his lips these lines of Euripides,[b] of which Cicero himself adds a version :

" If wrong may e'er be right, for a throne's sake
Were wrong most right :—be God in all else
      feared." [c]

43

XXXI. Cum ergo sublatam tribunorum intercessionem ipsosque urbe cessisse nuntiatum esset,[1] praemissis confestim clam cohortibus, ne qua suspicio moveretur, et spectaculo publico per dissimulationem interfuit et formam, qua ludum gladiatorium erat aedificaturus, consideravit et ex consuetudine convivio 2 se frequenti dedit.   Dein post solis occasum mulis e proximo pistrino ad vehiculum iunctis occultissimum iter modico comitatu ingressus est ; et cum luminibus extinctis decessisset via, diu errabundus tandem ad lucem duce reperto per angustissimos tramites pedibus evasit.   Consecutusque cohortis ad Rubiconem flumen, qui provinciae eius finis erat, paulum constitit, ac reputans quantum moliretur, conversus ad proximos : " Etiam nunc," inquit, " regredi possumus ; quod si ponticulum transierimus, omnia armis agenda erunt."

XXXII. Cunctanti ostentum tale factum est. Quidam eximia magnitudine et forma in proximo sedens repente apparuit harundine canens ; ad quem audiendum cum praeter pastores plurimi etiam ex stationibus milites concurrissent interque eos et aeneatores, rapta ab uno tuba prosilivit [2] ad flumen et ingenti spiritu classicum exorsus pertendit ad alteram ripam.   Tunc Caesar : " Eatur," inquit, "quo deorum ostenta et inimicorum iniquitas vocat.   Iacta alea est," inquit.

XXXIII. Atque ita traiecto exercitu, adhibitis tribunis plebis, qui pulsi supervenerant, pro contione

---

[1] esset, *G.* ; est, *Υ'* ; *the other mss. omit the word.*
[2] prosilivit, *MΠT* ; *the other mss. have* prosiluit.

XXXI. Accordingly, when word came that the veto of the tribunes had been set aside and they themselves had left the city, he at once sent on a few cohorts with all secrecy, and then, to disarm suspicion, concealed his purpose by appearing at a public show, inspecting the plans of a gladiatorial school which he intended building, and joining as usual in a banquet with a large company. It was not until after sunset that he set out very privily with a small company, taking the mules from a bakeshop hard by and harnessing them to a carriage ; and when his lights went out and he lost his way, he was astray for some time, but at last found a guide at dawn and got back to the road on foot by narrow by-paths. Then, overtaking his cohorts at the river Rubicon, which was the boundary of his province, he paused for a while, and realising what a step he was taking, he turned to those about him and said : " Even yet we may draw back ; but once cross yon little bridge, and the whole issue is with the sword."

XXXII. As he stood in doubt, this sign was given him. On a sudden there appeared hard by a being of wondrous stature and beauty, who sat and played upon a reed ; and when not only the shepherds flocked to hear him, but many of the soldiers left their posts, and among them some of the trumpeters, the apparition snatched a trumpet from one of them, rushed to the river, and sounding the war-note with mighty blast, strode to the opposite bank. Then Caesar cried : " Take we the course which the signs of the gods and the false dealing of our foes point out. The die is cast," said he.

XXXIII. Accordingly, crossing with his army, and welcoming the tribunes of the commons, who had

fidem militum flens ac veste a pectore discissa
invocavit. Existimatur etiam equestres census pollicitus singulis ; quod accidit opinione falsa. Nam
cum in adloquendo adhortandoque saepius digitum
laevae manus ostentans adfirmaret se ad satis facien-
dum omnibus, per quos dignitatem suam defensurus
esset, anulum quoque aequo animo detracturum sibi,
extrema contio, cui facilius erat videre contionantem
quam audire, pro dicto accepit, quod visu suspicabatur;
promissumque ius anulorum cum milibus quadringenis
fama distulit.

XXXIV. Ordo et summa rerum, quas deinceps
gessit, sic se habent. Picenum Umbriam Etruriam
occupavit et Lucio Domitio, qui per tumultum
successor ei nominatus Corfinium praesidio tenebat,
in dicionem redacto atque dimisso secundum Superum
mare Brundisium tetendit, quo consules Pompeiusque
2 confugerant quam primum transfretaturi. Hos frustra
per omnis moras exitu prohibere conatus Romam iter
convertit appellatisque de re publica patribus validis-
simas Pompei copias, quae sub tribus legatis M. Pe-
treio et L. Afranio et M. Varrone in Hispania erant,
invasit, professus ante inter suos, ire se ad exercitum
sine duce et inde reversurum ad ducem sine exercitu.
Et quanquam obsidione Massiliae, quae sibi in itinere

---

^a Knights (as well as senators) had the privilege of wearing
a gold ring, and must possess an estate of 400,000 sesterces.
^b *Per tumultum* is a strong expression for *contra legem* or
extra ordinem, since the Lex Sempronia provided that the
consuls be appointed to their provinces before election ; cf.
xix. 2.

come to him after being driven from Rome, he harangued the soldiers with tears, and rending his robe from his breast besought their faithful service. It is even thought that he promised every man a knight's estate, but that came of a misunderstanding ; for since he often pointed to the finger of his left hand as he addressed them and urged them on, declaring that to satisfy all those who helped him to defend his honour he would gladly tear his very ring from his hand, those on the edge of the assembly, who could see him better than they could hear his words, assumed that he said what his gesture seemed to mean ; and so the report went about that he had promised them the right of the ring and four hundred thousand sesterces [a] as well.

XXXIV. The sum total of his movements after that is, in their order, as follows : He overran Umbria, Picenum, and Etruria, took prisoner Lucius Domitius, who had been irregularly [b] named his successor, and was holding Corfinium with a garrison, let him go free, and then proceeded along the Adriatic to Brundisium, where Pompey and the consuls had taken refuge, intending to cross the sea as soon as might be. After vainly trying by every kind of hindrance to prevent their sailing, he marched off to Rome, and after calling the senate together to discuss public business, went to attack Pompey's strongest forces, which were in Spain under command of three of his lieutenants—Marcus Petreius, Lucius Afranius, and Marcus Varro—saying to his friends before he left "I go to meet an army without a leader, and I shall return to meet a leader without an army." And in fact, though his advance was delayed by the siege of Massilia, which had shut

portas clauserat, summaque frumentariae rei penuria
retardante brevi tamen omnia subegit.

XXXV. Hinc urbe repetita in Macedoniam transgressus Pompeium, per quattuor paene menses
maximis obsessum operibus, ad extremum Pharsalico
proelio fudit et· fugientem Alexandriam persecutus,
ut occisum deprehendit, cum Ptolemaeo rege, a quo
sibi quoque insidias tendi videbat, bellum sane
difficillimum gessit, neque loco neque tempore aequo,
sed hieme anni et intra moenia copiosissimi ac
sollertissimi hostis, inops ipse omnium rerum atque
inparatus. Regnum Aegypti victor Cleopatrae fra-
trique eius minori permisit, veritus provinciam
facere, ne quandoque violentiorem praesidem nacta
2 novarum rerum materia esset. Ab Alexandria in
Syriam et inde Pontum transiit urgentibus de
Pharnace nuntiis, quem Mithridatis Magni filium ac
tunc occasione temporum bellantem[1] iamque multiplici successu praeferocem, intra quintum quam
adfuerat diem, quattuor quibus in conspectum venit
horis, una profligavit acie ; crebro commemorans
Pompei felicitatem, cui praecipua militiae laus de
tam inbelli genere hostium contigisset. Dehinc
Scipionem ac Iubam reliquias partium in Africa
refoventis devicit, Pompei liberos in Hispania.

XXXVI. Omnibus civilibus bellis nullam cladem
nisi per legatos suos passus est, quorum C. Curio in

[1] rebellantem, *Bentley; cf. Eutr.* 6.22.3.

its gates against him, and by extreme scarcity of supplies, he nevertheless quickly gained a complete victory.

XXXV. Returning thence to Rome, he crossed into Macedonia, and after blockading Pompey for almost four months behind mighty ramparts, finally routed him in the battle at Pharsalus, followed him in his 48 b.c flight to Alexandria, and when he learned that his rival had been slain, made war on King Ptolemy, whom he perceived to be plotting against his own safety as well ; a war in truth of great difficulty, convenient neither in time nor place, but carried on during the winter season, within the walls of a well-provisioned and crafty foeman, while Caesar himself was without supplies of any kind and ill-prepared. Victor in spite of all, he turned over the rule of 47 b.c. Egypt to Cleopatra and her younger brother, fearing that if he made a province of it, it might one day under a headstrong governor be a source of revolution. From Alexandria he crossed to Syria, and from there went to Pontus, spurred on by the news that Pharnaces, son of Mithridates the Great, had taken advantage of the situation to make war, and was already flushed with numerous successes ; but Caesar vanquished him in a single battle within five days after his arrival and four hours after getting sight of him, often remarking on Pompey's good luck in gaining his principal fame as a general by victories over such feeble foemen. Then he over- 46 b.c came Scipio and Juba, who were patching up the remnants of their party in Africa, and the sons of Pompey in Spain. 45 b.c

XXXVI. In all the civil wars he suffered not a single disaster except through his lieutenants, of

49

Africa periit, C. Antonius in Illyrico in adversariorum devenit potestatem, P. Dolabella classem in eodem Illyrico, Cn. Domitius Calvinus in Ponto exercitum amiserunt. Ipse prosperrime semper ac ne ancipiti quidem umquam fortuna praeterquam bis dimicavit : semel ad Dyrrachium, ubi pulsus non instante Pompeio negavit eum vincere scire, iterum in Hispania ultimo proelio, cum desperatis rebus etiam de consciscenda nece cogitavit.

XXXVII. Confectis bellis quinquiens triumphavit, post devictum Scipionem quater eodem mense, sed interiectis diebus, et rursus semel post superatos Pompei liberos. Primum et excellentissimum triumphum egit Gallicum, sequentem Alexandrinum, deinde Ponticum, huic proximum Africanum, novissimum Hispaniensem, diverso quemque apparatu et
2 instrumento. Gallici triumphi die Velabrum praetervehens paene curru excussus est axe diffracto ascenditque Capitolium ad lumina, quadraginta elephantis dextra sinistraque lychnuchos gestantibus. Pontico triumpho inter pompae fercula trium verborum praetulit titulum VENI·VIDI·VICI non acta belli significantem sicut ceteris, sed celeriter confecti notam.

XXXVIII. Veteranis legionibus praedae nomine in pedites singulos super bina sestertia, quae initio civilis tumultus numeraverat, vicena quaterna milia nummum dedit. Adsignavit et agros, sed non

50

whom Gaius Curio perished in Africa, Gaius Antonius fell into the hands of the enemy in Illyricum, Publius Dolabella lost a fleet also off Illyricum, and Gnaeus Domitius Calvinus an army in Pontus. Personally he always fought with the utmost success, and the issue was never even in doubt save twice : once at Dyrrachium, where he was put to flight, and said of Pompey, who failed to follow up his success, that he did not know how to use a victory ; again in Spain, in the final struggle, when, believing the battle lost, he actually thought of suicide.

XXXVII. Having ended the wars, he celebrated five triumphs, four in a single month, but at intervals of a few days, after vanquishing Scipio ; and another on defeating Pompey's sons. The first and most splendid was the Gallic triumph, the next the Alexandrian, then the Pontic, after that the African, and finally the Spanish, each differing from the rest in its equipment and display of spoils. As he rode through the Velabrum on the day of his Gallic triumph, the axle of his chariot broke, and he was all but thrown out ; and he mounted the Capitol by torchlight, with forty elephants bearing lamps on his right and his left. In his Pontic triumph he displayed among the show-pieces of the procession an inscription of but three words, " I came, I saw, I conquered," not indicating the events of the war, as the others did, but the speed with which it was finished.

XXXVIII. To each and every foot-soldier of his veteran legions he gave twenty-four thousand sesterces by way of booty, over and above the two thousand apiece which he had paid them at the beginning of the civil strife. He also assigned them lands, but

continuos, ne quis possessorum expelleretur. Populo praeter frumenti denos modios ac totidem olei libras trecenos quoque nummos, quos pollicitus olim erat, viritim divisit et hoc amplius centenos pro mora.
2 Annuam etiam habitationem Romae usque ad bina milia nummum, in Italia non ultra quingenos sestertios remisit. Adiecit epulum ac viscerationem et post Hispaniensem victoriam duo prandia ; nam cum prius parce neque pro liberalitate sua praebitum iudicaret, quinto post die aliud largissimum praebuit.

XXXIX. Edidit spectacula varii generis : munus gladiatorium, ludos etiam regionatim urbe tota et quidem per omnium linguarum histriones, item circenses athletas naumachiam. Munere in Foro depugnavit Furius Leptinus stirpe praetoria et Q. Calpenus senator quondam actorque causarum. Pyrricham saltaverunt Asiae Bithyniaeque principum
2 liberi. Ludis Decimus Laberius eques Romanus mimum suum egit donatusque quingentis sestertiis et anulo aureo sessum in quattuordecim e scaena per orchestram transiit. Circensibus spatio Circi ab utraque parte producto et in gyrum euripo addito quadrigas bigasque et equos desultorios agitaverunt nobilissimi iuvenes. Troiam lusit turma duplex

---

[a] The *prandium* was the first substantial meal of the day, taken about noon ; the translation "dinner" is used advisedly.

[b] In token of his restoration to the rank of knight, which he forfeited by appearing on the stage ; see chap. xxxiii.

[c] The first fourteen rows above the orchestra, reserved for the knights by the law of L. Roscius Otho, tribune of the commons, 67 B.C.

[d] *Euripus*, the strait between Euboea and Boeotia, was used also as a common noun, meaning "a ditch" or "canal."

not side by side, to avoid dispossessing any of the
former owners. To every man of the people, besides
ten pecks of grain and the same number of pounds
of oil, he distributed the three hundred sesterces
which he had promised at first, and one hundred
apiece to boot because of the delay. He also
remitted a year's rent in Rome to tenants who paid
two thousand sesterces or less, and in Italy up to five
hundred sesterces. He added a banquet and a dole
of meat, and after his Spanish victory two dinners;[a]
for deeming that the former of these had not been
served with a liberality creditable to his generosity,
he gave another five days later on a most lavish
scale.

XXXIX. He gave entertainments of divers kinds:
a combat of gladiators and also stage-plays in every
ward all over the city, performed too by actors of
all languages, as well as races in the circus, athletic
contests, and a sham sea-fight. In the gladiatorial
contest in the Forum Furius Leptinus, a man of
praetorian stock, and Quintus Calpenus, a former
senator and pleader at the bar, fought to a finish. A
Pyrrhic dance was performed by the sons of the
princes of Asia and Bithynia. During the plays
Decimus Laberius, a Roman knight, acted a farce of
his own composition, and having been presented with
five hundred thousand sesterces and a gold ring,[b]
passed from the stage through the orchestra and took
his place in the fourteen rows.[c] For the races the
circus was lengthened at either end and a broad canal[d]
was dug all about it; then young men of the highest
rank drove four-horse and two-horse chariots and
rode pairs of horses, vaulting from one to the other.
The game called Troy was performed by two troops, of

53

3 maiorum minorumque puerorum. Venationes editae
per dies quinque ac novissime pugna divisa in duas
acies, quingenis peditibus, elephantis vicenis, tricenis
equitibus hinc et inde commissis. Nam quo laxius
dimicaretur, sublatae metae inque earum locum bina
castra exadversum constituta erant. Athletae stadio
ad tempus exstructo regione Marti campi certaverunt

4 per triduum. Navali proelio in minore Codeta
defosso lacu biremes ac triremes quadriremesque
Tyriae et Aegyptiae classis magno pugnatorum
numero conflixerunt. Ad quae omnia spectacula
tantum undique confluxit hominum, ut plerique
advenae aut inter vicos aut inter vias tabernaculis
positis manerent, ac saepe prae turba elisi exanimati-
que sint plurimi et in his duo senatores.

XL. Conversus hinc ad ordinandum rei publicae
statum fastos correxit iam pridem vitio pontificum
per intercalandi licentiam adeo turbatos, ut neque
messium feriae aestate neque vindemiarum autumno
conpeterent; annumque ad cursum solis accommodavit, ut trecentorum sexaginta quinque dierum
esset et intercalario mense sublato unus dies quarto

2 quoque anno intercalaretur. Quo autem magis in
posterum ex Kalendis Ianuariis novis[1] temporum ratio
congrueret, inter Novembrem ac Decembrem mensem interiecit duos alios; fuitque is annus, quo
haec constituebantur, quindecim mensium cum

---

[1] novis, *Ursinus;* nobis, Ω.

[a] The year had previously consisted of 355 days, and the
deficiency of about eleven days was made up by inserting an
intercalary month of twenty-two or twenty-three days after
February.

54

younger and of older boys. Combats with wild beasts
were presented on five successive days, and last of all
there was a battle between two opposing armies, in
which five hundred foot-soldiers, twenty elephants,
and thirty horsemen engaged on each side. To make
room for this, the goals were taken down and in their
place two camps were pitched over against each
other. The athletic competitions lasted for three days
in a temporary stadium built for the purpose in the
region of the Campus Martius. For the naval battle
a pool was dug in the lesser Codeta and there was a
contest of ships of two, three, and four banks of oars,
belonging to the Tyrian and Egyptian fleets, manned
by a large force of fighting men. Such a throng
flocked to all these shows from every quarter, that
many strangers had to lodge in tents pitched in the
streets or along the roads, and the press was often
such that many were crushed to death, including
two senators.

XL. Then turning his attention to the reorgani-
sation of the state, he reformed the calendar, which
the negligence of the pontiffs had long since so
disordered, through their privilege of adding months
or days at pleasure, that the harvest festivals did not
come in summer nor those of the vintage in the
autumn ; and he adjusted the year to the sun's
course by making it consist of three hundred and
sixty-five days, abolishing the intercalary month,[a]
and adding one day every fourth year. Furthermore, that the correct reckoning of seasons might
begin with the next Kalends of January, he inserted
two other months between those of November and
December ; hence the year in which these arrangements were made was one of fifteen months,

intercalario, qui ex consuetudine in eum annum inciderat.

XLI. Senatum supplevit, patricios adlegit, praetorum aedilium quaestorum, minorum etiam magistratuum numerum ampliavit; nudatos opere censorio aut sententia iudicum de ambitu condemnatos re-
2 stituit. Comitia cum populo partitus est, ut exceptis consulatus conpetitoribus de cetero numero candidatorum pro parte dimidia quos populus vellet pronuntiarentur, pro parte altera quos ipse dedisset. Et edebat per libellos circum[1] tribum missos scriptura brevi : "Caesar dictator illi tribui. Commendo vobis illum et illum, ut vestro suffragio suam dignitatem teneant." Admisit ad honores et proscriptorum liberos. Iudicia ad duo genera iudicum redegit, equestris ordinis ac senatorii ; tribunos aerarios, quod erat tertium, sustulit.
3 Recensum populi nec more nec loco solito, sed vicatim per dominos insularum egit atque ex viginti trecentisque milibus accipientium frumentum e publico ad centum quinquaginta retraxit; ac ne qui novi coetus recensionis causa moveri quandoque possent, instituit, quotannis in demortuorum locum ex iis, qui recensi non essent, subsortitio a praetore fieret.

XLII. Octoginta autem civium milibus in transmarinas colonias distributis, ut exhaustae quoque

---

[1] circum tribum] circum tribus, *Venetian ed. of* 1510, *Casaubon ;* tributim circummissos, *Bentley ; the early Roman editions have* cuique tribui.

---

[a] Plebeians, connected in some way with the treasury.
[b] *I.e.*, of the commons, with reference to the distribution of grain.

including the intercalary month, which belonged to
that year according to the former custom.

XLI. He filled the vacancies in the senate, enrolled additional patricians, and increased the number
of praetors, aediles, and quaestors, as well as of the
minor officials ; he reinstated those who had been
degraded by official action of the censors or found
guilty of bribery by verdict of the jurors. He
shared the elections with the people on this basis :
that except in the case of the consulship, half of the
magistrates should be appointed by the people's
choice, while the rest should be those whom he had
personally nominated. And these he announced in
brief notes like the following, circulated in each
tribe : " Caesar the Dictator to this or that tribe. I
commend to you so and so, to hold their positions by
your votes." He admitted to office even the sons of
those who had been proscribed. He limited the
right of serving as jurors to two classes, the
equestrian and senatorial orders, disqualifying the
third class, the tribunes of the treasury.[a]

He made the enumeration of the people [b] neither
in the usual manner nor place, but from street to
street aided by the owners of blocks of houses, and
reduced the number of those who received grain at
public expense from three hundred and twenty
thousand to one hundred and fifty thousand. And
to prevent the calling of additional meetings at any
future time for purposes of enrolment, he provided
that the places of such as died should be filled each
year by the praetors from those who were not on
the list.

XLII. Moreover, to keep up the population of
the city, depleted as it was by the assignment of

urbis frequentia suppeteret, sanxit, ne quis civis maior annis viginti minorve quadraginta,[1] qui sacramento non teneretur, plus triennio continuo Italia abesset, neu qui senatoris filius nisi contubernalis aut comes magistratus peregre proficisceretur ; neve ii, qui pecuariam facerent, minus tertia parte puberum ingenuorum inter pastores haberent. Omnisque medicinam Romae professos et liberalium artium doctores, quo libentius et ipsi urbem incolerent et ceteri adpeterent, civitate donavit.

2 De pecuniis mutuis disiecta novarum tabularum expectatione, quae crebro movebatur, decrevit tandem, ut debitores creditoribus satis facerent per aestimationem possessionum, quanti quasque ante civile bellum comparassent, deducto summae aeris alieni, si quid usurae nomine numeratum aut perscriptum fuisset ; qua condicione quarta pars fere 3 crediti deperibat. Cuncta collegia praeter antiquitus constituta distraxit. Poenas facinorum auxit ; et cum locupletes eo facilius scelere se obligarent, quod integris patrimoniis exsulabant, parricidas, ut Cicero scribit, bonis omnibus, reliquos dimidia parte multavit.

XLIII. Ius laboriosissime ac severissime dixit. Repetundarum convictos etiam ordine senatorio movit. Diremit nuptias praetorii viri, qui digressam a marito post biduum statim duxerat, quamvis sine

---

[1] quadraginta, *Basle ed. of* 1533 ; LX, *Casaubon* ; L, *Oudendorp;* decem, Ω.

---

[a] The derivation of *parricida* is uncertain, but it cannot come from *pater* and *caedo*. In early times it meant wilful murder of a freeman ; XII. Tab. ap. Fest. *s.v.*, *si qui hominem liberum dolo sciens morti duit, paricidas esto* ; later, it was associated by popular etymology with *pater* and *caedo*, and used also in the modern sense of the word.

eighty thousand citizens to colonies across the sea, he made a law that no citizen older than twenty or younger than forty, who was not detained by service in the army, should be absent from Italy for more than three successive years; that no senator's son should go abroad except as the companion of a magistrate or on his staff; and that those who made a business of grazing should have among their herdsmen at least one-third who were men of free birth. He conferred citizenship on all who practised medicine at Rome, and on all teachers of the liberal arts, to make them more desirous of living in the city and to induce others to resort to it.

As to debts, he disappointed those who looked for their cancellation, which was often agitated, but finally decreed that the debtors should satisfy their creditors according to a valuation of their possessions at the price which they had paid for them before the civil war, deducting from the principal whatever interest had been paid in cash or pledged through bankers; an arrangement which wiped out about a fourth part of their indebtedness. He dissolved all guilds, except those of ancient foundation. He increased the penalties for crimes; and inasmuch as the rich involved themselves in guilt with less hesitation because they merely suffered exile, without any loss of property, he punished murderers of freemen [a] by the confiscation of all their goods, as Cicero writes, and others by the loss of one-half.

XLIII. He administered justice with the utmost conscientiousness and strictness. Those convicted of extortion he even dismissed from the senatorial order. He annulled the marriage of an ex-praetor, who had married a woman the very day after her

59

probri suspicione. Peregrinarum mercium portoria
instituit. Lecticarum usum, item conchyliatae vestis
et margaritarum nisi certis personis et aetatibus
2 perque certos dies ademit. Legem praecipue
sumptuariam exercuit dispositis circa macellum custodibus, qui obsonia contra vetitum proposita[1] retinerent
deportarentque ad se, submissis nonnumquam lictoribus atque militibus, qui, si qua custodes fefellissent,
iam adposita e triclinio auferrent.

XLIV. Nam de ornanda instruendaque urbe, item
de tuendo ampliandoque imperio plura ac maiora in
dies destinabat: in primis Martis templum, quantum
nusquam esset, exstruere repleto et conplanato lacu,
in quo naumachiae spectaculum ediderat, theatrumque
2 summae magnitudinis Tarpeio monti accubans; ius
civile ad certum modum redigere atque ex immensa
diffusaque legum copia optima quaeque et necessaria
in paucissimos conferre libros; bibliothecas Graecas
Latinasque quas maximas posset publicare data
Marco Varroni cura comparandarum ac digerendarum;
3 siccare Pomptinas paludes; emittere Fucinum lacum;
viam munire a mari Supero per Appennini dorsum ad
Tiberim usque; perfodere Isthmum; Dacos, qui se
in Pontum et Thraciam effuderant, coercere; mox
Parthis inferre bellum per Armeniam minorem nec
nisi ante expertos adgredi proelio.

---

[1] proposita, *an addition to the text suggested by Ihm.*

60

divorce, although there was no suspicion of adultery. He imposed duties on foreign wares. He denied the use of litters and the wearing of scarlet robes or pearls to all except to those of a designated position and age, and on set days. In particular he enforced the law against extravagance, setting watchmen in various parts of the market, to seize and bring to him dainties which were exposed for sale in violation of the law; and sometimes he sent his lictors and soldiers to take from a dining-room any articles which had escaped the vigilance of his watchmen, even after they had been served.

XLIV. In particular, for the adornment and convenience of the city, also for the protection and extension of the Empire, he formed more projects and more extensive ones every day: first of all, to rear a temple to Mars, greater than any in existence, filling up and levelling the pool in which he had exhibited the sea-fight, and to build a theatre of vast size, sloping down from the Tarpeian rock; to reduce the civil code to fixed limits, and of the vast and prolix mass of statutes to include only the best and most essential in a limited number of volumes; to open to the public the greatest possible libraries of Greek and Latin books, assigning to Marcus Varro the charge of procuring and classifying them; to drain the Pomptine marshes; to let out the water from Lake Fucinus; to make a highway from the Adriatic across the summit of the Apennines as far as the Tiber; to cut a canal through the Isthmus; to check the Dacians, who had poured into Pontus and Thrace; then to make war on the Parthians by way of Lesser Armenia, but not to risk a battle with them until he had first tested their mettle.

4   Talia agentem atque meditantem mors praevenit.
De qua prius quam dicam, ea quae ad formam et
habitum et cultum et mores, nec minus quae ad
civilia et bellica eius studia pertineant, non alienum
erit summatim exponere.

   XLV. Fuisse traditur excelsa statura, colore
candido, teretibus membris, ore paulo pleniore, nigris
vegetisque oculis, valitudine prospera, nisi quod
tempore extremo repente animo linqui atque etiam
per somnum exterreri solebat.   Comitiali quoque
2 morbo bis inter res agendas correptus est. Circa
corporis curam morosior, ut non solum tonderetur
diligenter ac raderetur, sed velleretur etiam, ut
quidam exprobraverunt, calvitii vero deformitatem
iniquissime ferret, saepe obtrectatorum iocis obnoxiam
expertus.   Ideoque et deficientem capillum revocare
a vertice adsueverat et ex omnibus decretis sibi a
senatu populoque honoribus non aliud aut recepit aut
usurpavit libentius quam ius laureae coronae perpetuo
gestandae.

3   Etiam cultu notabilem ferunt; usum enim lato
clavo ad manus fimbriato nec umquam aliter quam ut[1]
super eum cingeretur, et quidem fluxiore cinctura ;
unde emanasse Sullae dictum optimates saepius ad-
monentis, ut male praecinctum puerum caverent.

---

[1] ut, *supplied by Bentley,* ΠQ*ς insert after* nec.

---

[a] Epilepsy, called *morbus comitialis*, because an attack was
regarded as sufficient cause for the postponement of elections,
or other public business.   Sometimes a seizure was feigned
for political reasons.

[b] *Latus clavus*, the broad purple stripe, is also applied to
a tunic with the broad stripe.   All senators had the right to

All these enterprises and plans were cut short by his death. But before I speak of that, it will not be amiss to describe briefly his personal appearance, his dress, his mode of life, and his character, as well as his conduct in civil and military life.

XLV. He is said to have been tall of stature, with a fair complexion, shapely limbs, a somewhat full face, and keen black eyes; sound of health, except that towards the end he was subject to sudden fainting fits and to nightmare as well. He was twice attacked by the falling sickness[a] during his campaigns. He was somewhat overnice in the care of his person, being not only carefully trimmed and shaved, but even having superfluous hair plucked out, as some have charged; while his baldness was a disfigurement which troubled him greatly, since he found that it was often the subject of the gibes of his detractors. Because of it he used to comb forward his scanty locks from the crown of his head, and of all the honours voted him by the senate and people there was none which he received or made use of more gladly than the privilege of wearing a laurel wreath at all times. They say, too, that he was remarkable in his dress; that he wore a senator's tunic[b] with fringed sleeves reaching to the wrist, and always had a girdle[c] over it, though rather a loose one; and this, they say, was the occasion of Sulla's *mot*, when he often warned the nobles to keep an eye on the ill-girt boy.

wear this; the peculiarity in Caesar's case consisted in the long fringed sleeves.

[c] While a girdle was commonly worn with the ordinary tunic, it was not usual to wear one with the *latus clavus*; *Quint.* XI. 3. 138. The looseness of the girdle was an additional peculiarity.

XLVI. Habitavit primo in Subura modicis aedibus, post autem pontificatum maximum in Sacra via domo publica. Munditiarum lautitiarumque studiossimum multi prodiderunt ; villam in Nemorensi a fundamentis incohatam magnoque sumptu absolutam, quia non tota ad animum ei responderat, totam diruisse, quanquam tenuem adhuc et obaeratum ; in expeditionibus tessellata et sectilia pavimenta circumtulisse.

XLVII. Britanniam petisse spe margaritarum, quarum amplitudinem conferentem interdum sua manu exegisse pondus ; gemmas, toreumata, signa, tabulas operis antiqui semper animosissime comparasse ; servitia rectiora politioraque inmenso pretio, et cuius ipsum etiam puderet, sic ut rationibus vetaret inferri.

XLVIII. Convivatum assidue per provincias duobus tricliniis, uno quo sagati palliative, altero quo togati cum inlustrioribus provinciarum discumberent. Domesticam disciplinam in parvis ac maioribus rebus diligenter adeo severeque rexit, ut pistorem alium quam sibi panem convivis subicientem compedibus vinxerit, libertum gratissimum ob adulteratam equitis Romani uxorem, quamvis nullo querente, capitali poena adfecerit.

XLIX. Pudicitiae eius famam nihil quidem

XLVI. He lived at first in the Subura in a modest house, but after he became pontifex maximus, in the official residence on the Sacred Way. Many have written that he was very fond of elegance and luxury ; that having laid the foundations of a country-house on his estate at Nemi and finished it at great cost, he tore it all down because it did not suit him in every particular, although at the time he was still poor and heavily in debt; and that he carried tesselated and mosaic floors about with him on his campaigns.

XLVII. They say that he was led to invade Britain by the hope of getting pearls, and that in comparing their size he sometimes weighed them with his own hand ; that he was always a most enthusiastic collector of gems, carvings, statues, and pictures by early artists ; also of slaves of exceptional figure and training at enormous prices, of which he himself was so ashamed that he forbade their entry in his accounts.

XLVIII. It is further reported that in the provinces he gave banquets constantly in two dining-halls, in one of which his officers or Greek companions, in the other Roman civilians and the more distinguished of the provincials reclined at table. He was so punctilious and strict in the management of his household, in small matters as well as in those of greater importance, that he put his baker in irons for serving him with one kind of bread and his guests with another ; and he inflicted capital punishment on a favourite freedman for adultery with the wife of a Roman knight, although no complaint was made against him.

XLIX. There was no stain on his reputation for

praeter Nicomedis contubernium laesit, gravi tamen
et perenni obprobrio et ad omnium convicia exposito.
Omitto Calvi Licini notissimos versus :

> " Bithynia quicquid
> et pedicator [1] Caesaris umquam habuit."

Praetereo actiones Dolabellae et Curionis patris, in
quibus eum Dolabella " paelicem reginae, spondam
interiorem regiae lecticae," at Curio " stabulum Nico-
2 medis et Bithynicum fornicem " dicunt. Missa etiam
facio edicta Bibuli, quibus proscripsit : collegam
suum Bithynicam reginam, eique antea regem
fuisse cordi, nunc esse regnum. Quo tempore, ut
Marcus Brutus refert, Octavius etiam quidam
valitudine mentis liberius dicax conventu maximo,
cum Pompeium regem appellasset, ipsum reginam
salutavit. Séd C. Memmius etiam ad cyathum et
vinum [2] Nicomedi stetisse obicit, cum reliquis exoletis,
pleno convivio, accubantibus nonnullis urbicis nego-
3 tiatoribus, quorum refert nomina. Cicero vero non
contentus in quibusdam epistulis scripsisse a satelliti-
bus eum in cubiculum regium eductum in aureo lecto
veste purpurea decubuisse floremque aetatis a Venere
orti in Bithynia contaminatum, quondam etiam in
senatu defendenti ei Nysae causam, filiae Nicomedis,
beneficiaque regis in se commemoranti : " Remove,"
inquit, " istaec, oro te, quando notum est, et quid
4 ille tibi et quid illi tute dederis." Gallico denique
triumpho milites eius inter cetera carmina, qualia

---

[1] pedicator] predicator, Ω.
[2] et vinum, Υ′ ; et vina, G ; et vi, MVL²δ.

chastity except his intimacy with King Nicomedes, but that was a deep and lasting reproach, which laid him open to insults from every quarter. I say nothing of the notorious lines of Licinius Calvus:

"Whate'er Bithynia had, and Caesar's paramour."

I pass over, too, the invectives of Dolabella and the elder Curio, in which Dolabella calls him "the queen's rival, the inner partner of the royal couch," and Curio, "the brothel of Nicomedes and the stew of Bithynia." I take no account of the edicts of Bibulus, in which he posted his colleague as "the queen of Bithynia," saying that "of yore he was enamoured of a king, but now of a king's estate." At this same time, so Marcus Brutus declares, one Octavius, a man whose disordered mind made him somewhat free with his tongue, after saluting Pompey as "king" in a crowded assembly, greeted Caesar as "queen." But Gaius Memmius makes the direct charge that he acted as cup-bearer to Nicomedes with the rest of his wantons at a large dinner-party, and that among the guests were some merchants from Rome, whose names Memmius gives. Cicero, indeed, is not content with having written in sundry letters that Caesar was led by the king's attendants to the royal apartments, that he lay on a golden couch arrayed in purple, and that the virginity of this son of Venus was lost in Bithynia; but when Caesar was once addressing the senate in defence of Nysa, daughter of Nicomedes, and was enumerating his obligations to the king, Cicero cried: "No more of that, pray, for it is well known what he gave you, and what you gave him in turn." Finally, in his Gallic triumph his soldiers, among the bantering

currum prosequentes ioculariter canunt, etiam illud
vulgatissimum pronuntiaverunt :

" Gallias Caesar subegit, Nicomedes Caesarem :
  Ecce Caesar nunc triumphat qui subegit Gallias,[1]
  Nicomedes non triumphat qui subegit Caesarem."

L. Pronum et sumptuosum in libidines fuisse
constans opinio est, plurimasque et illustres feminas
corrupisse, in quibus Postumiam Servi Sulpici,
Lolliam Auli Gabini, Tertullam Marci Crassi, etiam
Cn. Pompei Muciam. Nam certe Pompeio et a
Curionibus patre et filio et a multis exprobratum
est, quod cuius causa post tres liberos exegisset
uxorem et quem gemens Aegisthum appellare
consuesset, eius postea filiam potentiae cupiditate
2 in matrimonium recepisset. Sed ante alias dilexit
Marci Bruti matrem Serviliam, cui et primo [2] suo
consulatu sexagiens sestertium margaritam mercatus
est et bello civili super alias donationes amplissima
praedia ex auctionibus hastae minimo addixit ; cum
quidem plerisque vilitatem mirantibus facetissime
Cicero : " Quo melius," inquit, " emptum sciatis, tertia
deducta ; " existimabatur enim Servilia etiam filiam
suam Tertiam Caesari conciliare.

----

[1] *The second line is omitted by MHGVPO'δ, while Q (and ε
in the margin) add*

    Et quare triumphat Caesar qui subegit Gallias ?
    Nicomedes non triumphat qui subegit Caesarem.

[2] primo, *Torrentius;* proximo, *mss.*

----

[a] The word play on *tertia (pars)* and *Tertia*, daughter of
Servilia, as well as on the two senses of *deducta*, is quite
untranslatable. The first meaning is given in the translation,
and the second is implied in the following sentence. Cf.
Macrobius, *Saturnalia*, 2. 2. 5.

songs which are usually sung by those who follow the chariot, shouted these lines, which became a by-word :

" All the Gauls did Caesar vanquish, Nicomedes
    vanquished him ;
  Lo ! now Caesar rides in triumph, victor over all
    the Gauls,
  Nicomedes does not triumph, who subdued the
    conqueror."

L. That he was unbridled and extravagant in his intrigues is the general opinion, and that he seduced many illustrious women, among them Postumia, wife of Servius Sulpicius, Lollia, wife of Aulus Gabinius, Tertulla, wife of Marcus Crassus, and even Gnaeus Pompey's wife Mucia. At all events there is no doubt that Pompey was taken to task by the elder and the younger Curio, as well as by many others, because through a desire for power he had afterwards married the daughter of a man on whose account he divorced a wife who had borne him three children, and whom he had often referred to with a groan as an Aegisthus. But beyond all others Caesar loved Servilia, the mother of Marcus Brutus, for whom in his first consulship he bought a pearl costing six million sesterces. During the civil war, too, besides other presents, he knocked down some fine estates to her in a public auction at a nominal price, and when some expressed their surprise at the low figure, Cicero wittily remarked : " It's a better bargain than you think, for there is a third off." [a] And in fact it was thought that Servilia was prostituting her own daughter Tertia to Caesar.

LI. Ne provincialibus quidem matrimoniis abstinuisse vel hoc disticho apparet iactato aeque a militibus per Gallicum triumphum :

" Urbani, servate uxores : moechum calvom adducimus.
Aurum in Gallia effutuisti, hic sumpsisti mutuum."

LII. Dilexit et reginas, inter quas Eunoen Mauram Bogudis uxorem, cui maritoque eius plurima et immensa tribuit, ut Naso[1] scripsit ; sed maxime Cleopatram, cum qua et convivia in primam lucem saepe protraxit et eadem nave thalamego paene Aethiopia tenus Aegyptum penetravit, nisi exercitus sequi recusasset, quam denique accitam in urbem non nisi maximis honoribus praemiisque auctam remisit filiumque natum appellare nomine suo passus 2 est. Quem quidem nonnulli Graecorum similem quoque Caesari et forma et incessu tradiderunt. M. Antonius adgnitum etiam ab eo senatui adfirmavit, idque[2] scire C. Matium et C. Oppium reliquosque Caesaris amicos ; quorum Gaius Oppius, quasi plane defensione ac patrocinio res egeret, librum edidit, non esse Caesaris filium, quem 3 Cleopatra dicat. Helvius Cinna tr. pl. plerisque confessus est habuisse se scriptam paratamque legem, quam Caesar ferre iussisset cum ipse abesset, uti uxores liberorum quaerendorum causa quas et quot

---

[1] Naso, ς (*Mancinellus*); vasa, Ω (*apparently corrected from* vasu *in* M ; vasas, G).
[2] idque, *Modderman ; the greater number of the mss. have* que (= quae).

---

a M. Actorius Naso ; see chap. ix, 3.

LI. That he did not refrain from intrigues in the provinces is shown in particular by this couplet, which was also shouted by the soldiers in his Gallic triumph :

" Men of Rome, keep close your consorts, here's a
    bald adulterer.
Gold in Gaul you spent in dalliance, which you
    borrowed here in Rome."

LII. He had love affairs with queens too, including Eunoe the Moor, wife of Bogudes, on whom, as well as on her husband, he bestowed many splendid presents, as Naso writes ;[a] but above all with Cleopatra, with whom he often feasted until daybreak, and he would have gone through Egypt with her in her state-barge almost to Aethiopia, had not his soldiers refused to follow him. Finally he called her to Rome and did not let her leave until he had ladened her with high honours and rich gifts, and he allowed her to give his name to the child which she bore. In fact, accordding to certain Greek writers, this child was very like Caesar in looks and carriage. Mark Antony declared to the senate that Caesar had really acknowledged the boy, and that Gaius Matius, Gaius Oppius, and other friends of Caesar knew this. Of these Gaius Oppius, as if admitting that the situation required apology and defence, published a book, to prove that the child whom Cleopatra fathered on Caesar was not his. Helvius Cinna, tribune of the commons, admitted to several that he had a bill drawn up in due form, which Caesar had ordered him to propose to the people in his absence, making it lawful for Caesar to marry what wives he wished, and as many as he wished, " for the purpose of be-

vellet ducere liceret. At ne cui dubium omnino
sit et impudicitiae et adulteriorum flagrasse infamia,
Curio pater quadam eum oratione omnium mulierum
virum et omnium virorum mulierem appellat.

LIII. Vini parcissimum ne inimici quidem ne-
gaverunt. Marci Catonis est : unum ex omnibus
Caesarem ad evertendam rem publicam sobrium
accessisse. Nam circa victum Gaius Oppius adeo
indifferentem docet, ut quondam ab hospite conditum
oleum pro viridi adpositum aspernantibus ceteris
solum etiam largius appetisse scribat, ne hospitem
aut neglegentiae aut rusticitatis videretur arguere.

LIV. Abstinentiam neque in imperiis neque in
magistratibus praestitit. Ut enim quidam monumentis suis testati sunt, in Hispania pro consule et
a sociis pecunias accepit emendicatas in auxilium
aeris alieni et Lusitanorum quaedam oppida, quanquam nec imperata detrectarent et advenienti portas
2 patefacerent, diripuit hostiliter. In Gallia fana
templaque deum donis referta expilavit, urbes diruit
saepius ob praedam quam ob delictum ; unde factum,
ut auro abundaret ternisque milibus nummum in
libras promercale per Italiam provinciasque diven-
3 deret. In primo consulatu tria milia pondo auri
furatus e Capitolio tantundem inaurati aeris reposuit.
Societates ac regna pretio dedit, ut qui uni Ptolemaeo
prope sex milia talentorum suo Pompeique nomine

---

^a The words *liberorum quaerendorum causa* are a legal
formula indicating that the purpose of marriage is to beget
legal heirs.

^b Caesar was in reality *propraetor*, but *proconsul* (*pro
consule*) is sometimes used of the governor of a province,
regardless of his rank.

^c Apparently about half the usual price : see Index, *s.v.
sestertius.*

getting children." [a] But to remove all doubt that he had an evil reputation both for shameless vice and for adultery, I have only to add that the elder Curio in one of his speeches calls him "every woman's man and every man's woman."

LIII. That he drank very little wine not even his enemies denied. There is a saying of Marcus Cato that Caesar was the only man who undertook to overthrow the state when sober. Even in the matter of food Gaius Oppius tells us that he was so indifferent, that once when his host served stale oil instead of fresh, and the other guests would have none of it, Caesar partook even more plentifully than usual, not to seem to charge his host with carelessness or lack of manners.

LIV. Neither when in command of armies nor as a magistrate at Rome did he show a scrupulous integrity; for as certain men have declared in their memoirs, when he was proconsul in Spain,[b] he not only begged money from the allies, to help pay his debts, but also attacked and sacked some towns of the Lusitanians although they did not refuse his terms and opened their gates to him on his arrival. In Gaul he pillaged shrines and temples of the gods filled with offerings, and oftener sacked towns for the sake of plunder than for any fault. In consequence he had more gold than he knew what to do with, and offered it for sale throughout Italy and the provinces at the rate of three thousand sesterces the pound.[c] In his first consulship he stole three thousand pounds of gold from the Capitol, replacing it with the same weight of gilded bronze. He made alliances and thrones a matter of barter, for he extorted from Ptolemy alone in his own name

abstulerit. Postea vero evidentissimis rapinis ac sacrilegis et onera bellorum civilium et triumphorum ac munerum sustinuit impendia.

LV. Eloquentia militarique[1] re aut aequavit praestantissimorum gloriam aut excessit. Post accusationem Dolabellae haud dubie principibus patronis adnumeratus est. Certe Cicero ad Brutum oratores enumerans negat se videre, cui debeat Caesar cedere, aitque eum elegantem, splendidam quoque atque etiam magnificam et generosam quodam modo rationem dicendi tenere ; et ad Cornelium Nepotem

2 de eodem ita scripsit : " Quid ? oratorem quem huic antepones eorum, qui nihil aliud egerunt ? Quis sententiis aut acutior aut crebrior ? Quis verbis aut ornatior aut elegantior ? " Genus eloquentiae dumtaxat adulescens adhuc Strabonis Caesaris secutus videtur, cuius etiam ex oratione, quae inscribitur " pro Sardis," ad verbum nonnulla transtulit in divinationem suam. Pronuntiasse autem dicitur voce acuta,

3 ardenti motu gestuque, non sine venustate. Orationes aliquas reliquit, inter quas temere quaedam feruntur. " Pro Quinto Metello " non immerito Augustus existimat magis ab actuariis exceptam male subsequentibus verba dicentis, quam ab ipso editam ; nam in quibusdam exemplaribus invenio ne inscriptam quidem " pro Metello," sed " quam scripsit Metello," cum ex persona Caesaris sermo sit Metellum seque adversus

---

[1] militarique re, *Lipsius;* militari quare, Ω (*G omits* quare).

[a] Cic. *Brut.* 261.
[b] That is, a speech in which he competed with other advocates for the right to conduct a prosecution.

and that of Pompey nearly six thousand talents, while later on he met the heavy expenses of the civil wars and of his triumphs and entertainments by the most bare-faced pillage and sacrilege.

LV. In eloquence and in the art of war he either equalled or surpassed the fame of their most eminent representatives. After his accusation of Dolabella, he was without question numbered with the leading advocates. At all events when Cicero reviews the orators in his *Brutus*,[a] he says that he does not see to whom Caesar ought to yield the palm, declaring that his style is elegant as well as transparent, even grand and in a sense noble. Again in a letter to Cornelius Nepos he writes thus of Caesar: "Come now, what orator would you rank above him of those who have devoted themselves to nothing else? Who has cleverer or more frequent epigrams? Who is either more picturesque or more choice in diction?" He appears, at least in his youth, to have imitated the manner of Caesar Strabo, from whose speech entitled "For the Sardinians" he actually transferred some passages word for word to a trial address[b] of his own. He is said to have delivered himself in a high-pitched voice with impassioned action and gestures, which were not without grace. He left several speeches, including some which are attributed to him on insufficient evidence. Augustus had good reason to think that the speech "For Quintus Metellus" was rather taken down by shorthand writers who could not keep pace with his delivery, than published by Caesar himself; for in some copies I find that even the title is not "For Metellus," but, "Which he wrote for Metellus," although the discourse purports to be from Caesar's lips, defending Metellus and himself

communium obtrectatorum criminationes purgantis.
4 "Apud milites" quoque "in Hispania" idem Augustus
vix ipsius putat, quae tamen duplex fertur: una
quasi priore habita proelio, altera posteriore, quo
Asinius Pollio ne tempus quidem contionandi habuisse
eum dicit subita hostium incursione.

LVI. Reliquit et rerum suarum commentarios*
Gallici civilisque belli Pompeiani.   Nam Alexandrini
Africique et Hispaniensis incertus auctor est; alii
Oppium putant, alii Hirtium, qui etiam Gallici belli
novissimum imperfectumque librum suppleverit.   De
commentariis Caesaris Cicero in eodem Bruto sic
2 refert: "Commentarios scripsit valde quidem pro-
bandos; nudi sunt, recti et venusti, omni ornatu
orationis tamquam veste detracta; sed dum voluit
alios habere parata, unde sumerent qui vellent
scribere historiam, ineptis gratum fortasse fecit, qui
illa volent calamistris inurere, sanos quidem homines
3 a scribendo deterruit."   De isdem commentariis Hirtius ita praedicat: "Adeo probantur omnium iudicio, ut
praerepta, non praebita facultas scriptoribus videatur.
Cuius[1] tamen rei maior nostra quam reliquorum est
admiratio; ceteri enim, quam bene atque emendate,
nos etiam, quam facile atque celeriter eos perscrip-
4 serit, scimus."   Pollio Asinius parum diligenter
parumque integra veritate compositos putat, cum

[1] Cuius . . . emendate, *found only in* ς; *cf. praef. ad B.G.* viii.

[a] Cic. *Brut.* 262.   [b] *De Bell. Gall.* viii, preface, 5–6.

against the charges of their common detractors. Augustus also questions the authenticity of the address " To his Soldiers in Spain," although there are two sections of it, one purporting to have been spoken at the first battle, the other at the second, when Asinius Pollio writes that because of the sudden onslaught of the enemy he actually did not have time to make an harangue.

LVI. He left memoirs too of his deeds in the Gallic war and in the civil strife with Pompey; for the author of the Alexandrian, African, and Spanish Wars is unknown; some think it was Oppius, others Hirtius, who also supplied the final book of the Gallic War, which Caesar left unwritten. With regard to Caesar's memoirs Cicero, also in the *Brutus*[a] speaks in the following terms : "He wrote memoirs which deserve the highest praise ; they are naked in their simplicity, straightforward yet graceful, stripped of all rhetorical adornment, as of a garment ; but while his purpose was to supply material to others, on which those who wished to write history might draw, he haply gratified silly folk, who will try to use the curling-irons on his narrative, but he has kept men of any sense from touching the subject." Of these same memoirs Hirtius uses this emphatic language[b]: "They are so highly rated in the judgment of all men, that he seems to have deprived writers of an opportunity, rather than given them one ; yet our admiration for this feat is greater than that of others ; for they know how well and faultlessly he wrote, while we know besides how easily and rapidly he finished his task." Asinius Pollio thinks that they were put together somewhat carelessly and without strict regard for truth ; since in many cases Caesar was too

Caesar pleraque et quae per alios erant gesta temere crediderit et quae per se, vel consulto vel etiam memoria lapsus perperam ediderit; existimatque
5 rescripturum et correcturum fuisse. Reliquit et "de Analogia" duos libros et "Anticatones" totidem ac praeterea poema quod inscribitur "Iter." Quorum librorum primos in transitu Alpium, cum ex citeriore Gallia conventibus peractis ad exercitum rediret, sequentes sub tempus Mundensis proelii fecit; novissimum, dum ab urbe in Hispaniam ulteriorem
6 quarto et vicensimo die pervenit. Epistulae quoque eius ad senatum extant, quas primum videtur ad paginas et formam memorialis libelli convertisse, cum antea consules et duces non nisi transversa charta scriptas mitterent. Exstant et ad Ciceronem, item ad familiares domesticis de rebus, in quibus, si qua occultius perferenda erant, per notas scripsit, id est sic structo litterarum ordine, ut nullum verbum effici posset; quae si qui investigare et persequi velit,[1] quartam elementorum litteram, id est D pro A et
7 perinde reliquas commutet. Feruntur a puero et ab[2] adulescentulo quaedam scripta, ut "Laudes Herculis," tragoedia "Oedipus," item "Dicta collectanea": quos omnis libellos vetuit Augustus publicari in epistula, quam brevem admodum ac simplicem ad Pompeium Macrum, cui ordinandas bibliothecas delegaverat, misit.

[1] velit, ς; vellet, Ω; volet, *Stephanus*.
[2] et a puero et ab, ΠQ; et a puero ab, R; et aituero ab, MV.

---

a That is, Caesar reduced his reports to book form. If the book was a *roll*, the writing was arranged in columns, parallel with the edges (or long sides) of the roll. If it was a *codex*, several sheets were folded and fastened together and the writing was arranged on each page in one or two columns. His predecessors merely took a sheet, or sheets, and wrote from side to side and from top to bottom, without columns or margins.

ready to believe the accounts which others gave of
their actions, and gave a perverted account of his own,
either designedly or perhaps from forgetfulness; and
he thinks that he intended to rewrite and revise them.
He left besides a work in two volumes "On Analogy,"
the same number of "Speeches criticising Cato,"
in addition to a poem, entitled "The Journey."
He wrote the first of these works while crossing the
Alps and returning to his army from Hither Gaul,
where he had held the assizes; the second about
the time of the battle of Munda, and the third in
the course of a twenty-four days' journey from Rome
to Farther Spain. Some letters of his to the senate
are also preserved, and he seems to have been the
first to reduce such documents to pages and the
form of a note-book,[a] whereas previously consuls and
generals sent their reports written right across the
sheet. There are also letters of his to Cicero, as
well as to his intimates on private affairs, and in the
latter, if he had anything confidential to say, he
wrote it in cipher, that is, by so changing the order of
the letters of the alphabet, that not a word could be
made out. If anyone wishes to decipher these, and
get at their meaning, he must substitute the fourth
letter of the alphabet, namely D, for A, and so with
the others. We also have mention of certain
writings of his boyhood and early youth, such as the
" Praises of Hercules," a tragedy "Oedipus," and
a " Collection of Apophthegms"; but Augustus forbade the publication of all these minor works in
a very brief and frank letter sent to Pompeius
Macer, whom he had selected to set his libraries
in order.

LVII. Armorum et equitandi peritissimus, laboris
ultra fidem patiens erat. In agmine nonnumquam
equo, saepius pedibus anteibat, capite detecto, seu
sol seu imber esset; longissimas vias incredibili
celeritate confecit, expeditus, meritoria raeda, centena
passuum milia in singulos dies; si flumina morarentur,
nando traiciens vel innixus inflatis utribus, ut persaepe
nuntios de se praevenerit.

LVIII. In obeundis expeditionibus dubium cautior
an audentior, exercitum neque per insidiosa itinera
duxit umquam nisi perspeculatus locorum situs, neque
in Britanniam transvexit, nisi ante per se portus et
navigationem et accessum ad insulam explorásset.[a]
At idem obsessione castrorum in Germania nuntiata
per stationes hostium Gallico habitu penetravit ad
2 suos. A Brundisio Dyrrachium inter oppositas classes
hieme transmisit cessantibusque copiis, quas subsequi
iusserat, cum ad accersendas frustra saepe misisset,
novissime ipse clam noctu parvulum navigium solus
obvoluto capite conscendit, neque aut quis esset
ante detexit aut gubernatorem cedere adversae
tempestati passus est quam paene obrutus fluctibus.

LIX. Ne religione quidem ulla a quoquam incepto
absterritus umquam vel retardatus est. Cum immolanti aufugisset hostia, profectionem adversus
Scipionem et Iubam non distulit. Prolapsus etiam

---

[a] Through Gaius Volusenus (Caes. *B. G.* 4. 21. 1). Suetonius's
words *per se* do not necessarily imply that Caesar went to
Britain himself for this purpose.

LVII. He was highly skilled in arms and horsemanship, and of incredible powers of endurance. On the march he headed his army, sometimes on horseback, but oftener on foot, bareheaded both in the heat of the sun and in rain. He covered great distances with incredible speed, making a hundred miles a day in a hired carriage and with little baggage, swimming the rivers which barred his path or crossing them on inflated skins, and very often arriving before the messengers sent to announce his coming.

LVIII. In the conduct of his campaigns it is a question whether he was more cautious or more daring, for he never led his army where ambuscades were possible without carefully reconnoitring the country, and he did not cross to Britain without making personal inquiries[a] about the harbours, the course, and the approach to the island. But on the other hand, when news came that his camp in Germany was beleaguered, he made his way to his men through the enemies' pickets, disguised as a Gaul. He crossed from Brundisium to Dyrrachium in winter time, running the blockade of the enemy's fleets; and when the troops which he had ordered to follow him delayed to do so, and he had sent to fetch them many times in vain, at last in secret and alone he boarded a small boat at night with his head muffled up; and he did not reveal who he was, or suffer the helmsman to give way to the gale blowing in their teeth, until he was all but overwhelmed by the waves.

LIX. No regard for religion ever turned him from any undertaking, or even delayed him. Though the victim escaped as he was offering sacrifice, he did not put off his expedition against Scipio and Juba. Even

81

in egressu navis verso ad melius omine : " Teneo te,"
inquit, " Africa." Ad eludendas autem vaticinationes,
quibus felix et invictum in ea provincia fataliter
Scipionum nomen ferebatur, despectissimum quendam
ex Corneliorum genere, cui ad opprobrium vitae
Salvitoni [1] cognomen erat, in castris secum habuit.

LX. Proelia non tantum destinato, sed ex occasione
sumebat ac saepe ab itinere statim, interdum spurcissi-
mis tempestatibus, cum minime quis moturum putaret ;
nec nisi tempore extremo ad dimicandum cunctatior
factus est, quo saepius vicisset, hoc minus experien-
dos casus opinans nihilque se tantum adquisiturum
victoria, quantum auferre [2] calamitas posset. Nullum
umquam hostem fudit, quin castris quoque exueret ;
ita nullum spatium perterritis dabat. Ancipiti proelio
equos dimittebat et in primis suum, quo maior
permanendi necessitas imponeretur auxilio fugae
erepto.

LXI. Utebatur autem equo insigni, pedibus prope
humanis et in modum digitorum ungulis fissis, quem
natum apud se, cum haruspices imperium orbis terrae
significare domino pronuntiassent, magna cura aluit
nec patientem sessoris alterius primus ascendit ; cuius
etiam instar pro aede Veneris Genetricis postea
dedicavit.

---

[1] Salvitem, *L'*; Salutioni, ς. [2] auferre ... umquam, *only in* ς.

---

[a] The significance of this name can only be conjectured.
Salutio was an actor of mimes, mentioned by Pliny, *N.H.*
7. 10 and 35. 2.

when he had a fall as he disembarked, he gave the omen a favourable turn by crying: " I hold thee fast, Africa." Furthermore, to make the prophecies ridiculous which declared that the stock of the Scipios was fated to be fortunate and invincible in that province, he kept with him in camp a contemptible fellow belonging to the Cornelian family, to whom the nickname Salvito[a] had been given as a reproach for his manner of life.

LX. He joined battle, not only after planning his movements in advance but on a sudden opportunity, often immediately at the end of a march, and sometimes in the foulest weather, when one would least expect him to make a move. It was not until his later years that he became slower to engage, through a conviction that the oftener he had been victor, the less he ought to tempt fate, and that he could not possibly gain as much by success as he might lose by a defeat. He never put his enemy to flight without also driving him from his camp, thus giving him no respite in his panic. When the issue was doubtful, he used to send away the horses, and his own among the first, to impose upon his troops the greater necessity of standing their ground by taking away that aid to flight.

LXI. He rode a remarkable horse, too, with feet that were almost human; for its hoofs were cloven in such a way as to look like toes. This horse was foaled on his own place, and since the soothsayers had declared that it foretold the rule of the world for its master, he reared it with the greatest care, and was the first to mount it, for it would endure no other rider. Afterwards, too, he dedicated a statue of it before the temple of Venus Genetrix.

LXII. Inclinatam aciem solus saepe restituit obsistens fugientibus retinensque singulos et contortis faucibus convertens in hostem et quidem adeo plerumque trepidos, ut aquilifer [1] moranti se cuspide sit comminatus, alius in manu detinentis reliquerit signum.

LXIII. Non minor illa constantia eius, maiora [2] etiam indicia fuerint. Post aciem Pharsalicam cum praemissis in Asiam copiis per angustias Hellesponti vectoria navicula traiceret, L. Cassium partis adversae cum decem rostratis navibus obvium sibi neque refugit et comminus tendens, ultro ad deditionem hortatus, supplicem ad se recepit.

LXIV. Alexandriae circa oppugnationem pontis eruptione hostium subita conpulsus in scapham pluribus eodem praecipitantibus, cum desiluisset [3] in mare, nando per ducentos passus evasit ad proximam navem, elata laeva, ne libelli quos tenebat madefierent, paludamentum mordicus trahens, ne spolio poteretur hostis.

LXV. Militem neque a moribus neque a fortuna [4] probabat, sed tantum a viribus, tractabatque pari severitate atque indulgentia. Non enim ubique ac semper, sed cum hostis in proximo esset, coercebat ;

[1] aquilifer, *Egnatius*; aquilifero, Ω.
[2] minora, Υ′; constantiae, ΠQSTς ; immo maiora etiam, Υ′.
[3] dedisset, *P′O* ; *the other mss. have* desilisset.
[4] fortuna, *M* ; *the other mss. have* fortuna ; forma, *Torrentius.*

---

[a] The standard of the legion was a silver eagle with outstretched wings, mounted on a pole which had a sharp point at the other end, so that it could be set firmly in the ground.

[b] *Rostratae naves,* ships of war provided with brazen beaks (*rostra*) or rams.

LXII. When his army gave way, he often rallied it single-handed, planting himself in the way of the fleeing men, laying hold of them one by one, and even catching them by the throat and forcing them to face the enemy; that, too, when they were in such a panic that an eagle-bearer made a pass at him with the point[a] as he tried to stop him, while another left the standard in Caesar's hand when he would hold him back.

LXIII. His presence of mind was no less renowned, and the instances of it will appear even more striking. After the battle of Pharsalus, when he had sent on his troops and was crossing the strait of the Hellespont in a small passenger boat, he met Lucius Cassius, of the hostile party, with ten armoured ships,[b] and made no attempt to escape, but went to meet Cassius and actually urged him to surrender; and Cassius sued for mercy and was taken on board.

LXIV. At Alexandria, while assaulting a bridge, he was forced by a sudden sally of the enemy to take to a small skiff; when many others threw themselves into the same boat, he plunged into the sea, and after swimming for two hundred paces, got away to the nearest ship, holding up his left hand all the way, so as not to wet some papers which he was carrying, and dragging his cloak after him with his teeth, to keep the enemy from getting it as a trophy.

LXV. He valued his soldiers neither for their personal character nor their fortune, but solely for their prowess, and he treated them with equal strictness and indulgence; for he did not curb them everywhere and at all times, but only in the presence

tum maxime exactor gravissimus disciplinae, ut
neque itineris neque proelii tempus denuntiaret, sed
paratum et intentum momentis omnibus quo vellet
subito educeret. Quod etiam sine causa plerumque
faciebat, praecipue pluviis et festis diebus. Ac
subinde observandum se admonens repente interdiu
vel nocte subtrahebat, augebatque iter, ut serius
subsequentis defetigaret.

LXVI. Fama vero hostilium copiarum perterritos
non negando minuendove, sed insuper amplificando
ementiendoque confirmabat. Itaque cum expectatio
adventus Iubae terribilis esset, convocatis ad contionem militibus : " Scitote," inquit, " paucissimis his
diebus regem adfuturum cum decem legionibus,
equitum triginta, levis armaturae centum milibus,
elephantis trecentis. Proinde desinant quidam
quaerere ultra aut opinari mihique, qui compertum
habeo, credant ; aut quidem vetustissima nave im-
positos quocumque vento in quascumque terras
iubebo avehi."

LXVII. Delicta neque observabat omnia neque pro
modo exsequebatur, sed desertorum ac seditiosorum
et inquisitor et punitor acerrimus conivebat in ceteris.
Ac nonnumquam post magnam pugnam atque
victoriam remisso officiorum munere licentiam
omnem passim lasciviendi permittebat, iactare
solitus milites suos etiam unguentatos bene pug-

of the enemy. Then he required the strictest discipline, not announcing the time of a march or a battle, but keeping them ready and alert to be led on a sudden at any moment wheresoever he might wish. He often called them out even when there was no occasion for it, especially on rainy days and holidays. And warning them every now and then that they must keep close watch on him, he would steal away suddenly by day or night and make a longer march than usual, to tire out those who were tardy in following.

LXVI. When they were in a panic through reports about the enemy's numbers, he used to rouse their courage not by denying or discounting the rumours, but by falsely exaggerating the true danger. For instance, when the anticipation of Juba's coming filled them with terror, he called the soldiers together and said: "Let me tell you that within the next few days the king will be here with ten legions, thirty thousand horsemen, a hundred thousand light-armed troops, and three hundred elephants. Therefore some of you may as well cease to ask further questions or make surmises and may rather believe me, since I know all about it. Otherwise, I shall surely have them shipped on some worn out craft and carried off to whatever lands the wind may blow them."

LXVII. He did not take notice of all their offences or punish them by rule, but he kept a sharp look out for deserters and mutineers, and chastised them most severely, shutting his eyes to other faults. Sometimes, too, after a great victory he relieved them of all duties and gave them full licence to revel, being in the habit of boasting that his soldiers could fight well even when reeking of per-

2 nare posse. Nec milites eos pro contione, sed
blandiore nomine commilitones appellabat habebat-
que tam cultos, ut argento et auro politis armis
ornaret, simul et ad speciem et quo tenaciores eorum
in proelio essent metu damni. Diligebat quoque
usque adeo, ut audita clade Tituriana barbam capil-
lumque summiserit nec ante dempserit quam vindi-
casset.

LXVIII. Quibus rebus et devotissimos sibi et
fortissimos reddidit. Ingresso civile bellum centuriones cuiusque legionis singulos equites e viatico
suo optulerunt, universi milites gratuitam et sine
frumento stipendioque operam, cum tenuiorum
tutelam locupletiores in se contulissent. Neque in
tam diuturno spatio quisquam omnino descivit,
plerique capti concessam sibi sub condicione vitam,
2 si militare adversus eum vellent, recusarunt. Famem
et ceteras necessitates, non cum obsiderentur modo
sed et si ipsi alios obsiderent, tanto opere tolerabant,
ut Dyrrachina munitione Pompeius viso genere panis
ex herba, quo sustinebantur, cum feris sibi rem
esse dixerit amoverique ocius nec cuiquam ostendi
iusserit, ne patientia et pertinacia hostis animi
suorum frangerentur.

3 Quanta fortitudine dimicarint, testimonio est
quod adverso semel apud Dyrrachium proelio poenam
in se ultro depoposcerunt, ut consolandos eos magis
imperator quam puniendos habuerit. Ceteris proeliis
88

fumes. In the assembly he addressed them not as " soldiers," but by the more flattering term " comrades," and he kept them in fine trim, furnishing them with arms inlaid with silver and gold, both for show and to make them hold the faster to them in battle, through fear of the greatness of the loss. Such was his love for them that when he heard of the disaster to Titurius, he let his hair and beard grow long, and would not cut them until he had taken vengeance.

LXVIII. In this way he made them most devoted to his interests as well as most valiant. When he began the civil war, every centurion of each legion proposed to supply a horseman from his own savings, and the soldiers one and all offered their service without pay and without rations, the richer assuming the care of the poorer. Throughout the long struggle not one deserted and many of them, on being taken prisoner, refused to accept their lives, when offered them on the condition of consenting to serve against Caesar. They bore hunger and other hardships, both when in a state of siege and when besieging others, with such fortitude, that when Pompey saw in the works at Dyrrachium a kind of bread made of herbs, on which they were living, he said that he was fighting wild beasts; and he gave orders that it be put out of sight quickly and shown to none of his men, for fear that the endurance and resolution of the foe would break their spirit.

How valiantly they fought is shown by the fact that when they suffered their sole defeat before Dyrrachium, they insisted on being punished, and their commander felt called upon rather to console than to chastise them. In the other battles they

innumeras adversariorum copias multis partibus ipsi pauciores facile superarunt. Denique una sextae legionis cohors praeposita castello quattuor Pompei legiones per aliquot horas sustinuit paene omnis confixa multitudine hostilium sagittarum, quarum centum ac triginta milia [1] intra vallum reperta sunt.

4 Nec mirum, si quis singulorum facta respiciat, vel Cassi Scaevae centurionis vel Gai Acili militis, ne de pluribus referam. Scaeva excusso oculo, transfixus femore et umero, centum et viginti ictibus scuto perforato, custodiam portae commissi castelli retinuit. Acilius navali ad Massiliam proelio iniecta in puppem hostium dextera et abscisa memorabile illud apud Graecos Cynegiri exemplum imitatus transiliit in navem umbone obvios agens.

LXIX. Seditionem per decem annos Gallicis bellis nullam omnino moverunt, civilibus aliquas, sed ut celeriter ad officium redierint, nec tam indulgentia ducis quam auctoritate. Non enim cessit umquam tumultuantibus atque etiam obviam semper iit; et nonam quidem legionem apud Placentiam, quanquam in armis adhuc Pompeius esset, totam cum ignominia missam fecit aegreque post multas et supplicis preces, nec nisi exacta de sontibus poena, restituit.

LXX. Decimanos autem Romae cum ingentibus minis summoque etiam urbis periculo missionem et praemia flagitantes, ardente tunc in Africa bello,

---

[1] *Since Caesar* (*B.C.* 3.53) *gives the number as* milia . . . circiter xxx, *Ernesti proposed to omit* centum *and read* ad *for* ac.

overcame with ease countless forces of the enemy,
though decidedly fewer in number themselves.
Indeed one cohort of the sixth legion, when set to
defend a redoubt, kept four legions of Pompey at bay
for several hours, though almost all were wounded by
the enemy's showers of arrows, of which a hundred
and thirty thousand were picked up within the
ramparts. And no wonder, when one thinks of the
deeds of individual soldiers, either of Cassius Scaeva
the centurion, or of Gaius Acilius of the rank and file,
not to mention others. Scaeva, with one eye gone,
his thigh and shoulder wounded, and his shield bored
through in a hundred and twenty places, continued
to guard the gate of a fortress put in his charge.
Acilius in the sea-fight at Massilia grasped the stern
of one of the enemy's ships, and when his right hand
was lopped off, rivalling the famous exploit of the
Greek hero Cynegirus, boarded the ship and drove
the enemy before him with the boss of his shield.

LXIX. They did not mutiny once during the
ten years of the Gallic war; in the civil wars they
did so now and then, but quickly resumed their
duty, not so much owing to any indulgence of their
general as to his authority. For he never gave way
to them when they were insubordinate, but always
boldly faced them, discharging the entire ninth
legion in disgrace before Placentia, though Pompey
was still in the field, reinstating them unwillingly
and only after many abject entreaties, and insisting
on punishing the ringleaders.

LXX. Again at Rome, when the men of the
Tenth clamoured for their discharge and rewards
with terrible threats and no little peril to the city,
though the war in Africa was then raging, he did

neque adire cunctatus est, quanquam deterrentibus amicis, neque dimittere; sed una voce, qua "Quirites" eos pro militibus appellarat, tam facile circumegit et flexit, ut ei milites esse confestim responderint et quamvis recusantem ultro in Africam sint secuti; ac sic quoque seditiosissimum quemque et praedae et agri destinati tertia parte multavit.

LXXI. Studium et fides erga clientis ne iuveni quidem defuerunt. Masintham nobilem iuvenem, cum adversus Hiempsalem regem tam enixe defendisset, ut Iubae regis filio in altercatione barbam invaserit, stipendiarium quoque pronuntiatum et abstrahentibus statim eripuit occultavitque apud se diu et mox ex praetura proficiscens in Hispaniam inter officia prosequentium fascesque lictorum lectica sua avexit.

LXXII. Amicos tanta semper facilitate indulgentiaque tractavit, ut Gaio Oppio comitanti se per silvestre iter correptoque subita valitudine deversoriolo eo,[1] quod unum erat, cesserit et ipse humi ac sub divo cubuerit. Iam autem rerum potens quosdam etiam infimi generis ad amplissimos honores provexit, cum ob id culparetur, professus palam, si grassatorum et sicariorum ope in tuenda sua dignitate usus esset, talibus quoque se parem gratiam relaturum.

[1] deversoriolo eo, *Politianus*; deversoriolo, *Casaubon*; deversorio loco, Ω.

[a] Probably some woodcutter's hut; *deversorium* means 'inn, lodging.'

not hesitate to appear before them, against the advice of his friends, and to disband them. But with a single word, calling them " citizens," instead of " soldiers," he easily brought them round and bent them to his will ; for they at once replied that they were his " soldiers" and insisted on following him to Africa, although he refused their service. Even then he punished the most insubordinate by the loss of a third part of the booty and of the land intended for them.

LXXI. Even when a young man he showed no lack of devotion and fidelity to his dependents. He defended Masintha, a youth of high birth, against king Hiempsal with such spirit, that in the dispute he caught the king's son Juba by the beard. On Masintha's being declared tributary to the king, he at once rescued him from those who would carry him off and kept him hidden for some time in his own house ; and when presently he left for Spain after his praetorship, he carried the young man off in his own litter, unnoticed amid the crowd that came to see him off and the lictors with their fasces.

LXXII. His friends he treated with invariable kindness and consideration. When Gaius Oppius was his companion on a journey through a wild, woody country and was suddenly taken ill, Caesar gave up to him the only shelter[a] there was, while he himself slept on the ground out-of-doors. Moreover, when he came to power, he advanced some of his friends to the highest positions, even though they were of the humblest origin, and when taken to task for it, flatly declared that if he had been helped in defending his honour by brigands and cut-throats, he would have requited even such men in the same way.

93

LXXIII. Simultates contra nullas tam graves excepit umquam, ut non occasione oblata libens deponeret. Gai Memmi, cuius asperrimis orationibus non minore acerbitate rescripserat, etiam suffragator mox in petitione consulatus fuit. Gaio Calvo post famosa epigrammata de reconciliatione per amicos agenti ultro ac prior scripsit. Valerium Catullum, a quo sibi versiculis de Mamurra perpetua stigmata imposita non dissimulaverat, satis facientem eadem die adhibuit cenae hospitioque patris eius, sicut consuerat, uti perseveravit.

LXXIV. Sed et in ulciscendo natura lenissimus piratas, a quibis captus est, cum in dicionem redegisset, quoniam suffixurum se cruci ante iuraverat, iugulari prius iussit, deinde suffigi ; Cornelio Phagitae, cuius quondam nocturnas insidias aeger ac latens, ne perduceretur ad Sullam, vix praemio dato evaserat, numquam nocere sustinuit ; Philemonem a manu servum, qui necem suam per venenum inimicis promiserat, non gravius quam simplici morte puniit ;

2 in Publium Clodium Pompeiae uxoris suae adulterum atque eadem de causa pollutarum caerimoniarum reum testis citatus negavit se quicquam comperisse, quamvis et mater Aurelia et soror Iulia apud eosdem iudices omnia ex fide rettulissent ; interrogatusque,

---

LXXIII. On the other hand he never formed such bitter enmities that he was not glad to lay them aside when opportunity offered. Although Gaius Memmius had made highly caustic speeches against him, to which he had replied with equal bitterness, he went so far as to support Memmius afterwards in his suit for the consulship. When Gaius Calvus, after some scurrilous epigrams, took steps through his friends towards a reconciliation, Caesar wrote to him first and of his own free will. Valerius Catullus, as Caesar himself did not hesitate to say, inflicted a lasting stain on his name by the verses about Mamurra[a]; yet when he apologised, Caesar invited the poet to dinner that very same day, and continued his usual friendly relations with Catullus's father.

LXXIV. Even in avenging wrongs he was by nature most merciful, and when he got hold of the pirates who had captured him, he had them crucified, since he had sworn beforehand that he would do so, but ordered that their throats be cut first. He could never make up his mind to harm Cornelius Phagites, although when he was sick and in hiding,[b] the man had waylaid him night after night, and even a bribe had barely saved him from being handed over to Sulla. The slave Philemon, his amanuensis, who had promised Caesar's enemies that he would poison him, he merely punished by death, without torture. When summoned as a witness against Publius Clodius, the paramour of his wife Pompeia, charged on the same count with sacrilege, Caesar declared that he had no evidence, although both his mother Aurelia and his sister Julia had given the same jurors a faithful account of the whole affair; and on being asked why it was then that he had put away his

cur igitur repudiasset uxorem : "Quoniam," inquit,
"meos tam suspicione quam crimine iudico carere
oportere."

LXXV. Moderationem vero clementiamque cum
in administratione tum in victoria belli civilis
admirabilem exhibuit. Denuntiante Pompeio pro
hostibus se habiturum qui rei publicae defuissent,
ipse medios et neutrius partis suorum sibi numero
futuros pronuntiavit. Quibus autem ex commendatione Pompei ordines dederat, potestatem transeundi
2 ad eum omnibus fecit. Motis apud Ilerdam de-
ditionis condicionibus, cum, assiduo inter utrasque
partes usu atque commercio, Afranius et Petreius
deprehensos intra castra Iulianos subita paenitentia
interfecissent, admissam in se perfidiam non sustinuit
imitari. Acie Pharsalica proclamavit, ut civibus
parceretur, deincepsque nemini non suorum quem
3 vellet unum partis adversae servare concessit. Nec
ulli perisse nisi in proelio reperientur, exceptis dum
taxat Afranio et Fausto et Lucio Caesare iuvene ; ac
ne hos quidem voluntate ipsius interemptos putant,
quorum tamen et priores post impetratam veniam
rebellaverant [1] et Caesar libertis servisque eius ferro
et igni crudelem in modum enectis bestias quoque
4 ad munus populi comparatas contrucidaverat. Denique tempore extremo etiam quibus nondum igno-
verat, cunctis in Italiam redire permisit [2] magi-
stratusque et imperia capere ; sed et statuas Luci

---

[1] rebellaverant, *Stephanus* (ς); rebellaverunt, Ω.
[2] permisit, Nς ; permiserat, Ω.

wife, he replied: "Because I maintain that the members of my family should be free from suspicion, as well as from accusation."

LXXV. He certainly showed admirable self-restraint and mercy, both in his conduct of the civil war and in the hour of victory. While Pompey announced that he would treat as enemies those who did not take up arms for the government, Caesar gave out that those who were neutral and of neither party should be numbered with his friends. He freely allowed all those whom he had made centurions on Pompey's recommendation to go over to his rival. When conditions of surrender were under discussion at Ilerda, and friendly intercourse between the two parties was constant, Afranius and Petreius, with a sudden change of purpose, put to death all of Caesar's soldiers whom they found in their camp; but Caesar could not bring himself to retaliate in kind. At the battle of Pharsalus he cried out, " Spare your fellow citizens," and afterwards allowed each of his men to save any one man he pleased of the opposite party. And it will be found that no Pompeian lost his life except in battle, save only Afranius and Faustus, and the young Lucius Caesar; and it is believed that not even these men were slain by his wish, even though the two former had taken up arms again after being pardoned, while Caesar had not only cruelly put to death the dictator's slaves and freedmen with fire and sword, but had even butchered the wild beasts which he had procured for the entertainment of the people. At last, in his later years, he went so far as to allow all those whom he had not yet pardoned to return to Italy, and to hold magistracies and the command of armies:

Sullae atque Pompei a plebe disiectas reposuit; ac si qua posthac aut cogitarentur gravius adversus se aut dicerentur, inhibere maluit quam vindicare.

5 Itaque et detectas coniurationes conventusque nocturnos non ultra arguit, quam ut edicto ostenderet esse sibi notas, et acerbe loquentibus satis habuit pro contione denuntiare ne perseverarent, Aulique Caecinae criminosissimo libro et Pitholai carminibus maledicentissimis laceratam existimationem suam civili animo tulit.

LXXVI. Praegravant tamen cetera facta dictaque eius, ut et abusus dominatione et iure caesus existimetur. Non enim honores modo nimios recepit: continuum consulatum, perpetuam dictaturam praefecturamque morum, insuper praenomen Imperatoris, cognomen Patris patriae, statuam inter reges, suggestum in orchestra; sed et ampliora etiam humano fastigio decerni sibi passus est: sedem auream in curia et pro tribunali, tensam et ferculum circensi pompa, templa, aras, simulacra iuxta deos, pulvinar, flaminem, lupercos, appellationem mensis e suo nomine; ac nullos non honores ad libidinem cepit et

2 dedit. Tertium et quartum consulatum titulo tenus gessit contentus dictaturae potestate decretae cum

---

^a At the theatre.
^b For carrying his statue among those of the gods.

and he actually set up the statues of Lucius Sulla and Pompey, which had been broken to pieces by the populace. After this, if any dangerous plots were formed against him, or slanders uttered, he preferred to quash rather than to punish them. Accordingly, he took no further notice of the conspiracies which were detected, and of meetings by night, than to make known by proclamation that he was aware of them; and he thought it enough to give public warning to those who spoke ill of him, not to persist in their conduct, bearing with good nature the attacks on his reputation made by the scurrilous volume of Aulus Caecina and the abusive lampoons of Pitholaus.

LXXVI. Yet after all, his other actions and words so turn the scale, that it is thought that he abused his power and was justly slain. For not only did he accept excessive honours, such as an uninterrupted consulship, the dictatorship for life, and the censorship of public morals, as well as the forename Imperator, the surname of Father of his Country, a statue among those of the kings, and a raised couch in the orchestra[a]; but he also allowed honours to be bestowed on him which were too great for mortal man: a golden throne in the House and on the judgment seat; a chariot and litter[b] in the procession at the circus; temples, altars, and statues beside those of the gods; a special priest, an additional college of the Luperci, and the calling of one of the months by his name. In fact, there were no honours which he did not receive or confer at pleasure.

He held his third and fourth consulships in name only, content with the power of the dictatorship

consulatibus simul atque utroque anno binos consules
substituit sibi in ternos novissimos menses, ita ut
medio tempore comitia nulla habuerit praeter tribunorum et aedilium plebis praefectosque pro praetoribus constituerit, qui apsente se res urbanas adminis-
trarent.   Pridie autem Kalendas Ianuarias repentina
consulis morte cessantem honorem in paucas horas
3 petenti dedit.   Eadem licentia spreto patrio more
magistratus in pluris annos ordinavit, decem praetoriis[1]
viris consularia ornamenta tribuit, civitate donatos et
quosdam e semibarbaris Gallorum recepit in curiam.
Praeterea monetae publicisque vectigalibus peculiares
servos praeposuit.   Trium legionum, quas Alexandreae
relinquebat, curam et imperium Rufioni liberti sui
filio exoleto suo demandavit.

LXXVII. Nec minoris inpotentiae voces propalam
edebat, ut Titus Ampius[2] scribit : nihil esse rem
publicam, appellationem modo sine corpore ac specie.
Sullam nescisse litteras, qui dictaturam deposuerit.
Debere homines consideratius iam loqui secum ac
pro legibus habere quae dicat.   Eoque arrogantiae
progressus est, ut haruspice tristia et sine corde exta
quondam nuntiante, futura diceret laetiora, cum
vellet ; nec pro ostento ducendum, si pecudi cor
defuisset.

LXXVIII. Verum praecipuam et exitiabilem sibi
invidiam hinc maxime movit.   Adeuntis se cum plurimis honorificentissimisque decretis universos patres

---

[1] pretoris, MV (S erased in M) ; the other mss. have -iis.
[2] Ampius, Pulmann, Torrentius ; Amprius, Ω (Amplius, QT).

---

[a] Playing on the double meaning of cor, also regarded as
the seat of intelligence.

conferred on him at the same time as the consulships. Moreover, in both years he substituted two consuls for himself for the last three months, in the meantime holding no elections except for tribunes and plebeian aediles, and appointing praefects instead of the praetors, to manage the affairs of the city during his absence. When one of the consuls suddenly died the day before the Kalends of January, he gave the vacant office for a few hours to a man who asked for it. With the same disregard of law and precedent he named magistrates for several years to come, bestowed the emblems of consular rank on ten ex-praetors, and admitted to the House men who had been given citizenship, and in some cases half-civilised Gauls. He assigned the charge of the mint and of the public revenues to his own slaves, and gave the oversight and command of the three legions which he had left at Alexandria to a favourite of his called Rufio, son of one of his freedmen.

LXXVII. No less arrogant were his public utterances, which Titus Ampius records: that the state was nothing, a mere name without body or form; that Sulla did not know his A. B. C. when he laid down his dictatorship; that men ought now to be more circumspect in addressing him, and to regard his word as law. So far did he go in his presumption, that when a soothsayer once reported direful inwards without a heart, he said: " They will be more favourable when I wish it; it should not be regarded as a portent, if a beast has no heart." [a]

LXXVIII. But it was the following action in particular that roused deadly hatred against him. When the Senate approached him in a body with many highly honorary decrees, he received them

conscriptos sedens pro aede Veneris Genetricis
excepit. Quidam putant retentum a Cornelio Balbo,
cum conaretur assurgere; alii, ne conatum quidem
omnino, sed etiam admonentem Gaium Trebatium ut
2 assurgeret minus familiari vultu respexisse. Idque
factum eius tanto intolerabilius est visum, quod ipse
triumphanti et subsellia tribunicia praetervehenti sibi
unum e collegio Pontium Aquilam non assurrexisse
adeo indignatus sit, ut proclamaverit: " Repete ergo
a me Aquila rem publicam tribunus!" Et nec
destiterit per continuos dies quicquam cuiquam nisi
sub exceptione polliceri: " Si tamen per Pontium
Aquilam licuerit."

LXXIX. Adiecit ad tam insignem despecti senatus
contumeliam multo arrogantius factum. Nam cum
in sacrificio Latinarum revertente eo inter inmodicas
ac novas populi acclamationes quidam e turba statuae
eius coronam lauream candida fascia praeligata[1] in-
posuisset et tribuni plebis Epidius Marullus Caesetius-
que Flavus coronae fasciam detrahi hominemque duci
in vincula iussissent, dolens seu parum prospere
motam regni mentionem sive, ut ferebat, ereptam
sibi gloriam recusandi, tribunos graviter increpitos
2 potestate privavit. Neque ex eo infamiam affectati
etiam regii nominis discutere valuit,[2] quanquam et
plebei regem se salutanti Caesarem se, non regem
esse responderit et Lupercalibus pro rostris a consule

---

[1] praeligata, M; the other mss. have praeligatam.
[2] valuit, ς; voluit, Ω.

[a] That is, "make me restore the republic."
[b] The white fillet was emblematic of royalty.
[c] With a pun on Rex as a Roman name; cf. Horace, Serm.
1. 7, etc.

before the temple of Venus Genetrix without rising. Some think that when he attempted to get up, he was held back by Cornelius Balbus; others, that he made no such move at all, but on the contrary frowned angrily on Gaius Trebatius when he suggested that he should rise. And this action of his seemed the more intolerable, because when he himself in one of his triumphal processions rode past the benches of the tribunes, he was so incensed because a member of the college, Pontius Aquila by name, did not rise, that he cried: "Come then, Aquila. take back the republic from me,[a] you tribune"; and for several days he would not make a promise to any one without adding, "That is, if Pontius Aquila will allow me."

LXXIX. To an insult which so plainly showed his contempt for the Senate he added an act of even greater insolence; for at the Latin Festival, as he was returning to the city, amid the extravagant and unprecedented demonstrations of the populace, someone in the press placed on his statue a laurel wreath with a white fillet tied to it[b]; and when Epidius Marullus and Caesetius Flavus, tribunes of the commons, gave orders that the ribbon be removed from the wreath and the man taken off to prison, Caesar sharply rebuked and deposed them, either offended that the hint at regal power had been received with so little favour, or, as he asserted, that he had been robbed of the glory of refusing it. But from that time on he could not rid himself of the odium of having aspired to the title of monarch, although he replied to the commons, when they hailed him as king, "I am Caesar and no king,"[c] and at the Lupercalia, when

Antonio admotum saepius capiti suo diadema rep-
pulerit atque in Capitolium Iovi Optimo Maximo
3 miserit.   Quin etiam varia fama percrebruit migratu-
rum Alexandream vel Ilium, translatis simul opibus
imperii exhaustaque Italia dilectibus et procuratione
urbis amicis permissa, proximo autem senatu Lucium
Cottam quindecimvirum sententiam dicturum, ut,
quoniam fatalibus libris contineretur,[1] Parthos nisi
a rege non posse vinci, Caesar rex appellaretur.
LXXX. Quae causa coniuratis maturandi fuit destinata negotia, ne assentiri necesse esset.

Consilia igitur dispersim antea habita et quae
saepe bini ternive ceperant, in unum omnes contulerunt, ne populo quidem iam praesenti statu
laeto, sed clam palamque detrectante dominationem
2 atque assertores flagitante. Peregrinis in senatum
allectis libellus propositus est : " Bonum factum : ne
quis senatori novo curiam monstrare velit ! "   Et
illa vulgo canebantur :

"Gallos Caesar in triumphum ducit, idem   in
     curiam ;
   Galli   bracas   deposuerunt, latum clavum sum-
     pserunt."

3 Quinto Maximo suffecto trimenstrique consule theatrum introeunte, cum lictor animadverti ex more

---

[1] detineretur, *MV*; continetur *GT*.

[a] The college of fifteen priests (*quindecimviri sacris
faciundis*) in charge of the Sybilline books.
[b] *Bonum factum* (*sit*) was a formula prefixed to edicts, here
used in jest ; cf. the similar formulas in proposals to the
senate, *Aug.* lviii. 3, *Calig.* xv. 3.   [c] See note on xlv. 3.

the consul Antony several times attempted to place a crown upon his head as he spoke from the rostra, he put it aside and at last sent it to the Capitol, to be offered to Jupiter Optimus Maximus. Nay, more, the report had spread in various quarters that he intended to move to Ilium or Alexandria, taking with him the resources of the state, draining Italy by levies, and leaving the charge of the city to his friends; also that at the next meeting of the Senate Lucius Cotta would announce as the decision of the Fifteen,[a] that inasmuch as it was written in the books of fate that the Parthians could be conquered only by a king, Caesar should be given that title. LXXX. It was this that led the conspirators to hasten in carrying out their designs, in order to avoid giving their assent to this proposal.

Therefore the plots which had previously been formed separately, often by groups of two or three, were united in a general conspiracy, since even the populace no longer were pleased with present conditions, but both secretly and openly rebelled at his tyranny and cried out for defenders of their liberty. On the admission of foreigners to the Senate, a placard was posted: "God bless the Commonwealth![b] let no one consent to point out the House to a newly made senator." The following verses too were sung everwhere :—

"Caesar led the Gauls in triumph, led them to the senate house ;
Then the Gauls put off their breeches, and put on the laticlave."[c]

When Quintus Maximus, whom he had appointed consul in his place for three months, was entering

iussisset, ab universis conclamatum est non esse eum
consulem. Post remotos Caesetium et Marullum
tribunos reperta sunt proximis comitiis complura
suffragia consules eos declarantium. Subscripsere
quidam Luci Bruti statuae : "Utinam viveres!" item
ipsius Caesaris :

> "Brutus, quia reges eiecit, consul primus factus
>   est ;
> Hic, quia consules eiecit, rex postremo factus
>   est."

4 Conspiratum est in eum a sexaginta amplius, Gaio
Cassio Marcoque et Decimo Bruto principibus con-
spirationis. Qui primum cunctati utrumne in Campo
per comitia tribus ad suffragia vocantem partibus di-
visis e ponte deicerent atque exceptum trucidarent,
an in Sacra Via vel in aditu theatri adorirentur, postquam senatus Idibus Martiis in Pompei curiam
edictus est, facile tempus et locum praetulerunt.

LXXXI. Sed Caesari futura caedes evidentibus
prodigiis denuntiata est. Paucos ante menses, cum
in colonia Capua deducti lege Iulia coloni ad
exstruendas villas vetustissima sepulcra disicerent
idque eo studiosius facerent, quod aliquantum vascu-
lorum operis antiqui scrutantes reperiebant, tabula
aenea in monimento, in quo dicebatur Capys conditor
Capuae sepultus, inventa est conscripta litteris

" The *pons suffragiorum*, a temporary bridge of planks
over which the voters passed one by one, to cast their
ballots ; Cic. *Ad Att.* i. 14 ; Ovid, *Fasti*, v. 634.

the theatre, and his lictor called attention to his
arrival in the usual manner, a general shout was
raised: "He's no consul!" At the first election
after the deposing of Caesetius and Marullus, the
tribunes, several votes were found for their appointment as consuls. Some wrote on the base of
Lucius Brutus' statue, "Oh, that you were still
alive"; and on that of Caesar himself:

"First of all was Brutus consul, since he drove the
    kings from Rome;
Since this man drove out the consuls, he at last is
    made our king."

More than sixty joined the conspiracy against him,
led by Gaius Cassius and Marcus and Decimus Brutus.
At first they hesitated whether to form two divisions
at the elections in the Campus Martius, so that while
some hurled him from the bridge a as he summoned
the tribes to vote, the rest might wait below and
slay him; or to set upon him in the Sacred Way or
at the entrance to the theatre. When, however, a
meeting of the Senate was called for the Ides of
March in the Hall of Pompey, they readily gave
that time and place the preference.

LXXXI. Now Caesar's approaching murder was
foretold to him by unmistakable signs. A few
months before, when the settlers assigned to the
colony at Capua by the Julian Law were demolishing
some tombs of great antiquity, to build country
houses, and plied their work with the greater vigour
because as they rummaged about they found a
quantity of vases of ancient workmanship, there was
discovered in a tomb, which was said to be that of
Capys, the founder of Capua, a bronze tablet,

verbisque Graecis hac sententia : quandoque ossa
Capyis detecta essent, fore ut illo[1] prognatus manu
consanguineorum necaretur magnisque mox Italiae
2 cladibus vindicaretur.   Cuius rei, ne quis fabulosam
aut commenticiam putet, auctor est Cornelius Balbus,
familiarissimus Caesaris.   Proximis diebus equorum
greges, quos in traiciendo Rubiconi flumini con-
secrarat ac vagos et sine custode dimiserat, comperit
pertinacissime pabulo abstinere ubertimque flere.
Et immolantem haruspex Spurinna monuit, caveret
periculum, quod non ultra Martias Idus profer-
3 retur.   Pridie autem easdem Idus avem regaliolum
cum laureo ramulo Pompeianae curiae se inferentem
volucres varii generis ex proximo nemore persecutae
ibidem discerpserunt.   Ea vero nocte, cui inluxit
dies caedis, et ipse sibi visus est per quietem interdum supra nubes volitare, alias cum Iove dextram
iungere ; et Calpurnia uxor imaginata est conlabi
fastigium domus maritumque in gremio suo confodi ;
ac subito cubiculi fores sponte patuerunt.
4 Ob haec simul et ob infirmam valitudinem diu
cunctatus an se contineret et quae apud senatum
proposuerat agere differret, tandem Decimo Bruto
adhortante, ne frequentis ac iam dudum opperientis
destitueret, quinta fere hora progressus est libel-
lumque insidiarum indicem ab obvio quodam por-

---

[1] illo, *Turnebus, Bentley* ; ilio, *MHGϓ* ; *the other mss.
have* iulo *or* iulio.

---

[a] Properly said of a temple ; according to Florus, 4. 2. 91;
one of the honours bestowed on Caesar was *fastigium in domo*;
cf. Plutarch, *Caesar*, lxiii.

inscribed with Greek words and characters to this purport: "Whenever the bones of Capys shall be moved, it will come to pass that a son of Ilium shall be slain at the hands of his kindred, and presently avenged at heavy cost to Italy." And let no one think this tale a myth or a lie, for it is vouched for by Cornelius Balbus, an intimate friend of Caesar. Shortly before his death, as he was told, the herds of horses which he had dedicated to the river Rubicon when he crossed it, and had let loose without a keeper, stubbornly refused to graze and wept copiously. Again, when he was offering sacrifice, the soothsayer Spurinna warned him to beware of danger, which would come not later than the Ides of March; and on the day before the Ides of that month a little bird called the king-bird flew into the Hall of Pompey with a sprig of laurel, pursued by others of various kinds from the grove hard by, which tore it to pieces in the hall. In fact the very night before his murder he dreamt now that he was flying above the clouds, and now that he was clasping the hand of Jupiter; and his wife Calpurnia thought that the pediment *a* of their house fell, and that her husband was stabbed in her arms; and on a sudden the door of the room flew open of its own accord. March 15

Both for these reasons and because of poor health he hesitated for a long time whether to stay at home and put off what he had planned to do in the senate; but at last, urged by Decimus Brutus not to disappoint the full meeting which had for some time been waiting for him, he went forth almost at the end of the fifth hour; and when a note revealing the plot was handed him by someone on the way, he

rectum libellis ceteris, quos sinistra manu tenebat, quasi mox lecturus commiscuit. Dein pluribus hostiis caesis, cum litare non posset, introiit curiam spreta religione Spurinnamque irridens et ut falsum arguens, quod sine ulla sua noxa Idus Martiae adessent; quanquam is venisse quidem eas diceret, sed non praeterisse.

LXXXII. Assidentem conspirati specie officii circumsteterunt, ilicoque Cimber Tillius, qui primas partes susceperat, quasi aliquid rogaturus propius accessit renuentique et gestu in aliud tempus differenti ab utroque umero togam adprehendit; deinde clamantem: "Ista quidem vis est!" alter e Cascis

2 aversum[1] vulnerat paulum infra iugulum. Caesar Cascae brachium arreptum graphio traiecit conatusque prosilire alio vulnere tardatus est; utque animadvertit undique se strictis pugionibus peti, toga caput obvolvit, simul sinistra manu sinum ad ima crura deduxit, quo honestius caderet etiam inferiore corporis parte velata. Atque ita tribus et viginti plagis confossus est uno modo ad primum ictum gemitu sine voce edito, etsi tradiderunt quidam

3 Marco Bruto irruenti dixisse: καὶ σὺ τέκνον; Exanimis diffugientibus cunctis aliquamdiu iacuit, donec lecticae impositum, dependente brachio, tres servoli domum rettulerunt. Nec in tot vulneribus, ut

[1] adversum, *GVO′ΠR*.

---

[a] Possibly "from behind," though it is hard to see how a wound *paulo infra iugulum* could have been dealt from that position. *Aversum* has better mss. authority than *adversum*, is *a priori* more probable, and is supported by Plutarch's version; but it may mean "turned away."

[b] A pointed instrument of bone or metal, for writing on waxen tablets.

put it with others which he held in his left hand,
intending to read them presently. Then, after
several victims had been slain, and he could not get
favourable omens, he entered the House in defiance
of portents, laughing at Spurinna and calling him a
false prophet, because the Ides of March were come
without bringing him harm; though Spurinna replied
that they had of a truth come, but they had not
gone.

LXXXII. As he took his seat, the conspirators   44 B.C.
gathered about him as if to pay their respects, and
straightway Tillius Cimber, who had assumed the
lead, came nearer as though to ask something; and
when Caesar with a gesture put him off to another
time, Cimber caught his toga by both shoulders;
then as Caesar cried, "Why, this is violence!" one of
the Cascas stabbed him from one side just below the
throat.[a] Caesar caught Casca's arm and ran it through
with his stylus,[b] but as he tried to leap to his feet,
he was stopped by another wound. When he saw
that he was beset on every side by drawn daggers, he
muffled his head in his robe, and at the same time
drew down its lap to his feet with his left hand, in
order to fall more decently, with the lower part of
his body also covered. And in this wise he was
stabbed with three and twenty wounds, uttering not
a word, but merely a groan at the first stroke, though
some have written that when Marcus Brutus rushed
at him, he said in Greek, "You too, my child?"
All the conspirators made off, and he lay there life-
less for some time, until finally three common slaves
put him on a litter and carried him home, with one
arm hanging down. And of so many wounds none
turned out to be mortal, in the opinion of the

Antistius medicus existimabat, letale ullum repertum est, nisi quod secundo loco in pectore acceperat.

4 Fuerat animus coniuratis corpus occisi in Tiberim trahere, bona publicare, acta rescindere, sed metu Marci Antoni consulis et magistri equitum Lepidi destiterunt.

LXXXIII. Postulante ergo Lucio Pisone socero testamentum eius aperitur recitaturque in Antoni domo, quod Idibus Septembribus proximis in Lavicano suo fecerat demandaveratque virgini Vestali maximae. Quintus Tubero tradit heredem ab eo scribi solitum ex consulatu ipsius primo usque ad initium civilis belli Cn. Pompeium, idque militibus pro contione 2 recitatum. Sed novissimo testamento tres instituit heredes sororum nepotes, Gaium Octavium ex dodrante, et Lucium Pinarium et Quintum Pedium ex quadrante reliquo[1]; in ima cera Gaium Octavium etiam in familiam nomenque adoptavit; plerosque percussorum in tutoribus fili, si qui sibi nasceretur, nominavit, Decimum Brutum etiam in secundis heredibus. Populo hortos circa Tiberim publice et viritim trecenos sestertios legavit.

LXXXIV. Funere indicto rogus extructus est in Martio campo iuxta Iuliae tumulum et pro rostris aurata aedes ad simulacrum templi Veneris Genetricis collocata; intraque lectus eburneus auro ac purpura stratus et ad caput tropaeum cum veste, in qua fuerat occisus. Praeferentibus munera, quia suffec-

---

[1] reliquo, *T* (*Lipsius*); *the other mss. have* reliquos.

" To inherit a share of his estate in the event of the death of the heirs in the first degree or their refusal to accept the inheritance; it was often a mere compliment.

physician Antistius, except the second one in the breast.

The conspirators had intended after slaying him to drag his body to the Tiber, confiscate his property, and revoke his decrees; but they forebore through fear of Marcus Antonius the consul, and Lepidus, the master of horse.

LXXXIII. Then at the request of his father-in-law, Lucius Piso, the will was unsealed and read in Antony's house, which Caesar had made on the preceding Ides of September at his place near Lavicum, Sept. 13, and put in the care of the chief of the Vestals. Quintus 45 B.C. Tubero states that from his first consulship until the beginning of the civil war it was his wont to write down Gnaeus Pompeius as his heir, and to read this to the assembled soldiers. In his last will, however, he named three heirs, his sisters' grandsons, Gaius Octavius, to three-fourths of his estate, and Lucius Pinarius and Quintus Pedius to share the remainder. At the end of the will, too, he adopted Gaius Octavius into his family and gave him his name. He named several of his assassins among the guardians of his son, in case one should be born to him, and Decimus Brutus even among his heirs in the second degree.[a] To the people he left his gardens near the Tiber for their common use and three hundred sesterces to each man.

LXXXIV. When the funeral was announced, a pyre was erected in the Campus Martius near the tomb of Julia, and on the rostra a gilded shrine was placed, made after the model of the temple of Venus Genetrix; within was a couch of ivory with coverlets of purple and gold, and at its head a pillar hung with the robe in which he was slain. Since it was clear

113

turus dies non videbatur, praeceptum, ut omisso
ordine, quibus quisque vellet itineribus urbis, portaret
2 in Campum.   Inter ludos cantata sunt quaedam ad
miserationem et invidiam caedis eius accommodata,
ex Pacuvi Armorum iudicio :

" Men servasse, ut essent qui me perderent " ?

et ex Electra Atili [1] ad similem sententiam.   Lauda-
tionis loco consul Antonius per praeconem pronuntiavit senatus consultum, quo omnia simul ei divina
atque humana decreverat, item ius iurandum, quo se
cuncti pro salute unius astrinxerant ; quibus perpauca
3 a se verba addidit.   Lectum pro rostris in Forum
magistratus et honoribus functi detulerunt.   Quem
cum pars in Capitolini Iovis cella cremare pars in
curia Pompei destinaret, repente duo quidam gladiis
succincti ac bina iacula gestantes ardentibus cereis
succenderunt confestimque circumstantium turba
virgulta arida et cum subselliis tribunalia, quicquid
4 praeterea ad donum aderat, congessit.   Deinde
tibicines et scaenici artifices vestem, quam ex
triumphorum instrumento ad praesentem usum
induerant, detractam sibi atque discissam iniecere
flammae et veteranorum militum legionarii arma sua,
quibus exculti funus celebrabant ; matronae etiam
pleraeque ornamenta sua, quae gerebant, et liberorum
bullas atque praetextas.

[1] Atilii, ς ; Acilii, Ω.

---

[a] Cf. the apparition at the Rubicon ; chap. xxxii.

that the day would not be long enough for those who offered gifts, they were directed to bring them to the Campus by whatsoever streets of the city they wished, regardless of any order of precedence. At the funeral games, to rouse pity and indignation at his death, these words from the " Contest for the Arms" of Pacuvius were sung :—

"Saved I these men that they might murder me?"

and words of a like purport from the " Electra" of Atilius. Instead of a eulogy the consul Antonius caused a herald to recite the decree of the Senate in which it had voted Caesar all divine and human honours at once, and likewise the oath with which they had all pledged themselves to watch over his personal safety; to which he added a very few words of his own. The bier on the rostra was carried down into the Forum by magistrates and ex-magistrates; and while some were urging that it be burned in the temple of Jupiter of the Capitol, and others in the Hall of Pompey, on a sudden two beings [a] with swords by their sides and brandishing a pair of darts set fire to it with blazing torches, and at once the throng of bystanders heaped upon it dry branches, the judgment seats with the benches, and whatever else could serve as an offering. Then the musicians and actors tore off their robes, which they had taken from the equipment of his triumphs and put on for the occasion, rent them to bits and threw them into the flames, and the veterans of the legions the arms with which they had adorned themselves for the funeral; many of the women too, offered up the jewels which they wore and the amulets and robes of their children.

5   In summo publico luctu exterarum gentium multitudo circulatim suo quaeque more lamentata est
praecipueque Iudaei, qui etiam noctibus continuis
bustum frequentarunt.

LXXXV. Plebs statim a funere ad domum Bruti
et Cassi cum facibus tetendit atque aegre repulsa
obvium sibi Helvium Cinnam per errorem nominis,
quasi Cornelius is esset, quem graviter pridie contio-
natum de Caesare requirebat, occidit caputque eius
praefixum hastae circumtulit.   Postea solidam colum-
nam prope viginti pedum lapidis Numidici in Foro
statuit inscripsitque[1] PARENTI PATRIAE.   Apud eam
longo tempore sacrificare, vota suscipere, controversias
quasdam interposito per Caesarem iure iurando dis-
trahere perseveravit.

LXXXVI. Suspicionem Caesar quibusdam suorum
reliquit neque voluisse se diutius vivere neque curasse
quod valitudine minus prospera uteretur, ideoque et
quae religiones monerent et quae renuntiarent amici
neglexisse.   Sunt qui putent, confisum eum novissimo
illo senatus consulto ac iure iurando etiam custodias
Hispanorum cum gladiis †adsectantium[2] se removisse.
2   Alii e diverso opinantur insidias undique imminentis
subire semel quam cavere semper sollicitum maluisse.
Quidam dicere etiam[3] solitum ferunt: non tam sua

---

[1] inscripsitque, *Bentley* ; scripsitque, Ω.
[2] adsectantium, *conjecture of Ihm*; inspectantium, X' ;
sectantium, *Casaubon* ; adinspectantium, *MGϒ.*
[3] sollicitum . . . etiam, *supplied by Roth, except* semper,
which was added by Ihm.

---

[a] Caesar was beloved by the Jews, not only because he had
overthrown Pompey, who had violated their Holy of Holies,
but because of many acts of kindness besides.

At the height of the public grief a throng of foreigners went about lamenting each after the fashion of his country, above all the Jews,[a] who even flocked to the place for several successive nights.

LXXXV. Immediately after the funeral the commons ran to the houses of Brutus and Cassius with firebrands, and after being repelled with difficulty, they slew Helvius Cinna when they met him, through a mistake in the name, supposing that he was Cornelius Cinna, who had the day before made a bitter indictment of Caesar and for whom they were looking; and they set his head upon a spear and paraded it about the streets. Afterwards they set up in the Forum a solid column of Numidian marble almost twenty feet high, and inscribed upon it, "To the Father of his Country." At the foot of this they continued for a long time to sacrifice, make vows, and settle some of their disputes by an oath in the name of Caesar.

LXXXVI. Caesar left in the minds of some of his friends the suspicion that he did not wish to live longer and had taken no precautions, because of his failing health; and that therefore he neglected the warnings which came to him from portents and from the reports of his friends. Some think that it was because he had full trust in that last decree of the senators and their oath that he dismissed even the armed bodyguard of Spanish soldiers that formerly attended him. Others, on the contrary, believe that he elected to expose himself once for all to the plots that threatened him on every hand, rather than to be always anxious and on his guard. Some, too, say that he was wont to declare that it was not so much to his own interest

quam rei publicae interesse, uti salvus esset; se iam pridem potentiae gloriaeque abunde adeptum; rem publicam, si quid sibi eveniret, neque quietam fore et aliquanto deteriore condicione civilia bella subituram.

LXXXVII. Illud plane inter omnes fere constitit, talem ei mortem paene ex sententia obtigisse. Nam et quondam, cum apud Xenophontem legisset Cyrum ultima valitudine mandasse quaedam de funere suo, aspernatus tam lentum mortis genus subitam sibi celeremque optaverat; et pridie quam occideretur, in sermone nato super cenam apud Marcum Lepidum, quisnam esset finis vitae commodissimus, repentinum inopinatumque praetulerat.

LXXXVIII. Periit sexto et quinquagensimo aetatis anno atque in deorum numerum relatus est, non ore modo decernentium sed et persuasione volgi. Siquidem ludis, quos primos consecrato[1] ei heres Augustus edebat, stella crinita per septem continuos dies fulsit exoriens circa undecimam horam, creditumque est animam esse Caesaris in caelum recepti; et hac de causa simulacro eius in vertice additur stella.

Curiam, in qua occisus est, obstrui placuit Idusque Martias Parricidium nominari, ac ne umquam eo die senatus ageretur.

LXXXIX. Percussorum autem fere neque triennio quisquam amplius supervixit neque sua morte defunctus est. Damnati omnes alius alio casu periit, pars naufragio, pars proelio; nonnulli semet eodem illo pugione, quo Caesarem violaverant, interemerunt.

[1] primos consecrato, *Basle ed. of* 1546; primo consecratos, Ω.

[a] *Cyropedeia*, 8. 7.   [b] About an hour before sunset.

as to that of his country that he remain alive; he had long since had his fill of power and glory; but if aught befell him, the commonwealth would have no peace, but would be plunged in civil strife under much worse conditions.

LXXXVII. About one thing almost all are fully agreed, that he all but desired such a death as he met; for once when he read in Xenophon[a] how Cyrus in his last illness gave directions for his funeral, he expressed his horror of such a lingering kind of end and his wish for one which was swift and sudden. And the day before his murder, in a conversation which arose at a dinner at the house of Marcus Lepidus, as to what manner of death was most to be desired, he had given his preference to one which was sudden and unexpected.

LXXXVIII. He died in the fifty-sixth year of his age, and was numbered among the gods, not only by a formal decree, but also in the conviction of the common people. For at the first of the games which his heir Augustus gave in honour of his apotheosis, a comet shone for seven successive days, rising about the eleventh hour,[b] and was believed to be the soul of Caesar, who had been taken to heaven; and this is why a star is set upon the crown of his head in his statue. 44 B.C.

It was voted that the hall in which he was slain be walled up, that the Ides of March be called the Day of Parricide, and that a meeting of the senate should never be called on that day.

LXXXIX. Hardly any of his assassins survived him for more than three years, or died a natural death. They were all condemned, and they perished in various ways—some by shipwreck, some in battle; some took their own lives with the self-same dagger with which they had impiously slain Caesar.

BOOK II

THE DEIFIED AUGUSTUS

LIBER II

DIVUS AUGUSTUS

I. Gentem Octaviam Velitris praecipuam olim fuisse multa declarant. Nam et vicus celeberrima parte oppidi iam pridem Octavius vocabatur et ostendebatur ara Octavio consecrata, qui bello dux finitimo, cum forte Marti rem divinam faceret, nuntiata repente hostis incursione semicruda exta rapta foco prosecuit atque ita proelium ingressus victor redit. Decretum etiam publicum exstabat, quo cavebatur, ut in posterum quoque simili modo exta Marti redderentur reliquiaeque ad Octavios referrentur.

II. Ea gens a Tarquinio Prisco rege inter minores gentis adlecta in senatum, mox a Servio[1] Tullio in patricias traducta, procedente tempore ad plebem se contulit ac rursus · magno[2] intervallo per Divum Iulium in patriciatum redit. Primus ex hac magis-
2 tratum populi suffragio cepit C. Rufus. Is quaestorius

---

[1] Servio] servilio, *mss.*
[2] magno intervallo per, ς *(also V in a correction by a late hand).*

---

[a] A term applied to the plebeian families in the senate enrolled in addition to the patricians.

BOOK II

THE DEIFIED AUGUSTUS

I. THERE are many indications that the Octavian family was in days of old a distinguished one at Velitrae; for not only was a street in the most frequented part of the town long ago called Octavian, but an altar was shown there besides, consecrated by an Octavius. This man was leader in a war with a neighbouring town, and when news of a sudden onset of the enemy was brought to him just as he chanced to be sacrificing to Mars, he snatched the inwards of the victim from the fire and offered them up half raw; and thus he went forth to battle, and returned victorious. There was, besides, a decree of the people on record, providing that for the future too the inwards should be offered to Mars in the same way, and the rest of the victims be handed over to the Octavii.

II. The family was admitted to the senate by king Tarquinius Priscus among the lesser clans;[a] was later enrolled by Servius Tullius among the patricians; in course of time returned to the ranks of the plebeians; and after a long interval was restored to patrician rank by the Deified Julius. The first of the house to be elected by the people to a magistracy was Gaius Rufus, who became quaestor. He begot

Cn. et C. procreavit, a quibus duplex Octaviorum familia defluxit condicione diversa, siquidem Gnaeus et deinceps ab eo reliqui omnes functi sunt honoribus summis; at C. eiusque posteri, seu fortuna seu voluntate, in equestri ordine constiterunt usque ad Augusti patrem. Proavus Augusti secundo Punico bello stipendia in Sicilia tribunus militum fecit Aemilio Papo imperatore. Avus municipalibus magisteriis contentus abundante patrimonio tranquil-

3 lissime senuit. Sed haec alii; ipse Augustus nihil amplius quam equestri familia ortum se scribit vetere ac locuplete, et in qua primus senator pater suus fuerit. M. Antonius libertinum ei proavum exprobrat, restionem e pago Thurino, avum argentarium. Nec quicquam ultra de paternis Augusti maioribus repperi.

III. C. Octavius pater a principio aetatis et re et existimatione magna fuit, ut equidem mirer hunc quoque a nonnullis argentarium atque etiam inter divisores operasque campestres proditum; amplis enim innutritus opibus honores et adeptus est facile et egregie administravit. Ex praetura Macedoniam sortitus fugitivos, residuam Spartaci et Catilinae manum, Thurinum agrum tenentis in itinere delevit,

2 negotio sibi in senatu [1] extra ordinem dato. Pro-

---

[1] in senatu] a senatu, *Mommsen* (*P. Thomas*).

---

[a] In his Memoirs; see chap. lxxxv. 1.

Gnaeus and Gaius, from whom two branches of the Octavian family were derived, of very different standing; for Gnaeus and all his scions in turn held the highest offices, but Gaius and his progeny, whether from chance or choice, remained in the equestrian order down to the father of Augustus. Augustus's great grandfather served in Sicily in the second Punic war as tribune of the soldiers under the command of Aemilius Papus. His grandfather, 205 B C. content with the offices of a municipal town and possessing an abundant income, lived to a peaceful old age. This is the account given by others; Augustus himself merely writes [a] that he came of an old and wealthy equestrian family, in which his own father was the first to become a senator. Marcus Antonius taunts him with his great-grandfather, saying that he was a freedman and a rope-maker from the country about Thurii, while his grandfather was a money-changer. This is all that I have been able to learn about the paternal ancestors of Augustus.

III. His father Gaius Octavius was from the beginning of his life a man of wealth and repute, and I cannot but wonder that some have said that he too was a money-changer, and was even employed to distribute bribes at the elections and perform other services in the Campus; for as a matter of fact, being brought up in affluence, he readily attained to high positions and filled them with distinction. Macedonia fell to his lot at the end of his praetorship; on his way to the province, executing a special commission from the senate, he wiped out a band of runaway slaves, refugees from the armies of Spartacus and Catiline, who held possession of the country about Thurii. In governing his province he

125

vinciae praefuit non minore iustitia quam fortitudine ;
namque Bessis ac Thracibus magno proelio fusis ita
socios tractavit, ut epistulae M. Ciceronis exstent,
quibus Quintum fratrem eodem tempore parum
secunda fama proconsulatum Asiae administrantem
hortatur et monet, imitetur in promerendis sociis
vicinum suum Octavium.

IV. Decedens Macedonia, prius quam profiteri[1]
se candidatum consulatus posset, mortem obiit
repentinam, superstitibus liberis Octavia maiore,
quam ex Ancharia, et Octavia minore item Augusto,
quos ex Atia tulerat. Atia M. Atio Balbo et Iulia,
sorore C. Caesaris, genita est. Balbus, paterna stirpe
Aricinus, multis in familia senatoriis imaginibus, a
matre Magnum Pompeium artissimo contingebat
gradu, functusque honore praeturae inter vigintiviros
2 agrum Campanum plebi Iulia lege divisit. Verum
idem Antonius, despiciens etiam maternam Augusti
originem, proavum eius Afri generis fuisse et modo
unguentariam tabernam modo pistrinum Ariciae
exercuisse obicit. Cassius quidem Parmensis quadam
epistula non tantum ut pistoris, sed etiam ut num-
mulari nepotem sic taxat Augustum : " Materna tibi
farina est ex crudissimo Ariciae pistrino ; hanc finxit
manibus collybo decoloratis Nerulonensis mensarius."

---

[1] profiteri, ς ; confiteri, Ω.

[a] *Ad Quint. Frat.* 1. 1. 21.
[b] Q. Cicero was really *propraetor* ; see note on *Jul.* liv. 1.
[c] *Imagines* were waxen masks of ancestors of noble (*i.e.*,
senatorial) rank, kept in the hall (*atrium*) of their descendants.   [d] See *Jul.* xx. 3, note.
[e] According to the *Thes. Ling. Lat. s.v. collybus*, Suetonius

showed equal justice and courage ; for besides rout-
ing the Bessi and the other Thracians in a great
battle, his treatment of our allies was such, that
Marcus Cicero, in letters which are still in existence,[a]
urges and admonishes his brother Quintus, who at
the time was serving as proconsular governor [b] of
Asia with no great credit to himself, to imitate his
neighbour Octavius in winning the favour of our
allies.

61/58
B.C.

IV. While returning from Macedonia, before he
could declare himself a candidate for the consulship,
he died suddenly, survived by three children, an
elder Octavia by Ancharia, and by Atia a younger
Octavia and Augustus. Atia was the daughter of
Marcus Atius Balbus and Julia, sister of Gaius Caesar.
Balbus, a native of Aricia on his father's side, and of
a family displaying many senatorial portraits,[c] was
closely connected on his mother's side with Pompey
the Great. After holding the office of praetor, he
was one of the commission of twenty [d] appointed by
the Julian law to distribute lands in Campania to the
commons. But Antonius again, trying to disparage
the maternal ancestors of Augustus as well, twits
him with having a great-grandfather of African
birth, who kept first a perfumery shop and then a
bakery at Aricia. Cassius of Parma also taunts
Augustus with being the grandson both of a baker
and of a money-changer, saying in one of his letters :
" Your mother's meal came from a vulgar bakeshop
of Aricia ; this a money-changer from Nerulum
kneaded into shape with hands stained with filthy
lucre." [e]

misunderstood Cassius, who used *collybus* of a kind of cake.
In general, see Scott, *Mem. Amer. Acad. in Rome*, xi. 12 f.

127

V. Natus est Augustus M. Tullio Cicerone C. Antonio conss. VIIII. Kal. Octob. paulo ante solis exortum, regione Palati ad Capita Bubula, ubi nunc sacrarium habet, aliquanto post quam excessit constitutum. Nam ut senatus actis continetur, cum C. Laetorius, adulescens patricii generis, in deprecanda graviore adulterii poena praeter aetatem atque natales hoc quoque patribus conscriptis allegaret, esse possessorem ac velut aedituum soli, quod primum Divus Augustus nascens attigisset, peteretque donari quasi proprio suo ac peculiari deo, decretum est ut ea pars domus consecraretur.

VI. Nutrimentorum eius ostenditur adhuc locus in avito suburbano iuxta Velitras permodicus et cellae penuariae instar, tenetque vicinitatem opinio tamquam et natus ibi sit. Huc introire nisi necessario et caste religio est, concepta opinione veteri, quasi temere adeuntibus horror quidam et metus obiciatur, sed et mox confirmata. Nam cum possessor villae novus seu forte seu temptandi causa cubitum se eo contulisset, evenit ut post paucissimas noctis horas exturbatus inde subita vi et incerta paene semianimis cum strato simul ante fores inveniretur.

VII. Infanti cognomen Thurino inditum est, in memoriam maiorum originis, vel quod regione Thurina

THE DEIFIED AUGUSTUS

V. Augustus was born just before sunrise on the ninth day before the Kalends of October in the consulship of Marcus Tullius Cicero and Gaius Antonius, at the Ox-Heads in the Palatine quarter, where he now has a shrine, built shortly after his death. For it is recorded in the proceedings of the senate, that when Gaius Laetorius, a young man of patrician family, was pleading for a milder punishment for adultery because of his youth and position, he further urged upon the senators that he was the possessor and as it were the warden of the spot which the deified Augustus first touched at his birth, and begged that he be pardoned for the sake of what might be called his own special god. Whereupon it was decreed that that part of his house should be consecrated.

VI. A small room like a pantry is shown to this day as the emperor's nursery in his grandfather's country-house near Velitrae, and the opinion prevails in the neighbourhood that he was actually born there. No one ventures to enter this room except of necessity and after purification, since there is a conviction of long-standing that those who approach it without ceremony are seized with shuddering and terror; and what is more, this has recently been shown to be true. For when a new owner, either by chance or to test the matter, went to bed in that room, it came to pass that, after a very few hours of the night, he was thrown out by a sudden mysterious force, and was found bedclothes and all half-dead before the door.

VII. In his infancy he was given the surname Thurinus in memory of the home of his ancestors, or else because it was near Thurii that his father

recens eo nato pater Octavius adversus fugitivos rem
prospere gesserat. Thurinum cognominatum satis
certa probatione tradiderim nactus puerilem imagun-
culam eius aeream veterem ferreis et paene iam
exolescentibus litteris hoc nomine inscriptam, quae
dono a me principi data inter cubiculi [1] Lares colitur.
Sed et a M. Antonio in epistulis per contumeliam
saepe Thurinus appellatur et ipse nihil amplius quam
mirari se rescribit pro obprobrio sibi prius nomen obici.
2 Postea Gai Caesaris et deinde Augusti cognomen
assumpsit, alterum testamento maioris avunculi,
alterum Munati Planci sententia, cum quibusdam
censentibus Romulum appellari oportere quasi et
ipsum conditorem urbis, praevaluisset, ut Augustus
potius vocaretur, non tantum [2] novo sed etiam
ampliore cognomine, quod loca quoque religiosa et
in quibus augurato quid consecratur augusta dicantur,
ab auctu vel ab avium gestu gustuve, sicut etiam
Ennius docet scribens :

" Augusto augurio postquam incluta condita Roma
    est."

VIII. Quadrimus patrem amisit. Duodecimum
annum agens aviam Iuliam defunctam pro contione
laudavit. Quadriennio post virili toga sumpta militaribus donis triumpho Caesaris Africano donatus est,

---

[1] cubiculi Lares, *Lipsius* ; cubiculares, Ω.
[2] tantum, ς (*Erasmus*) ; eum, *MQ* ; cum, *G*ΠR ; enim, *V* ;
autem, X ; solum, ς (*omitted by* δ).

---

[a] *i.e.* Hadrian.   [b] *Annales*, 502, Vahlen.[2]

Octavius, shortly after the birth of his son, had gained his victory over the runaway slaves. That he was surnamed Thurinus I may assert on very trustworthy evidence, since I once obtained a bronze statuette, representing him as a boy and inscribed with that name in letters of iron almost illegible from age. This I presented to the emperor,[a] who cherishes it among the Lares of his bed-chamber. Furthermore, he is often called Thurinus in Mark Antony's letters by way of insult; to which Augustus merely replied that he was surprised that his former name was thrown in his face as a reproach. Later he took the name of Gaius Caesar and then the surname Augustus, the former by the will of his 27 B.C. great-uncle, the latter on the motion of Munatius Plancus. For when some expressed the opinion that he ought to be called Romulus as a second founder of the city, Plancus carried the proposal that he should rather be named Augustus, on the ground that this was not merely a new title but a more honourable one, inasmuch as sacred places too, and those in which anything is consecrated by augural rites are called "august" (*augusta*), from the increase (*auctus*) in dignity, or from the movements or feeding of the birds (*avium gestus gustusve*), as Ennius[b] also shows when he writes:

"After by augury august illustrious Rome had been founded."

VIII. At the age of four he lost his father. In 59 B.C. his twelfth year he delivered a funeral oration to the assembled people in honour of his grandmother Julia. Four years later, after assuming the gown of manhood, he received military prizes at Caesar's

quanquam expers belli propter aetatem. Profectum
mox avunculum in Hispanias adversus Cn. Pompei
liberos vixdum firmus a gravi valitudine per infestas
hostibus vias paucissimis comitibus naufragio etiam
facto subsecutus, magno opere demeruit, approbata
cito etiam morum indole super itineris industriam.

2 Caesare post receptas Hispanias expeditionem in
Dacos et inde Parthos [1] destinante praemissus Apolloniam studiis vacavit. Utque primum occisum eum
heredemque se comperit, diu cunctatus an proximas
legiones imploraret, id quidem consilium ut praeceps
inmaturumque omisit. Ceterum urbe repetita hereditatem adiit, dubitante matre, vitrico vero Marcio
3 Philippo consulari multum dissuadente. Atque ab eo
tempore exercitibus comparatis primum cum M.
Antonio M. que Lepido, deinde [2] tantum cum Antonio
per duodecim fere annos, novissime per quattuor et
quadraginta solus rem p. tenuit.

IX. Proposita vitae eius velut summa partes [3]
singillatim neque per tempora sed per species
exsequar, quo distinctius demonstrari cognoscique
possint.

Bella civilia quinque gessit: Mutinense, Philippense, Perusinum, Siculum, Actiacum; e quibus primum ac novissimum adversus M. Antonium, secundum

---

[1] Parthos, *M*; *the other mss. have* in Parthos.
[2] deinde, *M*; *the other mss. have* dein.
[3] parte, Ω. *Corrected in* 15*th century.*

African triumph, although he had taken no part in
the war on account of his youth. When his uncle
presently went to Spain to engage the sons of Pompey,
although Augustus had hardly yet recovered his 46 B.C.
strength after a severe illness, he followed over roads
beset by the enemy with only a very few companions,
and that too after suffering shipwreck, and thereby
greatly endeared himself to Caesar, who soon formed
a high opinion of his character over and above the
energy with which he had made the journey.

When Caesar, after recovering the Spanish provinces, planned an expedition against the Dacians
and then against the Parthians, Augustus, who
had been sent on in advance to Apollonia, devoted his leisure to study. As soon as he learned
that his uncle had been slain and that he was his 44 B.C.
heir, he was in doubt for some time whether to
appeal to the nearest legions, but gave up the
idea as hasty and premature. He did, however,
return to the city and enter upon his inheritance, in
spite of the doubts of his mother and the strong
opposition of his stepfather, the ex-consul Marcius
Philippus. Then he levied armies and henceforth
ruled the State, at first with Marcus Antonius and
Marcus Lepidus, then with Antony alone for nearly
twelve years, and finally by himself for forty-four.

IX. Having given as it were a summary of his life,
I shall now take up its various phases one by one,
not in chronological order, but by classes, to make
the account clearer and more intelligible.

The civil wars which he waged were five, called by
the names of Mutina, Philippi, Perusia, Sicily, and
Actium; the first and last of these were against
Marcus Antonius, the second against Brutus and

adversus Brutum et Cassium, tertium adversus L. Antonium triumviri fratrem, quartum adversus Sextum Pompeium Cn. filium.

X. Omnium bellorum initium et causam hinc sumpsit: nihil convenientius ducens quam necem avunculi vindicare tuerique acta, confestim ut Apollonia rediit, Brutum Cassiumque et vi necopinantis et, quia provisum periculum subterfugerant, legibus adgredi reosque caedis absentis deferre statuit. Ludos autem victoriae Caesaris non audentibus facere quibus
2 optigerat id munus, ipse edidit. Et quo constantius cetera quoque exsequeretur, in locum tr. pl. forte demortui candidatum se ostendit, quanquam patricius necdum senator. Sed adversante conatibus suis M. Antonio consule, quem vel praecipuum adiutorem speraverat, ac ne publicum quidem et translativum ius ulla in re sibi sine pactione gravissimae mercedis impertiente, ad optimates se contulit, quibus eum invisum sentiebat, maxime quod D. Brutum obsessum Mutinae provincia a Caesare data et per senatum
3 confirmata expellere armis niteretur. Hortantibus itaque nonnullis percussores ei subornavit, ac fraude deprehensa periculum in vicem metuens veteranos simul in suum ac rei p. auxilium quanta potuit largitione contraxit; iussusque comparato exercitui

---

ᵃ Since the time of Sulla only senators were eligible for the position of tribune.

Cassius, the third against Lucius Antonius, brother of the triumvir, and the fourth against Sextus Pompeius, son of Gnaeus.

X. The initial reason for all these wars was this: since he considered nothing more incumbent on him than to avenge his uncle's death and maintain the validity of his enactments, immediately on returning from Apollonia he resolved to surprise Brutus and Cassius by taking up arms against them; and when they foresaw the danger and fled, to resort to law and prosecute them for murder in their absence. Furthermore, since those who had been appointed to celebrate Caesar's victory by games did not dare to do so, he gave them himself. To be able to carry out his other plans with more authority, he announced his candidature for the position of one of the tribunes of the people, who happened to die; though he was a patrician, and not yet a senator.[a] But when his designs were opposed by Marcus Antonius, who was then consul, and on whose help he had especially counted, and Antony would not allow him even common and ordinary justice without the promise of a heavy bribe, he went over to the aristocrats, who he knew detested Antony, especially because he was besieging Decimus Brutus at Mutina, and trying to drive him by force of arms from the province given him by Caesar and ratified by the senate. Accordingly at the advice of certain men he hired assassins to kill Antony, and when the plot was discovered, fearing retaliation he mustered veterans, by the use of all the money he could command, both for his own protection and that of the State. Put in command of the army which he had raised, with the rank of propraetor, and bidden

pro praetore praeesse et cum Hirtio ac Pansa, qui
consulatum susceperant, D. Bruto opem ferre, deman-
datum bellum tertio mense confecit duobus proeliis.
4 Priore Antonius fugisse eum scribit ac sine paluda-
mento equoque post biduum demum apparuisse,
sequenti satis constat non modo ducis, sed etiam
militis functum munere atque in media dimicatione,
aquilifero legionis suae graviter saucio, aquilam
umeris subisse diuque portasse.

XI. Hoc bello cum Hirtius in acie, Pansa paulo
post ex vulnere perissent, rumor increbruit ambos
opera eius occisos, ut Antonio fugato, re p. consulibus
orbata solus victores exercitus occuparet. Pansae
quidem adeo suspecta mors fuit, ut Glyco medicus
custoditus sit, quasi venenum vulneri indidisset.
Adicit his Aquilius Niger alterum e consulibus
Hirtium in pugnae tumultu ab ipso interemptum.

XII. Sed ut cognovit Antonium post fugam a M.
Lepido receptum ceterosque duces et exercitus
consentire pro partibus, causam optimatium sine
cunctatione deseruit, ad praetextum mutatae volun-
tatis dicta factaque quorundam calumniatus, quasi alii
se puerum, alii ornandum tollendumque iactassent,
ne aut sibi aut veteranis par gratia referretur.   Et

---

[a] Cic. *Epist. ad Fam.* 11. 20. 1; according to Vell. Paterc.
2. 62. 6, Cicero punned on the double meaning of *tollo*, " raise "
and " put out of the way."

136

to join with Hirtius and Pansa, who had become
consuls, in lending aid to Decimus Brutus, he finished
the war which had been entrusted to him within
three months in two battles. In the former of these,
so Antony writes, he took to flight and was not seen
again until the next day, when he returned without
his cloak and his horse; but in that which followed
all agree that he played the part not only of a
leader, but of a soldier as well, and that, in the
thick of the fight, when the eagle-bearer of his
legion was sorely wounded, he shouldered the eagle
and carried it for some time.

XI. As Hirtius lost his life in battle during this
war, and Pansa shortly afterwards from a wound, the
rumour spread that he had caused the death of both,
in order that after Antony had been put to flight and
the state bereft of its consuls, he might gain sole
control of the victorious armies. The circumstances
of Pansa's death in particular were so suspicious, that
the physician Glyco was imprisoned on the charge of
having applied poison to his wound. Aquilius Niger
adds to this that Augustus himself slew the other
consul Hirtius amid the confusion of the battle.

XII. But when he learned that Antony after his
flight had found a protector in Marcus Lepidus, and
that the rest of the leaders and armies were coming
to terms with them, he abandoned the cause of
the nobles without hesitation, alleging as a pretext
for his change of allegiance the words and acts of
certain of their number, asserting that some had
called him a boy, while others had openly said that
he ought to be honoured and got rid of,[a] to escape
the necessity of making suitable recompense to him
or to his veterans. To show more plainly that he

quo magis paenitentiam prioris sectae approbaret,
Nursinos grandi pecunia et quam pendere nequirent
multatos extorres oppido egit, quod Mutinensi acie
interemptorum civium tumulo publice exstructo
ascripserant pro libertate eos occubuisse.

XIII. Inita cum Antonio et Lepido societate
Philippense quoque bellum, quamquam invalidus
atque aeger, duplici proelio transegit, quorum priore
castris exutus vix ad Antoni cornu fuga evaserat.
Nec successum victoriae moderatus est, sed capite
Bruti Romam misso, ut statuae Caesaris subiceretur,
in splendidissimum quemque captivum non sine
2 verborum contumelia saeviit; ut quidem uni suppliciter sepulturam precanti respondisse dicitur[1] iam
istam volucrum fore potestatem; alios, patrem et
filium, pro vita rogantis sortiri vel micare iussisse, ut
alterutri concederetur, ac spectasse utrumque mori-
entem, cum patre, quia se optulerat, occiso filius
quoque voluntariam occubuisset necem. Quare
ceteri, in his M. Favonius ille Catonis aemulus, cum
catenati producerentur, imperatore Antonio honorifice salutato, hunc foedissimo convicio coram
prosciderunt.

3   Partitis post victoriam officiis cum Antonius Orientem ordinandum, ipse veteranos in Italiam
reducendos et municipalibus agris collocandos

---

[1] dicitur, *MV*; dicatur *GXΥ and the editors, except Ihm.*

[a] A game still common in Italy, in which the contestants
thrust out their fingers (*micare digitis*), the one naming
correctly the number thrust out by his opponent being the
winner.
[b] The term applied to a victorious general by his soldiers.

regretted his connection with the former party, he imposed a heavy fine on the people of Nursia and banished them from their city when they were unable to pay it, because they had at public expense erected a monument to their citizens who were slain in the battles at Mutina and inscribed upon it: " they fell for liberty."

XIII. Then, forming a league with Antony and Lepidus, he finished the war of Philippi also in two 42 b.c. battles, although weakened by illness, being driven from his camp in the first battle and barely making his escape by fleeing to Antony's division. He did not use his victory with moderation, but after sending Brutus's head to Rome, to be cast at the feet of Caesar's statue, he vented his spleen upon the most distinguished of his captives, not even sparing them insulting language. For instance, to one man who begged humbly for burial, he is said to have replied : "The birds will soon settle that question." When two others, father and son, begged for their lives, he is said to have bidden them cast lots or play mora,[a] to decide which should be spared, and then to have looked on while both died, since the father was executed because he offered to die for his son, and the latter thereupon took his own life. Because of this the rest, including Marcus Favonius, the well-known imitator of Cato, saluted Antony respectfully as Imperator,[b] when they were led out in chains, but lashed Augustus to his face with the foulest abuse.

When the duties of administration were divided after the victory, Antony undertaking to restore order in the East, and Augustus to lead the veterans back to Italy and assign them lands in the munici-palities, he could neither satisfy the veterans nor the

139

recepisset, neque veteranorum neque possessorum
gratiam tenuit, alteris pelli se, alteris non pro spe
meritorum tractari querentibus.

XIV. Quo tempore L. Antonium fiducia consulatus,
quem gerebat, ac fraternae potentiae res novas
molientem confugere Perusiam coegit et ad deditionem fame conpulit, non tamen sine magnis suis
et ante bellum et in bello discriminibus. Nam cum
spectaculo ludorum gregarium militem in quattuordecim ordinibus sedentem excitari per apparitorem
iussisset, rumore ab obtrectatoribus dilato quasi
eundem mox et discruciatum necasset, minimum
afuit quin periret concursu et indignatione turbae
militaris. Saluti fuit, quod qui desiderabatur repente
comparuit incolumis ac sine iniuria. Circa Perusinum autem murum sacrificans paene interceptus est
a manu gladiatorum, quae oppido eruperat.

XV. Perusia capta in plurimos animadvertit, orare
veniam vel excusare se conantibus una voce oc-
currens "moriendum esse." Scribunt quidam tre-
centos ex dediticiis electos utriusque ordinis ad aram
Divo Iulio exstructam Idibus Martiis hostiarum more
mactatos. Exstiterunt qui traderent conpecto[1] eum
ad arma isse, ut occulti adversarii et quos metus
magis quam voluntas contineret, facultate L. Antoni
ducis praebita, detegerentur devictisque iis et con-
fiscatis promissa veteranis praemia solverentur.

---

[1] conpecto, *Lipsius* ; conspecto Ω (conspectu, *Q*).

---

[a] See note on *Jul.* xxxix. 2.

landowners, since the latter complained that they were driven from their homes, and the former that they were not being treated as their services had led them to hope.

XIV. When Lucius Antonius at this juncture attempted a revolution, relying on his position as consul and his brother's power, he forced him to take refuge in Perusia, and starved him into surrender, not, however, without great personal danger both before and during the war. For at an exhibition of games, when he had given orders that a common soldier who was sitting in the fourteen rows [a] be put out by an attendant, the report was spread by his detractors that he had had the man killed later and tortured as well; whereupon he all but lost his life in a furious mob of soldiers, owing his escape to the sudden appearance of the missing man safe and sound. Again, when he was sacrificing near the walls of Perusia, he was well nigh cut off by a band of gladiators, who had made a sally from the town.

XV. After the capture of Perusia he took vengeance on many, meeting all attempts to beg for pardon or to make excuses with the one reply, " You must die." Some write that three hundred men of both orders were selected from the prisoners of war and sacrificed on the Ides of March like so many victims at the altar raised to the Deified Julius. Some have written that he took up arms of a set purpose, to unmask his secret opponents and those whom fear rather than good-will kept faithful to him, by giving them the chance to follow the lead of Lucius Antonius; and then by vanquishing them and confiscating their estates to pay the rewards promised to his veterans.

XVI. Siculum bellum incohavit in primis, sed diu traxit intermissum saepius, modo reparandarum classium causa, quas tempestatibus duplici naufragio et quidem per aestatem amiserat, modo pace facta, flagitante populo ob interclusos commeatus famemque ingravescentem; donec navibus ex integro fabricatis ac viginti servorum milibus manumissis et ad remum datis portum Iulium apud Baias inmisso in Lucrinum et Avernum lacum mari effecit. In quo cum hieme tota copias exercuisset, Pompeium inter Mylas et Naulochum superavit, sub horam pugnae tam arto repente somno devinctus, ut ad dandum 2 signum ab amicis excitaretur. Unde praebitam Antonio materiam putem exprobrandi: ne rectis quidem oculis eum aspicere potuisse instructam aciem, verum supinum, caelum intuentem, stupidum cubuisse nec prius surrexisse ac militibus in conspectum venisse quam a M. Agrippa fugatae sint hostium naves. Alii dictum factumque eius criminantur, quasi classibus tempestate perditis exclamaverit etiam invito Neptuno victoriam se adepturum, ac die circensium proximo sollemni pompae 3 simulacrum dei detraxerit. Nec temere plura ac maiora pericula ullo alio bello adiit. Traiecto in Siciliam exercitu, cum partem reliquam copiarum continenti repeteret, oppressus ex inproviso a Demochare et Apollophane praefectis Pompei uno demum navigio aegerrime effugit. Iterum cum praeter Locros Regium pedibus iret et prospectis biremibus

XVI. The Sicilian war was among the first that he
began, but it was long drawn out by many interrup-
tions, now for the purpose of rebuilding his fleets,
which he twice lost by shipwreck due to storms, and
that, too, in the summer; and again by making peace
at the demand of the people, when supplies were cut
off and there was a severe famine. Finally, after
new ships had been built and twenty thousand slaves
set free and trained as oarsmen, he made the Julian
harbour at Baiae by letting the sea into the Lucrine
lake and lake Avernus. After drilling his forces
there all winter, he defeated Pompey between Mylae
and Naulochus, though just before the battle he was
suddenly held fast by so deep a sleep that his
friends had to awaken him to give the signal. And
it was this, I think, that gave Antony opportunity for
the taunt: "He could not even look with steady
eyes at the fleet when it was ready for battle, but
lay in a stupor on his back, looking up at the sky,
and did not rise or appear before the soldiers until
the enemy's ships had been put to flight by Marcus
Agrippa." Some censured an act and saying of his,
declaring that when his fleets were lost in the storm,
he cried out, "I will have the victory spite of
Neptune," and that on the day when games in the
Circus next occurred, he removed the statue of that
god from the sacred procession. And it is safe to
say that in none of his wars did he encounter more
dangers or greater ones. For when he had transported an army to Sicily and was on his way back to
the rest of his forces on the mainland, he was
surprised by Pompey's admirals Demochares and
Apollophanes and barely escaped with but a single
ship. Again, as he was going on foot to Regium by

Pompeianis terram legentibus suas ratus descendisset ad litus, paene exceptus est. Tunc etiam per devios tramites refugientem servus Aemili Pauli comitis eius, dolens proscriptum olim ab eo patrem Paulum et quasi occasione ultionis oblata, interficere conatus est.

4 Post Pompei fugam collegarum alterum M. Lepidum, quem ex Africa in auxilium evocarat, superbientem viginti legionum fiducia summasque sibi partes terrore et minis vindicantem spoliavit exercitu supplicemque concessa vita Cerceios in perpetuum relegavit.

XVII. M. Antoni societatem semper dubiam et incertam reconciliationibusque variis male focilatam abrupit tandem, et quo magis degenerasse eum a civili more approbaret, testamentum, quod is Romae etiam de Cleopatra liberis inter heredes nuncupatis reliquerat, aperiundum recitandumque pro contione 2 curavit. Remisit tamen hosti iudicato[1] necessitudines amicosque omnes atque inter alios C. Sosium et T.[2] Domitium tunc adhuc consules. Bononiensibus quoque publice, quod in Antoniorum clientela antiquitus erant, gratiam fecit coniurandi cum tota Italia pro partibus suis. Nec multo post navali proelio apud Actium vicit in serum dimicatione protracta, ut 3 in nave victor pernoctaverit. Ab Actio cum Samum

---

[1] iudicato] indicato, Ω.

[2] *So the manuscripts ; the consul was Gnaeus Domitius Ahenobarbus.*

way of Locri, he saw some of Pompey's biremes coasting along the shore, and taking them for his own ships and going down to the beach, narrowly escaped capture. At that same time, too, as he was making his escape by narrow bypaths, a slave of his companion Aemilius Paulus, nursing a grudge because Augustus had proscribed his master's father some time before, and thinking that he had an opportunity for revenge, attempted to slay him.

After Pompey's flight, Augustus' other colleague, Marcus Lepidus, whom he had summoned from Africa to help him, was puffed up by confidence in his twenty legions and claimed the first place with terrible threats; but Augustus stripped him of his army; and though he granted him his life when he sued for it, he banished him for all time to Circei.

XVII. At last he broke off his alliance with Marcus Antonius, which was always doubtful and uncertain, and with difficulty kept alive by various reconciliations; and the better to show that his rival had fallen away from conduct becoming a citizen, he had the will which Antony had left in Rome, naming his children by Cleopatra among his heirs, opened and read before the people. But when Antony was declared a public enemy, he sent back to him all his kinsfolk and friends, among others Gaius Sosius and Titus Domitius, who were still consuls at the time. He also excused the community of Bononia from joining in the rally of all Italy to his standards, since they had been from ancient days dependents of the Antonii. Not long afterwards he won 31 B.C. the sea-fight at Actium, where the contest continued to so late an hour that the victor passed the night on board. Having gone into winter quarters at Samos

145

in hiberna se recepisset, turbatus nuntiis de seditione
praemia et missionem poscentium, quos ex omni
numero confecta victoria Brundisium praemiserat,
repetita Italia[1] tempestate in traiectu bis conflictatus,
primo inter promunturia Peloponnesi atque Aetoliae,
rursus circa montes Ceraunios utrubique parte
liburnicarum demersa, simul eius, in qua vehebatur,
fusis armamentis et gubernaculo diffracto; nec
amplius quam septem et viginti dies, donec ad
desideria militum omnia[2] ordinarentur, Brundisii com-
moratus, Asiae Syriaeque circuitu Aegyptum petit
obsessaque Alexandrea, quo Antonius cum Cleopatra
4 confugerat, brevi potitus est.   Et Antonium quidem
seras condiciones pacis temptantem ad mortem
adegit viditque mortuum.   Cleopatrae, quam ser-
vatam triumpho magno opere cupiebat, etiam Psyllos
admovit, qui venenum ac virus exsugerent, quod
perisse morsu aspidis putabatur.   Ambobus com-
munem sepulturae honorem tribuit ac tumulum ab
5 ipsis incohatum perfici iussit.   Antonium iuvenem,
maiorem de duobus Fulvia genitis, simulacro Divi
Iuli, ad quod post multas et irritas preces confugerat, abreptum interemit.   Item Caesarionem, quem
ex Caesare patre Cleopatra concepisse praedicabat,
retractum e fuga supplicio adfecit.   Reliquos Antoni
reginaeque communes liberos non secus ac necessitudine iunctos sibi et conservavit et mox pro
condicione cuiusque sustinuit ac fovit.

---

[1] repetita Italia ς (*Schiffer*) ; repetit alia, *mss.*
[2] omnia, *an addition to the text suggested by Ihm.*

after Actium, he was disturbed by the news of a mutiny of the troops that he had selected from every division of his army and sent on to Brundisium after the victory, who demanded their rewards and discharge; and on his way back to Italy he twice encountered storms at sea, first between the headlands of the Peloponnesus and Aetolia, and again off the Ceraunian mountains. In both places a part of his galleys were sunk, while the rigging of the ship in which he was sailing was carried away and its rudder broken. He delayed at Brundisium only twenty-seven days— just long enough to satisfy all the demands of the soldiers—and then went to Egypt by a roundabout way through Asia and Syria, laid siege to Alexandria, where Antony had taken refuge with Cleopatra, and soon took the city. Although Antony tried to make terms at the eleventh hour, Augustus forced him to commit suicide, and viewed his corpse. He greatly desired to save Cleopatra alive for his triumph, and even had Psylli brought to her, to suck the poison from her wound, since it was thought that she died from the bite of an asp. He allowed them both the honour of burial, and in the same tomb, giving orders that the mausoleum which they had begun should be finished. The young Antony, the elder of Fulvia's two sons, he dragged from the image of the Deified Julius, to which he had fled after many vain entreaties, and slew him. Caesarion, too, whom Cleopatra fathered on Caesar, he overtook in his flight, brought back, and put to death. But he spared the rest of the offspring of Antony and Cleopatra, and afterwards maintained and reared them according to their several positions, as carefully as if they were his own kin.

XVIII. Per idem tempus conditorium et corpus
Magni Alexandri, cum prolatum e penetrali subie-
cisset oculis, corona aurea imposita ac floribus
aspersis veneratus est consultusque, num et Ptolemaeum inspicere vellet, regem se voluisse ait
2 videre, non mortuos. Aegyptum in provinciae
formam redactam ut feraciorem habilioremque
annonae urbicae redderet, fossas omnis, in quas
Nilus exaestuat, oblimatas longa vetustate militari
opere detersit. Quoque Actiacae victoriae memoria
celebratior et in posterum esset, urbem Nicopolim
apud Actium condidit ludosque illic quinquennales
constituit et ampliato vetere Apollinis templo locum
castrorum, quibus fuerat usus, exornatum navalibus
spoliis Neptuno ac Marti consecravit.

XIX. Tumultus posthac et rerum novarum initia
coniurationesque complures, prius quam invalescerent
indicio detectas, compressit alias alio tempore;
Lepidi iuvenis, deinde Varronis Murenae et Fanni
Caepionis, mox M. Egnati, exin Plauti Rufi Lucique
Pauli progeneri sui, ac praeter has L. Audasi falsarum
tabularum rei ac neque aetate neque corpore integri,
item Asini Epicadi ex gente Parthina ibridae, ad
extremum Telephi, mulieris servi nomenculatoris.
Nam ne ultimae quidem sortis hominum con-
2 spiratione et periculo caruit. Audasius atque
Epicadus Iuliam filiam et Agrippam nepotem ex

---

^a The sacred precinct at Alexandria (τὸ καλούμενον Σῆμα, ὃ
περίβολος ἦν, Strabo, 17. 1. 8) containing the tombs of
Alexander and of the kings.

^b The *nomenclator* (*nomenculator*) was a slave whose duty it
was to remind his master, or mistress, of the names of persons.

XVIII. About this time he had the sarcophagus and body of Alexander the Great brought forth from its shrine,[a] and after gazing on it, showed his respect by placing upon it a golden crown and strewing it with flowers; and being then asked whether he wished to see the tomb of the Ptolemies as well, he replied, " My wish was to see a king, not corpses." He reduced Egypt to the form of a province, and then to make it more fruitful and better adapted to supply the city with grain, he set his soldiers at work cleaning out all the canals into which the Nile overflows, which in the course of many years had become choked with mud. To extend the fame of his victory at Actium and perpetuate its memory, he founded a city called Nicopolis near Actium, and provided for the celebration of games there every five years; enlarged the ancient temple of Apollo; and after adorning the site of the camp which he had occupied with naval trophies, consecrated it to Neptune and Mars.

XIX. After this he nipped in the bud at various times several outbreaks, attempts at revolution, and conspiracies, which were betrayed before they became formidable. The ringleaders were, first the young Lepidus, then Varro Murena and Fannius Caepio, later Marcus Egnatius, next Plautius Rufus and Lucius Paulus, husband of the emperor's granddaughter, and besides these Lucius Audasius, who had been charged with forgery, and was moreover old and feeble; also Asinius Epicadus, a half-breed of Parthian descent, and finally Telephus, slave and page[b] of a woman; for even men of the lowest condition conspired against him and imperilled his safety. Audasius and Epicadus had planned to take his daughter Julia

insulis, quibus continebantur, rapere ad exercitus, Telephus quasi debita sibi fato dominatione et ipsum et senatum adgredi destinarant. Quin etiam quondam iuxta cubiculum eius lixa quidam ex Illyrico exercitu, ianitoribus deceptis, noctu deprehensus est cultro venatorio cinctus, imposne mentis an simulata dementia incertum; nihil enim exprimi quaestione potuit.

XX. Externa bella duo omnino per se gessit, Delmaticum adulescens adhuc et Antonio devicto Cantabricum. Delmatico etiam vulnera excepit, una acie dextrum genu lapide ictus, altera et crus et utrumque brachium ruina pontis consauciatus. Reliqua per legatos administravit, ut tamen quibusdam Pannonicis atque Germanicis aut interveniret aut non longe abesset, Ravennam vel Mediolanum vel Aquileiam usque ab urbe progrediens.

XXI. Domuit autem partim ductu partim auspiciis suis Cantabriam, Aquitaniam, Pannoniam, Delmatiam cum Illyrico omni, item Raetiam et Vindelicos ac Salassos, gentes Inalpinas. Coercuit et Dacorum incursiones tribus eorum ducibus cum magna copia caesis, Germanosque ultra Albim fluvium summovit, ex quibus Suebos et Sigambros dedentis se traduxit in Galliam atque in proximis Rheno agris conlocavit. Alias item nationes male quietas ad obsequium

_____

^a Applied to expeditions commanded by others, since as commander-in-chief he took the auspices before the army set out.

and his grandson Agrippa by force to the armies from the islands where they were confined, Telephus to set upon both Augustus and the senate, under the delusion that he himself was destined for empire. Even a soldier's servant from the army in Illyricum, who had escaped the vigilance of the door-keepers, was caught at night near the emperor's bed-room, armed with a hunting knife ; but whether the fellow was crazy or feigned madness is a question, since nothing could be wrung from him by torture.

XX. He carried on but two foreign wars in person : in Dalmatia, when he was but a youth, and with the Cantabrians after the overthrow of Antony. He was wounded, too, in the former campaign, being struck on the right knee with a stone in one battle, and in another having a leg and both arms severely injured by the collapse of a bridge. His other wars he carried on through his generals, although he was either present at some of those in Pannonia and Germany, or was not far from the front, since he went from the city as far as Ravenna, Mediolanum, or Aquileia.

XXI. In part as leader, and in part with armies serving under his auspices,[a] he subdued Cantabria, Aquitania, Pannonia, Dalmatia, and all Illyricum, as well as Raetia and the Vindelici and Salassi, which are Alpine tribes. He also put a stop to the inroads of the Dacians, slaying great numbers of them, together with three of their leaders, and forced the Germans back to the farther side of the river Albis, with the exception of the Suebi and Sigambri, who submitted to him and were taken into Gaul and settled in lands near the Rhine. He reduced to submission other peoples, too, that were in a state of unrest.

151

2 redegit. Nec ulli genti sine iustis et necessariis
causis bellum intulit, tantumque afuit a cupiditate
quoquo modo imperium vel bellicam gloriam augendi,
ut quorundam barbarorum principes in aede Martis
Ultoris iurare coegerit mansuros se in fide ac pace
quam peterent, a quibusdam vero novum genus
obsidum, feminas, exigere temptaverit, quod negle-
gere marum pignera sentiebat ; et tamen potestatem
semper omnibus fecit, quotiens vellent obsides
recipiendi. Neque aut crebrius aut perfidiosius
rebellantis graviore umquam ultus est poena, quam
ut captivos sub lege venundaret, ne in vicina regione
servirent neve intra tricensimum annum liberarentur.

3 Qua virtutis moderationisque fama Indos etiam ac
Scythas auditu modo cognitos pellexit ad amicitiam
suam populique Rom. ultro per legatos petendam.
Parthi quoque et Armeniam vindicanti facile cesse-
runt et signa militaria, quae M. Crasso et M.
Antonio ademerant, reposcenti reddiderunt obsides-
que insuper optulerunt, denique pluribus quondam
de regno concertantibus, non nisi ab ipso electum
probaverunt.

XXII. Ianum Quirinum semel atque iterum a[1]
condita urbe ante memoriam suam clausum in multo
breviore temporis spatio terra marique pace parta ter
clusit. Bis ovans ingressus est urbem, post Philippense

---

[1] a, Υ´ ; *omitted by the other mss.*

[a] Crassus lost his standards at the battle of Carrhae in 53,
and Antony through the defeat of his lieutenants in 40 and
36 B.C.

[b] In the reign of Numa, and in 235 B.C., after the first
Punic war.

But he never made war on any nation without just and due cause, and he was so far from desiring to increase his dominion or his military glory at any cost, that he forced the chiefs of certain barbarians to take oath in the temple of Mars the Avenger that they would faithfully keep the peace for which they asked; in some cases, indeed, he tried exacting a new kind of hostages, namely women, realizing that the barbarians disregarded pledges secured by males; but all were given the privilege of reclaiming their hostages whenever they wished. On those who rebelled often or under circumstances of especial treachery he never inflicted any severer punishment than that of selling the prisoners, with the condition that they should not pass their term of slavery in a country near their own, nor be set free within thirty years. The reputation for prowess and moderation which he thus gained led even the Indians and the Scythians, nations known to us only by hearsay, to send envoys of their own free will and sue for his friendship and that of the Roman people. The Parthians, too, readily yielded to him, when he laid claim to Armenia, and at his demand surrendered the stand- 20 B.C. ards which they had taken from Marcus Crassus and Marcus Antonius[a]; they offered him hostages besides, and once when there were several claimants of their throne, they would accept only the one whom he selected.

XXII. The temple of Janus Quirinus, which had been closed but twice before his time since the founding of the city,[b] he closed three times in a far shorter period, having won peace on land and sea. He twice entered the city in an ovation, after the war of Philippi, and again after that in Sicily,

et rursus post Siculum bellum. Curulis triumphos tris egit, Delmaticum, Actiacum, Alexandrinum continuo triduo omnes.

XXIII. Graves ignominias cladesque duas omnino nec alibi quam in Germania accepit, Lollianam et Varianam, sed Lollianam maioris infamiae quam detrimenti, Varianam paene exitiabilem tribus legionibus cum duce legatisque et auxiliis omnibus caesis. Hac nuntiata excubias per urbem indixit, ne quis tumultus exsisteret, et praesidibus provinciarum propagavit imperium, ut a peritis et assuetis socii continerentur. Vovit et magnos ludos Iovi Optimo Maximo, si res p. in meliorem statum vertisset : quod factum Cimbrico Marsicoque bello erat. Adeo denique consternatum ferunt, ut per continuos menses barba capilloque summisso caput interdum foribus illideret vociferans : " Quintili Vare, legiones redde! " diemque cladis quotannis maestum habuerit ac lugubrem.

XXIV. In re militari et commutavit multa et instituit atque etiam ad antiquum morem nonnulla revocavit. Disciplinam severissime rexit. Ne legatorum quidem cuiquam, nisi gravate hibernisque demum mensibus, permisit uxorem intervisere. Equitem R., quod duobus filiis adulescentibus causa detrectandi sacramenti pollices amputasset, ipsum bonaque subiecit hastae ; quem tamen, quod inminere

---

^a The ovation was a lesser triumph, in which the general entered the city on foot, instead of in a chariot drawn by four horses (whence the term *triumphus curulis*), and with other difference described by Gellius, 5. 6.

and he celebrated three regular triumphs^a for his
victories in Dalmatia, at Actium, and at Alexandria,
all on three successive days.

XXIII. He suffered but two severe and ignominious defeats, those of Lollius and Varus, both of
which were in Germany. Of these the former was 15 B.C.
more humiliating than serious, but the latter was 9 A.D.
almost fatal, since three legions were cut to pieces
with their general, his lieutenants, and all the
auxiliaries. When the news of this came, he ordered
that watch be kept by night throughout the city, to
prevent any outbreak, and he prolonged the terms
of the governors of the provinces, that the allies
might be held to their allegiance by experienced
men with whom they were acquainted. He also
vowed great games to Jupiter Optimus Maximus, in
case the condition of the commonwealth should im-
prove, a thing which had been done in the Cimbric
and Marsic wars. In fact, they say that he was so
greatly affected that for several months in succession
he cut neither his beard nor his hair, and sometimes
he would dash his head against a door, crying :
"Quintilius Varus, give me back my legions!"
And he observed the day of the disaster each year
as one of sorrow and mourning.

XXIV. He made many changes and innovations
in the army, besides reviving some usages of former
times. He exacted the strictest discipline. It was
with great reluctance that he allowed even his
generals to visit their wives, and then only in the
winter season. He sold a Roman knight and his
property at public auction, because he had cut off the
thumbs of two young sons, to make them unfit for
military service ; but when he saw that some tax-

emptioni publicanos videbat, liberto suo addixit, ut
2 relegatum in agros pro libero esse sineret. Decimam
legionem contumacius parentem cum ignominia totam
dimisit, item alias immodeste missionem postulantes
citra commoda emeritorum praemiorum exauctoravit.
Cohortes, si quae cessissent loco, decimatas hordeo
pavit.   Centuriones statione deserta, itidem ut
manipulares, capitali animadversione puniit, pro
cetero delictorum genere variis ignominiis adfecit,
ut stare per totum diem iuberet ante praetorium,
interdum tunicatos discinctosque, nonnumquam cum
decempedis vel etiam caespitem portantes.

XXV. Neque post bella civilia aut in contione aut
per edictum ullos militum commilitones appellabat,
sed milites, ac ne a filiis quidem aut privignis suis
imperio praeditis aliter appellari passus est, ambitiosius
id existimans, quam aut ratio militaris aut temporum
quies aut sua domusque suae maiestas postularet.
2 Libertino milite, praeterquam Romae incendiorum
causa et si tumultus in graviore annona metueretur,
bis[1] usus est: semel ad praesidium coloniarum
Illyricum contingentium, iterum ad tutelam ripae
Rheni fluminis ; eosque, servos adhuc viris feminisque
pecuniosioribus indictos ac sine mora manumissos, sub

---

[1] bis] urbis, *MGVLP*[1]*T.*

---

[a] That is, executed every tenth man, selected by lot.

[b] Instead of the usual rations of wheat.

[c] Carrying the pole to measure off the camp, or clods for
building the rampart, was the work of common soldiers ;
hence degrading for officers.   [d] Cf. *Jul.* lxvii. 2.

gatherers were intent upon buying him, he knocked him down to a freeman of his own, with the understanding that he should be banished to the country districts, but allowed to live in freedom. He dismissed the entire tenth legion in disgrace, because they were insubordinate, and others, too, that demanded their discharge in an insolent fashion, he disbanded without the rewards which would have been due for faithful service. If any cohorts gave way in battle, he decimated them,[a] and fed the rest on barley.[b] When centurions left their posts, he punished them with death, just as he did the rank and file; for faults of other kinds he imposed various ignominious penalties, such as ordering them to stand all day long before the general's tent, sometimes in their tunics without their sword-belts, or again holding ten-foot poles or even a clod of earth.[c]

XXV. After the civil wars he never called any of the troops "comrades," either in the assembly or in an edict, but always "soldiers"[d]; and he would not allow them to be addressed otherwise, even by those of his sons or stepsons who held military commands, thinking the former term too flattering for the requirements of discipline, the peaceful state of the times, and his own dignity and that of his household. Except as a fire-brigade at Rome, and when there was fear of riots in times of scarcity, he employed freedmen as soldiers only twice: once as a guard for the colonies in the vicinity of Illyricum, and again to defend the bank of the river Rhine; even these he levied, when they were slaves, from men and women of means, and at once gave them freedom; and he kept them under their original

priore vexillo habuit, neque aut commixtos cum in-
genuis aut eodem modo armatos.

3   Dona militaria aliquanto facilius phaleras et tor-
ques, quicquid auro argentoque constaret, quam val-
lares ac murales coronas, quae honore praecellerent,
dabat ; has quam parcissime et sine ambitione ac
saepe etiam caligatis tribuit. M. Agrippam in Sicilia
post navalem victoriam caeruleo vexillo donavit. Solos
triumphales, quamquam et socios expeditionum et
participes victoriarum suarum, numquam donis imper-
tiendos putabat, quod ipsi quoque ius habuissent
4 tribuendi ea quibus vellent. Nihil autem minus perfecto [1] duci quam festinationem temeritatemque con-
venire arbitrabatur. Crebro itaque illa iactabat :
σπεῦδε βραδέως·

    ἀσφαλὴς γάρ ἐστ᾽ ἀμείνων ἢ θρασὺς στρατηλάτης.

et : " sat celeriter fieri quidquid fiat satis bene."
Proelium quidem aut bellum suscipiendum omnino
negabat, nisi cum maior emolumenti spes quam
damni metus ostenderetur. Nam minima commoda
non minimo sectantis discrimine similes aiebat esse
aureo hamo piscantibus, cuius abrupti damnum nulla
captura pensari posset.

    XXVI. Magistratus atque honores et ante tempus
et quosdam novi generis perpetuosque cepit.
Consulatum vicesimo aetatis anno invasit admotis
hostiliter ad urbem legionibus missisque qui sibi
nomine exercitus deposcerent ; cum quidem cunctante

---

    [1] perfecto, *Bentley* ; inperfecto, *mss.*

    [a] That is, he kept them apart from the rest in the companies
in which they were first enrolled.
    [b] The *phalerae* were discs or plates of metal attached to a
belt or to the harness of horses.

standard,[a] not mingling them with the soldiers of free birth or arming them in the same fashion.

As military prizes he was somewhat more ready to give trappings[b] or collars, valuable for their gold and silver, than crowns for scaling ramparts or walls, which conferred high honour; the latter he gave as sparingly as possible and without favouritism, often even to the common soldiers. He presented Marcus Agrippa with a blue banner in Sicily after his naval victory. Those who had celebrated triumphs were the only ones whom he thought ineligible for prizes, even though they had been the companions of his campaigns and shared in his victories, on the ground that they themselves had the privilege of bestowing such honours wherever they wished. He thought nothing less becoming in a well-trained leader than haste and rashness, and, accordingly, favourite sayings of his were : " More haste, less speed " ; " Better a safe commander than a bold " ; and " That is done quickly enough which is done well enough." He used to say that a war or a battle should not be begun under any circumstances, unless the hope of gain was clearly greater than the fear of loss ; for he likened such as grasped at slight gains with no slight risk to those who fished with a golden hook, the loss of which, if it were carried off, could not be made good by any catch.

XXVI. He received offices and honours before the usual age, and some of a new kind and for life. He usurped the consulship in the twentieth year of his age, leading his legions against the city as if it were 43 B.C. that of an enemy, and sending messengers to demand the office for him in the name of his army ; and

senatu Cornelius centurio, princeps legationis, reiecto sagulo ostendens gladii capulum non dubitasset in curia dicere: "Hic faciet, si vos non feceritis."

2 Secundum consulatum post novem annos, tertium anno interiecto gessit, sequentis usque ad undecimum continuavit, multisque mox, cum deferrentur, recusatis duodecimum magno, id est septemdecim annorum, intervallo et rursus tertium decimum biennio post ultro petit, ut C. et Lucium filios amplissimo praeditus magistratu suo quemque

3 tirocinio deduceret in Forum. Quinque medios consulatus a sexto ad decimum annuos gessit, ceteros aut novem aut sex aut quattuor aut tribus mensibus, secundum vero paucissimis horis. Nam die Kal. Ian. cum mane pro aede Capitolini Iovis paululum curuli sella praesedisset, honore abiit suffecto alio in locum suum. Nec omnes Romae, sed quartum consulatum in Asia, quintum in insula Samo, octavum et nonum Tarracone init.

XXVII. Triumviratum rei p. constituendae per decem annos administravit; in quo restitit quidem aliquamdiu collegis ne qua fieret proscriptio, sed inceptam utroque acerbius exercuit. Namque illis in multorum saepe personam per gratiam et preces exorabilibus solus magno opere contendit ne cui parceretur, proscripsitque etiam C. Toranium tutorem suum, eundem collegam patris sui Octavi in

when the Senate hesitated, his centurion, Cornelius, leader of the deputation, throwing back his cloak and showing the hilt of his sword, did not hesitate to say in the House, " This will make him consul, if you do not." He held his second consulship nine years later, and a third after a year's interval ; the rest up to the eleventh were in successive years, then after declining a number of terms that were offered him, he asked of his own accord for a twelfth after a long interval, no less than seventeen years, and two years later for a thirteenth, wishing to hold the highest magistracy at the time when he introduced each of his sons Gaius and Lucius to public life upon their coming of age. The five consulships from the sixth to the tenth he held for the full year, the rest for nine, six, four, or three months, except the second, which lasted only a few hours ; for after sitting for a short time on the curule chair in front of the temple of Jupiter Capitolinus in the early morning, he resigned the honour on the Kalends of January and appointed another in his place. He did not begin all his consulships in Rome, but the fourth in Asia, the fifth on the Isle of Samos, the eighth and ninth at Tarraco.

XXVII. He was for ten years a member of the triumvirate for restoring the State to order, and though he opposed his colleagues for some time and tried to prevent a proscription, yet when it was begun, he carried it through with greater severity than either of them. For while they could oftentimes be moved by personal influence and entreaties, he alone was most insistent that no one should be spared, even adding to the list his guardian Gaius Toranius, who had also been the colleague of his father

33 B.C.

31 B.C

30/23 B.C.

5 B.C.

2 B.C.

2 aedilitate. Iulius Saturninus hoc amplius tradit, cum peracta proscriptione M. Lepidus in senatu excusasset praeterita et spem clementiae in posterum fecisset, quoniam satis poenarum exactum esset, hunc e diverso professum, ita modum se proscribendi statuisse, ut omnia sibi reliquerit libera. In cuius tamen pertinaciae paenitentiam postea T. Vinium Philopoemenem, quod patronum suum proscriptum celasse olim diceretur, equestri dignitate honoravit.

3 In eadem hac potestate multiplici flagravit invidia. Nam et Pinarium equitem R., cum contionante se admissa turba paganorum apud milites subscribere quaedam animadvertisset, curiosum ac speculatorem ratus coram confodi imperavit; et Tedium Afrum consulem designatum, quia factum quoddam suum maligno sermone carpsisset, tantis conterruit minis,

4 ut is se praecipitaverit; et Quintum Gallium praetorem, in officio salutationis tabellas duplices veste tectas tenentem, suspicatus gladium occulere, nec quicquam statim, ne aliud inveniretur, ausus inquirere, paulo post per centuriones et milites raptum e tribunali servilem in modum torsit ac fatentem nihil iussit occidi, prius oculis eius sua manu effossis; quem tamen scribit conloquio petito insidiatum sibi coniectumque a se in custodiam, deinde urbe interdicta dimissum naufragio vel

---

a Se precipitaverit means "hurled himself headlong," perhaps into the Tiber; more probably from some high place such as the Tarpeian Rock, or the roof of a building.

Octavius in the aedileship. Julius Saturninus adds
that after the proscription was over Marcus Lepidus
addressed the senate in justification of the past and
held out hope of leniency thereafter, since enough
punishment had been inflicted ; but that Augustus
on the contrary declared that he had consented to
end the proscription only on condition that he was
allowed a free hand for the future. However, to
show his regret for this inflexibility, he later
honoured Titus Vinius Philopoemen with equestrian
rank, because it was said that he had hidden his
patron, who was on the list.

While he was triumvir, Augustus incurred general
detestation by many of his acts. For example, when
he was addressing the soldiers and a throng of civilians
had been admitted to the assembly, noticing that
Pinarius, a Roman knight, was taking notes, he ordered
that he be stabbed on the spot, thinking him an eaves-
dropper and a spy. Because Tedius Afer, consul elect,
railed at some act of his in spiteful terms, he uttered
such terrible threats that Afer committed suicide.[a]
Again, when Quintus Gallius, a praetor, held some
folded tablets under his robe as he was paying his
respects, Augustus, suspecting that he had a sword
concealed there, did not dare to make a search on the
spot for fear it should turn out to be something else ;
but a little later he had Gallius hustled from the tribunal by some centurions and soldiers, tortured him
as if he were a slave, and though he made no confession,
ordered his execution, first tearing out the man's eyes
with his own hand. He himself writes, however,
that Gallius made a treacherous attack on him after
asking for an audience, and was haled to prison ;
and that after he was dismissed under sentence of

5 latronum insidiis perisse. Tribuniciam potestatem
perpetuam recepit, in qua semel atque iterum per
singula lustra collegam sibi cooptavit. Recepit et
morum legumque regimen aeque perpetuum, quo
iure, quamquam sine censurae honore, censum tamen
populi ter egit, primum ac tertium cum collega,
medium solus.

XXVIII. De reddenda re p. bis cogitavit:
primum[1] post oppressum statim Antonium, memor
obiectum sibi ab eo saepius, quasi per ipsum staret
ne redderetur; ac rursus taedio diuturnae valitudinis, cum etiam magistratibus ac senatu domum
accitis rationarium imperii tradidit. Sed reputans
et se privatum non sine periculo fore et illam
plurium arbitrio temere committi, in retinenda
perseveravit, dubium eventu meliore an voluntate.

2 Quam voluntatem, cum prae se identidem[2] ferret,
quodam etiam edicto his verbis testatus est: " Ita
mihi salvam ac sospitem rem p. sistere in sua sede
liceat atque eius rei fructum percipere, quem peto,
ut optimi status auctor dicar et moriens ut feram
mecum spem, mansura in vestigio suo fundamenta
rei p. quae iecero." Fecitque ipse se compotem voti
nisus omni modo, ne quem novi status paeniteret.

---

[1] primum, *M* ; *the other mss. have* primo.
[2] prae se identidem, *LP*[1]; *the other mss. have* praesident
(praesidens) idem.

---

[a] See chap. ci.
[b] Suetonius is brief to the point of obscurity. The idea
seems to be that the intentions of Augustus in establishing
the principate, and the effect of the new régime on the public
welfare, were equally good.

banishment, he either lost his life by shipwreck or was waylaid by brigands.

He received the tribunician power for life, and once or twice chose a colleague in the office for periods of five years each. He was also given the supervision of morals and of the laws for all time, and by the virtue of this position, although without the title of censor, he nevertheless took the census thrice, the first and last time with a colleague, the second time alone.

XXVIII. He twice thought of restoring the republic; first immediately after the overthrow of Antony, remembering that his rival had often made the charge that it was his fault that it was not restored; and again in the weariness of a lingering illness, when he went so far as to summon the magistrates and the senate to his house, and submit an account of the general condition of the empire.[a] Reflecting, however, that as he himself would not be free from danger if he should retire, so too it would be hazardous to trust the State to the control of more than one, he continued to keep it in his hands; and it is not easy to say whether his intentions or their results were the better.[b] His good intentions he not only expressed from time to time, but put them on record as well in an edict in the following words: "May it be my privilege to establish the State in a firm and secure position, and reap from that act the fruit that I desire; but only if I may be called the author of the best possible government, and bear with me the hope when I die that the foundations which I have laid for the State will remain unshaken." And he realized his hope by making every effort to prevent any dissatisfaction with the new régime.

3   Urbem neque pro maiestate imperii ornatam et
inundationibus incendiisque obnoxiam excoluit adeo,
ut iure sit gloriatus marmoream se relinquere, quam
latericiam accepisset.[a] Tutam uero, quantum pro-
videri humana ratione potuit, etiam in posterum
praestitit.

XXIX. Publica opera plurima exstruxit, e quibus
vel praecipua: forum cum aede Martis Ultoris, templum
Apollinis in Palatio, aedem Tonantis Iovis in Capitolio.
Fori exstruendi causa fuit hominum et iudiciorum
multitudo, quae videbatur non sufficientibus duobus
etiam tertio indigere; itaque festinatius necdum per-
fecta Martis aede publicatum est cautumque, ut
separatim in eo publica iudicia et sortitiones iudicum
2 fierent. Aedem Martis bello Philippensi pro ultione[1]
paterna suscepto voverat; sanxit ergo, ut de bellis
triumphisque hic consuleretur senatus, provincias cum
imperio petituri hinc deducerentur, quique victores
redissent, huc insignia triumphorum conferrent.
3 Templum Apollinis in ea parte Palatinae domus
excitavit, quam fulmine ictam desiderari a deo
haruspices pronuntiarant[2]; addidit porticus cum
bibliotheca Latina Graecaque, quo loco iam senior
saepe etiam senatum habuit decuriasque iudi-

¹ ultione, ς (ρ); visione, Ω.
² pronuntiarant, *Stephanus*; pronuntiarent, Ω (-runt *T*,
Bentley).

ᵃ *Latericiam* is strictly "of sun-dried brick."
ᵇ See *Jul.* lxxi.

Since the city was not adorned as the dignity of the empire demanded, and was exposed to flood and fire, he so beautified it that he could justly boast that he had found it built of brick[a] and left it in marble. He made it safe too for the future, so far as human foresight could provide for this.

XXIX. He built many public works, in particular the following: his forum with the temple of Mars the Avenger, the temple of Apollo on the Palatine, and the fane of Jupiter the Thunderer on the Capitol. His reason for building the forum was the increase in the number of the people and of cases at law, which seemed to call for a third forum, since two were no longer adequate. Therefore it was opened to the public with some haste, before the temple of Mars was finished, and it was provided that the public prosecutions be held there apart from the rest, as well as the selection of jurors by lot. He had made a vow to build the temple of Mars in the war of Philippi, which he undertook to avenge his father; accordingly he decreed that in it the senate should consider wars and claims for triumphs, from it those who were on their way to the provinces with military commands should be escorted,[b] and to it victors on their return should bear the tokens of their triumphs. He reared the temple of Apollo in that part of his house on the Palatine for which the soothsayers declared that the god had shown his desire by striking it with lightning. He joined to it colonnades with Latin and Greek libraries, and when he was getting to be an old man he often held meetings of the senate there as well, and revised the lists of jurors. He dedicated the

24 B.C.
28 B.C.
22 B.C.

cum recognovit. Tonanti Iovi aedem consecravit
liberatus periculo, cum expeditione Cantabrica per
nocturnum iter lecticam eius fulgur praestrinxisset
4 servumque praelucentem exanimasset. Quaedam
etiam opera sub nomine alieno, nepotum scilicet et
uxoris sororisque fecit, ut porticum basilicamque Gai
et Luci, item porticus Liviae et Octaviae theatrumque Marcelli. Sed et ceteros principes viros saepe
hortatus est, ut pro facultate quisque monimentis vel
novis vel refectis et excultis urbem adornarent.
5 Multaque a multis tunc exstructa sunt, sicut a Marcio
Philippo aedes Herculis Musarum, a L. Cornificio
aedes Dianae, ab Asinio Pollione atrium Libertatis, a
Munatio Planco aedes Saturni, a Cornelio Balbo
theatrum, a Statilio Tauro amphitheatrum, a M. vero
Agrippa complura et egregia.

XXX. Spatium urbis in regiones vicosque divisit in-
stituitque, ut illas annui magistratus sortito tuerentur,
hos magistri e plebe cuiusque viciniae lecti. Adversus
incendia excubias nocturnas vigilesque commentus est;
ad coercendas inundationes alveum Tiberis laxavit ac
repurgavit completum olim ruderibus et aedificiorum
prolationibus coartatum. Quo autem facilius undique
urbs adiretur, desumpta sibi Flaminia via Arimino

shrine to Jupiter the Thunderer because of a narrow escape; for on his Cantabrian expedition during a march by night, a flash of lightning grazed his litter and struck the slave dead who was carrying a torch before him. He constructed some works too in the name of others, his grandsons and nephew to wit, his wife and his sister, such as the colonnade and basilica 12 B.C. of Gaius and Lucius; also the colonnades of Livia and 15 & 33 B.C. Octavia, and the theatre of Marcellus. More than 13 B.C. that, he often urged other prominent men to adorn the city with new monuments or to restore and embellish old ones, each according to his means. And many such works were built at that time by many men; for example, the temple of Hercules and the Muses by Marcius Philippus, the temple of Diana by Lucius Cornificius, the Hall of Liberty by Asinius Pollio, the temple of Saturn by Munatius Plancus, a theatre by Cornelius Balbus, an amphitheatre by Statilius Taurus, and by Marcus Agrippa in particular many magnificent structures.

XXX. He divided the area of the city into regions and wards, arranging that the former should be under the charge of magistrates selected each year by lot, and the latter under "masters" elected by the inhabitants of the respective neighbourhoods. To guard against fires he devised a system of stations of night watchmen, and to control the floods he widened and cleared out the channel of the Tiber, which had for some time been filled with rubbish and narrowed by jutting buildings. Further, to make the approach to the city easier from every direction, he personally undertook to rebuild the Flaminian Road all the way to Ariminum, and assigned the rest of the high-ways to others who had

tenus munienda reliquas triumphalibus viris ex ma-
nubiali pecunia sternendas distribuit.

2   Aedes sacras vetustate conlapsas aut incendio ab-
sumptas refecit easque et ceteras opulentissimis donis
adornavit, ut qui in cellam Capitolini Iovis sedecim
milia pondo auri gemmasque ac margaritas quingenties
sestertium una donatione contulerit.

XXXI. Postquam vero pontificatum maximum,
quem numquam vivo Lepido auferre sustinuerat,
mortuo demum suscepit, quidquid fatidicorum librorum Graeci Latinique generis nullis vel parum
idoneis auctoribus vulgo ferebatur, supra duo milia
contracta undique cremavit ac solos retinuit Sibyllinos,
hos quoque dilectu habito ; condiditque duobus

2 forulis auratis sub Palatini Apollinis basi.   Annum a[1]
Divo Iulio ordinatum, sed postea neglegentia contur-
batum atque confusum, rursus ad pristinam rationem
redegit ; in cuius ordinatione Sextilem mensem e suo
cognomine nuncupavit magis quam Septembrem quo
erat natus, quod hoc sibi et primus consulatus et in-

3 signes victoriae optigissent.   Sacerdotum et numerum
et dignitatem sed et commoda auxit, praecipue Vesta-
lium virginum.   Cumque in demortuae locum aliam
capi oporteret ambirentque multi ne filias in sortem
darent, adiuravit, si cuiusquam neptium suarum

------

[1] *MGV omit* a.

been honoured with triumphs, asking them to use their prize-money in paving them.

He restored sacred edifices which had gone to ruin through lapse of time or had been destroyed by fire, and adorned both these and the other temples with most lavish gifts, depositing in the shrine of Jupiter Capitolinus as a single offering sixteen thousand pounds of gold, besides pearls and other precious stones to the value of fifty million sesterces.

XXXI. After he finally had assumed the office of 13 B.C. pontifex maximus on the death of Lepidus (for he could not make up his mind to deprive him of the honour while he lived) he collected whatever prophetic writings of Greek or Latin origin were in circulation anonymously or under the names of authors of little repute, and burned more than two thousand of them, retaining only the Sibylline books and making a choice even among those; and he deposited them in two gilded cases under the pedestal of the Palatine Apollo. Inasmuch as the calendar, which had been set in order by the Deified Julius, had later been confused and disordered through negligence, he restored it to its former system; and in making this arrangement he called the month 8 B.C. Sextilis by his own surname, rather than his birth-month September, because in the former he had won his first consulship and his most brilliant victories. He increased the number and importance of the priests, and also their allowances and privileges, in particular those of the Vestal virgins. Moreover, when there was occasion to choose another vestal in place of one who had died, and many used all their influence to avoid submitting their daughters to the hazard of the lot, he solemnly swore that if

4 competeret aetas, oblaturum se fuisse eam. Nonnulla
etiam ex antiquis caerimoniis paulatim abolita restituit,
ut Salutis augurium, Diale flamonium, sacrum Luper-
cale, ludos Saeculares et Compitalicios. Lupercalibus
vetuit currere inberbes, item Saecularibus ludis iuvenes utriusque sexus prohibuit ullum nocturnum
spectaculum frequentare nisi cum aliquo maiore natu
propinquorum. Compitales Lares ornari bis anno instituit vernis floribus et aestivis.

5 Proximum a dis immortalibus honorem memoriae
ducum praestitit, qui imperium p. R. ex minimo maximum reddidissent. Itaque et opera cuiusque manenti-
bus titulis restituit et statuas omnium triumphali
effigie in utraque fori sui porticu dedicavit, professus
et [1] edicto : commentum id se, ut ad illorum vitam [2]
velut ad exemplar et ipse, dum viveret, et insequentium aetatium principes exigerentur a civibus.
Pompei quoque statuam contra theatri eius regiam
marmoreo Iano superposuit translatam e curia, in qua
C. Caesar fuerat occisus.

XXXII. Pleraque pessimi exempli in perniciem
publicam aut ex consuetudine licentiaque bellorum
civilium duraverant aut per pacem etiam exstiterant.
Nam et grassatorum plurimi palam se ferebant
succincti ferro, quasi tuendi sui causa, et rapti per

---

[1] et, *Bentley* ; est, Ω.
[2] vitam, *supplied by Bücheler* ; normam, *Oudendorp.*

---

[a] See Index under Salus, and Dio 37. 24.
[b] *Exigere* is the technical term for making weights and
measures correspond with the standards in charge of the
aediles ; see *C.I.L.* XIV. 4124 1, 2 ; X. 8067. 2 ; etc.
[c] According to Richter, *Topographie von Rom*, p. 229, the
regia was the main door, leading from the stage of the theatre
to the colonnade.

anyone of his grand-daughters were of eligible age, he would have proposed her name. He also revived some of the ancient rites which had gradually fallen into disuse, such as the augury of Safety,[a] the office of Flamen Dialis, the ceremonies of the Lupercalia, the Secular Games, and the festival of the Compitalia. At the Lupercalia he forbade beardless youths to join in the running, and at the Secular Games he would not allow young people of either sex to attend any entertainment by night except in company with some adult relative. He provided that the Lares of the Crossroads should be crowned twice a year, with spring and summer flowers.

Next to the immortal Gods he honoured the memory of the leaders who had raised the estate of the Roman people from obscurity to greatness. Accordingly he restored the works of such men with their original inscriptions, and in the two colonnades of his forum dedicated statues of all of them in triumphal garb, declaring besides in a proclamation : " I have contrived this to lead the citizens to require [b] me, while I live, and the rulers of later times as well, to attain the standard set by those worthies of old." He also moved the statue of Pompey from the hall in which Gaius Caesar had been slain and placed it on a marble arch opposite the grand door [c] of Pompey's theatre.

XXXII. Many pernicious practices militating against public security had survived as a result of the lawless habits of the civil wars, or had even arisen in time of peace. Gangs of footpads openly went about with swords by their sides, ostensibly to protect themselves, and travellers in the country, freemen and slaves alike, were seized and kept in confinement

agros viatores sine discrimine liberi servique ergastulis
possessorum supprimebantur, et plurimae factiones
titulo collegi novi ad nullius non facinoris societatem
coibant. Igitur grassaturas [1] dispositis per opportuna
loca stationibus inhibuit, ergastula recognovit, collegia
2 praeter antiqua et legitima dissolvit. Tabulas veterum
aerari debitorum, vel praecipuam calumniandi materiam, exussit ; [2] loca in urbe publica iuris ambigui
possessoribus adiudicavit ; diuturnorum reorum et ex
quorum sordibus nihil aliud quam voluptas inimicis
quaereretur nomina abolevit condicione proposita, ut
si quem quis repetere vellet, par periculae poenae
subiret. Ne quod autem maleficium negotiumve in-
punitate vel mora elaberetur, triginta amplius dies,
qui honoraris ludis occupabantur, actui rerum ac-
3 commodavit. Ad tris iudicum decurias quartam
addidit [3] ex inferiore censu, quae ducenariorum
vocaretur iudicaretque de levioribus summis. Iudices
a tricensimo [4] aetatis anno adlegit, id est quinquennio
maturius quam solebant. Ac plerisque iudicandi
munus detractantibus vix concessit, ut singulis decuriis

[1] grassaturas, *V* ; grassatur ad, *M* ; grassaturam, *G* ; *the
other mss. have* grassatores.
[2] exussit, *Beroaldus* (*cf.* ἔκαυσε, *Dio*, 53.2) ; excussit, *mss.*
[3] addidit, *Stephanus* ; addixit, Ω.
[4] tricensimo, *M* (*the other mss. have* tricesimo) ; vicesimo,
Cuiacius ; xxv. *Shuckburgh. The number is apparently wrong,
but the error may have been made by Suetonius himself.*

[a] The *ergastula* were prisons for slaves, who were made to
work in chains in the fields.
[b] *Collegia*, or guilds, of workmen were allowed and were
numerous ; not infrequently they were a pretext for some
illegal secret organization.
[c] *Sordibus* refers especially to the mourning garb in which
it was usual for the accused to appear in public.

in the workhouses [a] of the land owners; numerous leagues, too, were formed for the commission of crimes of every kind, assuming the title of some new guild.[b] Therefore to put a stop to brigandage, he stationed guards of soldiers wherever it seemed advisable, inspected the workhouses, and disbanded all guilds, except such as were of long standing and formed for legitimate purposes. He burned the records of old debts to the treasury, which were by far the most frequent source of blackmail. He made over to their holders places in the city to which the claim of the state was uncertain. He struck off the lists the names of those who had long been under accusation, from whose humiliation [c] nothing was to be gained except the gratification of their enemies, with the stipulation that if anyone was minded to renew the charge, he should be liable to the same penalty.[d] To prevent any action for damages or on a disputed claim from falling through or being put off, he added to the term of the courts thirty more days, which had before been taken up with honorary games. To the three divisions of jurors he added a fourth of a lower estate, to be called *ducenarii* [e] and to sit on cases involving trifling amounts. He enrolled as jurors men of thirty years or more, that is five years younger than usual. But when many strove to escape court duty, he reluctantly consented that each division in turn should have a year's exemption, and that the custom of holding court during the

[d] That is, if he failed to win his suit, he should suffer the penalty that would have been inflicted on the defendant, if he had been convicted.

[e] Men whose property amounted to 200,000 sesterces, or half of a knight's estate.

per vices annua vacatio esset et ut solitae agi Novembri ac Decembri mense res omitterentur.

XXXIII. Ipse ius dixit assidue et in noctem nonnumquam, si parum corpore valeret lectica pro tribunali collocata, vel etiam domi cubans. Dixit autem ius non diligentia modo summa sed et lenitate, siquidem manifesti parricidii reum, ne culleo insueretur, quod non nisi confessi adficiuntur hac poena, ita fertur interrogasse : "Certe patrem tuum non

2 occidisti?" Et cum de falso testamento ageretur omnesque signatores [1] lege Cornelia tenerentur, non tantum duas tabellas, damnatoriam et absolutoriam, simul cognoscentibus dedit, sed tertiam quoque, qua ignosceretur iis, quos fraude ad signandum vel errore

3 inductos constitisset. Appellationes quotannis urbanorum quidem litigatorum praetori delegabat urbano, at provincialium consularibus viris, quos singulos cuiusque provinciae negotiis praeposuisset.

XXXIV. Leges retractavit et quasdam ex integro sanxit, ut sumptuariam et de adulteriis et de pudicitia, de ambitu, de maritandis ordinibus. Hanc cum aliquanto severius quam ceteras emendasset, prae tumultu recusantium perferre non potuit nisi adempta demum lenitave parte poenarum et

---

[1] signatores, *Beroaldus* ; senatores, Ω.

---

[a] Parricides were sewn up in a sack with a dog, a cock, a snake, and a monkey, and thrown into the sea or a river. The word is here used in its modern sense ; cf. *Jul.* xlii. 3.

[b] These consisted of various immunities, especially those connected with the *ius trium liberorum* (see Introd. p. x).

months of November and December should be given up.

XXXIII. He himself administered justice regularly and sometimes up to nightfall, having a litter placed upon the tribunal, if he was indisposed, or even lying down at home. In his administration of justice he was both highly conscientious and very lenient; for to save a man clearly guilty of parricide from being sewn up in the sack,[a] a punishment which was inflicted only on those who pleaded guilty, he is said to have put the question to him in this form: "You surely did not kill your father, did you?" Again, in a case touching a forged will, in which all the signers were liable to punishment by the Cornelian Law, he distributed to the jury not merely the two tablets for condemnation or acquittal, but a third as well, for the pardon of those who were shown to have been induced to sign by misrepresentation or misunderstanding. Each year he referred appeals of cases involving citizens to the city praetor, but those between foreigners to ex-consuls, of whom he had put one in charge of the business affairs of each province.

XXXIV. He revised existing laws and enacted some new ones, for example, on extravagance, on adultery and chastity, on bribery, and on the encouragement of marriage among the various classes of citizens. Having made somewhat more stringent changes in the last of these than in the others, he was unable to carry it out because of an open revolt against its provisions, until he had abolished or mitigated a part of the penalties, besides increasing the rewards[b] and allowing a three years' exemption from the obligation to marry after the death of a husband

2 vacatione trienni data auctisque praemiis. Sic quoque abolitionem eius publico spectaculo pertinaciter postulante equite, accitos Germanici liberos receptosque partim ad se partim in patris gremium ostentavit, manu vultuque significans ne gravarentur imitari iuvenis exemplum. Cumque etiam inmaturitate sponsarum et matrimoniorum crebra mutatione vim legis eludi sentiret, tempus sponsas habendi coartavit, divortiis modum imposuit.

XXXV. Senatorum affluentem numerum deformi et incondita turba — erant enim super mille, et quidam indignissimi et post necem Caesaris per gratiam et praemium adlecti, quos orcinos [1] vulgus vocabat — ad modum pristinum et splendorem redegit duabus lectionibus : prima ipsorum arbitratu, quo vir virum legit, secunda suo et Agrippae ; quo tempore existimatur lorica sub veste munitus ferroque cinctus praesedisse decem valentissimis senatorii

2 ordinis amicis sellam suam circumstantibus. Cordus Cremutius scribit ne admissum quidem tunc quemquam senatorum nisi solum et praetemptato sinu. Quosdam ad excusandi se verecundiam compulit servavitque etiam excusantibus [2] insigne vestis et spectandi in orchestra epulandique publice ius.

3 Quo autem lecti probatique et religiosius et minore molestia senatoria munera fungerentur, sanxit, ut prius quam consideret quisque ture ac mero sup-

---

[1] orcivos, *MGV*ϒ. abortivos, X ; orcinos, ς.
[2] excusantibus, *Roman and first Venetian editions* ; excusantis, Ω ; excusatis, *Ts, Gruter.*

---

^a Orcivi or Orcini, "freedmen by the grace of Orcus," were slaves set free by their master's will. The *Orcivi senatores* were those admitted by Mark Antony under pretence that they had been named in the papers left by Caesar.

or wife. When the knights even then persistently called for its repeal at a public show, he sent for the children of Germanicus and exhibited them, some in his own lap and some in their father's, intimating by his gestures and expression that they should not refuse to follow that young man's example. And on finding that the spirit of the law was being evaded by betrothal with immature girls and by frequent changes of wives, he shortened the duration of betrothals and set a limit on divorce.

XXXV. Since the number of the senators was swelled by a low-born and ill-assorted rabble (in fact, the senate numbered more than a thousand, some of whom, called by the vulgar Orcivi,*a* were wholly unworthy, and had been admitted after Caesar's death through favour or bribery) he restored it to its former limits and distinction by two enrolments, one according to the choice of the members themselves, each man naming one other, and a second made by Agrippa and himself. On the latter occasion it is thought that he wore a coat of mail under his tunic as he presided, and a sword by his side, while ten of the most robust of his friends among the senators stood by his chair. Cremutius Cordus writes that even then the senators were not allowed to approach except one by one, and after the folds of their robes had been carefully searched. Some he shamed into resigning, but he allowed even these to retain their distinctive dress, as well as the privilege of viewing the games from the orchestra and taking part in the public banquets of the order. Furthermore, that those who were chosen and approved might perform their duties more conscientiously, and also with less inconvenience, he provided that before taking his seat each member

179

plicaret apud aram eius dei, in cuius templo coiretur,
et ne plus quam bis in mense legitimus senatus
ageretur, Kalendis et Idibus, neve Septembri
Octobrive mense ullos adesse alios necesse esset
quam sorte ductos, per quorum numerum decreta
confici possent; sibique instituit consilia sortiri
semenstria, cum quibus de negotiis ad frequentem
4 senatum referendis ante tractaret. Sententias de
maiore negotio non more atque ordine sed prout
libuisset perrogabat, ut perinde quisque animum
intenderet ac si censendum magis quam adsentien-
dum esset.

XXXVI. Auctor et aliarum rerum fuit, in quis:
ne acta senatus publicarentur, ne magistratus deposito[1] honore statim in provincias mitterentur, ut
proconsulibus ad mulos et tabernacula, quae publice
locari solebant, certa pecunia constitueretur, ut cura
aerari a quaestoribus urbanis ad praetorios praeto-
resve transiret, ut centumviralem hastam quam quaesturam functi consuerant cogere decemviri cogerent.

XXXVII. Quoque plures partem administrandae
rei p. caperent, nova officia excogitavit: curam
operum publicorum, viarum, aquarum, alvei Tiberis,
frumenti populo dividundi, praefecturam urbis, trium-

---

[1] deposito, ç; disposito, Ω.

[a] Cf. *Jul.* xx. 1.

[b] A very ancient tribunal, consisting at first of 105 members, three from each tribe, but later of 180. It sat in the
Basilica Julia, with a spear (*hasta*), the ancient symbol of
Quiritary ownership, planted before it. It was divided into
four chambers, which usually sat separately, but sometimes
altogether, or in two divisions.

[c] The *decemviri stlitibus iudicandis.*

should offer incense and wine at the altar of the god
in whose temple the meeting was held; that regular
meetings of the senate should be held not oftener
than twice a month, on the Kalends and the Ides;
and that in the months of September and October
only those should be obliged to attend who were
drawn by lot, to a number sufficient for the passing
of decrees. He also adopted the plan of privy
councils chosen by lot for terms of six months, with
which to discuss in advance matters which were
to come before the entire body. On questions of
special importance he called upon the senators to
give their opinions, not according to the order
established by precedent, but just as he fancied, to
induce each man to keep his mind on the alert, as if
he were to initiate action rather than give assent to
others.

XXXVI. He introduced other innovations too,
among them these: that the proceedings of the senate
should not be published [a]; that magistrates should
not be sent to the provinces immediately after laying
down their office; that a fixed sum should be allowed
the proconsuls for mules and tents, which it was the
custom to contract for and charge to the State; that
the management of the public treasury should be
transferred from the city quaestors to ex-praetors or
praetors; and that the centumviral court,[b] which it
was usual for ex-quaestors to convoke, should be
summoned by the Board of Ten.[c]

XXXVII. To enable more men to take part in
the administration of the State, he devised new
offices: the charge of public buildings, of the roads,
of the aqueducts, of the channel of the Tiber, of the
distribution of grain to the people, as well as the

viratum legendi senatus et alterum recognoscendi turmas equitum, quotiensque opus esset. Censores creari desitos longo intervallo creavit. Numerum praetorum auxit. Exegit etiam, ut quotiens consulatus sibi daretur, binos pro singulis collegas haberet, nec optinuit, reclamantibus cunctis satis maiestatem eius imminui, quod honorem eum non solus sed cum altero gereret.

XXXVIII. Nec parcior in bellica virtute honoranda, super triginta ducibus iustos triumphos et aliquanto pluribus triumphalia ornamenta decernenda curavit.

2   Liberis senatorum, quo celerius rei p. assuescerent, protinus a[1] virili toga latum clavum induere et curiae interesse permisit militiamque auspicantibus non tribunatum modo legionum, sed et praefecturas alarum dedit; ac ne qui expers castrorum esset, binos plerumque laticlavios praeposuit singulis alis.

3   Equitum turmas frequenter recognovit, post longam intercapedinem reducto more travectionis. Sed neque detrahi quemquam in travehendo ab accusatore passus est, quod fieri solebat, et senio vel aliqua corporis labe insignibus permisit, praemisso in ordine equo, ad respondendum quotiens citarentur pedibus venire; mox ˙ reddendi equi gratiam fecit

---

[1] a, *quidam apud Torrentium*; *Ihm suggests* sumpta.

---

[a] See note on chap. xxii.
[b] That is, were so old or infirm that they could not ride, or would cut a sorry figure if they did.

prefecture of the city, a board of three for choosing senators, and another for reviewing the companies of the knights whenever it should be necessary. He appointed censors, an office which had long been discontinued. He increased the number of praetors. He also demanded that whenever the consulship was conferred on him, he should have two colleagues instead of one; but this was not granted, since all cried out that it was a sufficient offence to his supreme dignity that he held the office with another and not alone.

XXXVIII. He was not less generous in honouring martial prowess, for he had regular triumphs [a] voted to above thirty generals, and the triumphal regalia to somewhat more than that number.

To enable senators' sons to gain an earlier acquaintance with public business, he allowed them to assume the broad purple stripe immediately after the gown of manhood and to attend meetings of the senate; and when they began their military career, he gave them not merely a tribunate in a legion, but the command of a division of cavalry as well; and to furnish all of them with experience in camp life, he usually appointed two senators' sons to command each division.

He reviewed the companies of knights at frequent intervals, reviving the custom of the procession after long disuse. But he would not allow an accuser to force anyone to dismount as he rode by, as was often done in the past; and he permitted those who were conspicuous because of old age or any bodily infirmity [b] to send on their horses in the review, and come on foot to answer to their names whenever they were summoned. Later he excused those who were over

eis, qui maiores annorum quinque et triginta retinere eum nollent.

XXXIX. Impetratisque a senatu decem adiutoribus unum quemque equitum rationem vitae reddere coegit atque ex improbatis [1] alios poena, alios ignominia notavit, plures admonitione, sed varia. Lenissimum genus admonitionis fuit traditio coram pugillarium, quos taciti et ibidem statim legerent [2]; notavitque aliquos, quod pecunias levioribus usuris mutuati graviore faenore collocassent.

XL. Ac comitiis tribuniciis si deessent candidati senatores, ex equitibus R. creavit, ita ut potestate transacta in utro vellent ordine manerent. Cum autem plerique equitum attrito bellis civilibus patrimonio spectare ludos e quattuordecim non auderent metu poenae theatralis, pronuntiavit non teneri ea, quibus ipsis parentibusve equester census umquam fuisset.

2   Populi recensum vicatim egit, ac ne plebs frumentationum causa frequentius ab negotiis avocaretur, ter in annum quaternum mensium tesseras dare destinavit ; sed desideranti consuetudinem veterem concessit rursus, ut sui cuiusque mensis acciperet. Comitiorum quoque pristinum ius reduxit ac multiplici poena coercito ambitu, Fabianis et Scaptiensibus

---

[1] ex improbatis, ς ; *the best mss. have* in exprobratis.
[2] legerent] legerint, *MGVL²S.*

---

[a] See note on chap. x. 2.
[b] See note on *Jul.* xxxix. 2, and cf. chap. xiv.
[c] Cf. *Jul.* xli.

thirty-five years of age and did not wish to retain their horses from formally surrendering them.

XXXIX. Having obtained ten assistants from the senate, he compelled each knight to render an account of his life, punishing some of those whose conduct was scandalous and degrading others; but the greater part he reprimanded with varying degrees of severity. The mildest form of reprimand was to hand them a pair of tablets publicly, which they were to read in silence on the spot. He censured some because they had borrowed money at low interest and invested it at a higher rate.

XL. At the elections for tribunes if there were not candidates enough of senatorial rank,[a] he made appointments from among the knights, with the understanding that after their term they might remain in whichever order they wished. Moreover, since many knights whose property was diminished during the civil wars did not venture to view the games from the fourteen rows[b] through fear of the penalty of the law regarding theatres, he declared that none were liable to its provisions, if they themselves or their parents had ever possessed a knight's estate.

He revised the lists of the people district by district, and to prevent the commons from being called away from their occupations too often because of the distributions of grain, he determined to give out tickets for four months' supply three times a year; but at their urgent request he allowed a return to the old custom of receiving a share every month. He also revived the old time election privileges,[c] trying to put a stop to bribery by numerous penalties, and distributing to his fellow members of the Fabian

tribulibus[1] suis die comitiorum, ne quid a quoquam
candidato desiderarent, singula milia nummum a se
dividebat.

3 Magni praeterea existimans sincerum atque ab
omni colluvione peregrini ac servilis sanguinis
incorruptum servare populum, et civitates Romanas
parcissime dedit et manumittendi modum termi-
navit. Tiberio pro cliente Graeco petenti rescripsit,
non aliter se daturum, quam si praesens sibi per-
suasisset, quam iustas petendi causas haberet; et
Liviae pro quodam tributario Gallo roganti civitatem
negavit, immunitatem optulit affirmans facilius se
passurum fisco detrahi aliquid, quam civitatis
4 Romanae vulgari honorem. Servos non contentus
multis difficultatibus a libertate et multo pluribus
a libertate iusta removisse, cum et de numero et de
condicione ac differentia eorum, qui manumitte-
rentur, curiose cavisset, hoc quoque adiecit, ne
vinctus umquam tortusve quis ullo libertatis genere
civitatem adipisceretur.

5 Etiam habitum vestitumque pristinum reducere
studuit, ac visa quondam pro contione pullatorum
turba indignabundus et clamitans : " en

Romanos, rerum dominos, gentemque togatam!"

negotium aedilibus dedit, ne quem posthac pate-

---

[1] Scaptiensibus   tribulibus,   *Beroaldus* ;   scaptensibus
tribubus, Ω.

---

[a] Augustus was a member of the latter because of his connection with the Octavian family ; of the former, through
his adoption into the Julian *gens*.

[b] That is, even by *iusta libertas*, which conferred citizenship. Slaves who had been punished for crimes (*facinora*)

and Scaptian tribes [a] a thousand sesterces a man from his own purse on the day of the elections, to keep them from looking for anything from any of the candidates.

Considering it also of great importance to keep the people pure and unsullied by any taint of foreign or servile blood, he was most chary of conferring Roman citizenship and set a limit to manumission. When Tiberius requested citizenship for a Grecian dependent of his, Augustus wrote in reply that he would not grant it unless the man appeared in person and convinced him that he had reasonable grounds for the request; and when Livia asked it for a Gaul from a tributary province, he refused, offering instead freedom from tribute, and declaring that he would more willingly suffer a loss to his privy purse than the prostitution of the honour of Roman citizenship. Not content with making it difficult for slaves to acquire freedom, and still more so for them to attain full rights, by making careful provision as to the number, condition, and status of those who were manumitted, he added the proviso that no one who had ever been put in irons or tortured should acquire citizenship by any grade of freedom.[b]

He desired also to revive the ancient fashion of dress, and once when he saw in an assembly a throng of men in dark cloaks, he cried out indignantly, " Behold them

Romans, lords of the world, the nation clad in the toga," [c]

and he directed the aediles never again to allow

or disgraceful acts (*flagitia*) became on manumission *dediticii*, "prisoners of war."   [c] Verg. *Aen.* 1. 282.

187

rentur in Foro circave [1] nisi positis lacernis togatum consistere.

XLI. Liberalitatem omnibus ordinibus per occasiones frequenter exhibuit. Nam et invecta urbi Alexandrino triumpho regia gaza tantam copiam nummariae rei effecit, ut faenore deminuto plurimum agrorum pretiis accesserit, et postea, quotiens ex damnatorum bonis pecunia superflueret, usum eius gratuitum iis, qui cavere in duplum possent, ad certum tempus indulsit. Senatorum censum ampliavit ac pro octingentorum milium summa duodecies sestertium taxavit supplevitque non habentibus.
2 Congiaria populo frequenter dedit, sed diversae fere summae : modo quadringenos, modo trecenos,[2] nonnumquam ducenos quinquagenosque nummos ; ac ne minores quidem pueros praeteriit, quamvis non nisi ab undecimo aetatis anno accipere consuessent. Frumentum quoque in annonae difficultatibus saepe levissimo, interdum nullo pretio viritim admensus est tesserasque nummarias duplicavit.

XLII. Sed ut salubrem magis quam ambitiosum principem scires, querentem de inopia et caritate vini populum severissima coercuit voce : satis provisum a genero suo Agrippa perductis pluribus aquis, ne
2 homines sitirent. Eidem populo promissum quidem

---

[1] circave] circove, *G*Υ.·
[2] trecenos, *Torrentius* (ς) ; tricenos, Ω.

---

[a] *Congiarium*, strictly a distribution of oil (from *congius*, a liquid measure) came to be used of any largess.
[b] The *tesserae nummulariae* were small tablets or round hollow balls of wood, marked with numbers. They were distributed to the people instead of money and entitled the holder to receive the sum inscribed upon them. Grain, oil,

anyone to appear in the Forum or its neighbour-hood except in the toga and without a cloak.

XLI. He often showed generosity to all classes when occasion offered. For example, by bringing the royal treasures to Rome in his Alexandrian triumph he made ready money so abundant, that the rate of interest fell, and the value of real estate rose greatly; and after that, whenever there was an excess of funds from the property of those who had been condemned, he loaned it without interest for fixed periods to any who could give security for double the amount. He increased the property qualification for senators, requiring one million two hundred thousand sesterces, instead of eight hundred thousand, and making up the amount for those who did not possess it. He often gave largess[a] to the people, but usually of different sums: now four hundred, now three hundred, now two hundred and fifty sesterces a man; and he did not even exclude young boys, though it had been usual for them to receive a share only after the age of eleven. In times of scarcity too he often distributed grain to each man at a very low figure, sometimes for nothing, and he doubled the money tickets.[b]

XLII. But to show that he was a prince who desired the public welfare rather than popularity, when the people complained of the scarcity and high price of wine, he sharply rebuked them by saying: "My son-in-law Agrippa has taken good care, by building several aqueducts, that men shall not go thirsty." Again, when the people demanded largess which he had in fact promised, he replied:

and various commodities were distributed by similar *tesserae*; cf. chap. xl. 2; *Nero*, xi; *Dom.* iv.

congiarium reposcenti bonae se fidei esse respondit ;
non promissum autem flagitanti turpitudinem et
impudentiam edicto exprobravit affirmavitque non
daturum se quamvis dare destinaret. Nec minore
gravitate atque constantia, cum proposito congiario
multos manumissos insertosque civium numero
comperisset, negavit accepturos quibus promissum
non esset, ceterisque minus quam promiserat dedit,
3 ut destinata summa sufficeret. Magna vero quondam
sterilitate ac difficili remedio cum venalicias et
lanistarum familias peregrinosque omnes exceptis
medicis et praeceptoribus partimque servitiorum urbe
expulisset, ut tandem annona convaluit, impetum
se cepisse scribit frumentationes publicas in perpetuum abolendi, quod earum fiducia cultura agrorum
cessaret [1] ; neque tamen perseverasse, quia certum
haberet posse per ambitionem quandoque restitui.
Atque ita posthac rem temperavit, ut non minorem
aratorum ac negotiantium quam populi rationem
deduceret.

XLIII. Spectaculorum et assiduitate et varietate
et magnificentia omnes antecessit. Fecisse se
ludos ait suo nomine quater, pro aliis magistratibus,
qui aut abessent aut non sufficerent, ter et vicies.
Fecitque nonnumquam etiam vicatim ac pluribus
scaenis per omnium linguarum histriones, munera [2]
non in Foro modo, nec in amphitheatro, sed et in

---

[1] cesseret, ς ; cesserat, Ω.

[2] munera, *added by Perizonius*; circensibus ludis gladitori-
isque muneribus frequentissime editis interiecit plerumque
bestiarum Africanarum venationes, *Roth* (cf. *Mon. Ancyr.* iv.
39 ff. and *Claud.* xxi.).

---

[a] Cf. *Jul.* xxxix. 1.

" I am a man of my word "; but when they called for one which had not been promised, he rebuked them in a proclamation for their shameless impudence, and declared that he would not give it, even though he was intending to do so. With equal dignity and firmness, when he had announced a distribution of money and found that many had been manumitted and added to the list of citizens, he declared that those to whom no promise had been made should receive nothing, and gave the rest less than he had promised, to make the appointed sum suffice. Once indeed in a time of great scarcity when it was difficult to find a remedy, he expelled from the city the slaves that were for sale, as well as the schools of gladiators, all foreigners with the exception of physicians and teachers, and a part of the household slaves; and when grain at last became more plentiful, he writes: " I was strongly inclined to do away forever with distributions of grain, because through dependence on them agriculture was neglected; but I did not carry out my purpose, feeling sure that they would one day be renewed through desire for popular favour." But from that time on he regulated the practice with no less regard for the interests of the farmers and grain-dealers than for those of the populace.

XLIII. He surpassed all his predecessors in the frequency, variety, and magnificence of his public shows. He says that he gave games four times in his own name and twenty-three times for other magistrates, who were either away from Rome or lacked means. He gave them sometimes in all the wards and on many stages with actors in all languages,[a] and combats of gladiators not only in the Forum or the amphi-

Circo et in Saeptis, et aliquando nihil praeter venationem edidit; athletas quoque exstructis in campo Martio sedilibus ligneis; item navale proelium circa Tiberim cavato solo, in quo nunc Caesarum nemus est. Quibus diebus custodes in urbe disposuit, ne raritate remanentium grassatoribus obnoxia esset.

2 In Circo aurigas cursoresque et confectores ferarum, et nonnumquam ex nobilissima iuventute, produxit. Sed et Troiae lusum edidit frequentissime maiorum[1] minorumque puerorum, prisci decorique moris existimans clarae stirpis indolem sic notescere. In hoc ludicro Nonium Asprenatem lapsu debilitatum aureo torque donavit passusque est ipsum posterosque Torquati ferre cognomen. Mox finem fecit talia edendi Asinio Pollione oratore graviter invidioseque in curia questo Aesernini[2] nepotis sui casum, qui et ipse crus fregerat.

3 Ad scaenicas quoque et gladiatorias operas et equitibus Romanis aliquando usus est, verum prius quam senatus consulto interdiceretur. Postea nihil sane praeterquam adulescentulum Lycium[3] honeste natum exhibuit, tantum ut ostenderet, quod erat bipedali minor, librarum septemdecim ac vocis immensae.

4 Quodam autem muneris die Parthorum obsides tunc

---

[1] maiorum, ς; magnorum, Ω.
[2] Aesernini, *Beroaldus*; Aserinini, Ω.
[3] Lycium, *mss.* (lucium, *R*; licium, *HT*[1]); L. Icium, *Roth.*

---

[a] Cf. *Jul.* xxxix. 2.

theatre, but in the Circus and in the Saepta; sometimes, however, he gave nothing except a fight with wild beasts. He gave athletic contests too in the Campus Martius, erecting wooden seats; also a seafight, constructing an artificial lake near the Tiber, where the grove of the Caesars now stands. On such occasions he stationed guards in various parts of the city, to prevent it from falling a prey to footpads because of the few people who remained at home. In the Circus he exhibited charioteers, runners, and slayers of wild animals, who were sometimes young men of the highest rank. Besides he gave frequent performances of the game of Troy ^a by older and younger boys, thinking it a time-honoured and worthy custom for the flower of the nobility to become known in this way. When Nonius Asprenas was lamed by a fall while taking part in this game, he presented him with a golden necklace and allowed him and his descendants to bear the surname Torquatus. But soon afterwards he gave up that form of entertainment, because Asinius Pollio the orator complained bitterly and angrily in the senate of an accident to his grandson Aeserninus, who also had broken his leg.

He sometimes employed even Roman knights in scenic and gladiatorial performances, but only before it was forbidden by decree of the senate. After that he exhibited no one of respectable parentage, with the exception of a young man named Lycius, whom he showed merely as a curiosity; for he was less than two feet tall, weighed but seventeen pounds, yet had a stentorian voice. He did however on the day of one of the shows make a display of the first Parthian hostages that had ever

primum missos per mediam harenam ad spectaculum
induxit superque se subsellio secundo collocavit.
Solebat etiam citra spectaculorum dies, si quando
quid invisitatum dignumque cognitu advectum esset,
id extra ordinem quolibet loco publicare, ut rhinoce-
rotem apud Saepta, tigrim in scaena, anguem quinquaginta cubitorum pro Comitio.

5   Accidit votivis circensibus, ut correptus valitudine
lectica cubans tensas deduceret; rursus commissione
ludorum, quibus theatrum Marcelli dedicabat, evenit
ut laxatis sellae curulis compagibus caderet supinus.
Nepotum quoque suorum munere cum consternatum
ruinae metu populum retinere et confirmare nullo
modo posset, transiit e loco suo atque in ea parte
consedit, quae suspecta maxime erat.

   XLIV. Spectandi confusissimum ac solutissimum
morem correxit ordinavitque, motus iniuria senatoris,
quem Puteolis per celeberrimos ludos consessu frequenti nemo receperat. Facto igitur decreto patrum
ut, quotiens quid spectaculi usquam publice ederetur,
primus subselliorum ordo vacaret senatoribus, Romae
legatos liberarum sociarumque gentium vetuit in
orchestra sedere, cum quosdam etiam libertini generis
mitti deprendisset. Militem secrevit a populo.
2 Maritis e plebe proprios ordines assignavit, praetextatis cuneum suum, et proximum paedagogis, sanxit-
que ne quis pullatorum media cavea sederet. Feminis

been sent to Rome, by leading them through the middle of the arena and placing them in the second row above his own seat. Furthermore, if anything rare and worth seeing was ever brought to the city, it was his habit to make a special exhibit of it in any convenient place on days when no shows were appointed. For example a rhinoceros in the Saepta, a tiger on the stage and a snake of fifty cubits in front of the Comitium.

It chanced that at the time of the games which he had vowed to give in the circus, he was taken ill and headed the sacred procession lying in a litter; again, at the opening of the games with which he dedicated the theatre of Marcellus, it happened that the joints of his curule chair gave way and he fell on his back. At the games for his grandsons, when the people were in a panic for fear the theatre should fall, and he could not calm them or encourage them in any way, he left his own place and took his seat in the part which appeared most dangerous.

XLIV. He put a stop by special regulations to the disorderly and indiscriminate fashion of viewing the games, through exasperation at the insult to a senator, to whom no one offered a seat in a crowded house at some largely attended games in Puteoli. In consequence of this the senate decreed that, whenever any public show was given anywhere, the first row of seats should be reserved for senators; and at Rome he would not allow the envoys of the free and allied nations to sit in the orchestra, since he was informed that even freedmen were sometimes appointed. He separated the soldiery from the people. He assigned special seats to the married men of the commons, to boys under age their own section and the adjoining one to their preceptors; and he decreed that no one

ne gladiatores quidem, quos promiscue spectari sollemne olim erat, nisi ex superiore loco spectare
3 concessit.   Solis virginibus Vestalibus locum in
theatro separatim et contra praetoris tribunal dedit.
Athletarum vero spectaculo muliebre secus omne
adeo summovit, ut pontificalibus ludis pugilum par
postulatum distulerit in insequentis diei matutinum
tempus edixeritque mulieres ante horam quintam
venire in theatrum non placere.

XLV. Ipse circenses ex amicorum fere libertorum-
que cenaculis spectabat, interdum ex pulvinari et
quidem cum coniuge ac liberis sedens. Spectaculo
plurimas horas, aliquando totos dies aberat, petita
venia commendatisque qui suam vicem praesidendo
fungerentur. Verum quotiens adesset, nihil praeterea
agebat, seu vitandi rumoris causa, quo patrem
Caesarem vulgo reprehensum commemorabat, quod
inter spectandum epistulis libellisque legendis aut
rescribendis vacaret, seu studio spectandi ac voluptate, qua teneri se neque dissimulavit umquam et
2 saepe ingenue professus est. Itaque corollaria et
praemia in alienis quoque muneribus ac ludis et
crebra et grandia de suo offerebat nullique Graeco
certamini interfuit, quo non pro merito quemque

---

[a] The auditorium was divided horizontally into three parts:
ima (prima), *media*, and *summa (ultima) cavea*.

[b] This puzzling statement is thus explained by Baum.-
Crusius: "*i.e.* ex aedibus proxime adjacentibus, unde pro-
spectus erat in Circum. Coenacula autem in summis aedibus
esse solebant.   Idem narrat Dio 57. 11 de Tiberio: τοὺς τῶν
ἵππων ἀγῶνας ἐξ οἰκίας καὶ αὐτὸς τῶν ἀπελευθέρων τινὸς πολ-
λάκις ἑώρα."

[c] *Pulvinar* was originally a sacred couch for a god.   The
honour was given to Julius Caesar (see *Jul.* lxxvi. 1) and the
term was later applied, as here, to the place reserved for the
emperor and his family ; cf. *Claud.* iv. 3.

[d] That is, given at Rome in the Greek language and dress.
Or *Graeco certamini* may mean "a contest in Greece."

wearing a dark cloak should sit in the middle of the house.[a] He would not allow women to view even the gladiators except from the upper seats, though it had been the custom for men and women to sit together at such shows. Only the Vestal virgins were assigned a place to themselves, opposite the praetor's tribunal. As for the contests of the athletes, he excluded women from them so strictly, that when a contest between a pair of boxers had been called for at the games in honour of his appointment as pontifex maximus, he postponed it until early the following day, making proclamation that it was his desire that women should not come to the theatre before the fifth hour.

XLV. He himself usually watched the games in the Circus from the upper rooms of his friends and freedmen,[b] but sometimes from the imperial box,[c] and even in company with his wife and children. He was sometimes absent for several hours, and now and then for whole days, making his excuses and appointing presiding officers to take his place. But whenever he was present, he gave his entire attention to the performance, either to avoid the censure to which he realized that his father Caesar had been generally exposed, because he spent his time in reading or answering letters and petitions ; or from his interest and pleasure in the spectacle, which he never denied but often frankly confessed. Because of this he used to offer special prizes and numerous valuable gifts from his own purse at games given by others, and he appeared at no contest in the Grecian fashion [d] without making a present to each of the participants according to his deserts.

certantium honorarit. Spectavit autem studiosissime
pugiles et maxime Latinos, non legitimos atque
ordinarios modo, quos etiam committere cum Graecis
solebat, sed et catervarios oppidanos inter angustias
3 vicorum pugnantis temere ac sine arte. Universum
denique genus operas aliquas publico spectaculo
praebentium etiam cura sua dignatus est ; athletis
et conservavit privilegia et ampliavit, gladiatores sine
missione edi prohibuit, coercitionem in histriones
magistratibus omni tempore et loco [1] lege vetere
permissam ademit praeterquam ludis et scaena.[2]
4 Nec tamen eo minus aut xysticorum certationes aut
gladiatorum pugnas severissime semper exegit. Nam
histrionum licentiam adeo compescuit, ut Stepha-
nionem togatarium, cui in puerilem habitum circum-
tonsam matronam ministrasse compererat, per trina
theatra virgis caesum relegaverit, Hylan pantomimum querente praetore in atrio domus suae nemine
excluso flagellis verberarit et Pyladen urbe atque
Italia summoverit, quod spectatorem, a quo exsibila-
batur, demonstrasset digito conspicuumque fecisset.

XLVI. Ad hunc modum urbe urbanisque rebus
administratis Italiam duodetriginta coloniarum numero deductarum a se frequentavit operibusque ac
vectigalibus publicis plurifariam instruxit, etiam iure
ac dignatione urbi quodam modo pro parte aliqua

---

[1] loco, *early editions* ; longo, Ω.
[2] ludis et scaena, *Stephanus* ; ludos et scenam, Ω.

---

[a] Those of Pompey, Balbus, and Marcellus.
[b] That is, his middle finger, *infamis digitus* ; it implied a
charge of obscenity ; cf. *Calig.* lvi. 2.

He was especially given to watching boxers, particularly those of Latin birth, not merely such as were recognized and classed as professionals, whom he was wont to match even with Greeks, but the common untrained townspeople that fought rough and tumble and without skill in the narrow streets. In fine, he honoured with his interest all classes of performers who took part in the public shows; maintained the privileges of the athletes and even increased them; forbade the matching of gladiators without the right of appeal for quarter; and deprived the magistrates of the power allowed them by an ancient law of punishing actors anywhere and everywhere, restricting it to the time of games and to the theatre. Nevertheless he exacted the severest discipline in the contests in the wrestling halls and the combats of the gladiators. In particular he was so strict in curbing the lawlessness of the actors, that when he learned that Stephanio, an actor of Roman plays, was waited on by a matron with hair cut short to look like a boy, he had him whipped with rods through the three theatres [a] and then banished him. Hylas, a pantomimic actor, was publicly scourged in the atrium of his own house, on complaint of a praetor, and Pylades was expelled from the city and from Italy as well, because by pointing at him with his finger [b] he turned all eyes upon a spectator who was hissing him.

XLVI. After having thus set the city and its affairs in order, he added to the population of Italy by personally establishing twenty-eight colonies; furnished many parts of it with public buildings and revenues; and even gave it, at least to some degree, equal rights and dignity with the city of Rome, by

adaequavit excogitato genere suffragiorum, quae de magistratibus urbicis decuriones colonici in sua quisque colonia ferrent et sub die comitiorum obsignata Romam mitterent. Ac necubi aut honestorum deficeret copia aut multitudinis suboles, equestrem militiam petentis etiam ex commendatione publica cuiusque oppidi ordinabat, at iis, qui e plebe regiones sibi revisenti filios filiasve approbarent, singula nummorum milia pro singulis dividebat.

XLVII. Provincias validiores et quas annuis magistratuum imperiis regi nec facile nec tutum erat, ipse suscepit, ceteras proconsulibus sortito permisit ; et tamen nonnullas commutavit interdum atque ex utroque genere plerasque saepius adiit. Urbium quasdam, foederatas sed ad exitium licentia praecipites, libertate privavit, alias aut aere alieno laborantis levavit aut terrae motu subversas denuo condidit aut merita erga populum R. adlegantes Latinitate vel civitate donavit. Nec est, ut opinor, provincia, excepta dum taxat Africa et Sardinia, quam non adierit. In has fugato Sex. Pompeio traicere ex Sicilia apparantem continuae et immodicae tempestates inhibuerunt nec mox occasio aut causa traiciendi fuit.

XLVIII. Regnorum quibus belli iure potitus est, praeter pauca, aut iisdem quibus ademerat reddidit

---

[a] That is, appointed them to the offices of *tribunus cohortis*, *praefectus alae*, and *tribunus legionis*, usually open only to knights.

[b] A limited citizenship, taking its name from the old Latin cities and varying in different cases and at different times.

devising a kind of votes which the members of the local senate were to cast in each colony for candidates for the city offices and send under seal to Rome against the day of the elections. To keep up the supply of men of rank and induce the commons to increase and multiply, he admitted to the equestrian military career [a] those who were recommended by any town, while to those of the commons who could lay claim to legitimate sons or daughters when he made his rounds of the districts he distributed a thousand sesterces for each child.

XLVII. The stronger provinces, which could 27 B.C. neither easily nor safely be governed by annual magistrates, he took to himself; the others he assigned to proconsular governors selected by lot. But he changed some of them at times from one class to the other, and often visited many of both sorts. Certain of the cities which had treaties with Rome, but were on the road to ruin through their lawlessness, he deprived of their independence; he relieved others that were overwhelmed with debt, rebuilt some which had been destroyed by earthquakes, and gave Latin rights [b] or full citizenship to such as could point to services rendered the Roman people. I believe there is no province, excepting only Africa and Sardinia, which he did not visit; and he was planning to cross to these from Sicily after his defeat of Sextus Pompeius, but was prevented by a series of violent storms, and later had neither opportunity nor occasion to make the voyage.

XLVIII. Except in a few instances he restored the kingdoms of which he gained possession by the right of conquest to those from whom he had taken

aut alienigenis contribuit. Reges socios etiam inter semet ipsos necessitudinibus mutuis iunxit, promptissimus affinitatis cuiusque atque amicitiae conciliator et fautor; nec aliter universos quam membra partisque imperii curae habuit, rectorem quoque solitus apponere aetate parvis aut mente lapsis, donec adolescerent aut resipiscerent; ac plurimorum liberos et educavit simul cum suis et instituit.

XLIX. Ex militaribus copiis legiones et auxilia provinciatim distribuit, classem Miseni et alteram Ravennae ad tutelam Superi et Inferi maris conlocavit, ceterum numerum partim in urbis partim in sui custodiam adlegit dimissa Calagurritanorum manu, quam usque ad devictum Antonium, item Germanorum, quam usque ad cladem Varianam inter armigeros circa se habuerat. Neque tamen umquam plures quam tres cohortes in urbe esse passus est easque sine castris, reliquas in hiberna et aestiva circa finitima oppida dimittere assuerat. 2 Quidquid autem ubique militum esset, ad certam stipendiorum praemiorumque formulam adstrinxit definitis pro gradu cuiusque et temporibus militiae et commodis missionum, ne aut aetate aut inopia post missionem sollicitari ad res novas possent. Utque perpetuo ac sine difficultate sumptus ad tuendos eos prosequendosque suppeteret, aerarium militare cum vectigalibus novis constituit.

them or joined them with other foreign nations. He also united the kings with whom he was in alliance by mutual ties, and was very ready to propose or favour intermarriages or friendships among them. He never failed to treat them all with consideration as integral parts of the empire, regularly appointing a guardian for such as were too young to rule or whose minds were affected, until they grew up or recovered; and he brought up the children of many of them and educated them with his own.

XLIX. Of his military forces he assigned legions and auxiliaries to the various provinces, stationed a fleet at Misenum and another at Ravenna, to defend the Upper and Lower seas, and employed the remainder partly in the defence of the city and partly in that of his own person, disbanding a troop of Calagurritani which had formed a part of his body-guard until the overthrow of Antony, and also one of Germans, which he had retained until the defeat of Varus. However, he never allowed more than three cohorts to remain in the city and even those were without a permanent camp; the rest he regularly sent to winter or summer quarters in the towns near Rome. Furthermore, he restricted all the soldiery everywhere to a fixed scale of pay and allowances, designating the duration of their service and the rewards on its completion according to each man's rank, in order to keep them from being tempted to revolution after their discharge either by age or poverty. To have funds ready at all times without difficulty for maintaining the soldiers and paying the rewards due to them, he established a military treasury, supported by new taxes,

3   Et quo celerius ac sub manum adnuntiari cognoscique posset, quid in provincia quaque gereretur, iuvenes primo modicis intervallis per militaris vias, dehinc vehicula disposuit. Commodius id visum est, ut qui a loco idem perferunt litteras, interrogari quoque, si quid res exigant, possint.

L. In diplomatibus libellisque et epistulis signandis initio sphinge usus est, mox imagine Magni Alexandri, novissime sua, Dioscuridis manu scalpta,[1] qua signare insecuti quoque principes perseverarunt. Ad epistulas omnis horarum quoque momenta nec diei modo sed et noctis, quibus datae significarentur, addebat.

LI. Clementiae civilitatisque eius multa et magna documenta sunt. Ne enumerem, quot et quos diversarum partium venia et incolumitate donatos principem etiam in civitate locum tenere passus sit: Iunium Novatum et Cassium Patavinum e plebe homines alterum pecunia, alterum levi exilio punire satis habuit, cum ille Agrippae iuvenis nomine asperrimam de se epistulam in vulgus edidisset, hic convivio pleno proclamasset neque votum sibi neque

2 animum deesse confodiendi eum. Quadam vero cognitione, cum Aemilio Aeliano Cordubensi inter cetera crimina vel maxime obiceretur quod male opinari de Caesare soleret, conversus ad accusatorem commotoque similis: "Velim," inquit, "hoc mihi

---

[1] scalpta, *Ernesti*; sculpta, Ω.

---

a Diploma, strictly any document written on a two-leaved tablet, is used especial'y of those which secured to travellers the use of the public post (see chap. xlix. 3) and other privileges; cf. Cic. *Ad Fam.* 6. 12.

To enable what was going on in each of
vinces to be reported and known more spee
promptly, he at first stationed young men ᵢ
intervals along the military roads, and aftᵢ
post-chaises. The latter has seemed the moɪᵤ convenient arrangement, since the same men who bring
the dispatches from any place can, if occasion demands, be questioned as well.

L. In passports,ᵃ dispatches, and private letters hᵤ
used as his seal at first a sphinx, later an image of
Alexander the Great, and finally his own, carved by
the hand of Dioscurides ; and this his successors continued to use as their seal. He always attached
to all letters the exact hour, not only of the day,
but even of the night, to indicate precisely when they
were written.

LI. The evidences of his clemency and moderation are numerous and strong. Not to give the
full list of the men of the opposite faction whom he
not only pardoned and spared, but allowed to hold
high positions in the state, I may say that he thought
it enough to punish two plebeians, Junius Novatus
and Cassius Patavinus, with a fine and with a mild
form of banishment respectively, although the former
had circulated a most scathing letter about him under
the name of the young Agrippa, while the latter had
openly declared at a large dinner party that he
lacked neither the earnest desire nor the courage to
kill him. Again, when he was hearing a case against
Aemilius Aelianus of Corduba and it was made the chief
offence, amongst other charges, that he was in the
habit of expressing a bad opinion of Caesar, Augustus
turned to the accuser with assumed anger and said :
" I wish you could prove the truth of that. I'll let

probes; faciam sciat Aelianus et me linguam habere, plura enim de eo loquar"; nec quicquam ultra aut
3 statim aut postea inquisiit. Tiberio quoque de eadem re, sed violentius[1] apud se per epistulam conquerenti ita rescripsit : "Aetati tuae, mi Tiberi, noli in hac re indulgere et nimium indignari quemquam esse, qui de me male loquatur ; satis est enim, si hoc habemus ne quis nobis male facere possit."

LII. Templa, quamvis sciret etiam proconsulibus decerni solere, in nulla tamen provincia nisi communi suo Romaeque nomine recepit. Nam in urbe quidem pertinacissime abstinuit hoc honore ; atque etiam argenteas statuas olim sibi positas conflavit omnis exque iis[2] aureas cortinas Apollini Palatino dedicavit.

Dictaturam magna vi offerente populo genu nixus deiecta ab umeris toga nudo pectore deprecatus est.

LIII. Domini appellationem ut maledictum et obprobrium semper exhorruit. Cum spectante eo ludos pronuntiatum esset in mimo :

"O dominum aequum et bonum ! "

et universi quasi de ipso dictum exsultantes comprobassent, et statim manu vultuque indecoras adulationes repressit et insequenti die gravissimo corripuit edicto ; dominumque se posthac appellari ne a liberis quidem aut nepotibus suis vel serio vel ioco

[1] sed violentius, *Pithoeus*; sedulo lentius, *MGVΥ*; sedulo violentius, *XN*; sed dolentius, *Bentley*.
[2] exque iis, *Casaubon*; ex quiis *MV* (ex quis, *M²*); *the other mss. have* ex quis (ex quib., *S*).

[a] *Dominus,* "master," in the time of the Republic indicated the relation between master and slaves. Tiberius also shrank from it (*Tib.* xxvii.), and it was first adopted by Caligula and Domitian. From the time of Trajan it was usual in the sense of "Lord" or "Sire."

Aelianus know that I have a tongue as well as he, for I'll say even more about him;" and he made no further inquiry either at the time or afterwards. When Tiberius complained to him of the same thing in a letter, but in more forcible language, he replied as follows: "My dear Tiberius, do not be carried away by the ardour of youth in this matter, or take it too much to heart that anyone speak evil of me; we must be content if we can stop anyone from doing evil to us."

LII. Although well aware that it was usual to vote temples even to proconsuls, he would not accept one even in a province save jointly in his own name and that of Rome. In the city itself he refused this honour most emphatically, even melting down the silver statues which had been set up in his honour in former times and with the money coined from them dedicating golden tripods to Apollo of the Palatine.

When the people did their best to force the dictatorship upon him, he knelt down, threw off his toga from his shoulders and with bare breast begged them not to insist.

LIII. He always shrank from the title of Lord [a] as reproachful and insulting. When the words

"O just and gracious Lord!"

were uttered in a farce at which he was a spectator and all the people sprang to their feet and applauded as if they were said of him, he at once checked their unseemly flattery by look and gesture, and on the following day sharply reproved them in an edict. After that he would not suffer himself to be called Sire even by his children or his grandchildren either in jest or earnest, and he forbade them to use

passus est atque eius modi blanditias etiam inter
2 ipsos prohibuit. Non temere urbe oppidove ullo
egressus aut quoquam ingressus est nisi vespera
aut noctu, ne quem officii causa inquietaret. In
consulatu pedibus fere, extra consulatum saepe
adoperta[1] sella per publicum incessit. Promiscuis
salutationibus admittebat et plebem, tanta comitate
adeuntium desideria excipiens, ut quendam ioco
corripuerit, quod sic sibi libellum porrigere dubitaret,
3 "quasi elephanto stipem." Die senatus numquam
patres nisi in curia salutavit et quidem sedentis ac
nominatim singulos nullo submonente ; etiam dis-
cedens eodem modo sedentibus valere dicebat.
Officia cum multis mutuo exercuit, nec prius dies
cuiusque sollemnes frequentare desiit, quam grandior
iam natu[2] et in turba quondam sponsaliorum die
vexatus. Gallum Cerrinium senatorem minus sibi
familiarem, sed captum repente oculis et ob id inedia[3]
mori destinantem praesens consolando revocavit
ad vitam.

LIV. In senatu verba facienti dictum est : " Non
intellexi," et ab alio : "Contra dicerem tibi, si locum
haberem." Interdum ob immodicas disceptantium
altercationes e curia per iram se proripienti quidam
ingesserunt licere oportere senatoribus de re p.

---

[1] adoperta, *mss.* ; adaperta, *Beroaldus* (*Shuckburgh*).
[2] grandior iam natu] grandi iam ornatu, Ω.
[3] id inedia, *Bologna ed. of* 1488 ; inediam, Ω.

---

[a] That is, they did not make a morning call on him, as in
other days.

such flattering terms even among themselves. He
did not if he could help it leave or enter any city or
town except in the evening or at night, to avoid dis-
turbing anyone by the obligations of ceremony.   In
his consulship he commonly went through the streets
on foot, and when he was not consul, generally in
a closed litter.   His morning receptions were open
to all, including even the commons, and he met
the requests of those who approached him with great
affability, jocosely reproving one man because he
presented a petition to him with as much hesitation
" as he would a penny to an elephant."   On the day
of a meeting of the senate he always greeted the
members in the House [a] and in their seats, calling
each man by name without a prompter; and when
he left the House, he used to take leave of them
in the same manner, while they remained seated.
He exchanged social calls with many, and did not
cease to attend all their anniversaries, until he was
well on in years and was once incommoded by the
crowd on the day of a betrothal.   When Gallus
Cerrinius, a senator with whom he was not at all
intimate, had suddenly become blind and had therefore resolved to end his life by starvation, Augustus
called on him and by his consoling words induced
him to live.

LIV. As he was speaking in the senate someone
said to him: " I did not understand," and another :
" I would contradict you if I had an opportunity."
Several times when he was rushing from the House
in anger at the excessive bickering of the disputants,
some shouted after him : " Senators ought to have
the right of speaking their mind on public affairs."
At the selection of senators when each member chose

loqui. Antistius Labeo senatus lectione, cum vir virum [1] legeret, M. Lepidum hostem olim eius et tunc exsulantem legit interrogatusque ab eo an essent alii digniores, suum quemque iudicium habere respondit. Nec ideo libertas aut contumacia fraudi cuiquam fuit.

LV. Etiam sparsos de se in curia famosos libellos nec expavit et magna cura redarguit ac ne requisitis quidem auctoribus id modo censuit, cognoscendum posthac de iis, qui libellos aut carmina ad infamiam cuiuspiam sub alieno nomine edant.

LVI. Iocis quoque quorundam invidiosis aut petulantibus lacessitus contra dixit edicto. Et tamen ne de inhibenda testamentorum licentia quicquam constitueretur intercessit. Quotiens magistratuum comitiis interesset, tribus cum candidatis suis circuibat supplicabatque more sollemni. Ferebat et ipse suffragium in tribu,[2] ut unus e populo. Testem se in iudiciis et interrogari et refelli aequissimo animo patiebatur. Forum angustius fecit non ausus extorquere possessoribus proximas domos. Numquam filios suos populo commendavit ut non adiceret: "Si merebuntur." Eisdem praetextatis adhuc assurrectum ab universis in theatro et a stantibus plausum gravissime questus est. Amicos ita magnos et potentes in civitate esse voluit, ut tamen pari iure essent quo ceteri legibusque iudiciariis aeque teneren-

---

[1] vir virum, *Torrentius*; triumvirum, Ω.
[2] tribu, *Erasmus*; tribus, Ω.

---

[a] See chap. xxxv. 1.
[b] The Romans in their wills often express their opinion freely about public men and affairs; cf. chap. lxvi., and Cassius Dio, 58. 25, where it is said that Fulcinius Tiro, who died in prison, bitterly assailed Tiberius in his will.

another,[a] Antistius Labeo named Marcus Lepidus, an old enemy of the emperor's who was at the time in banishment; and when Augustus asked him whether there were not others more deserving of the honour, Labeo replied that every man had his own opinion. Yet for all that no one suffered for his freedom of speech or insolence.

LV. He did not even dread the lampoons against him which were scattered in the senate house, but took great pains to refute them; and without trying to discover the authors, he merely proposed that thereafter such as published notes or verses defamatory of anyone under a false name should be called to account.

LVI. When he was assailed with scurrilous or spiteful jests by certain men, he made reply in a public proclamation; yet he vetoed a law to check freedom of speech in wills.[b] Whenever he took part in the election of magistrates, he went the round of the tribes with his candidates and appealed for them in the traditional manner. He also cast his own vote in his tribe, as one of the people. When he gave testimony in court, he was most patient in submitting to questions and even to contradiction. He made his forum narrower than he had planned, because he did not venture to eject the owners of the neighbouring houses. He never recommended his sons for office without adding "If they be worthy of it." When they were still under age and the audience at the theatre rose as one man in their honour, and stood up and applauded them, he expressed strong disapproval. He wished his friends to be prominent and influential in the state, but to be bound by the same laws as the rest and equally liable to

3 tur. Cum Asprenas Nonius artius ei iunctus causam
veneficii accusante Cassio Severo diceret, consuluit
senatum, quid officii sui putaret ; cunctari enim se,
ne si superesset, eripere [1] legibus reum, sin deesset,
destituere ac praedamnare amicum existimaretur ;
et consentientibus universis sedit in subselliis per
aliquot horas, verum tacitus et ne laudatione quidem
4 iudiciali data. Affuit et clientibus, sicut Scutario
cuidam evocato quondam suo, qui postulabatur
iniuriarum. Unum omnino e reorum numero ac ne
eum quidem nisi precibus eripuit, exorato coram
iudicibus accusatore, Castricium, per quem de coniuratione Murenae cognoverat.

LVII. Pro quibus meritis quanto opere dilectus sit,
facile est aestimare. Omitto senatus consulta, quia
possunt videri vel necessitate expressa vel verecundia.
Equites R. natalem eius sponte atque consensu [2] biduo
semper celebrarunt. Omnes ordines in lacum Curti
quotannis ex voto pro salute eius stipem iaciebant,
item Kal. Ian. strenam in Capitolio etiam absenti, ex
qua summa pretiosissima deorum simulacra mercatus
vicatim dedicabat, ut Apollinem Sandaliarium et
2 Iovem Tragoedum aliaque. In restitutionem Palatinae
domus incendio absumptae veterani, decuriae, tribus

---

[1] eripere, *Juncker* ; eriperet, Ω.
[2] consensu] concessu, Ω.

---

[a] The movable seats provided for the advocates, witnesses,
etc.
[b] The custom of defending an accused person by a general
eulogy of his character was forbidden by Pompey in his
third consulship (Dio, 40. 52), but was nevertheless resorted
to, even by Pompey himself (Dio, 40. 55).
[c] September 22 and 23.
[d] Probably of the scribes and other minor officials.

prosecution. When Nonius Asprenas, a close friend of his, was meeting a charge of poisoning made by Cassius Severus, Augustus asked the senate what they thought he ought to do; for he hesitated, he said for fear that if he should support him, it might be thought that he was shielding a guilty man, but if he failed to do so, that he was proving false to a friend and prejudicing his case. Then, since all approved of his appearing in the case, he sat on the benches [a] for several hours, but in silence and without even speaking in praise of the defendant.[b] He did however defend some of his clients, for instance a certain Scutarius, one of his former officers, who was accused of slander. But he secured the acquittal of no more than one single man, and then only by entreaty, making a successful appeal to the accuser in the presence of the jurors; this was Castricius, through whom he had learned of Murena's conspiracy.

LVII. It may readily be imagined how much he was beloved because of this admirable conduct. I say nothing of decrees of the senate, which might seem to have been dictated by necessity or by awe. The Roman knights celebrated his birthday of their own accord by common consent, and always for two successive days.[c] All sorts and conditions of men, in fulfilment of a vow for his welfare, each year threw a small coin into the Lacus Curtius, and also brought a New Year's gift to the Capitol on the Kalends of January, even when he was away from Rome. With this sum he bought and dedicated in each of the city wards costly statues of the gods, such as Apollo Sandaliarius, Jupiter Tragoedus, and others. To rebuild his house on the Palatine, which had been destroyed by fire, the veterans, the guilds,[d] the tribes,

atque etiam singillatim e cetero genere hominum
libentes ac pro facultate quisque pecunias contulerunt,
delibante tantum modo eo summarum acervos neque
ex quoquam plus denario auferente. Revertentem ex
provincia non solum faustis ominibus, sed et modulatis
carminibus prosequebantur. Observatum etiam est,
ne quotiens introiret urbem, supplicium de quoquam
sumeretur.

LVIII. Patris patriae cognomen universi repentino
maximoque consensu detulerunt ei : prima plebs
legatione Antium missa ; dein, quia non recipiebat,
ineunti Romae spectacula frequens et laureata ; mox
in curia senatus, neque decreto neque adclamatione,
2 sed per Valerium Messalam. Is mandantibus cunctis :
" Quod bonum," inquit, " faustumque sit tibi domui-
que tuae, Caesar Auguste ! Sic enim nos perpetuam
felicitatem rei p. et laeta huic precari existimamus :
senatus te consentiens cum populo R. consalutat
patriae patrem." Cui lacrimans respondit Augustus
his verbis—ipsa enim, sicut Messalae, posui— :
" Compos factus votorum meorum, p. c., quid habeo
aliud deos immortales precari, quam ut hunc con-
sensum vestrum ad ultimum finem vitae mihi perferre
liceat ? "

LIX. Medico Antonio Musae, cuius opera ex
ancipiti morbo convaluerat, statuam aere conlato
iuxta signum Aesculapi statuerunt. Nonnulli patrum
familiarum testamento caverunt, ut ab heredibus suis
praelato titulo victumae in Capitolium ducerentur

and even individuals of other conditions gladly contributed money, each according to his means; but he merely took a little from each pile as a matter of form, not more than a denarius from any of them. On his return from a province they received him not only with prayers and good wishes, but with songs. It was the rule, too, that whenever he entered the city, no one should suffer punishment.

LVIII. The whole body of citizens with a sudden unanimous impulse proffered him the title of Father of his Country: first the commons, by a deputation sent to Antium, and then, because he declined it, again at Rome as he entered the theatre, which they attended in throngs, all wearing laurel wreaths; the senate afterwards in the House, not by a decree or by acclamation, but through Valerius Messala. He, speaking for the whole body, said: "Good fortune and divine favour attend thee and thy house, Caesar Augustus; for thus we feel that we are praying for lasting prosperity for our country and happiness for our city. The senate in accord with the people of Rome hails thee Father of thy Country." Then Augustus with tears in his eyes replied as follows (and I have given his exact words, as I did those of Messala): "Having attained my highest hopes, Fathers of the Senate, what more have I to ask of the immortal gods than that I may retain this same unanimous approval of yours to the very end of my life."

LIX. In honour of his physician, Antonius Musa, through whose care he had recovered from a dangerous illness, a sum of money was raised and Musa's statue set up beside that of Aesculapius. Some householders provided in their wills that their heirs should drive victims to the Capitol and pay a thank-offering

votumque pro se solveretur, quod superstitem
Augustum reliquissent. Quaedam Italiae civitates
diem, quo primum ad se venisset, initium anni
fecerunt. Provinciarum pleraeque super templa et
aras ludos quoque quinquennales paene oppidatim
constituerunt.

LX. Reges amici atque socii et singuli in suo
quisque regno Caesareas urbes condiderunt et cuncti
simul aedem Iovis Olympii Athenis antiquitus incohatam perficere communi sumptu destinaverunt
Genioque eius dedicare ; ac saepe regnis relictis non
Romae modo sed et provincias peragranti cotidiana
officia togati ac sine regio insigni more clientium
praestiterunt.

LXI. Quoniam qualis in imperiis ac magistratibus
regendaque per terrarum orbem pace belloque re p.
fuerit, exposui, referam nunc interiorem ac familiarem
eius vitam quibusque moribus atque fortuna domi et
inter suos egerit a iuventa usque ad supremum vitae
diem.

2 Matrem amisit in primo consulatu, sororem Octaviam quinquagensimum et quartum agens aetatis annum. Utrique cum praecipua officia vivae praestitisset,
etiam defunctae honores maximos tribuit.

LXII. Sponsam habuerat adulescens P. Servili
Isaurici filiam, sed reconciliatus post primam discordiam Antonio, expostulantibus utriusque militibus

---

a One's tutelary divinity, or familiar spirit, closely identified
with the person himself.

in their behalf, because Augustus had survived them, and that a placard to this effect should be carried before them. Some of the Italian cities made the day on which he first visited them the beginning of their year. Many of the provinces, in addition to temples and altars, established quinquennial games in his honour in almost every one of their towns.

LX. His friends and allies among the kings each in his own realm founded a city called Caesarea, and all joined in a plan to contribute the funds for finishing the temple of Jupiter Olympius, which was begun at Athens in ancient days, and to dedicate it to his Genius [a]; and they would often leave their kingdoms and show him the attentions usual in dependents, clad in the toga and without the emblems of royalty, not only at Rome, but even when he was travelling through the provinces.

LXI. Now that I have shown how he conducted himself in civil and military positions, and in ruling the State in all parts of the world in peace and in war, I shall next give an account of his private and domestic life, describing his character and his fortune at home and in his household from his youth until the last day of his life.

He lost his mother during his first consulship and 43 B.C. his sister Octavia in his fifty-fourth year. To both 9 B.C. he showed marked devotion during their lifetime, and also paid them the highest honours after their death.

LXII. In his youth he was betrothed to the daughter of Publius Servilius Isauricus, but when he became reconciled with Antony after their first quarrel, and their troops begged that the rivals be further united by some tie of kinship, he took to

ut et necessitudine aliqua iungerentur, privignam eius Claudiam, Fulviae ex P. Clodio filiam, duxit uxorem vixdum nubilem ac simultate cum Fulvia socru orta dimisit intactam adhuc et virginem. 2 Mox Scriboniam in matrimonium accepit nuptam ante duobus consularibus, ex altero etiam matrem. Cum hac quoque divortium fecit, "pertaesus," ut scribit, "morum perversitatem eius," ac statim Liviam Drusillam matrimonio Tiberi Neronis et quidem praegnantem abduxit dilexitque et probavit unice ac perseveranter.

LXIII. Ex Scribonia Iuliam, ex Livia nihil liberorum tulit, cum maxime cuperet. Infans, qui conceptus erat, immaturus est editus. Iuliam primum Marcello Octaviae sororis suae filio tantum quod pueritiam egresso, deinde, ut is obiit, M. Agrippae nuptum dedit exorata sorore, ut sibi genero cederet; nam tunc Agrippa alteram Marcellarum habebat et 2 ex ea liberos. Hoc quoque defuncto, multis ac diu, etiam ex equestri ordine, circumspectis condicionibus, Tiberium privignum suum elegit coegitque praegnantem uxorem et ex qua iam pater erat dimittere. M. Antonius scribit primum eum Antonio filio suo despondisse Iuliam, dein Cotisoni Getarum regi, quo tempore sibi quoque in vicem filiam regis in matrimonium petisset.

LXIV. Nepotes ex Agrippa et Iulia tres habuit C. et L. et Agrippam, neptes duas Iuliam et Agrippinam. Iuliam L. Paulo censoris filio, Agrippinam

wife Antony's stepdaughter Claudia, daughter of 43 B.C.
Fulvia by Publius Clodius, although she was barely
of marriageable age; but because of a falling out
with his mother-in-law Fulvia, he divorced her before
they had begun to live together. Shortly after
that he married Scribonia, who had been wedded 40 B.C.
before to two ex-consuls, and was a mother by one
of them. He divorced her also, "unable to put
up with her shrewish disposition," as he himself
writes, and at once took Livia Drusilla from her 38 B.C.
husband Tiberius Nero, although she was with child
at the time; and he loved and esteemed her to the
end without a rival.

LXIII. By Scribonia he had a daughter Julia, by
Livia no children at all, although he earnestly desired
issue. One baby was conceived, but was prematurely
born. He gave Julia in marriage first to Marcellus,
son of his sister Octavia and hardly more than a
boy, and then after his death to Marcus Agrippa,
prevailing upon his sister to yield her son-in-law
to him; for at that time Agrippa had to wife one of
the Marcellas and had children from her. When
Agrippa also died, Augustus, after considering various
alliances for a long time, even in the equestrian
order, finally chose his stepson Tiberius, obliging
him to divorce his wife, who was with child and
by whom he was already a father. Mark Antony
writes that Augustus first betrothed his daughter to
his son Antonius and then to Cotiso, king of the
Getae, at the same time asking for the hand of the
king's daughter for himself in turn.

LXIV. From Agrippa and Julia he had three
grandsons, Gaius, Lucius, and Agrippa, and two
granddaughters, Julia and Agrippina. He married

Germanico sororis suae nepoti collocavit. Gaium et
L. adoptavit domi per assem et libram emptos a
patre Agrippa tenerosque adhuc ad curam rei p.
admovit et consules designatos circum provincias
2 exercitusque dimisit. Filiam et neptes ita instituit,
ut etiam lanificio assuefaceret vetaretque loqui aut
agere quicquam nisi propalam et quod in diurnos
commentarios referretur ; extraneorum quidem coetu
adeo prohibuit, ut L. Vinicio, claro decoroque iuveni,
scripserit quondam parum modeste fecisse eum, quod
3 filiam suam Baias salutatum venisset. Nepotes et
litteras et natare[1] aliaque rudimenta per se plerumque docuit, ac nihil aeque elaboravit quam ut imitar-
entur chirographum suum ; neque cenavit una, nisi ut
in imo lecto assiderent, neque iter fecit, nisi ut
vehiculo anteirent aut circa adequitarent.

LXV. Sed laetum eum atque fidentem et subole
et disciplina domus Fortuna destituit. Iulias, filiam
et neptem, omnibus probris contaminatas relegavit ;
G. et L. in duodeviginti mensium spatio amisit
ambos, Gaio in Lycia, Lucio Massiliae defunctis.
Tertium nepotem Agrippam simulque privignum
Tiberium adoptavit in foro lege curiata ; ex quibus

---

[1] natare, *mss.* ; notare, *Lipsius.*

---

[a] The form of purchase consisted in thrice touching a
balance (*libra*) with a penny (*as*), in the presence of the
praetor.

[b] A record of the events of the imperial household. The
custom of keeping such a day-book apparently dated from
the time of Augustus. See Friedländer, *Roman Life and
Manners* (Eng. Trans.), IV. p. 56.

[c] The host usually occupied the *summus locus* on the *imus
lectus*.

[d] Ancient divisions of the citizens for political purposes.
In cases of adoption the *curiae* were represented by thirty

Julia to Lucius Paulus, the censor's son, and
Agrippina to Germanicus his sister's grandson.
Gaius and Lucius he adopted at home, privately
buying them from their father by a symbolic sale,[a]
and initiated them into administrative life when they
were still young, sending them to the provinces and
the armies as consuls elect. In bringing up his
daughter and his granddaughters he even had them
taught spinning and weaving, and he forbade them
to say or do anything except openly and such as
might be recorded in the household diary.[b] He was
most strict in keeping them from meeting strangers,
once writing to Lucius Vinicius, a young man of
good position and character: "You have acted
presumptuously in coming to Baiae to call on my
daughter." He taught his grandsons reading, swimming, and the other elements of education, for the
most part himself, taking special pains to train them to
imitate his own handwriting; and he never dined
in their company unless they sat beside him on the
lowest couch,[c] or made a journey unless they preceded his carriage or rode close by it on either side.

LXV. But at the height of his happiness and his
confidence in his family and its training, Fortune 2 B.C.
proved fickle. He found the two Julias, his daughter 9 B.C.
and granddaughter, guilty of every form of vice, and
banished them. He lost Gaius and Lucius within
the span of eighteen months, for the former died in 2 A.D.
Lycia and the latter at Massilia. He then publicly 4 A.D.
adopted his third grandson Agrippa and at the same
time his stepson Tiberius by a bill passed in the
assembly of the *curiae*[d]; but he soon disowned

lictors, presided over by the pontifex maximus. This form
of adoption was usual with adults; cf. chap. lxiv. 1.

Agrippam brevi ob ingenium sordidum ac ferox abdicavit seposuitque Surrentum.

2 Aliquanto autem patientius mortem quam dedecora suorum tulit. Nam C. Lucique casu non adeo fractus, de filia absens ac libello per quaestorem recitato notum senatui fecit abstinuitque congressu hominum diu prae pudore, etiam de necanda deliberavit. Certe cum sub idem tempus una ex consciis liberta Phoebe [1] suspendio vitam finisset, maluisse se ait

3 Phoebes [2] patrem fuisse. Relegatae usum vini omnemque delicatiorem cultum ademit neque adiri a quoquam libero servove [3] nisi se consulto permisit, et ita ut certior fieret, qua is aetate, qua statura, quo colore esset, etiam quibus corporis notis vel cicatricibus. Post quinquennium demum ex insula in continentem lenioribusque paulo condicionibus transtulit eam. Nam ut omnino revocaret, exorari nullo modo potuit, deprecanti saepe p. R. et pertinacius instanti tales filias talesque coniuges pro contione

4 inprecatus. Ex nepte Iulia post damnationem editum infantem adgnosci alique vetuit. Agrippam nihilo tractabiliorem, immo in dies amentiorem, in insulam transportavit saepsitque insuper custodia militum. Cavit etiam s. c. ut eodem loci in perpetuum contine-

---

[1] Phoebe, *Pulmann* ; foede, Ω.
[2] Phoebes, *Pulmann* ; foedes (fedes, fede), *mss.*
[3] servove, *Basle ed. of* 1518, *in the margin* ; servoque, Ω.

---

[a] Pandataria.   [b] Planasia.

Agrippa because of his low tastes and violent temper, and sent him off to Surrentum.

He bore the death of his kin with far more resignation than their misconduct. For he was not greatly broken by the fate of Gaius and Lucius, but he informed the senate of his daughter's fall through a letter read in his absence by a quaestor, and for very shame would meet no one for a long time, and even thought of putting her to death. At all events, when one of her confidantes, a freedwoman called Phoebe, hanged herself at about that same time, he said: "I would rather have been Phoebe's father." After Julia was banished, he denied her the use of wine and every form of luxury, and would not allow any man, bond or free, to come near her without his permission, and then not without being informed of his stature, complexion, and even of any marks or scars upon his body. -It was not until five years later that he moved her from the island [a] to the mainland and treated her with somewhat less rigour. But he could not by any means be prevailed on to recall her altogether, and when the Roman people several times interceded for her and urgently pressed their suit, he in open assembly called upon the gods to curse them with like daughters and like wives. He would not allow the child born to his granddaughter Julia after her sentence to be recognized or reared. As Agrippa grew no more manageable, but on the contrary became madder from day to day, he transferred him to an island [b] and set a guard of soldiers over him besides. He also provided by a decree of

retur.   Atque ad omnem et eius et Iuliarum mentionem ingemiscens proclamare etiam solebat :

Αἴθ᾽ ὄφελον ἄγαμός τ᾽ ἔμεναι ἄγονός τ᾽ ἀπολέσθαι.

nec aliter eos appellare quam tris vomicas ac tria
carcinomata sua.

LXVI. Amicitias neque facile admisit et constantissime retinuit, non tantum virtutes ac merita cuiusque
digne prosecutus, sed vitia quoque et delicta, dum
taxat modica, perpessus.   Neque enim temere ex
omni numero in amicitia eius afflicti reperientur
praeter Salvidienum [1] Rufum, quem ad consulatum
usque, et Cornelium Gallum, quem ad praefecturam
Aegypti, ex infima utrumque fortuna provexerat.
2 Quorum alterum res novas molientem damnandum
senatui tradidit, alteri ob ingratum et malivolum
animum domo et provinciis suis interdixit.   Sed Gallo
quoque et accusatorum denuntiationibus et senatus
consultis ad necem conpulso laudavit quidem pieta-
tem tanto opere pro se indignantium, ceterum et
inlacrimavit et vicem suam conquestus est, quod
sibi soli non liceret amicis, quatenus vellet, irasci.
3 Reliqui potentia atque opibus ad finem vitae sui [2]
quisque ordinis principes floruerunt, quanquam et

---

[1] Salvidienus] Salvidenius, Ω, *corrected in the Basle ed. of*
1533.   [2] sui, ς ; suae, Ω.

---

[a] *Iliad* 3. 40, where the line is addressed by Hector to
Paris, with the verbs in the second person.

[b] See chap. xlvii., at the beginning.

[c] As well as Salvidienus.

[d] That is, while a private citizen could quarrel and make

the senate that he should be confined there for all time, and at every mention of him and of the Julias he would sigh deeply and even cry out:

"Would that I ne'er had wedded and would I had
    died without offspring";[a]

and he never alluded to them except as his three boils and his three ulcers.

LXVI. He did not readily make friends, but he clung to them with the utmost constancy, not only suitably rewarding their virtues and deserts but even condoning their faults, provided they were not too great. In fact one cannot readily name any of his numerous friends who fell into disgrace, except Salvidienus Rufus, whom he had advanced to a consul's rank, and Cornelius Gallus, whom he had raised to the prefecture of Egypt, both from the lowest estate. The former he handed over to the senate that it might condemn him to death, because he was plotting revolution; the latter he forbade his house and the privilege of residence in the imperial provinces,[b] because of his ungrateful and envious spirit. But when Gallus too[c] was forced to undergo death through the declarations of his accusers and the decrees of the senate, though commending their loyalty and their indignation on his account, Augustus yet shed tears and bewailed his lot, because he alone could not set what limits he chose to his anger with his friends.[d] All the rest continued to enjoy power and wealth to the end of their lives, each holding a leading place in his own class,[e] although up with his friends, the emperor's position made his anger fatal.

[e] That is to say, holding the highest place in the *ordo* (*senatorius, equestris, plebeius*) of which he was a member.

offensis intervenientibus.   Desideravit enim nonnumquam, ne de pluribus referam, et M. Agrippae
patientiam et Maecenatis taciturnitatem, cum ille ex
levi frigoris [1] suspicione et quod Marcellus sibi ante-
ferretur, Mytilenas se relictis omnibus contulisset,[2]
hic secretum de comperta Murenae coniuratione
uxori Terentiae prodidisset.

4   Exegit et ipse in vicem ab amicis benivolentiam
mutuam, tam a defunctis quam a vivis.   Nam
quamvis minime appeteret hereditates, ut qui
numquam ex ignoti testamento capere quicquam
sustinuerit, amicorum tamen suprema iudicia mo₋o-
sissime pensitavit, neque dolore dissimulato, si parcius
aut citra honorem verborum, neque gaudio, si grate
pieque quis se prosecutus fuisset.   Legata vel partes
hereditatium a quibuscumque parentibus relicta sibi
aut statim liberis eorum concedere aut, si pupillari
aetate essent, die virilis togae vel nuptiarum cum
incremento restituere consueverat.

LXVII. Patronus dominusque non minus severus
quam facilis et clemens multos libertorum in honore
et usu maximo habuit, ut Licinum [3] et Celadum
aliosque. Cosmum servum gravissime de se opinantem
non ultra quam compedibus coercuit.   Diomeden
dispensatorem, a quo simul ambulante incurrenti
repente fero apro per metum obiectus est, maluit
timiditatis arguere quam noxae, remque non minimi

---

[1] frigoris, *Lipsius* ; rigoris, *mss.*
[2] et *after* contulisset, *mss.* ; *omitted by Torrentius.*
[3] Licinum,. *Torrentius* ; Licinium, *mss.* ; et Celadum,
Casaubon ; enceladum, Ω.

---

[a] Cf. chap. lvi. 1 and the note.

sometimes differences arose. Not to mention the others, he occasionally found Agrippa lacking in patience and Maecenas in the gift of silence; for the former because of a slight suspicion of coolness and of a preference shewn for Marcellus, threw up everything and went off to Mytilene, while the latter betrayed to his wife Terentia the secret of the discovery of the conspiracy of Murena.

In return he demanded of his friends affection on their part, both in life and after death.[a] For though he was in no sense a legacy-hunter, and in fact could never bring himself to accept anything from the will of a stranger, yet he was highly sensitive in weighing the death-bed utterances of his friends, concealing neither his chagrin if he was left a niggardly bequest or one unaccompanied with compliments, nor his satisfaction, if he was praised in terms of gratitude and affection. Whenever legacies or shares in inheritances were left him by men of any station who had offspring, he either turned them over to the children at once, or if the latter were in their minority, paid the money back with interest on the day when they assumed the gown of manhood or married.

LXVII. As patron and master he was no less strict than gracious and merciful, while he held many of his freedmen in high honour and close intimacy, such as Licinus, Celadus, and others. His slave Cosmus, who spoke of him most insultingly, he merely put in irons. When he was walking with his steward Diomedes, and the latter in a panic got behind him when they were suddenly charged by a wild boar, he preferred to tax the man with timorousness rather than with anything more serious, and

periculi, quia tamen fraus aberat, in iocum vertit.
2 Idem Polum ex acceptissimis libertis mori coegit
compertum adulterare matronas; Thallo a manu,
quod pro epistula prodita denarios quingentos
accepisset, crura ei fregit; paedagogum ministrosque
C. fili, per occasionem valitudinis mortisque eius
superbe avareque in provincia grassatos, oneratis[1]
gravi pondere cervicibus praecipitavit in flumen.

LXVIII. Prima iuventa variorum dedecorum infamiam subiit. Sextus Pompeius ut effeminatum
insectatus est; M. Antonius adoptionem avunculi
stupro meritum; item L. Marci frater, quasi pudi-
citiam delibatam a Caesare Aulo etiam Hirtio in
Hispania trecentis milibus nummum substraverit
solitusque sit crura suburere nuce ardenti, quo
mollior pilus surgeret. Sed et populus quondam
universus ludorum die et accepit in contumeliam
eius et adsensu maximo conprobavit versum in
scaena pronuntiatum de gallo Matris Deum tym-
panizante:

"Videsne, ut cinaedus orbem digito temperat?"[a]

LXIX. Adulteria quidem exercuisse ne amici
quidem negant, excusantes sane non libidine, sed
ratione commissa, quo facilius consilia adversariorum
per cuiusque mulieres exquireret. M. Antonius
super festinatas Liviae nuptias obiecit et feminam

---

[1] oneratis, $T\varsigma$; onenitos, G; the other mss. have oneratos.

[a] A double word-play on orbem, "round drum" and "world," and temperat, "beats" and "sways."

turned a matter of grave danger into a jest, because after all there was no evil intent. But he forced Polus, a favourite freedman of his, to take his own life, because he was convicted of adultery with Roman matrons, and broke the legs of his secretary Thallus for taking five hundred denarii to betray the contents of a letter. Because the tutor and attendants of his son Gaius took advantage of their master's illness and death to commit acts of arrogance and greed in his province, he had them thrown into a river with heavy weights about their necks.

LXVIII. In early youth he incurred the reproach of sundry shameless acts. Sextus Pompey taunted him with effeminacy; Mark Antony with having earned adoption by his uncle through unnatural relations; and Lucius, brother of Mark Antony, that after sacrificing his honour to Caesar he had given himself to Aulus Hirtius in Spain for three hundred thousand sesterces, and that he used to singe his legs with red-hot nutshells, to make the hair grow softer. What is more, one day when there were plays in the theatre, all the people took as directed against him and loudly applauded the following line, spoken on the stage and referring to a priest of the Mother of the Gods, as he beat his timbrel:

"See'st how a wanton's finger sways the world?" [a]

LXIX. That he was given to adultery not even his friends deny, although it is true that they excuse it as committed not from passion but from policy, the more readily to get track of his adversaries' designs through the women of their households. Mark Antony charged him, besides his hasty marriage with Livia, with taking the wife

229

consularem e triclinio viri coram in cubiculum
abductam, rursus in convivium rubentibus auriculis
incomptiore capillo reductam ; dimissam Scriboniam,
quia liberius doluisset nimiam potentiam paelicis ;
condiciones quaesitas per amicos, qui matres familias
et adultas aetate virgines denudarent atque per-
spicerent, tamquam Toranio mangone vendente.

2 Scribit etiam ad ipsum haec familiariter adhuc
necdum plane inimicus aut hostis : "Quid te mutavit?
Quod reginam ineo ? Uxor mea est. Nunc coepi
an abhinc annos novem ? Tu deinde solam Drusillam
inis ? Ita valeas, uti tu, hanc epistulam cum leges,
non inieris Tertullam aut Terentillam aut Rufillam
aut Salviam Titiseniam aut omnes. An refert, ubi
et in qua arrigas ? "

LXX. Cena quoque eius secretior in fabulis fuit,
quae vulgo δωδεκάθεος vocabatur ; in qua deorum
dearumque habitu discubuisse convivas et ipsum
pro Apolline ornatum non Antoni modo epistulae
singulorum nomina amarissime enumerantis ex-
probrant, sed et sine auctore notissimi versus ;

"Cum primum istorum conduxit mensa choragum,
    Sexque deos vidit Mallia sexque deas,
Impia dum Phoebi Caesar mendacia ludit,
    Dum nova divorum cenat adulteria :
Omnia se a terris tunc numina declinarunt,
    Fugit et auratos Iuppiter ipse thronos."

---

    ^a Probably referring to Livia.
    ^b The *choragus* at Athens had charge of the costuming and
stage setting of plays. Hence the meaning is here " when
they had found someone to make them up."
    ^c According to some, the choragus ; others regard it as the
name of a place.

of an ex-consul from her husband's dining room
before his very eyes into a bed-chamber, and
bringing her back to the table with her hair
in disorder and her ears glowing; that Scribonia
was divorced because she expressed her resentment
too freely at the excessive influence of a rival;[a]
that his friends acted as his panders, and stripped
and inspected matrons and well-grown girls, as
if Toranius the slave-dealer were putting them up
for sale. Antony also writes to Augustus himself
in the following familiar terms, when he had not
yet wholly broken with him privately or publicly:
"What has made such a change in you? Because
I lie with the queen? She is my wife. Am I just
beginning this, or was it nine years ago? What
then of you—do you lie only with Drusilla? Good
luck to you if when you read this letter you have
not been with Tertulla or Terentilla or Rufilla
or Salvia Titisenia, or all of them. Does it matter
where or with whom you take your pleasure?"

LXX. There was besides a private dinner of his,
commonly called that of the "twelve gods," which was
the subject of gossip. At this the guests appeared
in the guise of gods and goddesses, while he himself
was made up to represent Apollo, as was charged
not merely in letters of Antony, who spitefully
gives the names of all the guests, but also in these
anonymous lines, which everyone knows:

"As soon as that table of rascals had secured a
choragus[b] and Mallia[c] saw six gods and six goddesses,
while Caesar impiously plays the false rôle of Apollo
and feasts amid novel debaucheries of the gods; then
all the deities turned their faces from the earth and
Jupiter himself fled from his golden throne."

2 Auxit cenae rumorem summa tunc in civitate penuria ac fames, adclamatumque est postridie: Omne frumentum deos comedisse et Caesarem esse plane Apollinem, sed Tortorem, quo cognomine is deus quadam in parte urbis colebatur. Notatus est et ut pretiosae supellectilis Corinthiorumque praecupidus et aleae indulgens: Nam et proscriptionis tempore ad statuam eius ascriptum est:

"Pater argentarius, ego Corinthiarius,"

cum existimaretur quosdam propter vasa Corinthia inter proscriptos curasse referendos; et deinde bello Siciliensi epigramma vulgatum est:

"Postquam bis classe victus naves perdidit,
Aliquando ut vincat, ludit assidue aleam."

LXXI. Ex quibus sive criminibus sive maledictis infamiam impudicitiae facillime refutavit et praesentis et posterae vitae castitate; item lautitiarum invidiam, cum et Alexandria capta nihil sibi praeter unum murrinum calicem ex instrumento regio retinuerit et mox vasa aurea assiduissimi usus conflaverit omnia. Circa libidines haesit, postea quoque, ut ferunt, ad vitiandas virgines promptior, quae sibi undique etiam ab uxore conquirerentur. Aleae

---

[a] *Corinthiarius*: coined in jest on the analogy of *argentarius*; used in inscr. of slaves in charge of the *vasa Corinthia*.
[b] Cf. chap. xli. 1.

The scandal of this banquet was the greater because of dearth and famine in the land at the time, and on the following day there was an outcry that the gods had eaten all the grain and that Caesar was in truth Apollo, but Apollo the Tormentor, a surname under which the god was worshipped in one part of the city. He was criticized too as over fond of costly furniture and Corinthian bronzes and as given to gaming. Indeed, as early as the time of the proscriptions there was written on his statue—

" In silver once my father dealt, now in Corin-
thians [a] I,"

since it was believed that he caused some men to be entered in the list of the proscribed because of their Corinthian vases. Later, during the Sicilian war, this epigram was current:

"After he has twice been beaten at sea and lost his ships, he plays at dice all the time, in the hope of winning one victory."

LXXI. Of these charges or slanders (whichever we may call them) he easily refuted that for unnatural vice by the purity of his life at the time and afterwards; so too the odium of extravagance by the fact that when he took Alexandria, he kept none of the furniture of the palace for himself [b] except a single agate cup, and presently melted down all the golden vessels intended for everyday use. He could not dispose of the charge of lustfulness and they say that even in his later years he was fond of deflowering maidens, who were brought together for him from all quarters, even by his own wife. He did not in the least

rumorem nullo modo expavit lusitque simpliciter
et palam oblectamenti causa etiam senex ac praeterquam Decembri mense aliis quoque festis et profestis
2 diebus. Nec id dubium est. Autographa quadam
epistula : "Cenavi," ait, "mi Tiberi, cum iisdem ;
accesserunt convivae Vinicius et Silius pater. Inter
cenam lusimus geronticos et heri et hodie ; talis
enim iactatis, ut quisque canem aut senionem
miserat, in singulos talos singulos denarios in
medium conferebat, quos tollebat universos, qui
3 Venerem iecerat." Et rursus aliis litteris : " Nos,
mi Tiberi, Quinquatrus satis iucunde egimus ;
lusimus enim per omnis dies forumque aleatorum [1]
calfecimus. Frater tuus magnis clamoribus rem
gessit ; ad summam tamen perdidit non multum,
sed ex magnis detrimentis praeter spem paulatim
retractum est. Ego perdidi viginti milia nummum
meo nomine, sed cum effuse in lusu liberalis fuissem,
ut soleo plerumque. Nam si quas manus remisi
cuique exegissem aut retinuissem quod cuique
donavi, vicissem vel quinquaginta milia. Sed hoc
malo ; benignitas enim mea me ad caelestem
4 gloriam efferet." Scribit ad filiam : " Misi tibi
denarios ducentos quinquaginta, quos singulis convivis dederam, si vellent inter se inter cenam vel
talis vel par impar ludere."

LXXII. In ceteris partibus vitae continentissimum
constat ac sine suspicione ullius vitii. Habitavit

---

[1] aleatorum, *mss.* ; aleatorium, *Venice ed. of 1420, and the
editors generally.*

[a] When the freedom of the Saturnalia justified it.
[b] When only aces appeared, the throw was called *canis* ;
when all the dice turned up different numbers, *Venus.*
[c] The " five-day " festival of Minerva, March 20–25.

shrink from a reputation for gaming, and played frankly and openly for recreation, even when he was well on in years, not only in the month of December,[a] but on other holidays as well, and on working days too. There is no question about this, for in a letter in his own handwriting he says: "I dined, dear Tiberius, with the same company; we had besides as guests Vinicius and the elder Silius. We gambled like old men during the meal both yesterday and to-day; for when the dice were thrown, whoever turned up the 'dog'[b] or the six, put a denarius in the pool for each one of the dice, and the whole was taken by anyone who threw the 'Venus.'" Again in another letter: "We spent the Quinquatria[c] very merrily, my dear Tiberius, for we played all day long and kept the gaming-board warm. Your brother made a great outcry about his luck, but after all did not come out far behind in the long run; for after losing heavily, he unexpectedly and little by little got back a good deal. For my part, I lost twenty thousand sesterces, but because I was extravagantly generous in my play, as usual. If I had demanded of everyone the stakes which I let go, or had kept all that I gave away, I should have won fully fifty thousand. But I like that better, for my generosity will exalt me to immortal glory." To his daughter he writes: "I send you two hundred and fifty denarii, the sum which I gave each of my guests, in case they wished to play at dice or at odd and even during the dinner."

LXXII. In the other details of his life it is generally agreed that he was most temperate and without even the suspicion of any fault. He lived at first

primo iuxta Romanum Forum supra Scalas anularias,
in domo quae Calvi oratoris fuerat; postea in
Palatio, sed nihilo minus aedibus modicis Horten-
sianis, et neque laxitate neque cultu conspicuis,
ut in quibus porticus breves essent Albanarum
columnarum et sine marmore ullo aut insigni
pavimento conclavia. Ac per annos amplius quadraginta eodem cubiculo hieme et aestate mansit,
quamvis parum salubrem valitudini suae urbem
hieme experiretur assidueque in urbe hiemaret.

2 Si quando quid secreto aut sine interpellatione
agere proposuisset, erat illi locus in edito singularis,
quem Syracusas et technyphion[1] vocabat; huc
transibat aut in alicuius libertorum suburbanum;
aeger autem in domo Maecenatis cubabat. Ex
secessibus praecipue frequentavit maritima insulasque
Campaniae aut proxima urbi oppida, Lanuvium,
Praeneste, Tibur, ubi etiam in porticibus Herculis

3 templi persaepe ius dixit. Ampla et operosa praetoria
gravabatur. Et neptis quidem suae Iuliae, profuse ab
ea exstructa, etiam diruit ad solum, sua vero quamvis
modica non tam statuarum tabularumque pictarum
ornatu quam xystis et nemoribus excoluit rebusque
vetustate ac raritate notabilibus, qualia sunt Capreis
immanium beluarum ferarumque membra praegrandia,
quae dicuntur gigantum ossa, et arma heroum.

LXXIII. Instrumenti eius et supellectilis parsi-
monia apparet etiam nunc residuis lectis atque

---

[1] technyphion (τεχνύφιον), *Bentley*; tegnophion, Ω.

---

[a] Commonly called *peperino*, a hard grey volcanic stone with
black nodules resembling peppercorns. [b] Cf. chap. lxxxii. 1.

[c] With reference to the study of Archimedes, or perhaps
to the general use of such elevated rooms in Syracuse.

[d] "Little workshop"; a diminutive from τέχνη.

near the Forum Romanum, above the Stairs of the
Ringmakers, in a house which had belonged to the
orator Calvus ; afterwards, on the Palatine, but in
the no less modest dwelling of Hortensius, which
was remarkable neither for size nor elegance, having
but short colonnades with columns of Alban stone,[a]
and rooms without any marble decorations or handsome pavements. For more than forty years too he
used the same bedroom in winter and summer ;[b]
although he found the city unfavourable to his
health in the winter, yet continued to winter there.
If ever he planned to do anything in private or
without interruption, he had a retired place at the
top of the house, which he called " Syracuse " [c] and
" technyphion." [d] In this he used to take refuge, or
else in the villa of one of his freedmen in the
suburbs ; but whenever he was not well, he slept
at Maecenas's house. For retirement he went most
frequently to places by the sea and the islands of
Campania, or to the towns near Rome, such as
Lanuvium, Praeneste or Tibur, where he very often
held court in the colonnades of the Temple of
Hercules. He disliked large and sumptuous country
palaces, actually razing to the ground one which his
granddaughter Julia built on a lavish scale. His own
villas, which were modest enough, he decorated not
so much with handsome statues and pictures as with
terraces, groves, and objects noteworthy for their
antiquity and rarity ; for example, at Capreae the
monstrous bones of huge sea monsters and wild
beasts, called the " bones of the giants," and the
weapons of the heroes.

LXXIII. The simplicity of his furniture and household goods may be seen from couches and tables still in

mensis, quorum[1] pleraque vix privatae elegantiae
sint. Ne toro quidem cubuisse aiunt nisi humili
et modice instrato. Veste non temere alia quam
domestica usus est, ab sorore et uxore et filia
neptibusque confecta; togis neque restrictis neque
fusis, clavo nec lato nec angusto, calciamentis altius-
culis, ut procerior quam erat videretur. Et forensia
autem et calceos numquam non intra cubiculum
habuit ad subitos repentinosque casus parata.

LXXIV. Convivabatur assidue nec umquam nisi
recta, non sine magno ordinum hominumque dilectu.
Valerius Messala tradit, neminem umquam liber-
tinorum adhibitum ab eo cenae excepto Mena, sed
asserto in ingenuitatem post proditam Sexti Pompei
classem. Ipse scribit, invitasse se quondam,[2] in
cuius villa maneret, qui speculator suus olim fuisset.
Convivia nonnumquam et serius inibat et maturius
relinquebat, cum convivae et cenare inciperent,
prius quam ille discumberet, et permanerent digresso
eo. Cenam ternis ferculis aut cum abundantissime
senis praebebat, ut non nimio sumptu, ita summa
comitate. Nam et ad communionem sermonis
tacentis vel summissim fabulantis provocabat, et
aut acroamata[3] et histriones aut etiam triviales ex
circo ludios[4] interponebat ac frequentius aretalogos.

---

[1] quorum, *Sabellicus*; quarum, Ω.
[2] quondam] quendam X̄ΠR.
[3] acroamata, *Sabellicus*; acromata, *mss.* (cromata, M^1).
[4] ludios, *Beroaldus*; ludos, *mss.*

---

[a] Opposed to *vestis forensis* or *forensia* (*vestimenta*); cf. *Vit.*
viii. 1.

[b] The *cena recta* was a regular dinner, at which the guests
reclined on couches at a table, contrasted with *sportula*, an in-
formal meal (*Claud.* xxi. 4) or a distribution of food. See Friedländer, *Roman Life and Manners* (Eng. trans.), IV. pp. 77 ff.

existence, many of which are scarcely fine enough for a private citizen. They say that he always slept on a low and plainly furnished bed. Except on special occasions he wore common clothes for the house,[a] made by his sister, wife, daughter or grand-daughters; his togas were neither close nor full, his purple stripe neither narrow nor broad, and his shoes somewhat high-soled, to make him look taller than he really was. But he always kept shoes and clothing to wear in public ready in his room for sudden and unexpected occasions.

LXXIV. He gave dinner parties constantly and always formally,[b] with great regard to the rank and personality of his guests. Valerius Messala writes that he never invited a freedman to dinner with the exception of Menas, and then only when he had been enrolled among the freeborn after betraying the fleet of Sextus Pompey. Augustus himself writes that he once entertained a man at whose villa he used to stop,[c] who had been one of his body-guard. He would sometimes come to table late on these occasions and leave early, allowing his guests to begin to dine before he took his place and keep their places after he went out. He served a dinner of three courses or of six when he was most lavish, without needless extravagance but with the greatest goodfellowship. For he drew into the general conversation those who were silent or chatted under their breath, and introduced music and actors, or even strolling players from the circus, and especially story-tellers.[d]

[c] See chap. lxxii. 2.
[d] Tellers of marvellous tales; cf. Juv. 15. 16, and Mayor *ad loc.* Doubtless the same as the *fabulatores*, lxxviii. 2, below.

LXXV. Festos et sollemnes dies profusissime,
nonnumquam tantum ioculariter celebrabat. Saturnalibus, et si quando alias libuisset, modo munera
dividebat, vestem et aurum et argentum, modo
nummos omnis notae, etiam veteres regios ac
peregrinos, interdum nihil praeter cilicia et spongias
et rutabula et forpices atque alia id genus titulis
obscuris et ambiguis. Solebat et inaequalissimarum
rerum sortes et aversas tabularum picturas in
convivio venditare incertoque casu spem mercantium
vel frustrari vel explere, ita ut per singulos lectos
licitatio fieret et seu iactura seu lucrum communi-
caretur.

LXXVI. Cibi—nam ne haec quidem omiserim
—minimi erat atque vulgaris fere. Secundarium
panem et pisciculos minutos et caseum bibulum [1]
manu pressum et ficos virides biferas maxime
appetebat; vescebaturque et ante cenam quocumque
tempore et loco, quo stomachus desiderasset. Verba
ipsius ex epistulis sunt: " Nos in essedo panem et
2 palmulas gustavimus." Et iterum : " Dum lectica
ex regia domum redeo, panis unciam cum paucis
acinis uvae duracinae comedi." Et rursus : " Ne
Iudaeus quidem, mi Tiberi, tam diligenter sabbatis
ieiunium servat quam ego hodie servavi, qui in balineo
demum post horam primam noctis duas buccas
manducavi prius quam ungui inciperem." Ex hac
inobservantia nonnumquam vel ante initum vel

---

[1] bibulum, Ω ; bubulum, ς and the editors.

[a] See chap. xxxi. 5 ; some think that the reference is to
the Regia in the Forum.
[b] That is, grapes suited for eating and not for making
wine ; cf. Mart. 13. 22 ; Colum. 3. 2.

LXXV. Festivals and holidays he celebrated lavishly as a rule, but sometimes only in a spirit of fun. On the Saturnalia, and at any other time when he took it into his head, he would now give gifts of clothing or gold and silver ; again coins of every device, including old pieces of the kings and foreign money ; another time nothing but hair cloth, sponges, pokers and tongs, and other such things under misleading names of double meaning. He used also at a dinner party to put up for auction lottery-tickets for articles of most unequal value, and paintings of which only the back was shown, thus by the caprice of fortune disappointing or filling to the full the expectations of the purchasers, requiring however that all the guests should take part in the bidding and share the loss or gain.

LXXVI. He was a light eater (for I would not omit even this detail) and as a rule ate of plain food. He particularly liked coarse bread, small fishes, hand-made moist cheese, and green figs of the second crop ; and he would eat even before dinner, wherever and whenever he felt hungry. I quote word for word from some of his letters : "I ate a little bread and some dates in my carriage." And again : "As I was on my homeward way from the Regia[a] in my litter, I devoured an ounce of bread and a few berries from a cluster of hard-fleshed grapes." [b] Once more : "Not even a Jew, my dear Tiberius, fasts so scrupulously on his sabbaths as I have to-day ; for it was not until after the first hour of the night that I ate two mouthfuls of bread in the bath before I began to be anointed." Because of this irregularity he sometimes ate alone either before a dinner party

post dimissum convivium solus cenitabat, cum pleno convivio nihil tangeret.

LXXVII. Vini quoque natura parcissimus erat. Non amplius ter bibere eum solitum super cenam in castris apud Mutinam, Cornelius Nepos tradit. Postea quotiens largissime se invitaret, senos sextantes non excessit, aut si excessisset, reiciebat. Et maxime delectatus est Raetico neque temere interdiu bibit. Pro potione sumebat perfusum aqua frigida panem aut cucumeris frustum vel lactuculae thyrsum aut recens aridumve pomum suci vinosioris.

LXXVIII. Post cibum meridianum, ita ut vestitus calciatusque erat, ·retectis pedibus paulisper conquiescebat opposita ad oculos manu. A cena in lecticulam se lucubratoriam recipiebat; ibi, donec residua diurni actus aut omnia aut ex maxima parte conficeret, ad multam noctem permanebat. In lectum inde transgressus non amplius cum plurimum quam septem horas dormiebat, ac ne eas quidem continuas, sed ut in illo temporis spatio ter aut

2 quater expergisceretur. Si interruptum somnum reciperare, ut evenit, non posset, lectoribus aut fabulatoribus arcessitis resumebat producebatque ultra primam saepe lucem. Nec in tenebris vigilavit umquam nisi assidente aliquo. Matutina vigilia offendebatur; ac si vel officii vel sacri causa maturius vigilandum esset, ne id contra commodum faceret, in proximo cuiuscumque domesticorum cenaculo manebat. Sic quoque saepe indigens somni, et dum

---

^a Like an acid wine.

^b That is, without a blanket over his feet, because he had his shoes on.

^c *Lucubratoriam*, "for working by lamp-light."

began or after it was over, touching nothing while it was in progress.

LXXVII. He was by nature most sparing also in his use of wine. Cornelius Nepos writes that in camp before Mutina it was his habit to drink not more than three times at dinner. Afterwards, when he indulged most freely he never exceeded a pint; or if he did, he used to throw it up. He liked Raetian wine best, but rarely drank before dinner. Instead he would take a bit of bread soaked in cold water, a slice of cucumber, a sprig of young lettuce, or an apple with a tart flavour,[a] either fresh or dried.

LXXVIII. After his midday meal he used to rest for a while just as he was, without taking off his clothes or his shoes, with his feet uncovered[b] and his hand to his eyes. After dinner he went to a couch in his study,[c] where he remained to late at night, until he had attended to what was left of the day's business, either wholly or in great part. Then he went to bed and slept not more than seven hours at most, and not even that length of time without a break, but waking three or four times. If he could not resume his sleep when it was interrupted, as would happen, he sent for readers or story-tellers, and when sleep came to him he often prolonged it until after daylight. He would never lie awake in the dark without having someone sit by his side. He detested early rising and when he had to get up earlier than usual because of some official or religious duty, to avoid inconveniencing himself he spent the night in the room of one of his friends near the appointed place. Even so, he often suffered from want of sleep, and he would drop off while he was being

per vicos deportaretur et deposita lectica inter aliquas
moras condormiebat.

LXXIX. Forma fuit eximia et per omnes aetatis
gradus venustissima, quamquam et omnis lenocinii
neglegens; in capite comendo tam incuriosus, ut
raptim compluribus simul tonsoribus operam daret
ac modo tonderet modo raderet barbam eoque ipso
tempore aut legeret aliquid aut etiam scriberet. Vultu
erat vel in sermone vel tacitus adeo tranquillo
serenoque, ut quidam e primoribus Galliarum confessus sit inter suos, eo se inhibitum ac remollitum
quo minus, ut destinarat, in transitu Alpium per
simulationem conloquii propius admissus in prae-
.2 cipitium propelleret. Oculos habuit claros ac nitidos,
quibus etiam existimari volebat inesse quiddam divini
vigoris, gaudebatque, si qui sibi acrius contuenti
quasi ad fulgorem solis vultum summitteret; sed in
senecta sinistro minus vidit; dentes raros et exiguos
et scabros; capillum leviter inflexum et subflavum;
supercilia coniuncta; mediocres aures; nasum et a
summo eminentiorem et ab imo deductiorem; colorem
inter aquilum candidumque; staturam brevem—
quam tamen Iulius Marathus libertus et a memoria [1]
eius quinque pedum et dodrantis fuisse tradit,—sed
quae commoditate et aequitate membrorum occulere-

---

[1] et a memoria, *Lipsius*; etiam memoriam, etiam in
memoriam, *mss.*

---

[a] The so-called " Roman nose."
[b] Roman measure; a little less than five feet seven inches
(5·58) English.

carried through the streets and when his litter was
set down because of some delay.

LXXIX. He was unusually handsome and exceedingly graceful at all periods of his life, though
he cared nothing for personal adornment. He was
so far from being particular about the dressing of his
hair, that he would have several barbers working in a
hurry at the same time, and as for his beard he now
had it clipped and now shaved, while at the very same
time he would either be reading or writing something.
His expression, whether in conversation or when
he was silent, was so calm and mild, that one of
the leading men of the Gallic provinces admitted
to his countrymen that it had softened his heart,
and kept him from carrying out his design of pushing
the emperor over a cliff, when he had been allowed
to approach him under the pretence of a conference,
as he was crossing the Alps. He had clear, bright
eyes, in which he liked to have it thought that
there was a kind of divine power, and it greatly
pleased him, whenever he looked keenly at anyone,
if he let his face fall as if before the radiance of the
sun ; but in his old age he could not see very well
with his left eye. His teeth were wide apart, small,
and ill-kept ; his hair was slightly curly and inclining
to golden ; his eyebrows met. His ears were of
moderate size, and his nose projected a little at the
top and then bent slightly inward.[a] His complexion
was between dark and fair. He was short of stature
(although Julius Marathus, his freedman and keeper
of his records, says that he was five feet and nine
inches in height [b]), but this was concealed by the
fine proportion and symmetry of his figure, and was

tur, ut non nisi ex comparatione astantis alicuius procerioris intellegi posset.

LXXX. Corpore traditur maculoso dispersis per pectus atque alvum genetivis notis in modum et ordinem ac numerum stellarum caelestis ursae, sed et callis quibusdam ex prurigine corporis adsiduoque et vehementi strigilis usu plurifariam concretis ad impetiginis formam.   Coxendice[1] et femore et crure sinistro non perinde valebat, ut saepe etiam inclaudicaret; sed remedio harenarum atque harundinum confirmabatur.   Dextrae quoque manus digitum salutarem tam imbecillum interdum sentiebat, ut torpentem contractumque frigore vix cornei circuli supplemento scripturae admoveret. Questus est et de vesica, cuius dolore calculis demum per urinam eiectis levabatur.

LXXXI. Graves et periculosas valitudines per omnem vitam aliquot expertus est; praecipue Cantabria domita, cum etiam destillationibus iocinere vitiato ad desperationem redactus contrariam et ancipitem rationem medendi necessario subiit; quia calida fomenta non proderant, frigidis curari coactus auctore Antonio Musa.

2   Quasdam et anniversarias ac tempore certo recurrentes experiebatur; nam sub natalem suum plerumque languebat; et initio veris praecordiorum inflatione temptabatur, austrinis autem tempestatibus gravedine. Quare quassato corpore neque frigora neque aestus facile tolerabat.

---

[1] coxendice] coxaindice, Ω ; *corrected in the fifteenth century.*

[a] Ursa major, Charles's Wain, the Great Dipper.
[b] Apparently a form of poultice ; some read *habenarum* and explain as a kind of truss.   [c] Cf. Hor. *Epist.* 1. 15. 2–3.

noticeable only by comparison with some tall
standing beside him.

LXXX. It is said that his body was cover
spots and that he had birthmarks scattered
breast and belly, corresponding in form, order and
number with the stars of the Bear in the heavens;[a]
also numerous callous places resembling ringworm,
caused by a constant itching of his body and a
vigorous use of the strigil. He was not very strong
in his left hip, thigh, and leg, and even limped
slightly at times; but he strengthened them by
treatment with sand and reeds.[b] He sometimes found
the forefinger of his right hand so weak, when it was
numb and shrunken with the cold, that he could
hardly use it for writing even with the aid of a
finger-stall of horn. He complained of his bladder
too, and was relieved of the pain only after passing
stones in his urine.

LXXXI. In the course of his life he suffered from
several severe and dangerous illnesses, especially
after the subjugation of Cantabria, when he was in   23 B.C.
such a desperate plight from abscesses of the liver,
that he was forced to submit to an unprecedented and
hazardous course of treatment. Since hot fomenta-
tions gave him no relief, he was led by the advice
of his physician Antonius Musa to try cold ones.[c]

He experienced also some disorders which recurred
every year at definite times; for he was commonly
ailing just before his birthday; and at the beginning
of spring he was troubled with an enlargement of
the diaphragm, and when the wind was in the
south, with catarrh. Hence his constitution was so
weakened that he could not readily endure either
cold or heat

LXXXII. Hieme quaternis cum pingui toga tunicis et subucula et thorace[1] laneo et feminalibus et tibialibus muniebatur, aestate apertis cubiculi foribus ac saepe in peristylo saliente aqua atque etiam ventilante aliquo cubabat. Solis vero ne hiberni quidem patiens, domi quoque non nisi petasatus sub divo spatiabatur. Itinera lectica et noctibus fere eaque lenta ac minuta faciebat, ut Praeneste vel Tibur biduo procederet; ac si quo pervenire mari posset,

2 potius navigabat. Verum tantam infirmitatem magna cura tuebatur, in primis lavandi raritate; unguebatur enim saepius aut sudabat ad flammam, deinde perfundebatur egelida aqua vel sole multo tepefacta. At quotiens nervorum causa marinis Albulisque calidis utendum esset, contentus hoc erat ut insidens ligneo solio, quod ipse Hispanico verbo duretam vocabat, manus ac pedes alternis iactaret.

LXXXIII. Exercitationes campestres equorum et armorum statim post civilia bella omisit et ad pilam primo folliculumque transiit, mox nihil aliud quam vectabatur et deambulabat, ita ut in extremis spatiis subsultim decurreret segestria[2] vel lodicula involutus. Animi laxandi causa modo piscabatur hamo, modo talis aut ocellatis nucibusque ludebat cum

---

[1] subucula et thorace, *Beroaldus*; subuculaethorace, Ω.
[2] segestria, *Roth* (segestro, *Cuiacius*); sestertio, *mss.*

---

[a] Cf. chap. lxxii. 1, note *b*.
[b] *Albulae aquae* were the sulphur springs which flow into the Anio between Rome and Tivoli (Tibur).
[c] The *pila* was a small hard ball. Three players stood at the three points of a triangle (whence the game was called *trigon*) and passed the ball from one to the other. A skilful player used his left hand as well as his right.

LXXXII. In winter he protected himself with four tunics and a heavy toga, besides an undershirt, a woollen chest-protector and wraps for his thighs and shins, while in summer he slept with the doors of his bed-room open, oftentimes in the open court near a fountain, besides having someone to fan him.[a] Yet he could not endure the sun even in winter, and never walked in the open air without wearing a broad-brimmed hat, even at home. He travelled in a litter, usually at night, and by such slow and easy stages that he took two days to go to Praeneste or Tibur ; and if he could reach his destination by sea, he preferred to sail. Yet in spite of all he made good his weakness by great care, especially by moderation in bathing ; for as a rule he was anointed or took a sweat by a fire, after which he was doused with water either lukewarm or tepid from long exposure to the sun. When however he had to use hot salt water and sulphur baths [b] for rheumatism, he contented himself with sitting on a wooden bath-seat, which he called by the Spanish name *dureta*, and plunging his hands and feet in the water one after the other.

LXXXIII. Immediately after the civil war he gave up exercise with horses and arms in the Campus Martius, at first turning to pass-ball [c] and balloon-ball,[d] but soon confining himself to riding or taking a walk, ending the latter by running and leaping, wrapped in a mantle or a blanket. To divert his mind he sometimes angled and sometimes played at dice, marbles and nuts [e] with little boys, searching

[d] The *folliculus* was a large light ball. The players wore a guard on the right arm, with which they struck the ball, as in the Italian *gioco del pallone*.

[e] Many games were played with nuts ; cf. Hor. *Serm.* 2. 3. 171, Mart. 5. 84, etc.

pueris minutis, quos facie et garrulitate amabilis undique conquirebat, praecipue Mauros et Syros. Nam pumilos atque distortos et omnis generis eiusdem ut ludibria naturae malique ominis abhorrebat.

LXXXIV. Eloquentiam studiaque liberalia ab aetate prima et cupide et laboriosissime exercuit. Mutinensi bello in tanta mole rerum et legisse et scripsisse et declamasse cotidie traditur. Nam deinceps neque in senatu neque apud populum neque apud milites locutus est umquam nisi meditata et composita oratione, quamvis non deficeretur ad subita 2 extemporali facultate. Ac ne periculum memoriae adiret aut in ediscendo tempus absumeret,[1] instituit recitare omnia. Sermones quoque cum singulis atque etiam cum Livia sua graviores non nisi scriptos [2] et e libello habebat, ne plus minusve loqueretur ex tempore. Pronuntiabat dulci et proprio quodam oris sono dabatque assidue phonasco operam ; sed nonnumquam infirmatis faucibus praeconis voce ad populum contionatus est.

LXXXV. Multa varii generis prosa oratione composuit, ex quibus nonnulla in coetu familiarium velut in auditorio recitavit, sicut " Rescripta Bruto de Catone," quae volumina cum iam senior ex magna parte legisset, fatigatus Tiberio tradidit perlegenda ; item " Hortationes ad Philosophiam," et aliqua " De

---

[1] absumeret, $S^2 \varsigma$; assumeret (adsumeret), Ω.
[2] scriptos, ς ; scriptis, Ω.

---

[a] See chap. lxxxi. at the end.
[b] Brutus published a eulogy of Cato in 46 B.C. ; cf. Cic. ad Att. 12. 21.

everywhere for such as were attractive for their pretty faces or their prattle, especially Syrians and Moors; for he abhorred dwarfs, cripples, and everything of that sort, as freaks of nature and of ill omen.

LXXXIV. From early youth he devoted himself eagerly and with the utmost diligence to oratory and liberal studies. During the war at Mutina, amid such a press of affairs, he is said to have read, written and declaimed every day. In fact he never afterwards spoke in the senate, or to the people or the soldiers, except in a studied and written address, although he did not lack the gift of speaking offhand without preparation. Moreover, to avoid the danger of forgetting what he was to say, or wasting time in committing it to memory, he adopted the practice of reading everything from a manuscript. Even his conversations with individuals and the more important of those with his own wife Livia, he always wrote out and read from a note-book, for fear of saying too much or too little if he spoke offhand. He had an agreeable and rather characteristic enunciation, and he practised constantly with a teacher of elocution; but sometimes because of weakness of the throat [a] he addressed the people through a herald.

LXXXV. He wrote numerous works of various kinds in prose, some of which he read to a group of his intimate friends, as others did in a lecture-room; for example, his "Reply to Brutus on Cato." [b] At the reading of these volumes he had all but come to the end, when he grew tired and handed them to Tiberius to finish, for he was well on in years. He also wrote "Exhortations to Philosophy"

Vita Sua," quam tredecim libris Cantabrico tenus
2 bello nec ultra exposuit.   Poetica summatim attigit.
Unus liber exstat scriptus ab eo hexametris versibus,
cuius et argumentum et titulus est " Sicilia " ; exstat
alter aeque modicus " Epigrammatum," quae fere
tempore balinei meditabatur. Nam tragoediam magno
impetu exorsus,   non   succedenti   stilo, abolevit
quaerentibusque   amicis,   quidnam   Aiax   ageret,
respondit Aiacem suum in spongiam incubuisse.

LXXXVI. Genus eloquendi secutus est elegans et
temperatum vitatis sententiarum ineptiis atque con-
cinnitate et " reconditorum verborum," ut ipse dicit,
" fetoribus " ; praecipuamque curam duxit sensum
animi quam apertissime exprimere.   Quod quo
facilius efficeret aut necubi lectorem vel auditorem
obturbaret ac moraretur, neque praepositiones urbi-
bus addere neque coniunctiones saepius iterare
dubitavit, quae detractae afferunt aliquid obscuritatis,
2 etsi gratiam augent.   Cacozelos et antiquarios, ut
diverso genere vitiosos, pari fastidio sprevit exagita-
batque nonnumquam ; in primis Maecenatem suum,
cuius "myrobrechis," ut ait, "cincinnos " usque quaque persequitur et imitando per iocum irridet.   Sed
nec Tiberio parcit et exoletas interdum et reconditas
voces aucupanti.   M. quidem Antonium ut insanum
increpat, quasi ea scribentem, quae mirentur potius

and some volumes of an Autobiography, giving an account of his life in thirteen books up to the time of the Cantabrian war, but no farther. His essays in poetry were but slight. One book has come down to us written in hexameter verse, of which the subject and the title is "Sicily." There is another, equally brief, of "Epigrams," which he composed for the most part at the time of the bath. Though he began a tragedy with much enthusiasm, he destroyed it because his style did not satisfy him, and when some of his friends asked him what in the world had become of Ajax, he answered that "his Ajax had fallen on his sponge."

LXXXVI. He cultivated a style of speaking that was chaste and elegant, avoiding the vanity of attempts at epigram and an artificial order, and as he himself expresses it, "the noisomeness of far-fetched words," making it his chief aim to express his thought as clearly as possible. With this end in view, to avoid confusing and checking his reader or hearer at any point, he did not hesitate to use prepositions with names of cities, nor to repeat conjunctions several times, the omission of which causes some obscurity, though it adds grace. He looked on innovators and archaizers with equal contempt, as faulty in opposite directions, and he sometimes had a fling at them, in particular his friend Maecenas, whose "unguent-dripping curls," as he calls them, he loses no opportunity of belabouring and pokes fun at them by parody. He did not spare even Tiberius, who sometimes hunted up obsolete and pedantic expressions; and as for Mark Antony, he calls him a madman, for writing rather to be admired than to be understood. Then

homines quam intellegant; deinde ludens malum et inconstans in eligendo genere dicendi iudicium[1] eius,

3 addit haec: " Tuque dubitas, Cimberne Annius an Veranius Flaccus imitandi sint tibi, ita ut verbis, quae Crispus Sallustius excerpsit ex Originibus Catonis, utaris? An potius Asiaticorum oratorum inanis sententiis verborum volubilitas in nostrum sermonem transferenda?" Et quadam epistula Agrippinae neptis ingenium conlaudans: " Sed opus est," inquit, "dare te operam, ne moleste scribas et loquaris."

LXXXVII. Cotidiano sermone quaedam frequentius et notabiliter usurpasse eum, litterae ipsius autographae ostentant, in quibus identidem, cum aliquos numquam soluturos significare vult, " ad Kalendas Graecas soluturos" ait; et cum hortatur ferenda esse praesentia, qualiacumque sint: " contenti simus hoc Catone"; et ad exprimendam festinatae rei velocitatem: " celerius quam asparagi

2 cocuntur." Ponit assidue et pro stulto "baceolum" et pro pullo[2] "pulleiaceum" et pro cerrito "vacerrosum" et " vapide" se habere pro male et " betizare" pro languere, quod vulgo " lachanizare" dicitur; item " simus" pro sumus et " domos" genetivo casu sin-

---

[1] iudicium, *Bentley* ; ingenium, Υ; *omitted by the other mss.*   [2] et pro pullo, *S⊊* ; apud pullum, Ω.

---

[a] Evidently two archaizing grammarians of the day.

[b] See *De Grammaticis*, x, at the end.

[c] Thus characterized in contrast with the studied simplicity of the Attic school of orators.   [d] See Index.

[e] Cf. Catull. 67. 21, *languidior tenera beta*. All these words, which Augustus is said to have used, are colloquialisms or

going on to ridicule his perverse and inconsistent taste in choosing an oratorical style, he adds the following: "Can you doubt whether you ought to imitate Annius Cimber or Veranius Flaccus,*a* that you use the words which Sallustius Crispus gleaned from Cato's *Origines*?*b* Or would you rather introduce into our tongue the verbose and unmeaning fluency of the Asiatic orators?"*c* And in a letter praising the talent of his granddaughter Agrippina he writes: "But you must take great care not to write and talk affectedly."

LXXXVII. That in his everyday conversation he used certain favourite and peculiar expressions appears from letters in his own hand, in which he says every now and then, when he wishes to indicate that certain men will never pay, that "they will pay on the Greek Kalends." Urging his correspondent to put up with present circumstances, such as they are, he says: "Let's be satisfied with the Cato we have;"*d* and to express the speed of a hasty action, "Quicker than you can cook asparagus." He continually used *baceolus* (dolt) for *stultus* (fool), for *pullus* (dark) *pulleiaceus* (darkish), and for *cerritus* (mad) *vacerrosus* (blockhead); also *vapide se habere* (feel flat) for *male se habere* (feel badly), and *betizare*/*e* (be like a beet) for *languere* (be weak), for which the vulgar term is *lachanizare*. Besides he used *simus* for *sumus*/*f* and *domos* in the genitive

slang, and the exact form and derivation of many of them are uncertain.

f Since *sumus* was originally enclitic, the forms *simus*, *sumus* may have represented the sound between *u* and *i* in *maximus*, *maxumus*, etc. Or *simus* may have been formed on the analogy of *agimus* and similar forms.

gulari pro domuos.ᵃ Nec umquam aliter haec duo, ne quis mendam magis quam consuetudinem putet.

3 Notavi et in chirographo eius illa praecipue : non dividit verba nec ab extrema parte versuum abundantis litteras in alterum transfert, sed ibidem statim subicit circumducitque.

LXXXVIII. Orthographiam, id est formulam rationemque scribendi a grammaticis institutam, non adeo custodit ac videtur eorum potius sequi opinionem, qui perinde scribendum ac loquamur existiment. Nam quod saepe non litteras modo sed syllabas aut permutat aut praeterit, communis hominum error est. Nec ego id notarem, nisi mihi mirum videretur tradidisse aliquos, legato eum consulari successorem dedisse ut rudi et indocto, cuius manu " ixi " pro " ipsi " scriptum animadverterit. Quotiens autem per notas scribit, B pro A, C pro B ac deinceps eadem ratione sequentis litteras ponit ; pro X autem duplex A.

LXXXIX. Ne Graecarum quidem disciplinarum leviore studio tenebatur. In quibus et ipsis praestabat largiter magistro dicendi usus Apollodoro Pergameno, quem iam grandem natu Apolloniam quoque secum ab urbe iuvenis adhuc eduxerat, deinde eruditione etiam varia repletus per Arei[1] philosophi filiorumque eius Dionysi et Nicanoris contubernium ; non tamen ut aut loqueretur expedite aut componere aliquid auderet ; nam et si quid res

---

[1] per Arei, *Salmasius*; sperarei, *MGVϒ*; *omitted by X.*

ᵃ *Domuos* is the earlier form of the genitive, with the suffix *-os*, *domus* the later, with the suffix *-s*. There was no form *domos*, and if Augustus used it, he probably did so on the analogy of *domos*, *domus* in the acc. plur.

ᵇ Cf. *Jul.* lvi. 6–7, and Aul. Gell. 17. 9. 1–5.

singular instead of *domuos.*[a] The last two forms he
wrote invariably, for fear they should be thought
errors rather than a habit.

I have also observed this special peculiarity in
his manner of writing: he does not divide words
or carry superfluous letters from the end of one
line to the beginning of the next, but writes them
just below the rest of the word and draws a loop
around them.

LXXXVIII. He does not strictly comply with
orthography, that is to say the theoretical rules
of spelling laid down by the grammarians, seeming
to be rather of the mind of those who believe that
we should spell exactly as we pronounce. Of course
his frequent transposition or omission of syllables
as well as of letters are slips common to all
mankind. I should not have noted this, did it not
seem to me surprising that some have written that
he cashiered a consular governor, as an uncultivated
and ignorant fellow, because he observed that he
had written *ixi* for *ipsi.* Whenever he wrote in
cipher,[b] he wrote B for A, C for B, and the rest
of the letters on the same principle, using AA for X.

LXXXIX. He was equally interested in Greek
studies, and in these too he excelled greatly. His
teacher of declamation was Apollodorus of Per-
gamon, whom he even took with him in his youthful
days from Rome to Apollonia, though Apollodorus
was an old man at the time. Later he became
versed in various forms of learning through association
with the philosopher Areus and his sons Dionysius
and Nicanor. Yet he never acquired the ability
to speak Greek fluently or to compose anything
in it; for if he had occasion to use the language,

exigeret, Latine formabat vertendumque alii dabat. Sed plane poematum quoque non imperitus, delectabatur etiam comoedia veteri et saepe eam exhibuit

2 spectaculis publicis. In evolvendis utriusque linguae auctoribus nihil aeque sectabatur, quam praecepta et exempla publice vel privatim salubria, eaque ad verbum excerpta aut ad domesticos aut ad exercituum provinciarumque rectores aut ad urbis magistratus plerumque mittebat, prout quique monitione indigerent. Etiam libros totos et senatui recitavit et populo notos per edictum saepe fecit, ut orationes Q. Metelli " de Prole Augenda" et Rutili " de Modo Aedificiorum," quo magis persuaderet utramque rem non a se primo animadversam, sed antiquis iam tunc curae fuisse.

3 Ingenia saeculi sui omnibus modis fovit. Recitantis et benigne et patienter audiit, nec tantum carmina et historias, sed et orationes et dialogos. Componi tamen aliquid de se nisi et serio et a praestantissimis offendebatur, admonebatque praetores ne paterentur nomen suum commissionibus obsolefieri.

XC. Circa religiones talem accepimus. Tonitrua et fulgura paulo infirmius expavescebat, ut semper et ubique pellem vituli marini circumferret pro remedio atque ad omnem maioris tempestatis suspicionem in

---

a Religiones includes both religious belief and regard for omens and portents.

he wrote what he had to say in Latin and gave it to someone else to translate. Still he was far from being ignorant of Greek poetry, even taking great pleasure in the Old Comedy and frequently staging it at his public entertainments. In reading the writers of both tongues there was nothing for which he looked so carefully as precepts and examples instructive to the public or to individuals; these he would often copy word for word, and send to the members of his household, or to his generals and provincial governors, whenever any of them required admonition. He even read entire volumes to the senate and called the attention of the people to them by proclamations; for example, the speeches of Quintus Metellus "On Increasing the Family," and of Rutilius "On the Height of Buildings"; to convince them that he was not the first to give attention to such matters, but that they had aroused the interest even of their forefathers.

He gave every encouragement to the men of talent of his own age, listening with courtesy and patience to their readings, not only of poetry and history, but of speeches and dialogues as well. But he took offence at being made the subject of any composition except in serious earnest and by the most eminent writers, often charging the praetors not to let his name be cheapened in prize declamations.

XC. This is what we are told of his attitude towards matters of religion.[a] He was somewhat weak in his fear of thunder and lightning, for he always carried a seal-skin about with him everywhere as a protection, and at any sign of a violent storm took refuge in an underground

abditum et concamaratum locum se reciperet, consternatus olim per nocturnum iter transcursu fulguris, ut praediximus.

XCI. Somnia neque sua neque aliena de se neglegebat. Philippensi acie quamvis statuisset non egredi tabernaculo propter valitudinem, egressus est tamen amici somnio monitus ; cessitque res prospere, quando captis castris lectica eius, quasi ibi cubans remansisset, concursu hostium confossa atque lacerata est. Ipse per omne ver plurima et formidulosissima et vana et irrita videbat, reliquo tempore rariora et minus vana. Cum dedicatam in Capitolio aedem Tonanti Iovi assidue frequentaret, somniavit queri Capitolinum Iovem cultores sibi abduci seque respondisse Tonantem pro ianitore ei appositum ; ideoque mox tintinnabulis fastigium aedis redimiit, quod ea fere ianuis dependebant. Ex nocturno visu etiam stipem quotannis die certo emendicabat a populo cavam manum asses porrigentibus praebens.

2

XCII. Auspicia et omina quaedam pro certissimis observabat : si mane sibi calceus perperam ac sinister pro dextro induceretur, ut dirum ; si terra marive ingrediente se longinquam profectionem forte rorasset,

---

[a] Pliny, *N. H.* 2. 55, says that the laurel tree (cf. *Tib.* lxix.) and the seal are never struck by lightning ; and also that lightning never goes more than five feet below the ground.

[b] Chap. xxix. 3.

[c] This is not in accordance with the emperor's character (cf. chap. lvii), and Suetonius may have confused him with Caligula ; see *Calig.* xlii. Yet there are records of many such acts of humility to propitiate Nemesis ; see Casaubon *ad loc.*

vaulted room;[a] for as I have said,[b] he was once badly frightened by a narrow escape from lightning during a journey by night.

XCI. He was not indifferent to his own dreams or to those which others dreamed about him. At the battle of Philippi, though he had made up his mind not to leave his tent because of illness, he did so after all when warned by a friend's dream; fortunately, as it turned out, for his camp was taken and when the enemy rushed in, his litter was stabbed through and through and torn to pieces, in the belief that he was still lying there ill. All through the spring his own dreams were very numerous and fearful, but idle and unfulfilled; during the rest of the year they were less frequent and more reliable. Being in the habit of making constant visits to the temple of Jupiter the Thunderer, which he had founded on the Capitol, he dreamed that Jupiter Capitolinus complained that his worshippers were being taken from him, and that he answered that he had placed the Thunderer hard by to be his doorkeeper; and accordingly he presently festooned the gable of the temple with bells, because these commonly hung at house-doors. It was likewise because of a dream that every year on an appointed day he begged alms of the people, holding out his open hand to have pennies dropped in it.[c]

XCII. Certain auspices and omens he regarded as infallible. If his shoes were put on in the wrong way in the morning, the left instead of the right, he considered it a bad sign. If there chanced to be a drizzle of rain when he was starting on a long journey by land or sea, he thought it a good omen, betoken-

ut laetum maturique et prosperi reditus. Sed et ostentis praecipue movebatur. Enatam inter iuncturas lapidum ante domum suam palmam in conpluvium deorum Penatium transtulit, utque coales-

2 ceret magno opere curavit. Apud insulam Capreas veterrimae ilicis demissos iam ad terram languentisque ramos convaluisse adventu suo, adeo laetatus est, ut eas cum re p. Neapolitanorum permutaverit Aenaria data. Observabat et dies quosdam, ne aut postridie nundinas quoquam proficisceretur aut Nonis quicquam rei seriae incoharet; nihil in hoc quidem aliud devitans, ut ad Tiberium scribit, quam δυσφημίαν nominis.

XCIII. Peregrinarum caerimoniarum sicut veteres ac praeceptas reverentissime coluit, ita ceteras contemptui habuit. Namque Athenis initiatus, cum postea Romae pro tribunali de privilegio sacerdotum Atticae Cereris cognosceret et quaedam secretiora proponerentur, dimisso consilio et corona circumstantium solus audiit disceptantes. At contra non modo in peragranda Aegypto paulo deflectere ad visendum Apin supersedit, sed et Gaium nepotem, quod Iudaeam praetervehens apud Hierosolyma[1] non supplicasset, conlaudavit.

XCIV. Et quoniam ad haec ventum est, non ab re fuerit subtexere, quae ei prius quam nasceretur et ipso natali die ac deinceps evenerint, quibus futura

[1] Hierosolyma, *Burmann*; Hierosolymam, *mss.*

---

[a] The Roman month was divided into periods of eight days, lettered in the Calendar from A to H. The last of these, every ninth day (*nundinae*) according to the Roman reckoning, was a market day.

[b] Because of its resemblance to *non is* (from *eo*); cf. Cic. *de Div.* 284; or perhaps merely because it contained *non*.

[c] Into the Eleusinian mysteries of Ceres.

ing a speedy and prosperous return. But he was especially affected by prodigies. When a palm tree sprang up between the crevices of the pavement before his house, he transplanted it to the inner court beside his household gods and took great pains to make it grow. He was so pleased that the branches of an old oak, which had already drooped to the ground and were withering, became vigorous again on his arrival in the island of Capreae, that he arranged with the city of Naples to give him the island in exchange for Aenaria. He also had regard to certain days, refusing ever to begin a journey on the day after a market day,[a] or to take up any important business on the Nones; though in the latter case, as he writes Tiberius, he merely dreaded the unlucky sound [b] of the name.

XCIII. He treated with great respect such foreign rites as were ancient and well established, but held the rest in contempt. For example, having been initiated at Athens[c] and afterwards sitting in judgment of a case at Rome involving the privileges of the priests of Attic Ceres, in which certain matters of secrecy were brought up, he dismissed his councillors and the throng of bystanders and heard the disputants in private. But on the other hand he not only omitted to make a slight detour to visit Apis, when he was travelling through Egypt, but highly commended his grandson Gaius for not offering prayers at Jerusalem as he passed by Judaea.

XCIV. Having reached this point, it will not be out of place to add an account of the omens which occurred before he was born, on the very day of his birth, and afterwards, from which it was

magnitudo eius et perpetua felicitas sperari animadvertique posset.

2   Velitris antiquitus tacta de caelo parte muri responsum est eius oppidi civem quandoque rerum potiturum ; qua fiducia Veliterni et tunc statim et postea saepius paene ad exitium sui cum populo R. belligeraverant ; sero tandem documentis apparuit ostentum illud Augusti potentiam portendisse.

3   Auctor est Iulius Marathus, ante paucos quam nasceretur menses prodigium Romae factum publice, quo denuntiabatur, regem populo Romano naturam parturire ; senatum exterritum censuisse, ne quis illo anno genitus educaretur ; eos qui gravidas uxores haberent, quod ad se quisque spem traheret, curasse ne senatus consultum ad aerarium deferretur.

4   In Asclepiadis Mendetis Theologumenon libris lego, Atiam, cum ad sollemne Apollinis sacrum media nocte venisset, posita in templo lectica, dum ceterae matronae dormirent,[1] obdormisse ; draconem repente irrepsisse ad eam pauloque post egressum ; illam expergefactam quasi a concubitu mariti purificasse se ; et statim in corpore eius exstitisse maculam velut picti draconis nec potuisse umquam

---

[1] Dormirent, *mss.* ; domum irent, *Gaevius* ; convenirent, *Bentley* ; <domi> dormirent, *Wissowa* ; *etc., etc.*

---

[a] The decree was not complete until this was done ; cf. *Jul.* xxviii. 3.

[b] *i.e.* "Discourses about the Gods." Aristotle wrote a work with the same title.

[c] The *genius*, or familiar spirit (see note on chap. lx.), was

possible to anticipate and perceive his future greatness and uninterrupted good fortune.

In ancient days, when a part of the wall of Velitrae had been struck by lightning, the prediction was made that a citizen of that town would one day rule the world. Through their confidence in this the people of Velitrae had at once made war on the Roman people and fought with them many times after that almost to their utter destruction; but at last long afterward the event proved that the omen had foretold the rule of Augustus.

According to Julius Marathus, a few months before Augustus was born a portent was generally observed at Rome, which gave warning that nature was pregnant with a king for the Roman people; thereupon the senate in consternation decreed that no male child born that year should be reared; but those whose wives were with child saw to it that the decree was not filed in the treasury,[a] since each one appropriated the prediction to his own family.

I have read the following story in the books of Asclepias of Mendes entitled *Theologumena*.[b] When Atia had come in the middle of the night to the solemn service of Apollo, she had her litter set down in the temple and fell asleep, while the rest of the matrons also slept. On a sudden a serpent[c] glided up to her and shortly went away. When she awoke, she purified herself,[d] as if after the embraces of her husband, and at once there appeared on her body a mark in colours like a serpent, and she could never get rid of it; so that presently she ceased

often represented by a serpent, and those of husband and wife by two serpents; *e. g.* in Pompeian frescoes.
[d] To avoid profanation of the sacred rites.

exigi, adeo ut mox publicis balineis perpetuo
abstinuerit; Augustum natum mense decimo et ob
hoc Apollinis filium existimatum. Eadem Atia,
prius quam pareret, somniavit intestina sua ferri ad
sidera explicarique per omnem terrarum et caeli
ambitum. Somniavit et pater Octavius utero Atiae
iubar solis exortum.

5 Quo natus est die, cum de Catilinae coniuratione
ageretur in curia et Octavius ob uxoris puerperium
serius affuisset, nota ac vulgata res est P. Nigidium
comperta morae causa, ut horam quoque partus ac-
ceperit, affirmasse dominum terrarum orbi natum.
Octavio postea, cum per secreta Thraciae exercitum
duceret, in Liberi patris luco barbara caerimonia de
filio consulenti, idem affirmatum est a sacerdotibus,
quod infuso super altaria mero tantum flammae[1]
emicuisset, ut supergressa fastigium templi ad caelum
usque ferretur, unique omnino Magno Alexandro
apud easdem aras sacrificanti simile provenisset
6 ostentum. Atque etiam sequenti statim nocte videre
visus est filium mortali specie ampliorem, cum fulmine et sceptro exuviisque Iovis Optimi Maximi ac
radiata corona, super laureatum currum, bis senis
equis candore eximio trahentibus. Infans adhuc, ut
scriptum apud C. Drusum exstat, repositus vespere
in cunas a nutricula loco plano, postera luce non

[1] flammae, *mss.*; flamma, *Modderman*.

---

a Otherwise unknown; Müller would read *Caesarem
Drusum.* Stahr believes that the reference is to the Eulogy
in chap. c. 3.

ever to go to the public baths. In the tenth month
after that Augustus was born and was therefore
regarded as the son of Apollo. Atia too, before she
gave him birth, dreamed that her vitals were borne
up to the stars and spread over the whole extent of
land and sea, while Octavius dreamed that the sun
rose from Atia's womb.

The day he was born the conspiracy of Catiline
was before the House, and Octavius came late
because of his wife's confinement; then Publius
Nigidius, as everyone knows, learning the reason for
his tardiness and being informed also of the hour of
the birth, declared that the ruler of the world had
been born. Later, when Octavius was leading an
army through remote parts of Thrace, and in the
grove of Father Liber consulted the priests about his
son with barbarian rites, they made the same prediction; since such a pillar of flame sprang forth
from the wine that was poured over the altar, that it
rose above the temple roof and mounted to the very
sky, and such an omen had befallen no one save
Alexander the Great, when he offered sacrifice at
the same altar. Moreover, the very next night he
dreamt that his son appeared to him in a guise more
majestic than that of mortal man, with the thunderbolt, sceptre, and insignia of Jupiter Optimus Maximus, wearing a crown begirt with rays and mounted
upon a laurel-wreathed chariot drawn by twelve
horses of surpassing whiteness. When Augustus was
still an infant, as is recorded by the hand of Gaius
Drusus,[a] he was placed by his nurse at evening in
his cradle on the ground floor and the next morning
had disappeared; but after long search he was at

comparuit diuque quaesitus tandem in altissima turri repertus est iacens contra solis exortum.

7   Cum primum fari coepisset, in avito suburbano obstrepentis forte ranas silere iussit, atque ex eo negantur ibi ranae coaxare. Ad quartum lapidem Campanae viae in nemore prandenti ex inproviso aquila panem ei e manu rapuit et, cum altissime evolasset, rursus ex inproviso leniter delapsa reddidit.

8   Q. Catulus post dedicatum Capitolium duabus continuis noctibus somniavit: prima, Iovem Optimum Maximum e praetextatis compluribus circum aram ludentibus unum secrevisse atque in eius sinum signum rei p. quod manu gestaret reposuisse; at insequenti, animadvertisse se in gremio Capitolini Iovis eundem puerum, quem cum detrahi iussisset, prohibitum monitu dei, tamquam is ad tutelam rei p. educaretur; ac die proximo obvium sibi Augustum, cum incognitum alias haberet, non sine admiratione contuitus simillimum dixit puero, de quo somniasset. Quidam prius somnium Catuli aliter exponunt, quasi Iuppiter compluribus praetextatis tutorem a se poscentibus unum ex eis demonstrasset, ad quem omnia desideria sua referrent, eiusque osculum delibatum digitis ad os suum rettulisset.

9   M. Cicero C. Caesarem in Capitolium prosecutus somnium pristinae noctis familiaribus forte narrabat:

---

a Apparently another name for the via Appia; see *C.I.L.* i. 1291.
b Instead of kissing him directly.   c See note on *Jul.* xv.
268

last found lying on a lofty tower with his face towards
the rising sun.

As soon as he began to talk, it chanced that the
frogs were making a great noise at his grandfather's
country place; he bade them be silent, and they say
that since then no frog has ever croaked there. As
he was lunching in a grove at the fourth milestone
on the Campanian road,[a] an eagle surprised him by
snatching his bread from his hand, and after flying
to a great height, equally to his surprise dropped
gently down again and gave it back to him.

After Quintus Catulus had dedicated the Capitol,
he had dreams on two nights in succession: first,
that Jupiter Optimus Maximus called aside one of a
number of boys of good family, who were playing
around his alter, and put in the fold of his toga
an image of Roma, which he was carrying in his
hand; the next night he dreamt that he saw this
same boy in the lap of Jupiter of the Capitol, and
that when he had ordered that he be removed, the
god warned him to desist, declaring that the boy was
being reared to be the saviour of his country. When
Catulus next day met Augustus, whom he had never
seen before, he looked at him in great surprise and
said that he was very like the boy of whom he
had dreamed.

Some give a different account of Catulus's first
dream: when a large group of well-born children
asked Jupiter for a guardian, he pointed out one of
their number, to whom they were to refer all their
wishes, and then, after lightly touching the boy's
mouth with his fingers, laid them on his own lips.[b]

As Marcus Cicero was attending Gaius Caesar
to the Capitol,[c] he happened to tell his friends a

puerum facie liberali demissum e caelo catena aurea
ad fores Capitoli constitisse eique Iovem flagellum
tradidisse ; deinde repente Augusto viso, quem
ignotum plerisque adhuc avunculus Caesar ad sacri-
ficandum acciverat, affirmavit ipsum esse, cuius
imago secundum quietem sibi obversata sit.

10   Sumenti virilem togam tunica lati clavi resuta ex
utraque parte ad pedes decidit.   Fuerunt qui inter-
pretarentur, non aliud significare, quam ut is ordo
cuius insigne id esset quandoque ei subiceretur.

11   Apud Mundam Divus Iulius castris locum capiens
cum silvam caederet, arborem palmae repertam con-
servari ut omen victoriae iussit ; ex ea continuo
enata suboles adeo in paucis diebus adolevit, ut non
aequiperaret modo matricem, verum et obtegeret
frequentareturque columbarum nidis, quamvis id
avium genus duram et asperam frondem maxime
vitet.   Illo et praecipue ostento motum Caesarem
ferunt, ne quem alium sibi succedere quam sororis
nepotem vellet.

12   In secessu Apolloniae Theogenis mathematici per-
gulam comite Agrippa ascenderat ; cum Agrippae,
qui prior consulebat, magna et paene incredibilia
praedicerentur, reticere ipse genituram suam nec
velle edere perseverabat, metu ac pudore ne minor
inveniretur.   Qua tamen post multas adhortationes

---

a Marked by the broad purple stripe (*latus clavus*).
Augustus was not yet a senator, but the privilege of wearing
the laticlave was doubtless one of the honours conferred on
him by Caesar.

270

dream ot the night before ; that a boy of noble countenance was let down from heaven on a golden chain and, standing at the door of the temple, was given a whip by Jupiter. Just then suddenly catching sight of Augustus, who was still unknown to the greater number of those present and had been brought to the ceremony by his uncle Caesar, he declared that he was the very one whose form had appeared to him in his dream.

When Augustus was assuming the gown of manhood, his senatorial tunic [a] was ripped apart on both sides and fell at his feet, which some interpreted as a sure sign that the order of which the tunic was the badge would one day be brought to his feet.

As the Deified Julius was cutting down a wood at Munda and preparing a place for his camp, coming across a palm tree, he caused it to be spared as an omen of victory. From this a shoot at once sprang forth and in a few days grew so great that it not only equalled the parent tree, but even overshadowed it ; moreover many doves built their nests there, although that kind of bird especially avoids hard and rough foliage. Indeed, it was that omen in particular, they say, that led Caesar to wish that none other than his sister's grandson should be his successor

While in retirement at Apollonia, Augustus mounted with Agrippa to the studio of the astrologer Theogenes. Agrippa was the first to try his fortune, and when a great and almost incredible career was predicted for him, Augustus persisted in concealing the time of his birth and in refusing to disclose it, through diffidence and fear that he might be found to be less eminent. When he at last gave it unwillingly and hesitatingly, and

vix et cunctanter edita exsilivit Theogenes adoravit-
que eum. Tantam mox fiduciam fati Augustus
habuit, ut thema suum vulgaverit nummumque
argenteum nota sideris Capricorni, quo natus est,
percusserit.

XCV. Post necem Caesaris reverso ab Apollonia
et ingrediente eo urbem repente liquido ac puro
sereno circulus ad speciem caelestis arcus orbem solis
ambiit ac subinde Iuliae Caesaris filiae monimentum
fulmine ictum est. Primo autem consulatu et
augurium capienti duodecim se vultures ut Romulo
ostenderunt et immolanti omnium victimarum
iocinera replicata intrinsecus ab ima fibra paruerunt,
nemine peritorum aliter coniectante quam laeta per
haec et magna portendi.

XCVI. Quin et bellorum omnium eventus ante
praesensit. Contractis ad Bononiam triumvirorum
copiis aquila tentorio eius supersedens duos corvos
hinc et inde infestantis afflixit et ad terram dedit,
notante omni exercitu futuram quandoque inter
collegas discordiam talem qualis secuta est, atque [1]
exitum praesagiente. Eunti [2] Philippos [3] Thessalus
quidam de futura victoria nuntiavit auctore Divo.
Caesare, cuius sibi species itinere avio occurrisset.

2   Circa Perusiam sacrificio non litanti cum augeri
hostias imperasset ac subita eruptione hostes omnem
rei divinae apparatum abstulissent, constitit inter
haruspices, quae periculosa et adversa sacrificanti

[1] atque exitum, *Torrentius* ; at exitum, Ω.
[2] Eunti, *supplied by Boot.*
[3] Philippos, *Boot* ; Philippo, Ω.

only after many urgent requests, Theogenes sprang up and threw himself at his feet. From that time on Augustus had such faith in his destiny, that he made his horoscope public and issued a silver coin stamped with the sign of the constellation Capricornus, under which he was born.

XCV. As he was entering the city on his return from Apollonia after Caesar's death, though the heaven was clear and cloudless, a circle like a rainbow suddenly formed around the sun's disc, and straightway the tomb of Caesar's daughter Julia was struck by lightning. Again, as he was taking the auspices in his first consulship, twelve vultures appeared to him, as to Romulus, and when he slew the victims, the livers within all of them were found to be doubled inward at the lower end, which all those who were skilled in such matters unanimously declared to be an omen of a great and happy future.

XCVI. He even divined beforehand the outcome of all his wars. When the forces of the triumvirs were assembled at Bononia, an eagle that had perched upon his tent made a dash at two ravens, which attacked it on either side, and struck them to the ground. From this the whole army inferred that there would one day be discord among the colleagues, as actually came to pass, and divined its result. As he was on his way to Philippi, a Thessalian gave him notice of his coming victory on the authority of the deified Caesar, whose shade had met him on a lonely road. When he was sacrificing at Perusia without getting a favourable omen, and so had ordered more victims to be brought, the enemy made a sudden sally and carried off all the equipment of the sacrifice; whereupon the

273

denuntiata essent, cuncta in ipsos recasura qui exta
haberent; neque aliter evenit. Pridie quam Sicilien-
sem pugnam classe committeret, deambulanti in litore
piscis e mari exsilivit et ad pedes iacuit. Apud
Actium descendenti in aciem asellus cum asinario
occurrit : homini Eutychus, bestiae Nicon erat nomen ; utriusque simulacrum aeneum victor posuit in
templo, in quod castrorum suorum locum vertit.

XCVII. Mors quoque eius, de qua dehinc dicam,
divinitasque post mortem evidentissimis ostentis
praecognita est. Cum lustrum in campo Martio
magna populi frequentia conderet, aquila eum
saepius circumvolavit transgressaque in vicinam
aedem super nomen Agrippae ad primam litteram
sedit ; quo animadverso vota, quae in proximum
lustrum suscipi mos est, collegam suum Tiberium
nuncupare iussit ; nam se, quamquam conscriptis
paratisque iam tabulis, negavit suscepturum quae
2 non esset soluturus. Sub idem tempus ictu fulminis
ex inscriptione statuae eius prima nominis littera
effluxit ; responsum est, centum solos dies posthac
victurum, quem numerum C littera notaret, futur-
umque ut inter deos referretur, quod aesar, id est
reliqua pars e Caesaris nomine, Etrusca lingua deus
vocaretur.

3   Tiberium igitur in Illyricum dimissurus et Bene-

---

[a] Prosper (εὐτυχής, "fortunate").   [b] Victor (νικῶν).

[c] The *lustrum* was a sacrifice of purification, made every
five years by one of the censors, after the completion of the
census, or enumeration of the Roman people. The sacrifice
consisted of the *suovetaurilia*, the offering of a pig, a sheep,
and a bull. *Lustrum* was also applied to the five-year period.

soothsayers agreed that all the dangers and
with which the sacrificer had been threaten
recoil on the heads of those who were in pos.
the entrails; and so it turned out. As he v
ing on the shore the day before the sea-fight on Sicily,
a fish sprang from the sea and fell at his feet. At
Actium, as he was going down to begin the battle, he
met an ass with his driver, the man having the name
Eutychus [a] and the beast that of Nicon [b]; and after
the victory he set up bronze images of the two in the
sacred enclosure into which he converted the site of
his camp.

XCVII. His death, too, of which I shall speak next,
and his deification after death, were known in
advance by unmistakable signs. As he was bringing
the lustrum [c] to an end in the Campus Martius before
a great throng of people, an eagle flew several times
about him and then going across to the temple hard
by, perched above the first letter of Agrippa's name.
On noticing this, Augustus bade his colleague
Tiberius recite the vows which it is usual to offer for
the next five years; for although he had them
prepared and written out on a tablet, he declared
that he would not be responsible for vows which
he should never pay. At about the same time
the first letter of his name was melted from the
inscription on one of his statues by a flash of lightning; this was interpreted to mean that he would
live only a hundred days from that time, the number
indicated by the letter C, and that he would be
numbered with the gods, since *aesar* (that is, the
part of the name Caesar which was left) is the word
for god in the Etruscan tongue.

Then, too, when he was on the point of sending

ventum usque prosecuturus, cum interpellatores aliis
atque aliis causis in iure dicendo detinerent, exclamavit, quod et ipsum mox inter omina relatum est :
non, si omnia morarentur, amplius se posthac
Romae futurum ; atque itinere incohato Asturam
perrexit et inde praeter consuetudinem de nocte ad
occasionem aurae evectus causam valitudinis contraxit ex profluvio alvi.

XCVIII. Tunc Campaniae ora proximisque insulis
circuitis Caprearum quoque secessui quadriduum
impendit remississimo ad otium et ad omnem com-
itatem animo.

2 Forte Puteolanum sinum praetervehenti vectores
nautaeque de navi Alexandrina, quae tantum quod
appulerat, candidati coronatique et tura libantes
fausta omina et eximias laudes congesserant : per
illum se vivere, per illum navigare, libertate atque
fortunis per illum frui. Qua re admodum exhilara-
tus quadragenos aureos comitibus divisit iusque
iurandum et cautionem exegit a singulis, non alio
datam summam quam in emptionem Alexandrinarum
3 mercium absumpturos. Sed et ceteros continuos
dies inter varia munuscula togas insuper ac pallia
distribuit, lege proposita ut Romani Graeco, Graeci
Romano habitu et sermone uterentur. Spectavit
assidue exercentes ephebos, quorum aliqua adhuc

---

^a The *pallium* was the distinctive dress of the Greeks, as
the *toga* was of the Romans.

^b Greek youths between the ages of eighteen and that of
full citizenship, who had regular gymnastic training as a part
of their education. The Greek training survived in Capreae,
which until recently (see chap. xcii. 2) had belonged to
Naples.

Tiberius to Illyricum and was proposing to escort him
as far as Beneventum, and litigants detained him on
the judgment seat by bringing forward case after case,
he cried out that he would stay no longer in Rome,
even if everything conspired to delay him—and
this too was afterwards looked upon as one of the
omens of his death. When he had begun the
journey, he went on as far as Astura and from
there, contrary to his custom, took ship by night
since it chanced that there was a favourable breeze,
and thus contracted an illness beginning with a
diarrhoea.

XCVIII. Then after skirting the coast of Campania
and the neighbouring islands, he spent four more
days at his villa in Capreae, where he gave himself
up wholly to rest and social diversions. As he sailed
by the gulf of Puteoli, it happened that from an
Alexandrian ship which had just arrived there, the
passengers and crew, clad in white, crowned with gar-
lands, and burning incense, lavished upon him good
wishes and the highest praise, saying that it was
through him they lived, through him that they sailed
the seas, and through him that they enjoyed their
liberty and their fortunes. Exceedingly pleased at
this, he gave forty gold pieces to each of his companions, exacting from every one of them a pledge
under oath not to spend the sum that had been given
them in any other way than in buying wares from
Alexandria. More than that, for the several remaining days of his stay, among little presents of various
kinds, he distributed togas and cloaks *a* as well, stipu-
lating that the Romans should use the Greek dress
and language and the Greeks the Roman. He continually watched the exercises of the ephebi,*b* of whom

copia ex vetere instituto Capreis erat; isdem etiam
epulum in conspectu suo praebuit permissa, immo
exacta iocandi licentia diripiendique pomorum et
obsoniorum rerumque omnium [1] missilia. Nullo
denique genere hilaritatis abstinuit.

4 Vicinam Capreis insulam Apragopolim appellabat
a desidia secedentium illuc e comitatu suo. Sed ex
dilectis unum, Masgaban nomine, quasi conditorem
insulae κτίστην vocare consueverat. Huius Masgabae
ante annum defuncti tumulum cum e triclinio animadvertisset magna turba multisque luminibus fre-
quentari, versum compositum ex tempore clare
pronuntiavit :

Κτίστου δὲ τύμβον εἰσορῶ πυρούμενον·

conversusque ad Thrasyllum Tiberi comitem contra
accubantem et ignarum rei interrogavit, cuiusnam
poetae putaret [2] esse ; quo haesitante subiecit alium :

Ὁρᾷς φάεσσι Μασγάβαν τιμώμενον;

ac de hoc quoque consuluit. Cum ille nihil aliud responderet quam, cuiuscumque essent optimos esse,
cachinnum sustulit atque in iocos effusus est.

5 Mox Neapolim traiecit quanquam etiam tum in-
firmis intestinis morbo variante ; tamen et quin-
quennale certamen gymnicum honori suo institutum

---

[1] omnium, *added by C. F. W. Müller* ; missilium, X'.
[2] putaret, ϒ ; *the other mss. have* putarit (putaverit, S).

---

[a] The City of Do-nothings. There is no island "near
Capreae," and "the neighbouring island of Capreae" is
meaningless ; if the text is sound, Suetonius is careless, or we
must take Capreis as a locative, and regard *vicinam* as used in
a partitive sense like *reliquus, primus,* etc.
[b] Κτίστης, the Greek name for the founder of a city or colony.

there was still a goodly number at Capreae according
to the ancient usage. He also gave these youths a
banquet at which he himself was present, and not
only allowed, but even required perfect freedom
in jesting and in scrambling for tickets for fruit,
dainties and all kinds of things, which he threw to
them. In short, there was no form of gaiety in
which he did not indulge.

He called the neighbouring part of the island of
Capreae Apragopolis [a] from the laziness of some of his
company who sojourned there. Besides he used to
call one of his favourites, Masgaba by name, Ktistes,[b]
as if he were the founder of the island. Noticing from
his dining-room that the tomb of this Masgaba, who
had died the year before, was visited by a large
crowd with many torches, he uttered aloud this
verse, composed offhand :

"I see the founder's tomb alight with fire ";

and turning to Thrasyllus, one of the suite of Tiberius
who was reclining opposite him and knew nothing
about the matter, he asked of what poet he thought
it was the work. When Thrasyllus hesitated, he
added another verse :

"See you with lights Masgaba honoured now ? "

and asked his opinion of this one also. When
Thrasyllus could say nothing except that they were
very good, whoever made them, he burst into a laugh
and fell a joking about it.

Presently he crossed over to Naples, although his
bowels were still weak from intermittent attacks. In
spite of this he witnessed a quinquennial gymnastic
contest which had been established in his honour,

perspectavit et cum Tiberio ad destinatum locum contendit. Sed in redeundo adgravata valitudine tandem Nolae succubuit revocatumque ex itinere Tiberium diu secreto sermone detinuit, neque post ulli maiori negotio animum accommodavit.

XCIX. Supremo die identidem exquirens, an iam de se tumultus foris esset, petito speculo capillum sibi comi ac malas labantes[1] corrigi praecepit et admissos amicos percontatus, ecquid iis videretur mimum[2] vitae commode transegisse, adiecit et clausulam :

> Ἐπεὶ δὲ πάνυ καλῶς πέπαισται, δότε κρότον
> Καὶ πάντες ἡμᾶς μετὰ χαρᾶς προπέμψατε.

Omnibus deinde dimissis, dum advenientes ab urbe[3] de Drusi filia aegra interrogat, repente in osculis Liviae et in hac voce defecit : " Livia, nostri coniugii memor vive, ac vale ! " sortitus exitum facilem et qualem semper optaverat. Nam fere quotiens audisset cito ac nullo cruciatu defunctum quempiam, sibi et suis εὐθανασίαν similem—hoc enim et verbo uti solebat— precabatur. Unum omnino ante efflatam animam signum alienatae mentis ostendit, quod subito pavefactus a quadraginta se iuvenibus abripi questus est. Id quoque magis praesagium quam mentis deminutio fuit, siquidem totidem milites praetoriani extulerunt eum in publicum.

C. Obiit in cubiculo eodem, quo pater Octavius,

---

[1] labantes, *the mss. except GP (corr. by first hand), which have* labentes.

[2] mimum, P^2 (*Beroaldus*) ; *the other mss. have* minimum.

[3] ab urbe, $L^3 S^2 \varsigma$; ad urbem, Ω.

---

[a] Beneventum ; chap. xcvii. 3.

[b]*i.e.* open through weakness.　　　[c] Or closed.

and then started with Tiberius for his destination.[a] But as he was returning his illness increased and he at last took to his bed at Nola, calling back Tiberius, who was on his way to Illyricum, and keeping him for a long time in private conversation, after which he gave attention to no business of importance.

XCIX. On the last day of his life he asked every now and then whether there was any disturbance without on his account; then calling for a mirror, he had his hair combed and his falling[b] jaws set straight.[c] After that, calling in his friends and asking whether it seemed to them that he had played the comedy of life fitly, he added the tag:

" Since well I've played my part, all clap your hands
     And from the stage dismiss me with applause."

Then he sent them all off, and while he was asking some newcomers from the city about the daughter of Drusus, who was ill, he suddenly passed away as he was kissing Livia, uttering these last words : " Live mindful of our wedlock, Livia, and farewell," thus blessed with an easy death and such a one as he had always longed for. For almost always on hearing that anyone had died swiftly and painlessly, he prayed that he and his might have a like *euthanasia*, for that was the term he was wont to use. He gave but one single sign of wandering before he breathed his last, calling out in sudden terror that forty young men were carrying him off. And even this was rather a premonition than a delusion, since it was that very number of soldiers of the pretorian guard that carried him forth to lie in state.

C. He died in the same room as his father Octavius, in the consulship of two Sextuses, Pompeius and

duobus Sextis, Pompeio et Appuleio,[1] cons. XIIII. Kal.
Septemb. hora diei nona, septuagesimo et sexto aetatis
anno, diebus V et XXX minus.

2   Corpus decuriones municipiorum et coloniarum a
Nola Bovillas usque deportarunt noctibus propter
anni tempus, cum interdiu in basilica cuiusque oppidi
vel in aedium sacrarum maxima reponeretur.   A
Bovillis equester ordo suscepit urbique intulit atque in
vestibulo domus conlocavit.   Senatus et in funere
ornando et in memoria honoranda eo studio certatim
progressus est, ut inter alia complura censuerint
quidam, funus triumphali porta ducendum, praecedente Victoria quae est in curia, canentibus neniam
principum liberis utriusque sexus ; alii, exsequiarum
die ponendos anulos aureos ferreosque sumendos ;
nonnulli, ossa legenda per sacerdotes summorum
3 collegiorum.   Fuit et qui suaderet, appellationem
mensis Augusti in Septembrem transferendam, quod
hoc genitus Augustus, illo defunctus esset ; alius, ut
omne tempus a primo die natali ad exitum eius
saeculum Augustum appellaretur et ita in fastos
referretur.   Verum adhibito honoribus modo bifariam
laudatus est : pro aede Divi Iuli a Tiberio et pro rostris
veteribus a Druso Tiberi filio, ac senatorum umeris
4 delatus in Campum crematusque.   Nec defuit vir
praetorius, qui se effigiem cremati euntem in caelum

---

[1] Appuleio, *Monumentum Ancyranum* ; Apuleio, Ω.

[a] See *Claud.* vi. 1.

Appuleius, on the fourteenth day before the Kalends
of September at the ninth hour, just thirty-five days
before his seventy-sixth birthday.

His body was carried by the senators of the
municipalities and colonies from Nola all the way to
Bovillae, in the night time because of the season of
the year, being placed by day in the basilica of the
town at which they arrived or in its principal temple.
At Bovillae the members of the equestrian order [a]
met it and bore it to the city, where they placed it
in the vestibule of his house.

In their desire to give him a splendid funeral and
honour his memory the senators so vied with one
another that among many other suggestions some
proposed that his cortege pass through the triumphal
gate, preceded by the statue of Victory which stands
in the House, while a dirge was sung by children of
both sexes belonging to the leading families; others,
that on the day of the obsequies golden rings be laid
aside and iron ones worn; and some, that his ashes
be collected by the priests of the highest colleges.
One man proposed that the name of the month
of August be transferred to September, because
Augustus was born in the latter, but died in the
former; another, that all the period from the day of
his birth until his demise be called the Augustan Age,
and so entered in the Calendar. But though a limit
was set to the honours paid him, his eulogy was twice
delivered: before the temple of the Deified Julius
by Tiberius, and from the old rostra by Drusus, son
of Tiberius; and he was carried on the shoulders of
senators to the Campus Martius and there cremated.
There was even an ex-praetor who took oath that he
had seen the form of the Emperor, after he had been

283

vidisse iuraret. Reliquias legerunt primores equestris
ordinis tunicati et discincti pedibusque nudis ac
Mausoleo condiderunt. Id opus inter Flaminiam viam
ripamque Tiberis sexto suo consulatu exstruxerat cir-
cumiectasque silvas et ambulationes in usum populi
iam tum publicarat.

CI. Testamentum L. Planco C. Silio cons. III. Non.
Apriles, ante annum et quattuor menses quam decederet, factum ab eo ac duobus codicibus partim
ipsius partim libertorum Polybi et Hilarionis manu
scriptum depositumque apud se virgines Vestales cum
tribus signatis aeque voluminibus protulerunt. Quae
2 omnia in senatu aperta atque recitata sunt. Heredes
instituit primos : Tiberium ex parte dimidia et sextante, Liviam ex parte tertia, quos et ferre nomen
suum iussit; secundos : Drusum Tiberi filium ex
triente, ex partibus reliquis Germanicum liberosque
eius tres sexus virilis ; tertio gradu propinquos,
amicosque compluris. Legavit populo R. quadringenties, tribubus tricies quinquies sestertium, praetorianis militibus singula milia nummorum, cohortibus
urbanis quingenos, legionaris trecenos nummos ; quam
summam repraesentari iussit, nam et confiscatam
3 semper repositamque habuerat. Reliqua legata varie
dedit perduxitque quaedam ad vicena sestertia, quibus solvendis annuum diem finiit, excusata rei familiaris mediocritate nec plus perventurum ad heredes

---

a Augustus and Augusta, but Tiberius did not assume the
title until it was conferred on him by the senate ; Dio 57.
2–3.   b See note on *Jul.* lxxxiii. 2.   c See chap. lxiv. 1.
   d Probably those with which he was connected (see chap
xl. 2) ; Lipsius suggested *tribulibus.*
234

reduced to ashes, on its way to heaven. His remains were gathered up by the leading men of the equestrian order, bare-footed and in ungirt tunics, and placed in the Mausoleum. This structure he had built in his sixth consulship between the Via Flaminia and the bank of the Tiber, and at the same time opened to the public the groves and walks by which it was surrounded.

CI. He had made a will in the consulship of Lucius Plancus and Gaius Silius on the third day before the Nones of April, a year and four months before he died, in two note-books, written in part in his own hand and in part in that of his freedmen Polybius and Hilarion. These the Vestal virgins, with whom they had been deposited, now produced, together with three rolls, which were sealed in the same way. All these were opened and read in the senate. He appointed as his chief heirs Tiberius, to receive two-thirds of the estate, and Livia, one-third; these he also bade assume his name.[a] His heirs in the second degree [b] were Drusus, son of Tiberius, for one-third, and for the rest Germanicus and his three male children.[c] In the third grade he mentioned many of his relatives and friends. He left to the Roman people forty million sesterces; to the tribes [d] three million five hundred thousand; to the soldiers of the pretorian guard a thousand each; to the city cohorts five hundred; and to the legionaries three hundred. This sum he ordered to be paid at once, for he had always kept the amount at hand and ready for the purpose. He gave other legacies to various individuals, some amounting to as much as twenty thousand sesterces, and provided for the payment of these a year later, giving as his excuse for the delay the small amount of

28 B.C.

April 3, 13 A.D.

285

suos quam milies et quingenties professus, quamvis
viginti proximis annis quaterdecies milies ex testa-
mentis amicorum percepisset, quod paene omne cum
duobus paternis patrimoniis ceterisque hereditatibus
in rem p. absumpsisset. Iulias filiam neptemque, si
4 quid iis accidisset, vetuit sepulcro suo inferri. Tribus
voluminibus, uno mandata de funere suo complexus
est, altero indicem rerum a se gestarum, quem
vellet incidi in aeneis tabulis, quae ante Mausoleum
statuerentur, tertio breviarium totius imperii, quantum
militum sub signis ubique esset, quantum pecuniae
in aerario et fiscis et vectigaliorum residuis. Adiecit
et libertorum servorumque nomina, a quibus ratio
exigi posset.

---

^a That is, on their death ; a common euphemism.
^b The original of this inscription is lost, but the greater
part of a copy inscribed in Greek and Latin on marble is
preserved at Ancyra in Asia Minor and is known as the
Monumentum Ancyranum.

his property, and declaring that not more than a hundred and fifty millions would come to his heirs; for though he had received fourteen hundred millions during the last twenty years from the wills of his friends, he said that he had spent nearly all of it, as well as the estates left him by his natural and his adoptive father, for the benefit of the State. He gave orders that his daughter and his granddaughter Julia should not be put in his Mausoleum, if anything befell them.[a] In one of the three rolls he included directions for his funeral; in the second, an account of what he had accomplished, which he desired to have cut upon bronze tablets and set up at the entrance to the Mausoleum[b]; in the third, a summary of the condition of the whole empire; how many soldiers there were in active service in all parts of it, how much money there was in the public treasury and in the privy-purse, and what revenues were in arrears. He added, besides, the names of the freedmen and slaves from whom the details could be demanded.

BOOK III

TIBERIUS

LIBER III

TIBERIUS

I. Patricia gens Claudia — fuit enim et alia
plebeia, nec potentia minor nec dignitate — orta
est ex Regillis oppido Sabinorum. Inde Romam
recens conditam cum magna clientium manu
conmigravit auctore Tito Tatio consorte Romuli,
vel, quod magis constat, Atta Claudio gentis
principe, post reges exactos sexto fere anno; atque
in patricias cooptata[1] agrum insuper trans Anienem
clientibus locumque sibi ad sepulturam sub Capitolio
2 publice accepit. Deinceps procedente tempore
duodetriginta consulatus, dictaturas quinque, cen-
suras septem, triumphos sex, duas ovationes adepta
est. Cum praenominibus cognominibusque variis
distingueretur, Luci praenomen consensu repudiavit,
postquam e duobus gentilibus praeditis eo alter
latrocinii, caedis alter convictus est. Inter co-
gnomina autem et Neronis assumpsit, quo[2] significatur
lingua Sabina fortis ac strenuus.

---

[1] cooptata, ς; coaptata, Ω.   [2] quo, ς; quod, Ω.

---

[a] 504 B.C. in the traditional chronology.
[b] See note on *Aug.* xxii.

BOOK III

TIBERIUS

I. The patrician branch of the Claudian family (for there was, besides, a plebeian branch of no less influence and prestige) originated at Regilli, a town of the Sabines. From there it moved to Rome shortly after the founding of the city with a large band of dependents, through the influence of Titus Tatius, who shared the kingly power with Romulus (or, according to the generally accepted view, of Atta Claudius, the head of the family) about six years after the expulsion of the kings.[a] It was admitted among the patrician families, receiving, besides, from the State a piece of land on the farther side of the Anio for its dependents, and a burial-site for the family at the foot of the Capitoline hill. Then as time went on it was honoured with twenty-eight consulships, five dictatorships, seven censorships, six triumphs, and two ovations.[b] While the members of the family were known by various forenames and surnames, they discarded the forename Lucius by common consent after two of the family who bore it had been found guilty, the one of highway robbery, and the other of murder. To their surnames, on the other hand, they added that of Nero, which in the Sabine tongue means "strong and valiant."

II. Multa multorum Claudiorum egregia merita,
multa etiam sequius admissa in rem p. exstant. Sed
ut praecipua commemorem, Appius Caecus societatem cum rege Pyrrho ut parum salubrem iniri
dissuasit. Claudius Caudex primus freto classe
traiecto Poenos Sicilia expulit. Tiberius[1] Nero
advenientem ex Hispania cum ingentibus copiis
Hasdrubalem, prius quam Hannibali fratri coniun-
2 geretur, oppressit. Contra Claudius Regillianus,
decemvir legibus scribendis, virginem ingenuam
per vim libidinis gratia in servitutem asserere
conatus causa plebi fuit secedendi rursus a patribus.
Claudius Russus[2] statua sibi diademata ad Appi
Forum posita Italiam per clientelas occupare temptavit. Claudius Pulcher apud Siciliam non pas-
centibus in auspicando pullis ac per contemptum
religionis mari demersis, quasi ut biberent quando
esse nollent, proelium navale iniit; superatusque,
cum dictatorem dicere a senatu iuberetur, velut
iterum inludens discrimini publico Glycian[3] viatorem
suum dixit.
3 Exstant et feminarum exempla diversa aeque,
siquidem gentis eiusdem utraque Claudia fuit, et
quae navem cum sacris Matris deum Idaeae obhae-
rentem Tiberino vado extraxit, precata propalam,
ut ita demum se sequeretur, si sibi pudicitia

---

[1] Tiberius] Tibus, *M*; tybus, *G*[1]; tyb̄us, *G*[2]; Tibĭ, *V*;
the other mss. have Tibius *or* Tiberius.
[2] Russus,*conjecture of Ihm, Hermes,* 36,303 ; Drusus, *mss.*
[3] Glycian, *Salmasius* ; ilycian, Ω.

---

[a] 449 B.C. in the traditional chronology.
[b] Cybele, a Phrygian goddess worshipped near Mount

II. There are on record many distinguished services of the Claudii to their country, as well as many deeds of the opposite character. But to mention only the principal instances, Appius the Blind advised against forming an alliance with king Pyrrhus 280 B.C. as not at all expedient. Claudius Caudex was the first to cross the straits with a fleet, and drove the 264 B.C. Carthaginians from Sicily. Tiberius Nero crushed Hasdrubal, on his arrival from Spain with a vast army, 207 B.C. before he could unite with his brother Hannibal. On the other hand, Claudius Regillianus, decemvir for codifying the laws, through his lawless attempt to enslave a freeborn maid, to gratify his passion for her, was the cause of the second secession of the plebeians from the patricians.[a] Claudius Russus, having set up his statue at Forum Appi with a crown upon its head, tried to take possession of Italy through his dependents. Claudius Pulcher began a sea-fight off Sicily, though 249 B.C. the sacred chickens would not eat when he took the auspices, throwing them into the sea in defiance of the omen, and saying that they might drink, since they would not eat. He was defeated, and on being bidden by the senate to appoint a dictator, he appointed his messenger Glycias, as if again making a jest of his country's peril.

The women also have records equally diverse, since both the famous Claudias belonged to that family : the one who drew the ship with the sacred proper- 204 B.C. ties of the Idaean Mother of the Gods[b] from the shoal in the Tiber on which it was stranded, after first publicly praying that it might yield to her efforts only if her chastity were beyond question ; and

Ida. In the year 204 B.C. her cult was introduced into Rome, where she was worshipped as the Magna Mater.

constaret ; et quae novo more iudicium maiestatis
apud populum mulier subiit, quod in conferta
multitudine aegre procedente carpento palam optaverat, ut frater suus Pulcher revivisceret atque
iterum classem amitteret, quo minor turba Romae
4 foret.   Praeterea notatissimum est, Claudios omnis,
excepto dum taxat P. Clodio, qui ob expellendum
urbe Ciceronem plebeio homini atque etiam natu
minori in adoptionem se dedit, optimates adserto-
resque unicos dignitatis ac potentiae patriciorum
semper fuisse atque adversus plebem adeo violentos
et contumaces, ut ne capitis quidem quisquam
reus apud populum mutare vestem aut deprecari
sustinuerit ; nonnulli in altercatione et iurgio tribunos plebi pulsaverint.   Etiam virgo Vestalis
fratrem[1] iniussu populi triumphantem ascenso simul
curru usque in Capitolium prosecuta est, ne vetare
aut intercedere fas cuiquam tribunorum esset.

III. Ex hac stirpe Tiberius Caesar genus trahit,
et quidem[2] utrumque : paternum a Tiberio Nerone,
maternum ab Appio Pulchro, qui ambo Appi Caeci
filii fuerunt.   Insertus est et Liviorum familiae
adoptato in eam materno avo.   Quae familia
quanquam plebeia, tamen et ipsa admodum floruit
octo consulatibus, censuris duabus, triumphis tribus,

[1] fratrem, *mss.* ; patrem, *Cic. Cael.* **34**.
[2] et quidem, ΠQ ; *the other mss. have* equidem.

a Cf. *Jul.* xx. **4**.

the one who was tried by the people for treason, 246 B.C. an unprecedented thing in the case of a woman, because when her carriage made but slow progress through the throng, she openly gave vent to the wish that her brother Pulcher might come to life and lose another fleet, to make less of a crowd in Rome. It is notorious besides that all the Claudii were aristocrats and staunch upholders of the prestige and influence of the patricians, with the sole exception of Publius Clodius, who for the sake of driving Cicero from the city had himself adopted by a 60 B.C. plebeian and one too who was younger than himself.[a] Their attitude towards the commons was so headstrong and stubborn that not even when on trial for his life before the people did any one of them deign to put on mourning or beg for mercy; and some of them during bickerings and disputes struck the tribunes of the commons. Even a Vestal virgin mounted her brother's chariot with him, when he 143 B.C. was celebrating a triumph without the sanction of the people, and attended him all the way to the Capitol, in order to make it an act of sacrilege for any one of the tribunes to forbid him or interpose his veto.

III. Such was the stock from which Tiberius Caesar derived his origin, and that too on both sides: on his father's from Tiberius Nero; on his mother's from Appius Pulcher, both of whom were sons of Appius Caecus. He was a member also of the family of the Livii, through the adoption into it of his maternal grandfather. This family too, though of plebeian origin, was yet of great prominence and had been honoured with eight consulships, two censorships, and three triumphs, as well as with the

dictatura etiam ac magisterio equitum honorata ;
clara et insignibus viris ac maxime Salinatore
2 Drusisque. Salinator universas tribus in censura
notavit levitatis nomine, quod, cum se post priorem
consulatum multa inrogata condemnassent, consulem
iterum censoremque fecissent. Drusus hostium duce
Drauso comminus trucidato sibi posterisque suis
cognomen invenit. Traditur etiam pro praetore ex
provincia Gallia rettulisse aurum Senonibus olim
in obsidione Capitolii datum nec, ut fama est,
extortum a Camillo. Eius abnepos ob eximiam
adversus Gracchos operam patronus senatus dictus
filium reliquit, quem in simili dissensione multa
varie molientem diversa factio per fraudem interemit.

IV. Pater Tiberi, Nero, quaestor C. Caesaris
Alexandrino bello classi praepositus, plurimum ad
victoriam contulit. Quare et pontifex in locum
P. Scipionis substitutus et ad deducendas in Galliam
colonias, in quis Narbo et Arelate erant, missus
est. Tamen Caesare occiso, cunctis turbarum metu
abolitionem facti decernentibus, etiam de praemiis
2 tyrannicidarum referendum censuit. Praetura deinde
functus, cum exitu anni discordia inter triumviros
orta esset, retentis ultra iustum tempus insignibus
L. Antonium consulem triumviri fratrem ad Perusiam

ᵃ That is, affixed the mark of ignominy (*nota*) to their
names on the census roll.

offices of dictator and master of the horse. It was
made illustrious too by distinguished members, in
particular Salinator and the Drusi. The former in
his censorship put the brand on all the tribes[a] on 204 B.C.
the charge of fickleness, because having convicted
and fined him after a previous consulship, they made
him consul a second time and censor as well. Drusus
gained a surname for himself and his descendants by
slaying Drausus, leader of the enemy, in single
combat. It is also said that when propraetor he
brought back from his province of Gaul the gold
which was paid long before to the Senones, when
they beleaguered the Capitol, and that this had not 390 B.C.
been wrested from them by Camillus, as tradition
has it. His grandson's grandson, called "Patron of
the Senate" because of his distinguished services
against the Gracchi, left a son who was treacher- 122 B.C.
ously slain by the party of his opponents, while he
was busily agitating many plans during a similar 91 B.C.
dissension.

IV. Nero, the father of Tiberius, as a quaestor of
Julius Caesar during the Alexandrian war and com- 48–47
mander of a fleet, contributed materially to the B.C.
victory. For this he was made pontiff in place of
Publius Scipio and sent to conduct colonies to Gaul,
among them Narbo and Arelate. Yet after the
murder of Caesar, when all the others voted for an
amnesty through fear of mob violence, he even
favoured a proposal for rewarding the tyrannicides.
Later on, having held the praetorship, since a dispute
arose among the triumvirs at the close of his term,
he retained the badges of his rank beyond the
legitimate time and followed Lucius Antonius, consul 41 B.C.
and brother of the triumvir, to Perusia. When the

secutus, deditione a ceteris facta, solus permansit in partibus ac primo Praeneste, inde Neapolim evasit servisque ad pilleum frustra vocatis in Siciliam 3 profugit. Sed indigne ferens nec statim se in conspectum Sexti Pompei admissum et fascium usu prohibitum, ad M. Antonium traiecit in Achaiam. Cum quo brevi reconciliata inter omnis pace Romam redit uxoremque Liviam Drusillam et tunc gravidam et ante iam apud se filium enixam petenti Augusto concessit. Nec multo post diem obiit, utroque liberorum superstite, Tiberio Drusoque Neronibus.

V. Tiberium quidam Fundis natum existimaverunt secuti levem coniecturam, quod materna eius avia Fundana fuerit et quod mox simulacrum Felicitatis ex s. c. publicatum ibi sit. Sed ut plures certioresque tradunt, natus est Romae in Palatio XVI. Kal. Dec. M. Aemilio Lepido iterum L. Munatio Planco conss. per bellum Philippense. Sic enim in fastos actaque in publica relatum est. Nec tamen desunt, qui partim antecedente anno, Hirti ac Pansae, partim insequenti, Servili Isaurici L.[1] que Antoni consulatu, genitum eum scribant.

VI. Infantiam pueritiamque habuit laboriosam [2] et exercitatam, comes usque quaque parentum fugae; quos quidem apud Neapolim sub inruptionem hostis navigium clam petentis vagitu suo paene bis prodidit,

[1] L., *added by Bentley and Roth.*

[2] laboriosam, *Pithoeus*; luxoriosam, *MG*; *the other mss. have* luxuriosam.

[a] *Ad pilleum*: the *pilleus*, a close-fitting felt cap, was given to slaves on manumission, as a token of freedom.

[b] See *Aug.* lxii. 2.

others capitulated, he alone held to his allegiance
and got away first to Praeneste and then to Naples;
and after vainly trying to enlist the slaves by a
promise of freedom,[a] he took refuge in Sicily. Piqued
however because he was not at once given an audience
with Sextus Pompeius, and was denied the use of the
fasces, he crossed to Achaia and joined Mark Antony.
With him he shortly returned to Rome, on the conclusion of a general peace, and gave up to Augustus
at his request his wife Livia Drusilla, who was
pregnant at the time and had already borne him
a son.[b] Not long afterward he died, survived by
both his sons, Tiberius Nero and Drusus Nero.

V. Some have supposed that Tiberius was born at
Fundi, on no better evidence than that his maternal
grandmother was a native of that place, and that
later a statue of Good Fortune was set up there by
decree of the senate. But according to the most
numerous and trustworthy authorities, he was born at
Rome, on the Palatine, the sixteenth day before the
Kalends of December, in the consulship of Marcus
Aemilius Lepidus and Lucius Munatius Plancus (the
former for the second time) while the war of Philippi
was going on. In fact it is so recorded both in the
calendar and in the public gazette. Yet in spite
of this some write that he was born in the preceding
year, that of Hirtius and Pansa, and others in the
following year, in the consulate of Servilius Isauricus
and Lucius Antonius.

VI. He passed his infancy and his youth amid
hardship and tribulation, since he was everywhere
the companion of his parents in their flight; at
Naples indeed he all but betrayed them twice by his
crying, as they were secretly on their way to a ship

Nov. 16, 42 B.C.

semel cum a nutricis ubere, iterum[1] cum a sinu
matris raptim auferretur ab iis, qui pro necessitate
2 temporis mulierculas levare onere temptabant.   Per
Siciliam quoque et per Achaiam circumductus ac
Lacedaemoniis publice, quod in tutela Claudiorum
erant, demandatus, digrediens inde itinere nocturno
discrimen vitae adiit flamma repente e silvis undique
exorta adeoque omnem comitatum circumplexa, ut
3 Liviae pars vestis et capilli amburerentur.   Munera,
quibus a Pompeia Sex. Pompei sorore in Sicilia donatus
est, chlamys et fibula, item bullae aureae, durant
ostendunturque adhuc Baiis.   Post reditum in urbem
a M. Gallio senatore testamento adoptatus hereditate
adita mox nomine abstinuit, quod Gallius adversarum
Augusto partium fuerat.

4   Novem natus annos defunctum patrem pro rostris
laudavit.   Dehinc pubescens Actiaco triumpho currum
Augusti comitatus est sinisteriore funali equo, cum
Marcellus Octaviae filius dexteriore veheretur.   Praesedit et asticis[2] ludis et Troiam circensibus lusit[3]
ductor turmae puerorum maiorum.

VII. Virili toga sumpta adulescentiam omnem
spatiumque insequentis aetatis usque ad principatus
initia per haec fere transegit.   Munus gladiatorium
in memoriam patris et alterum in avi Drusi dedit,
diversis temporibus ac locis, primum in Foro, se-

---

[1] iterum, *Ursinus* ; item, Ω.

[2] Atticis, Υ *and* V *in the margin* ; atricis, *LPS* (attricis,
L) ; acticis, *T.   The* astici (*from* ἄστυ) *were originally celebrated at Athens, in honour of Dionysus.*

[3] lusit, *supplied by Bentley and after* Troiam *by Roth.*

---

^a See *Aug.* xxii.   ^b Cf. *Jul.* xxxix. 2.

just as the enemy burst into the town, being suddenly
torn from his nurse's breast and again from his
mother's arms by those who tried to relieve the poor
women of their burden because of the imminent
danger. After being taken all over Sicily also and
Achaia, and consigned to the public care of the
Lacedaemonians, because they were dependents of
the Claudii, he almost lost his life as he was leaving
there by night, when the woods suddenly took fire
all about them, and the flames so encircled the whole
company that part of Livia's robe and her hair were
scorched. The gifts which were given him in Sicily
by Pompeia, sister of Sextus Pompeius, a cloak and
clasp, as well as studs of gold, are still kept and
exhibited at Baiae. Being adopted, after his return
to the city, in the will of Marcus Gallius, a senator,
he accepted the inheritance, but soon gave up the
name, because Gallius had been a member of the
party opposed to Augustus.

At the age of nine he delivered a eulogy of his
dead father from the rostra. Then, just as he was
arriving at puberty, he accompanied the chariot of
Augustus in his triumph after Actium,[a] riding the
left trace-horse, while Marcellus, son of Octavia,
rode the one on the right. He presided, too, at the
city festival, and took part in the game of Troy
during the performances in the circus, leading the
band of older boys.[b]

VII. The principal events of his youth and later
life, from the assumption of the gown of manhood
to the beginning of his reign, were these. He gave
a gladiatorial show in memory of his father, and a
second in honour of his grandfather Drusus, at different times and in different places, the former in the

cundum in amphitheatro, rudiariis quoque quibusdam revocatis auctoramento centenum milium; dedit et ludos, sed absens; cuncta magnifice, inpensa matris ac vitrici.

2 Agrippinam, Marco Agrippa genitam, neptem Caecili Attici equitis R., ad quem sunt Ciceronis epistulae, duxit uxorem; sublatoque ex ea filio Druso, quanquam bene convenientem rursusque gravidam dimittere ac Iuliam Augusti filiam confestim coactus est ducere non sine magno angore animi, cum et Agrippinae consuetudine teneretur et Iuliae mores improbaret, ut quam sensisset sui quoque sub priore marito appetentem, quod sane etiam vulgo existimabatur.

3 Sed Agrippinam et abegisse post divortium doluit et semel omnino ex occursu visam adeo contentis et umentibus[1] oculis prosecutus est, ut custoditum sit ne umquam in conspectum ei posthac veniret. Cum Iulia primo concorditer et amore mutuo vixit, mox dissedit et aliquanto gravius, ut etiam perpetuo secubaret, intercepto communis fili pignore, qui Aquileiae natus infans exstinctus est. Drusum fratrem in Germania amisit, cuius corpus pedibus toto itinere praegrediens Roman usque pervexit.

VIII. Civilium officiorum rudimentis regem Archelaum Trallianos et Thessalos, varia quosque de causa,

---

[1] umentibus, *Lipsius*; tumentibus, Ω.

[a] The one built by Statilius Taurus; see *Aug.* xxix. 5.
[b] *Rudiarius*: presented with the *rudis*, or wooden sword, a symbol of honourable discharge; cf. Hor. *Epist.* 1. 1. 2.
[c] A child at birth was laid at his father's feet. He then acknowledged him by taking him in his arms (*tollere*), or the child was disowned and cast out (*expositus*).
[d] Cf. *Aug.* lxiii. 2.

Forum and the latter in the amphitheatre,[a] inducing some retired gladiators [b] to appear with the rest by the payment of a hundred thousand sesterces to each. He also gave stage-plays, but without being present in person. All these were on a grand scale, at the expense of his mother and his stepfather.

He married Agrippina, daughter of Marcus Agrippa, and granddaughter of Caecilius Atticus, a Roman knight, to whom Cicero's letters are addressed; but after he had acknowledged [c] a son from her, Drusus, although she was thoroughly congenial and was a second time with child, he was forced to divorce her 11 B.C. and to contract a hurried marriage with Julia,[d] daughter of Augustus. This caused him no little distress of mind, for he was living happily with Agrippina, and disapproved of Julia's character, having perceived that she had a passion for him even during the lifetime of her former husband, as was in fact the general opinion. But even after the divorce he regretted his separation from Agrippina, and the only time that he chanced to see her, he followed her with such an intent and tearful gaze that care was taken that she should never again come before his eyes. With Julia he lived in harmony at first, and returned her love; but he soon grew cold, and went so far as to cease to live with her at all, after the severing of the tie formed by a child which was born to them, but died at Aquileia in infancy. He lost his brother Drusus in Germany and conveyed his 9 B.C. body to Rome, going before it on foot all the way.

VIII. He began his civil career by a defence of king Archelaus, the people of Tralles, and those of Thessaly, before the judgment seat of Augustus, the charge in each case being different. He made a plea to the

303

Augusto cognoscente defendit; pro Laodicenis Thyati-
renis Chiis terrae motu afflictis opemque implorantibus
senatum deprecatus est; Fannium Caepionem, qui
cum Varrone Murena in Augustum conspiraverat,
reum maiestatis apud iudices fecit et condemnavit.
Interque haec duplicem curam administravit, annonae
quae artior inciderat, et repurgandorum tota Italia
ergastulorum, quorum domini in invidiam venerant
quasi exceptos supprimerent non solum viatores sed
et quos sacramenti metus ad eius modi latebras compulisset.

IX. Stipendia prima expeditione Cantabrica tribunus militum fecit, dein ducto ad Orientem exercitu
regnum Armeniae Tigrani restituit ac pro tribunali
diadema imposuit. Recepit et signa, quae M. Crasso
ademerant Parthi. Post hoc Comatam Galliam⸏anno
fere rexit et barbarorum incursionibus et principum
discordia inquietam. Exin Raeticum Vindelicumque
bellum, inde Pannonicum, inde Germanicum gessit.
2 Raetico atque Vindelico gentis Alpinas, Pannonico
Breucos et Dalmatas subegit, Germanico quadraginta
milia dediticiorum traiecit in Galliam iuxtaque ripam
Rheni sedibus adsignatis conlocavit. Quas ob res et
ovans et curru urbem ingressus est, prius, ut quidam
putant, triumphalibus ornamentis honoratus, novo
nec antea cuiquam tributo genere honoris.

ᵃ See note on *Aug.* xxxii. 1.   ᵇ Cf. *Aug.* xxi. 3.
ᶜ Transalpine Gaul was called *Comata*, "long-haired."
The southern part was called *Braccata*, "breeches-wearing,"
and Cisalpine Gaul, *Togata.*
ᵈ *i.e.* celebrating a *iustum triumphum* ; see note on *Aug.*
xxii., and cf. Vell. 2. 121. For a different version see Dio, 54.
31.

senate in behalf of the citizens of Laodicea, Thyatira and Chios, who had suffered loss from an earthquake and begged for help. Fannius Caepio, who had conspired with Varro Murena against Augustus, he arraigned for high treason and secured his con- 23 a.c. demnation. In the meantime he undertook two public charges: that of the grain supply, which, as it happened, was deficient; and the investigation of the slave-prisons *a* throughout Italy, the owners of which had gained a bad reputation; for they were charged with holding in durance not only travellers, but also those whom dread of military service had driven to such places of concealment.

IX. His first military service was as tribune of the 25 a.c. soldiers in the campaign against the Cantabrians; then he led an army to the Orient and restored the throne of Armenia to Tigranes, crowning him on the tribunal. He besides recovered the standards which the Parthians had taken from Marcus Crassus.*b* Then for about a year he was governor of Gallia Comata,*c* which was in a state of unrest through the inroads of the barbarians and the dissensions of its chiefs. Next he carried on war with the Raeti and Vindelici, then in Pannonia, and finally in Germany. In the first of these wars he subdued the Alpine tribes, in the second the Breuci and Dalmatians, and in the third he brought forty thousand prisoners of war over into Gaul and assigned them homes near the bank of the Rhine. Because of these exploits he entered the city both in an 7 and 9 ovation and riding in a chariot,*d* having previously, B. C. as some think, been honoured with the triumphal regalia, a new kind of distinction never before conferred upon anyone.

3   Magistratus et maturius incohavit et paene
iunctim percucurrit, quaesturam praeturam consulatum; interpositoque tempore consul iterum etiam
tribuniciam potestatem in quinquennium accepit.

X. Tot prosperis confluentibus integra aetate ac
valitudine statuit repente secedere seque e medio
quam longissime amovere; dubium uxorisne taedio,
quam neque criminari aut dimittere auderet neque
ultra perferre posset, an ut vitato assiduitatis fastidio
auctoritatem absentia tueretur atque etiam augeret,
si quando indiguisset sui res p. Quidam existimant,
adultis iam Augusti liberis, loco et quasi possessione
usurpati a se diu secundi gradus sponte cessisse
exemplo M. Agrippae, qui M. Marcello ad munera
publica admoto Mytilenas abierit, ne aut obstare
2 aut obtrectare praesens videretur. Quam causam et
ipse, sed postea, reddidit. Tunc autem honorum
satietatem ac requiem laborum praetendens commeatum petit; neque aut matri suppliciter precanti
aut vitrico deseri se etiam in senatu conquerenti
veniam dedit. Quin et pertinacius retinentibus,
cibo per quadriduum [1] abstinuit. Facta tandem
abeundi potestate, relictis Romae uxore et filio confestim Ostiam descendit, ne verbo quidem cuiquam
prosequentium reddito paucosque admodum in di-
gressu exosculatus.

---

[1] quadriduum] quatriduum, Ω.

---

[a] Since he was quaestor in 23 B.C. and consul for the first
time in 13 B.C., *paene iunctim* is used loosely, to indicate a
general disregard of the ages required for the various offices
and the prescribed intervals.   [b] Cf. *Aug.* lxvi. 3.

He entered upon the offices of quaestor, praetor, and consul before the usual age, and held them almost without an interval^a; then after a time he was made consul again, at the same time receiving 6 B.C. the tribunicial power for five years.

X. At the flood-tide of success, though in the prime of life and health, he suddenly decided to go into retirement and to withdraw as far as possible from the centre of the stage; perhaps from disgust at his wife, whom he dared neither accuse nor put away, though he could no longer endure her; or perhaps, avoiding the contempt born of familiarity, to keep up his prestige by absence, or even add to it, in case his country should ever need him. Some think that, since the children of Augustus were now of age, he voluntarily gave up the position and the virtual assumption of the second rank which he had long held, thus following the example of Marcus Agrippa,^b who withdrew to Mytilene when Marcellus began his public career, so that he might not seem either to oppose or belittle him by his presence. This was, in fact, the reason which Tiberius himself gave, but afterwards. At the time he asked for leave of absence on the ground of weariness of office and a desire to rest; and he would not give way either to his mother's urgent entreaties or to the complaint which his step-father openly made in the senate, that he was being forsaken. On the contrary, when they made more strenuous efforts to detain him, he refused to take food for four days. Being at last allowed to depart, he left his wife and son in Rome and went down to Ostia in haste, without saying a single word to any of those who saw him off, and kissing only a very few when he left.

XI. Ab Ostia oram Campaniae legens inbecillitate Augusti nuntiata paulum substitit. Sed increbrescente rumore quasi ad occasionem maioris spei commoraretur, tantum non adversis tempestatibus Rhodum enavigavit, amoenitate et salubritate insulae iam inde captus cum ad eam ab Armenia rediens appulisset. Hic modicis contentus aedibus nec multo laxiore suburbano genus vitae civile admodum instituit, sine lictore aut viatore gymnasio interdum obambulans mutuaque cum Graeculis officia usurpans prope ex aequo.

2 Forte quondam in disponendo die mane praedixerat, quidquid aegrorum in civitate esset visitare se velle ; id a proximis aliter exceptum iussique sunt omnes aegri in publicam porticum deferri ac per valitudinum genera disponi. Perculsus ergo inopinata re diuque quid ageret incertus, tandem singulos circuit excusans factum etiam tenuissimo cuique et ignoto.

3 Unum hoc modo neque praeterea quicquam notatum est, in quo exseruisse ius tribuniciae potestatis visus sit : cum circa scholas et auditoria professorum assiduus esset, moto inter antisophistas graviore iurgio, non defuit qui eum intervenientem et quasi studiosiorem partis alterius convicio incesseret. Sensim itaque regressus domum repente cum

308

XI. From Ostia he coasted along the shore of Campania, and learning of an indisposition of Augustus, he stopped for a while. But since gossip was rife that he was lingering on the chance of realising his highest hopes, although the wind was all but dead ahead, he sailed directly to Rhodes, for he had been attracted by the charm and healthfulness of that island ever since the time when he put in there on his return from Armenia. Content there with a modest house and a villa in the suburbs not much more spacious, he adopted a most unassuming manner of life, at times walking in the gymnasium without a lictor or a messenger, and exchanging courtesies with the good people of Greece with almost the air of an equal.

It chanced one morning in arranging his programme for the day, that he had announced his wish to visit whatever sick folk there were in the city. This was misunderstood by his attendants, and orders were given that all the sick should be taken to a public colonnade and arranged according to the nature of their complaints. Whereupon Tiberius, shocked at this unexpected sight, and in doubt for some time what to do, at last went about to each one, apologizing for what had happened even to the humblest and most obscure of them.

Only one single instance was noticed of a visible exercise of the rights of the tribunicial authority. He was a constant attendant at the schools and lecture-rooms of the professors of philosophy, and once when a hot dispute had arisen among rival sophists, a fellow had the audacity to ply him with abuse when he took part and appeared to favour one side. Thereupon he gradually backed away to his

apparitoribus prodiit citatumque pro tribunali voce
praeconis conviciatorem rapi iussit in carcerem.

4 Comperit deinde Iuliam uxorem ob libidines atque
adulteria damnatam repudiumque ei suo nomine ex
auctoritate Augusti remissum ; et quamquam laetus
nuntio, tamen officii duxit, quantum in se esset, exo-
rare filiae patrem frequentibus litteris et vel ut-
cumque meritae, quidquid umquam dono dedisset,
5 concedere. Transacto autem tribuniciae potestatis
tempore, confessus tandem, nihil aliud secessu
devitasse se quam aemulationis cum C. Lucioque
suspicionem, petit ut sibi securo iam ab hac parte,
conroboratis his et secundum locum facile tutantibus
permitteretur revisere necessitudines, quarum de-
siderio teneretur. Sed neque impetravit ultroque
etiam admonitus est, dimitteret omnem curam
suorum, quos tam cupide reliquisset.

XII. Remansit igitur Rhodi contra voluntatem,
vix per matrem consecutus, ut ad velandam igno-
miniam quasi legatus Augusto abesset.

2 Enimvero tunc non privatum modo, sed etiam
obnoxium et trepidum egit, mediterraneis agris
abditus vitansque praeternavigantium officia, quibus
frequentabatur assidue, nemine cum imperio aut

ᵃ The title of *legatus* gave him an official position and concealed the fact that his absence was a forced one.

310

house, and then suddenly coming out with his lictors and attendants, and bidding his crier to summon the foul-mouthed fellow before his tribunal, he had him taken off to prison.

Shortly after this he learned that his wife Julia had been banished because of her immorality and adulteries, and that a bill of divorce had been sent her in his name by authority of Augustus; but welcome as this news was, he yet considered it his duty to make every possible effort in numerous letters to reconcile the father to his daughter; and regardless of her deserts, to allow her to keep any gifts which he had himself made her at any time. Moreover, when the term of his tribunicial power was at an end, at last admitting that the sole object of his retirement had been to avoid the suspicion of rivalry with Gaius and Lucius, he asked that inasmuch as he was free from care in that regard, since they were now grown up and had an undisputed claim on the succession, he be allowed to visit his relatives, whom he sorely missed. But his request was denied and he was besides admonished to give up all thought of his kindred, whom he had so eagerly abandoned.

XII. Accordingly he remained in Rhodes against his will, having with difficulty through his mother's aid secured permission that, while away from Rome, he should have the title of envoy[a] of Augustus, so as to conceal his disgrace.

Then in very truth he lived not only in private, but even in danger and fear, secluded in the country away from the sea, and shunning the attentions of those that sailed that way; these, however, were constantly thrust on him, since

magistratu tendente quoquam quin deverteret
Rhodum. Et accesserunt maioris sollicitudinis
causae. Namque privignum Gaium Orienti prae-
positum, cum visendi gratia traiecisset Samum,
alieniorem sibi sensit ex criminationibus M. Lolli
3 comitis et rectoris eius. Venit etiam in suspicionem
per quosdam beneficii sui centuriones a commeatu
castra repetentis mandata ad complures dedisse
ambigua et quae temptare singulorum animos ad
novas res viderentur. De qua suspicione certïor ab
Augusto factus non cessavit efflagitare aliquem
cuiuslibet ordinis custodem factis atque dictis suis.

XIII. Equi quoque et armorum solitas exercitationes omisit redegitque se deposito patrio habitu ad
pallium et crepidas atque in tali statu biennio fere
permansit, contemptior in dies et invisior, adeo ut
imagines eius et statuas Nemausenses [1] subverterint
ac familiari quondam convivio mentione eius orta
exstiterit qui Gaio polliceretur, confestim se, si
iuberet, Rhodum navigaturum caputque exsulis—sic
2 enim appellabatur—relaturum. Quo praecipue non
iam metu sed discrimine coactus est, tam suis quam
matris inpensissimis precibus reditum expostulare,
impetravitque adiutus aliquantum etiam casu. Destinatum Augusto erat, nihil super ea re nisi ex

---

[1] Nemausenses, Q²ς; Remausenses, Ω.

[a] The Greek dress; see note on *Aug.* xcviii. 3.
[b] In Gallia Comata, where Tiberius had been governor;
see chap. ix. 1.

no general or magistrate who was on his way to any province failed to put in at Rhodes. He had besides reasons for still greater anxiety; for when he had crossed to Samos to visit his stepson Gaius, who had been made governor of the Orient, he found him somewhat estranged through the slanders of Marcus Lollius, a member of Gaius' staff and his guardian. He also incurred the suspicion of having through some centurions of his appointment, who were returning to camp after a furlough, sent messages to several persons which were of an ambiguous character and apparently designed to incite them to revolution. On being informed by Augustus of this suspicion, he unceasingly demanded the appointment of someone, of any rank whatsoever, to keep watch over his actions and words.

XIII. He also gave up his usual exercises with horses and arms, and laying aside the garb of his country, took to the cloak and slippers ^a; and in this state he continued for upwards of two years, becoming daily an object of greater contempt and aversion. This went so far that the citizens of Nemausus ^b threw down his statues and busts, and when mention was once made of him at a private dinner party, a man got up and assured Gaius that if he would say the word, he would at once take ship for Rhodes and bring back the head of "the exile," as he was commonly called. It was this act especially, which made his position no longer one of mere fear but of actual peril, that drove Tiberius to sue for his recall with most urgent prayers, in which his mother joined; and he obtained it, although partly owing to a fortunate chance. Augustus had resolved to come to no decision of the question which was not agree-

voluntate maioris fili statuere ; is forte tunc M. Lollio
offensior, facilis exorabilisque in vitricum fuit.   Permittente ergo Gaio revocatus est, verum sub condicione ne quam partem curamve rei p. attingeret.

XIV. Rediit octavo post secessum anno, magna
nec incerta spe futurorum, quam et ostentis et
praedictionibus ab initio aetatis conceperat.

2   Praegnans eo [1] Livia cum an marem editura esset,
variis captaret ominibus, ovum incubanti gallinae
subductum nunc sua nunc ministrarum manu per
vices usque fovit, quoad pullus insigniter cristatus
exclusus est.   Ac de infante Scribonius mathematicus praeclara spopondit, etiam regnaturum quandoque, sed sine regio insigni, ignota scilicet tunc
3 adhuc Caesarum potestate.   Et ingresso primam
expeditionem ac per Macedoniam ducente exercitum
in Syriam, accidit ut apud Philippos sacratae olim
victricium legionum arae sponte subitis conlucerent
ignibus ; et mox, cum Illyricum petens iuxta
Patavium adisset Geryonis oraculum, sorte tracta,
qua monebatur ut de consultationibus in Aponi
fontem talos aureos iaceret, evenit ut summum
numerum iacti ab eo ostenderent ; hodieque sub
4 aqua visuntur hi tali.   Ante paucos vero quam
revocaretur dies aquila numquam antea Rhodi
conspecta in culmine domus eius assedit ; et pridie

---

[1] eo, *Bentley* ; eum, Ω.

---

[a] Gaius Caesar.

able to his elder son,[a] who, as it happened, was at the time somewhat at odds with Marcus Lollius, and accordingly ready to lend an ear to his stepfather's prayers. With his consent therefore Tiberius was recalled, but on the understanding that he should take no part or active interest in public affairs.

XIV. So he returned in the eighth year after his 2 A.D. retirement, with that strong and unwavering confidence in his destiny, which he had conceived from his early years because of omens and predictions.

When Livia was with child with him, and was trying to divine by various omens whether she would bring forth a male, she took an egg from under a setting-hen, and when she had warmed it in her own hand and those of her attendants in turn, a cock with a fine crest was hatched. In his infancy the astrologer Scribonius promised him an illustrious career and even that he would one day be king, but without the crown of royalty; for at that time of course the rule of the Caesars was as yet unheard of. Again, on his 42 B.C. first campaign, when he was leading an army through Macedonia into Syria, it chanced that at Philippi the altars consecrated in bygone days by the victorious legions gleamed of their own accord with sudden fires. When later, on his way to Illyricum, he visited the oracle of Geryon near Patavium, and drew a lot which advised him to seek an answer to his inquiries by throwing golden dice into the fount of Aponus, it came to pass that the dice which he threw showed the highest posssible number; and those dice may be seen to-day under the water. A few days before his recall an eagle, a bird never before seen in Rhodes, perched upon the roof of his house; and the day before he was notified that he

quam de reditu certior fieret, vestimenta mutanti tunica ardere visa est. Thrasyllum quoque mathematicum, quem ut sapientiae professorem contubernio admoverat, tum maxime expertus est affirmantem nave provisa gaudium afferri ; cum quidem illum durius et contra praedicta cadentibus rebus ut falsum et secretorum temere conscium, eo ipso momento, dum spatiatur una, praecipitare in mare destinasset.

XV. Romam reversus deducto in Forum filio Druso statim e Carinis ac Pompeiana domo Esquilias in hortos Maecenatianos transmigravit totumque se ad quietem contulit, privata modo officia obiens ac publicorum munerum expers.

2 Gaio et Lucio intra triennium defunctis adoptatur ab Augusto simul cum fratre eorum M. Agrippa, coactus prius ipse Germanicum fratris sui filium adoptare Nec quicquam postea pro patre familias egit aut ius, quod amiserat, ex ulla parte retinuit. Nam neque donavit neque manumisit, ne hereditatem quidem aut legata percepit ulla aliter quam ut peculio referret accepta. Nihil ex eo tempore praetermissum est ad maiestatem eius augendam ac multo magis, postquam Agrippa abdicato atque seposito certum erat, uni spem successionis incumbere.

XVI. Data rursus potestas tribunicia in quinquennium, delegatus pacandae Germaniae status,

---

a Cf. *Aug.* xxvi. 2.

b " The Keels," so-called from its shape, on the western slope of the Esquiline Hill, where the church of S. Pietro in Vincoli now stands.

c *Peculium* was the term applied to the savings of a slave or of a son under his father's control, which they were allowed to hold as their own property, though technically belonging to the master or father.

might return, his tunic seemed to blaze as he was changing his clothes. It was just at this time that he was convinced of the powers of the astrologer Thrasyllus, whom he had attached to his household as a learned man; for as soon as he caught sight of the ship, Thrasyllus declared that it brought good news—this too at the very moment when Tiberius had made up his mind to push the man off into the sea as they were strolling together, believing him a false prophet and too hastily made the confidant of his secrets, because things were turning out adversely and contrary to his predictions.

XV. On his return to Rome, after introducing his son Drusus to public life,[a] he at once moved from the Carinae [b] and the house of the Pompeys to the gardens of Maecenas on the Esquiline, where he led a very retired life, merely attending to his personal affairs and exercising no public functions.

When Gaius and Lucius died within three years, he was adopted by Augustus along with their brother Marcus Agrippa, being himself first compelled to adopt his nephew Germanicus. And from that time on he ceased to act as the head of a family, or to retain in any particular the privileges which he had given up. For he neither made gifts nor freed slaves, and he did not even accept an inheritance or any legacies, except to enter them as an addition to his personal property.[c] From this time on nothing was left undone which could add to his prestige, especially after the disowning and banishment of Agrippa made it clear that the hope of the succession lay in him alone.

XVI. He was given the tribunician power for a second term of three years, the duty of subjugating

Parthorum legati mandatis Augusto Romae redditis eum quoque adire in provincia iussi. Sed nuntiata Illyrici defectione transiit ad curam novi belli, quod gravissimum omnium externorum bellorum post Punica, per quindecim legiones paremque auxiliorum copiam triennio gessit in magnis omnium

2 rerum difficultatibus summaque frugum inopia. Et quanquam saepius revocaretur, tamen perseveravit, metuens ne vicinus et praevalens hostis instaret ultro cedentibus. Ac perseverantiae grande pretium tulit, toto Illyrico, quod inter Italiam regnumque Noricum et Thraciam et Macedoniam interque Danuvium [1] flumen et sinum maris Hadriatici patet, perdomito et in dicionem redacto.

XVII. Cui gloriae amplior adhuc ex opportunitate cumulus accessit. Nam sub id fere tempus Quintilius Varus cum tribus legionibus in Germania periit, nemine dubitante quin victores Germani iuncturi se Pannoniis fuerint, nisi debellatum prius Illyricum esset. Quas ob res triumphus ei decretus est

2 multique [2] et magni honores. Censuerunt etiam quidam ut Pannonicus, alii ut Invictus, nonnulli ut Pius cognominaretur. Sed de cognomine intercessit Augustus, eo contentum repromittens, quod se defuncto suscepturus esset. Triumphum ipse distulit maesta civitate clade Variana; nihilo minus urbem praetextatus et laurea coronatus intravit

[1] Danuvium] Danubium, Ω.
[2] est multique, 16*th century editions*; et multi, *Stephanus*; multi, Ω.

Germany was assigned him, and the envoys of the Parthians, after presenting their instructions to Augustus in Rome, were bidden to appear also before him in his province. But when the revolt of Illyricum was reported, he was transferred to the charge of a new war, the most serious of all foreign wars since those with Carthage, which he carried on for three years with fifteen legions and a corresponding force of auxiliaries, amid great difficulties of every kind and the utmost scarcity of supplies. But though he was often recalled, he none the less kept on, for fear that the enemy, who were close at hand and very strong, might assume the offensive if the Romans gave ground. He reaped an ample reward for his perseverance, for he completely subdued and reduced to submission the whole of Illyricum, which is bounded by Italy and the kingdom of Noricum, by Thrace and Macedonia, by the Danube, and by the Adriatic sea.

XVII. Circumstances gave this exploit a larger and crowning glory; for it was at just about that time that Quintilius Varus perished with three legions in Germany, and no one doubted that the victorious Germans would have united with the Pannonians, had not Illyricum been subdued first. Consequently a triumph was voted him and many high honours. Some also recommended that he be given the surname of Pannonicus, others of Invictus, others of Pius. Augustus however vetoed the surname, reiterating the promise that Tiberius would be satisfied with the one which he would receive at his father's death. Tiberius himself put off the triumph, because the country was in mourning for the disaster to Varus; but he entered the city clad in the purple-bordered toga and crowned with laurel, and mounting a

positumque in Saeptis tribunal senatu astante
conscendit ac medius inter duos consules cum
Augusto simul sedit; unde populo consalutato
circum templa deductus est.

XVIII. Proximo anno repetita Germania cum
animadverteret Varianam cladem temeritate et
neglegentia ducis accidisse, nihil non de consilii
sententia egit; semper alias sui arbitrii contentusque
se uno, tunc praeter consuetudinem cum compluribus
de ratione belli communicavit. Curam quoque solito
exactiorem praestitit. Traiecturus Rhenum commeatum omnem ad certam formulam adstrictum
non ante transmisit, quam consistens apud ripam
explorasset vehiculorum onera, ne qua deportarentur
2 nisi concessa aut necessaria. Trans Rhenum vero
eum vitae ordinem tenuit, ut sedens in caespite
nudo cibum caperet, saepe sine tentorio pernoctaret,
praecepta sequentis diei omnia, et si quid subiti
muneris iniungendum esset, per libellos daret;
addita monitione ut, de quo quisque dubitaret,
se nec alio interprete quacumque vel noctis hora
uteretur.

XIX. Disciplinam acerrime exegit animad-
versionum et ignominiarum generibus ex antiquitate
repetitis atque etiam legato legionis, quod paucos
milites cum liberto suo trans ripam venatum misisset,
ignominia notato. Proelia, quamvis minimum
fortunae casibusque permitteret, aliquanto con-

tribunal which had been set up in the Saepta, while the senate stood alongside, he took his seat beside Augustus between the two consuls. Having greeted the people from this position, he was escorted to the various temples.

XVIII. The next year he returned to Germany, and realising that the disaster to Varus was due to that general's rashness and lack of care, he took no step without the approval of a council; while he had always before been a man of independent judgment and self reliance, then contrary to his habit he consulted with many advisers about the conduct of the campaign. He also observed more scrupulous care than usual. When on the point of crossing the Rhine, he reduced all the baggage to a prescribed limit, and would not start without standing on the bank and inspecting the loads of the wagons, to make sure that nothing was taken except what was allowed or necessary. Once on the other side, he adopted the following manner of life: he took his meals sitting on the bare turf, often passed the night without a tent, and gave all his orders for the following day, as well as notice of any sudden emergency, in writing; adding the injunction that if anyone was in doubt about any matter, he was to consult him personally at any hour whatsoever, even of the night.

XIX. He required the strictest discipline, reviving bygone methods of punishment and ignominy, and even degrading the commander of a legion for sending a few soldiers across the river to accompany one of his freedmen on a hunting expedition. Although he left very little to fortune and chance, he entered battles with considerably greater confidence

stantius inibat, quotiens lucubrante se subito ac nullo
propellente decideret lumen et exstingueretur,
confidens, ut aiebat, ostento sibi a maioribus suis in
omni ducatu expertissimo. Sed re prospere gesta
non multum afuit quin a Bructero quodam occideretur, cui inter proximos versanti et trepidatione
detecto tormentis expressa confessio est cogitati
facinoris.

XX. A Germania in urbem post biennium
regressus triumphum, quem distulerat, egit prose-
quentibus etiam legatis, quibus triumphalia ornamenta impetrarat. Ac prius quam in Capitolium
flecteret, descendit e curru seque praesidenti patri
ad genua summisit. Batonem Pannonium ducem
ingentibus donatum praemiis Ravennam transtulit,
gratiam referens, quod se quondam cum exercitu
iniquitate loci circumclusum passus esset[1] evadere.
Prandium dehinc populo mille mensis et congiarium
trecenos nummos viritim dedit. Dedicavit et
Concordiae aedem, item Pollucis et Castoris suo
fratrisque nomine de manubiis.

XXI. Ac non multo post lege per consules lata, ut
provincias cum Augusto communiter administraret
simulque censum ageret,[2] condito lustro in Illyricum
profectus est. Et statim ex itinere revocatus iam
quidem adfectum, sed tamen spirantem adhuc
Augustum repperit fuitque una secreto per totum
diem.

[1] esset, *Stephanus* ; est, Ω.
[2] ageret, T⁵ ; *the other mss. have* augeret.

---

[a] At the Porta Triumphalis, at the head of the senate, who
met the triumphing general there, and joined in the procession.

[b] Ordinarily the leaders of the enemy were strangled in
the *carcer*, or dungeon, at the foot of the Capitoline Hill.

[c] See *Aug.* xcvii. 1.

whenever it happened that, as he was working at night, his lamp suddenly and without human agency died down and went out; trusting, as he used to say, to an omen in which he had great confidence, since both he and his ancestors had found it trustworthy in all of their campaigns. Yet in the very hour of victory he narrowly escaped assassination by one of the Bructeri, who got access to him among his attendants, but was detected through his nervousness; whereupon a confession of his intended crime was wrung from him by torture.

XX. After two years he returned to the city from Germany and celebrated the triumph which he had postponed, accompanied also by his generals, for whom he had obtained the triumphal regalia. And before turning to enter the Capitol, he dismounted from his chariot and fell at the knees of his father, who was presiding over the ceremonies.[a] He sent Bato, the leader of the Pannonians, to Ravenna,[b] after presenting him with rich gifts; thus showing his gratitude to him for allowing him to escape when he was trapped with his army in a dangerous place. Then he gave a banquet to the people at a thousand tables, and a largess of three hundred sesterces to every man. With the proceeds of his spoils he restored and dedicated the temple of Concord, as well as that of Pollux and Castor, in his own name and that of his brother.

XXI. Since the consuls caused a law to be passed soon after this that he should govern the provinces jointly with Augustus and hold the census with him, he set out for Illyricum on the conclusion of the lustral ceremonies[c]; but he was at once recalled, and finding Augustus in his last illness but still alive, he spent an entire day with him in private.

12 A.D.

2   Scio vulgo persuasum quasi egresso post secretum
sermonem Tiberio vox Augusti per cubicularios
excepta sit : " Miserum populum R., qui sub tam
lentis maxillis erit ! " Ne illud quidem ignoro aliquos
tradidisse, Augustum palam nec dissimulanter morum
eius diritatem adeo improbasse, ut nonnumquam
remissiores hilarioresque sermones superveniente eo
abrumperet ; sed expugnatum precibus uxoris
adoptionem non abnuisse, vel etiam ambitione
tractum, ut tali successore desiderabilior ipse quan-
3   doque fieret. Adduci tamen nequeo quin existimem,
circumspectissimum et prudentissimum principem in
tanto praesertim negotio nihil temere fecisse ; sed
vitiis Tiberi virtutibusque perpensis potiores duxisse
virtutes, praesertim cum et rei p. causa adoptare se
eum pro contione iuraverit et epistulis aliquot ut
peritissimum rei militaris utque unicum p. R.
praesidium prosequatur. Ex quibus in exemplum
pauca hinc inde subieci.

4   " Vale, iucundissime Tiberi, et feliciter rem gere,
ἐμοὶ καὶ ταῖς μούσαις [1] στρατηγῶν. Iucundissime et ita
sim felix, vir fortissime et dux νομιμώτατε, vale."

5   " Ordinem aestivorum tuorum ego vero laudo,[2] mi
Tiberi, et inter tot rerum difficultates καὶ τοσαύτην
ἀποθυμίαν τῶν στρατευομένων non potuisse quemquam
prudentius gerere se quam tu gesseris, existimo.   Ii

---

[1] μούσαις] μουιϲαϲαιϲτ, *mss.*   [2] laudo, *inserted by Stephanus.*

[a] If the text is correct, the reference is to Tiberius'
literary tastes ; cf. Horace, *Odes*, 3. 4. 37 ff. ; *Epist.* 1. 3.

TIBERIUS

I know that it is commonly believed, that when Tiberius left the room after this confidential talk, Augustus was overheard by his chamberlains to say : " Alas for the Roman people, to be ground by jaws that crunch so slowly !" I also am aware that some have written that Augustus so openly and unreservedly disapproved of his austere manners, that he sometimes broke off his freer and lighter conversation when Tiberius appeared ; but that overcome by his wife's entreaties he did not reject his adoption, or perhaps was even led by selfish considerations, that with such a successor he himself might one day be more regretted. But after all I cannot be led to believe that an emperor of the utmost prudence and foresight acted without consideration, especially in a matter of so great moment. It is my opinion that after weighing the faults and the merits of Tiberius, he decided that the latter preponderated, especially since he took oath before the people that he was adopting Tiberius for the good of the country, and alludes to him in several letters as a most able general and the sole defence of the Roman people. In illustration of both these points, I append a few extracts from these letters.

" Fare thee well, Tiberius, most charming of men, and success go with you, as you war for me and for the Muses.[a] Fare thee well, most charming and valiant of men and most conscientious of generals, or may I never know happiness."

" I have only praise for the conduct of your summer campaigns, dear Tiberius, and I am sure that no one could have acted with better judgment than you did amid so many difficulties and such apathy of your army.

325

quoque qui tecum fuerunt omnes confitentur, versum illum in te posse dici :

> Unus homo nobis vigilando restituit rem."

6   "Sive quid incidit de quo sit cogitandum diligentius, sive quid stomachor, valde medius Fidius Tiberium meum desidero succurritque versus ille Homericus :

> Τούτου γ' ἑσπομένοιο καὶ ἐκ πυρὸς αἰθομένοιο
> Ἄμφω νοστήσαιμεν, ἐπεὶ περίοιδε νοῆσαι.

"Attenuatum te esse continuatione laborum cum audio et lego, di me perdant nisi cohorrescit corpus meum ; teque oro ut parcas tibi, ne si te languere audierimus, et ego et mater tua expiremus et summa imperi sui populus R. periclitetur."

"Nihil interest valeam ipse necne, si tu non valebis."

"Deos obsecro, ut te nobis conservent et valere nunc et semper patiantur, si non p. R. perosi sunt."

XXII. Excessum Augusti non prius palam fecit, quam Agrippa iuvene interempto. Hunc tribunus militum custos appositus occidit lectis codicillis, quibus ut id faceret iubebatur ; quos codicillos dubium fuit, Augustusne moriens reliquisset, quo materiam

---

    ^a Cf. Enn. *Ann.* 370 V²; where *cunctando* takes the place of *vigilando*.

    ^b Literally, "by the god of Truth"; Fidius was one of the surnames of Jupiter.   ^c *Iliad*, 10. 246 f.

326

All who were with you agree that the well-known line could be applied to you:

" ' One man alone by his foresight has saved our dear country from ruin.[a] ' "

" If anything comes up that calls for careful thought, or if I am vexed at anything, I long mightily, so help me Heaven,[b] for my dear Tiberius, and the lines of Homer come to my mind:

" ' Let him but follow and we too, though flames round about us be raging,
Both may return to our homes, since great are his wisdom and knowledge.[c] ' "

" When I hear and read that you are worn out by constant hardships, may the Gods confound me if my own body does not wince in sympathy; and I beseech you to spare yourself, that the news of your illness may not kill your mother and me, and endanger the Roman people in the person of their future ruler."

" It matters not whether I am well or not, if you are not well."

" I pray the Gods to preserve you to us and to grant you good health now and forever, if they do not utterly hate the people of Rome."

XXII. Tiberius did not make the death of Augustus public until the young Agrippa had been disposed of. The latter was slain by a tribune of the soldiers appointed to guard him, who received a letter in which he was bidden to do the deed; but it is not known whether Augustus left this letter when he died, to remove a future source of discord, or whether Livia wrote it herself in the name of her

tumultus post se subduceret; an nomine Augusti Livia
et ea conscio Tiberio an ignaro, dictasset. Tiberius
renuntianti tribuno, factum esse quod imperasset,
neque imperasse se et rediturum eum senatui
rationem respondit, invidiam scilicet in praesentia
vitans. Nam mox silentio rem obliteravit.

XXIII. Iure autem tribuniciae potestatis coacto
senatu incohataque adlocutione derepente velut impar
dolori congemuit, utque non solum vox sed et spiritus
deficeret optavit ac perlegendum librum Druso filio
tradidit. Inlatum deinde Augusti testamentum, non
admissis signatoribus nisi senatorii ordinis, ceteris
extra curiam signa agnoscentibus, recitavit per libertum. Testamenti initium fuit: "Quoniam atrox
fortuna Gaium et Lucium filios mihi eripuit, Tiberius
Caesar mihi ex parte dimidia et sextante heres esto."
Quo et ipso aucta suspicio est opinantium successorem
ascitum eum necessitate magis quam iudicio, quando
ita praefari non abstinuerit.

XXIV. Principatum, quamvis neque occupare confestim neque agere dubitasset, et statione militum,
hoc est vi et specie dominationis assumpta, diu tamen
recusavit, impudentissimo mimo [1] nunc adhortantis
amicos increpans ut ignaros, quanta belua esset
imperium, nunc precantem senatum et procum-

---

[1] mimo, *J.F. Gronovius*; animo, Ω.

husband; and in the latter case, whether it was with or without the connivance of Tiberius. At all events, when the tribune reported that he had done his bidding, Tiberius replied that he had given no such order, and that the man must render an account to the senate; apparently trying to avoid odium at the time, for later his silence consigned the matter to oblivion.

XXIII. When, however, by virtue of his tribunicial power, he had convened the senate and had begun to address it, he suddenly groaned aloud, as if overcome by grief, and with the wish that not only his voice, but his life as well might leave him, handed the written speech to his son Drusus to finish. Then bringing in the will of Augustus, he had it read by a freedman, admitting of the signers only such as were of the senatorial order, while the others acknowledged their seals outside the House. The will began thus: "Since a cruel fate has bereft me of my sons Gaius and Lucius, be Tiberius Caesar heir to two-thirds of my estate." These words in themselves added to the suspicion of those who believed that he had named Tiberius his successor from necessity rather than from choice, since he allowed himself to write such a preamble.

XXIV. Though Tiberius did not hesitate at once to assume and to exercise the imperial authority, surrounding himself with a guard of soldiers, that is, with the actual power and the outward sign of sovereignty, yet he refused the title for a long time, with barefaced hypocrisy now upbraiding his friends who urged him to accept it, saying that they did not realise what a monster the empire was, and now by evasive answers and calculating hesitancy keeping

bentem sibi ad genua ambiguis responsis et callida
cunctatione suspendens, ut quidam patientiam rum-
perent atque unus in tumultu proclamaret: " Aut
agat aut desistat!" Alter coram exprobraret ceteros,
quod polliciti sint tarde praestare, sed[1] ipsum, quod

2 praestet tarde polliceri. Tandem quasi coactus et
querens miseram et onerosam iniungi sibi servitutem,
recepit imperium; nec tamen aliter, quam ut deposi-
turum se quandoque spem faceret. Ipsius verba sunt:
" Dum veniam ad id tempus, quo vobis aequum possit
videri dare vos aliquam senectuti meae requiem."

XXV. Cunctandi causa erat metus undique im-
minentium discriminum, ut saepe lupum se auribus
tenere diceret. Nam et servus Agrippae Clemens
nomine non contemnendam manum in ultionem
domini compararat et L. Scribonius Libo vir nobilis
res novas clam moliebatur et duplex seditio militum

2 in Illyrico et in Germania exorta est. Flagitabant
ambo exercitus multa extra ordinem, ante omnia ut
aequarentur stipendio praetorianis.[2] Germaniciani
quidem etiam principem detractabant non a se datum
summaque vi Germanicum, qui tum iis praeerat, ad
capessendam rem p. urgebant, quanquam obfirmate
resistentem. Quem maxime casum timens, partes
sibi quas senatui liberet, tuendas in re p. depoposcit,
quando universae sufficere solus nemo posset nisi cum

3 altero vel etiam cum pluribus. Simulavit et valitu-

---

[1] sed, ΠQRP[2]; *the other mss. have* se (se et, O); *omitted by*
Lipsius.   [2] praetorianis] praetoriani, *mss.*

[a] A Greek proverb; cf. Ter. *Phorm.* 506 and Donatus,
ad loc.

the senators in suspense when they implored him
to yield, and fell at his feet. Finally, some lost
patience, and one man cried out in the confusion:
"Let him take it or leave it." Another openly
voiced the taunt that others were slow in doing what
they promised, but that he was slow to promise what
he was already doing. At last, as though on
compulsion, and complaining that a wretched and
burdensome slavery was being forced upon him,
he accepted the empire, but in such fashion as to
suggest the hope that he would one day lay it down.
His own words are: "Until I come to the time
when it may seem right to you to grant an old man
some repose."

XXV. The cause of his hesitation was fear of the
dangers which threatened him on every hand, and
often led him to say that he was "holding a wolf by
the ears.[a]" For a slave of Agrippa, Clemens by name,
had collected a band of no mean size to avenge his
master; Lucius Scribonius Libo, one of the nobles,
was secretly plotting a revolution; and a mutiny of
the soldiers broke out in two places, Illyricum and
Germany. Both armies demanded numerous special
privileges—above all, that they should receive the
same pay as the praetorians. The army in Germany
was, besides, reluctant to accept an emperor who was
not its own choice, and with the greatest urgency
besought Germanicus, their commander at the time,
to assume the purple, in spite of his positive refusal.
Fear of this possibility in particular led Tiberius
to ask the senate for any part in the administration
that it might please them to assign him, saying that
no one man could bear the whole burden without a
colleague, or even several colleagues. He also

dinem, quo aequiore animo Germanicus celerem successionem vel certe societatem principatus opperiretur.
Compositis seditionibus Clementem quoque fraude
deceptum redegit in potestatem. Libonem, ne quid
in novitate acerbius fieret, secundo demum anno in
senatu coarguit, medio temporis spatio tantum cavere
contentus ; nam et inter pontifices sacrificanti simul
pro secespita plumbeum cultrum subiciendum curavit
et secretum petenti non nisi adhibito Druso filio dedit
dextramque obambulantis veluti incumbens, quoad
perageretur sermo, continuit.

XXVI. Verum liberatus metu civilem admodum
inter initia ac paulo minus quam privatum egit.   Ex
plurimis maximisque honoribus praeter paucos et
modicos non recepit.   Natalem suum plebeis in-
currentem circensibus vix unius bigae adiectione
honorari passus est.   Templa, flamines, sacerdotes
decerni sibi prohibuit, etiam statuas atque imagines
nisi permittente se poni ; permisitque ea sola condicione, ne inter simulacra deorum sed inter ornamenta
2 aedium ponerentur.   Intercessit et quo minus in acta
sua iuraretur, et ne mensis September Tiberius,
October Livius vocarentur.   Praenomen quoque
imperatoris cognomenque patris patriae et civicam

---

^a The *secespita*, or sacrificial knife, had a long, sharp
point and a double edge, with an ivory handle ornamented
with gold and silver.

^b *Civilis* means "suited to a citizen" (of the days of the
Republic).   His conduct was that of a magistrate of the
olden time, who had regard to the laws and the rights of his
fellow-citizens.

^c The reference is to an oath taken by all the citizens to
support what the emperor had done in the past and might do
in the future ; see Dio, 57. 8.   ^d Cf. *Jul.* lxxvi. 1.

^e See note on *Jul.* ii.   This had been conferred on Augustus
honoris causa, as the saviour of all the citizens.

feigned ill-health, to induce Germanicus to wait with
more patience for a speedy succession, or at least for
a share in the sovereignty. The mutinies were put
down, and he also got Clemens into his power, out-
witting him by stratagem. Not until his second year
did he finally arraign Libo in the senate, fearing to
take any severe measures before his power was secure,
and satisfied in the meantime merely to be on his
guard. Thus when Libo was offering sacrifice with
him among the pontiffs, he had a leaden knife
substituted for the usual one,[a] and when he asked
for a private interview, Tiberius would not grant it
except with his son Drusus present, and as long as
the conference lasted he held fast to Libo's right
arm, under pretence of leaning on it as they walked
together.

XXVI. Once relieved of fear, he at first played a
most unassuming [b] part, almost humbler than that of
a private citizen. Of many high honours he accepted
only a few of the more modest. He barely consented to allow his birthday, which came at the time
of the Plebeian games in the Circus, to be recognized
by the addition of a single two-horse chariot. He
forbade the voting of temples, flamens, and priests in
his honour, and even the setting up of statues and
busts without his permission ; and this he gave only
with the understanding that they were not to be
placed among the likenesses of the gods, but among
the adornments of the temples. He would not
allow an oath to be taken ratifying his acts,[c] nor the
name Tiberius to be given to the month of September,
or that of Livia to October. He also declined the
forename Imperator,[d] the surname of Father of his
Country, and the placing of the civic crown [e] at his

in vestibulo coronam recusavit ; ac ne Augusti quidem nomen, quanquam hereditarium, ullis [1] nisi ad reges ac dynastas epistulis addidit. Nec amplius quam mox tres consulatus, unum paucis diebus, alterum tribus mensibus, tertium absens usque in Idus Maias gessit.

XXVII. Adulationes adeo aversatus est, ut neminem senatorum aut officii aut negotii causa ad lecticam suam admiserit, consularem vero satisfacientem sibi ac per genua orare conantem ita suffugerit, ut caderet supinus ; atque etiam, si quid in sermone vel in continua oratione blandius de se diceretur, non dubitaret interpellare ac reprehendere et commutare continuo. Dominus appellatus a quodam denuntiavit, ne se amplius contumeliae causa nominaret. Alium dicentem sacras eius occupationes et rursus alium, auctore eo senatum se adisse,[2] verba mutare et pro auctore suasorem, pro sacris laboriosas dicere coegit.

XXVIII. Sed et adversus convicia malosque rumores et famosa de se ac suis carmina firmus ac patiens, subinde iactabat in civitate libera linguam mentemque liberas esse debere ; et quondam senatu cognitionem de eius modi criminibus ac reis flagitante : "Non tantum," inquit, "otii habemus, ut implicare nos pluribus negotiis debeamus ; si hanc fenestram aperueritis, nihil aliud agi sinetis ; omnium inimicitiae hoc praetexto ad vos deferentur." Exstat

---

[1] ullis] nullus, *M* ; *the other mss. have* nullis.
[2] adi(i)sse, *ς* ; audisse, *Ω*.

---

[a] See *Aug.* ci. 2. [b] See *Aug.* liii. 1.

door; and he did not even use the title of Augustus in any letters except those to kings and potentates, although it was his by inheritance.[a] He held but three consulships after becoming emperor—one for a few days, a second for three months, and a third, during his absence from the city, until the Ides of May.

18, 21, and 31 A.D.

XXVII. He so loathed flattery that he would not allow any senator to approach his litter, either to pay his respects or on business, and when an ex-consul in apologizing to him attempted to embrace his knees, he drew back in such haste that he fell over backward. In fact, if anyone in conversation or in a set speech spoke of him in too flattering terms, he did not hesitate to interrupt him, to take him to task, and to correct his language on the spot. Being once called "Lord,"[b] he warned the speaker not to address him again in an insulting fashion. When another spoke of his "sacred duties," and still another said that he appeared before the senate "by the emperor's authority," he forced them to change their language, substituting "advice" for "authority" and "laborious" for "sacred."

XXVIII. More than that, he was self-contained and patient in the face of abuse and slander, and of lampoons on himself and his family, often asserting that in a free country there should be free speech and free thought. When the senate on one occasion demanded that cognizance be taken of such offences and those guilty of them, he said: "We have not enough spare time to warrant involving ourselves in more affairs; if you open this loophole you will find no time for any other business; it will be an excuse for laying everybody's quarrels before

et sermo eius in senatu percivilis: "Siquidem locutus aliter fuerit, dabo operam ut rationem factorum meorum dictorumque reddam ; si perseveraverit, in vicem eum odero."

XXIX. Atque haec eo notabiliora erant, quod ipse in appellandis venerandisque et singulis et universis prope excesserat humanitatis modum. Dissentiens in curia a Q. Haterio : "Ignoscas," inquit, " rogo, si quid adversus te liberius sicut senator dixero." Et deinde omnis adloquens : " Dixi et nunc et saepe alias, p. c., bonum et salutarem principem, quem vos tanta et tam libera potestate instruxistis, senatui servire debere et universis civibus saepe et plerumque etiam singulis ; neque id dixisse me paenitet, et bonos et aequos et faventes vos habui dominos et adhuc habeo."

XXX. Quin etiam speciem libertatis quandam induxit conservatis senatui ac magistratibus et maiestate pristina et potestate. Neque tam parvum quicquam neque tam magnum publici privatique negotii fuit, de quo non ad patres conscriptos referretur : de vectigalibus ac monopoliis, de exstruendis reficiendisve operibus, etiam de legendo vel exauctorando milite ac legionum et auxiliorum discriptione, denique quibus imperium prorogari aut extraordinaria bella mandari, quid et qua forma[1] regum[2] litteris rescribi placeret. Praefectum alae

[1] et qua forma, ς ; ad quam formam, *Salmasius* ; et quam formam, Ω.   [2] regum, ς ; legum, Ω.

---

[a] See note on chap. xxvi. 1.

[b] The flattery of the term *dominos* is the more marked because Tiberius himself shrank from it ; cf. xxvii.

[c] That is, the granting to an individual or a company of the exclusive right to sell certain commodities.   Forbidden in *Cod. Just.* 4. 59. 1.

you." A most unassuming[a] remark of his in the senate is also a matter of record: "If so and so criticizes me I shall take care to render an account of my acts and words; if he persists, our enmity will be mutual."

XXIX. All this was the more noteworthy, because in addressing and in paying his respects to the senators individually and as a body he himself almost exceeded the requirements of courtesy. In a disagreement with Quintus Haterius in the House, he said: "I crave your pardon, if in my capacity as senator I use too free language in opposing you." Then addressing the whole body: " I say now and have often said before, Fathers of the Senate, that a well-disposed and helpful prince, to whom you have given such great and unrestrained power, ought to be the servant of the senate, often of the citizens as a whole, and sometimes even of individuals. I do not regret my words, but I have looked upon you as kind, just, and indulgent masters,[b] and still so regard you."

XXX. He even introduced a semblance of free government by maintaining the ancient dignity and powers of the senate and the magistrates; for there was no matter of public or private business so small or so great that he did not lay it before the senators, consulting them about revenues and monopolies,[c] constructing and restoring public buildings, and even about levying and disbanding the soldiers, and the disposal of the legionaries and auxiliaries; finally about the extension of military commands and appointments to the conduct of wars, and the form and content of his replies to the letters of kings. He forced the commander of a troop of horse, when

de vi et rapinis reum causam in senatu dicere coegit. Numquam curiam nisi solus intravit; lectica quondam intro latus aeger comites a se removit.

XXXI. Quaedam adversus sententiam suam decerni ne questus quidem est. Negante eo destinatos magistratus abesse[1] oportere, ut praesentes honori adquiescerent, praetor designatus liberam legationem impetravit. Iterum censente, ut Trebianis legatam in opus novi theatri pecuniam ad munitionem viae transferre concederetur, optinere non potuit quin rata voluntas legatoris esset. Cum senatus consultum per discessionem forte fieret, transeuntem eum in alteram partem, in qua pauciores erant, secutus est nemo.

2 Cetera quoque non nisi per magistratus et iure ordinario agebantur, tanta consulum auctoritate, ut legati ex Africa adierint eos querentes, trahi se a Caesare ad quem missi forent. Nec mirum, cum palam esset, ipsum quoque eisdem et assurgere et decedere via.

XXXII. Corripuit consulares exercitibus praepositos, quod non de rebus gestis senatui scriberent quodque de tribuendis quibusdam militaribus donis ad se referrent, quasi non omnium tribuendorum ipsi ius haberent. Praetorem conlaudavit, quod

---

[1] abesse, ς ; adesse, Ω.

[a] That is, to make use of the public post ; see *Aug.* xlix. 3, and Cic. *de Leg.* 3. 18.   [b] See *Aug.* xxv. 3.

charged with violence and robbery, to plead his cause before the senate. He always entered the House alone; and when he was brought in once in a litter because of illness, he dismissed his attendants.

XXXI. When certain decrees were passed contrary to his expressed opinion, he did not even remonstrate. Although he declared that those who were elected to office ought to remain in the city and give personal attention to their duties, a praetor elect obtained permission to travel abroad with the privileges of an ambassador.[a] On another occasion when he recommended that the people of Trebia be allowed to use, in making a road, a sum of money which had been left them for the construction of a new theatre, he could not prevent the wish of the testator from being carried out. When it happened that the senate passed a decree by division and he went over to the side of the minority, not a man followed him.

Other business as well was done solely through the magistrates and the ordinary process of law, while the importance of the consuls was such that certain envoys from Africa presented themselves before them with the complaint that their time was being wasted by Caesar, to whom they had been sent. And this was not surprising, for it was plain to all that he himself actually arose in the presence of the consuls, and made way for them on the street.

XXXII. He rebuked some ex-consuls in command of armies, because they did not write their reports to the senate, and for referring to him the award of some military prizes,[b] as if they had not themselves the right to bestow everything of the kind. He

honore inito consuetudinem antiquam rettulisset
de maioribus suis pro contione memorandi. Quorundam illustrium exsequias usque ad rogum frequentavit.

2   Parem moderationem minoribus quoque et personis
et rebus exhibuit. Cum Rhodiorum magistratus,
quod litteras publicas sine subscriptione ad se
dederant, evocasset, ne verbo quidem insectatus
ac tantum modo iussos subscribere remisit. Diogenes
grammaticus, disputare sabbatis Rhodi solitus, veni-
entem eum, ut se extra ordinem audiret, non
admiserat ac per servolum suum in septimum
diem distulerat; hunc Romae salutandi sui causa
pro foribus adstantem nihil amplius quam ut post
septimum annum rediret admonuit. Praesidibus
onerandas tributo provincias suadentibus rescripsit
boni pastoris esse tondere pecus, non deglubere.

XXXIII. Paulatim principem exseruit praestititque
etsi varium diu, commodiorem tamen saepius et
ad utilitates publicas proniorem. Ac primo eatenus
interveniebat, ne quid perperam fieret. Itaque
et constitutiones senatus quasdam rescidit et magistratibus pro tribunali cognoscentibus plerumque
se offerebat consiliarium assidebatque iuxtim vel
exadversum in parte primori; et si quem reorum
elabi gratia rumor esset, subitus aderat iudicesque

---

^a Consisting of prayers for the emperor's welfare ; see Dio,
57. 11, and cf. Plin. *Epist.* 10. 1, *Fortem te et hilarem, Imperator optime, et privatim et publice opto.*

^b The designation of the seventh day of the week (Saturday)
by the Jewish term "Sabbath" seems to have been common;
cf. *Aug.* lxxvi. 2.

^c That is, at one end of the curved platform, to leave room
for the praetor in the middle ; cf. Tac. *Ann.* 1. 75, *iudiciis
adsidebat* in cornu tribunalis, *ne praetorem curuli depelleret.*

highly complimented a praetor, because on entering
upon his office he had revived the custom of eulogiz-
ing his ancestors before the people. He attended
the obsequies of certain distinguished men, even
going to the funeral-pyre.

He showed equal modesty towards persons of
lower rank and in matters of less moment. When
he had summoned the magistrates of Rhodes, because
they had written him letters on public business
without the concluding formula,[a] he uttered not a
word of censure, but merely dismissed them with
orders to supply the omission. The grammarian
Diogenes, who used to lecture every Sabbath [b] at
Rhodes, would not admit Tiberius when he came to
hear him on a different day, but sent a message by a
common slave of his, putting him off to the seventh
day. When this man waited before the Emperor's door
at Rome to pay his respects, Tiberius took no further
revenge than to bid him return seven years later.
To the governors who recommended burdensome
taxes for his provinces, he wrote in answer that it
was the part of a good shepherd to shear his flock,
not skin it.

XXXIII. Little by little he unmasked the ruler,
and although for some time his conduct was variable,
yet he more often showed himself kindly and devoted
to the public weal. His intervention too was at first
limited to the prevention of abuses. Thus he revoked
some regulations of the senate and sometimes offered
the magistrates his services as adviser, when they
sat in judgment on the tribunal, taking his place beside
them or opposite them at one end of the platform [c];
and if it was rumoured that any of the accused were
being acquitted through influence, he would suddenly

aut e plano aut e quaesitoris tribunali legum et religionis et noxae, de qua cognoscerent, admonebat; atque etiam, si qua in publicis moribus desidia aut mala consuetudine labarent, corrigenda suscepit.

XXXIV. Ludorum ac munerum impensas corripuit mercedibus scaenicorum recisis paribusque gladiatorum ad certum numerum redactis. Corinthiorum vasorum pretia in immensum exarsisse tresque mullos triginta milibus nummum venisse graviter conquestus, adhibendum supellectili modum censuit annonamque macelli senatus arbitratu quotannis temperandam, dato aedilibus negotio popinas ganeasque usque eo inhibendi, ut ne opera quidem pistoria proponi venalia sinerent. Et ut parsimoniam publicam exemplo quoque iuvaret, sollemnibus ipse cenis pridiana saepe ac semesa obsonia apposuit dimidiatumque aprum, affirmans omnia eadem habere, quae totum.

2 Cotidiana oscula edicto prohibuit, item strenarum commercium ne ultra Kal. Ian. exerceretur. Consuerat quadriplam strenam, et de manu, reddere ; sed offensus interpellari se toto mense ab iis qui potestatem sui die festo non habuissent, ultra non tulit.

XXXV. Matronas prostratae pudicitiae, quibus accusator publicus deesset, ut propinqui more maiorum

---

¹ mullos, *ς*; *the other mss. have* mulos.

---

a See note on *Jul.* xvii. 1.   *b* Cf. *Aug.* lxx. 2.
c Both an hygienic and a moral measure, see Plin. *N.H.* 26. 1 ff., and Mart. xi. 99.
d *Strena*, Fr. étrenne, literally "an omen," meant strictly gifts given for good luck.
e That is, of four times the value of the one which he received.

appear, and either from the floor or from the judge's [a] tribunal remind the jurors of the laws and of their oath, as well as of the nature of the crime on which they were sitting in judgment. Moreover, if the public morals were in any way affected by laziness or bad habits he undertook to reform them.

XXXIV. He reduced the cost of the games and shows by cutting down the pay of the actors and limiting the pairs of gladiators to a fixed number. Complaining bitterly that the prices of Corinthian bronzes [b] had risen to an immense figure and that three mullets had been sold for thirty thousand sesterces, he proposed that a limit be set to household furniture and that the prices in the market should be regulated each year at the discretion of the senate; while the aediles were instructed to put such restrictions on cook-shops and eating-houses as not to allow even pastry to be exposed for sale. Furthermore, to encourage general frugality by his personal example, he often served at formal dinners meats left over from the day before and partly consumed, or the half of a boar, declaring that it had all the qualities of a whole one.

He issued an edict forbidding general kissing,[c] as well as the exchange of New Year's gifts [d] after the Kalends of January. It was his custom to return a gift of four-fold value,[e] and in person; but annoyed at being interrupted all through the month by those who did not have access to him on the holiday, he did not continue it.

XXXV. He revived the custom of our forefathers, that in the absence of a public prosecutor matrons of ill-repute be punished according to the decision of a

de communi sententia coercerent auctor fuit.   Equiti
Romano iuris iurandi gratiam fecit, uxorem in stupro
generi compertam dimitteret, quam se numquam
2 repudiaturum ante iuraverat.   Feminae famosae, ut
ad evitandas legum poenas iure ac dignitate matronali
exsolverentur, lenocinium profiteri coeperant, et ex
iuventute utriusque ordinis profligatissimus quisque,
quominus in opera scaenae harenaeque edenda
senatus consulto teneretur, famosi iudicii notam
sponte subibant ; eos easque omnes, ne quod
refugium in tali fraude cuiquam esset, exsilio adfecit.
Senatori latum clavum ademit, cum cognosset sub
Kal. Iul. demigrasse in hortos, quo vilius post diem
aedes in urbe conduceret.   Alium e quaestura removit, quod uxorem pridie sortitionem ductam
postridie repudiasset.

XXXVI. Externas caerimonias, Aegyptios Iudai-
cosque ritus compescuit, coactis qui superstitione ea
tenebantur religiosas vestes cum instrumento omni
comburere.   Iudaeorum iuventutem per speciem
sacramenti in provincias gravioris caeli distribuit,
reliquos gentis eiusdem vel similia sectantes urbe
summovit, sub poena perpetuae servitutis nisi
obtemperassent.   Expulit et mathematicos, sed de-

---

[a] The punishments for adultery had been made very severe
by Augustus (cf. *Aug.* xxxiv.).   To escape these some
matrons registered with the aediles as prostitutes, thereby
sacrificing their rights as matrons, as well as their responsi-
bilities ; cf. Tac. *Ann.* 2. 85.

[b] The first of July was the date for renting and hiring
houses and rooms ; hence it was "moving-day."   See Mart.
12. 32.

[c] To determine his province or the sphere of his duty.   The

council of their relatives. He absolved a Roman
knight from his oath and allowed him to put away
his wife, who was taken in adultery with her son-in-
law, even though he had previously sworn that he
would never divorce her. Notorious women had
begun to make an open profession of prostitution,
to avoid the punishment of the laws by giving up
the privileges and rank of matrons,[a] while the most
profligate young men of both orders voluntarily
incurred degradation from their rank, so as not to be
prevented by the decree of the senate from appearing on the stage and in the arena. All such men
and women he punished with exile, to prevent anyone from shielding himself by such a device. He
deprived a senator of his broad stripe on learning
that he had moved to his gardens just before the
Kalends of July,[b] with the design of renting a house
in the city at a lower figure after that date. He
deposed another from his quaestorship, because he
had taken a wife the day before casting lots[c] and
divorced her the day after.

XXXVI. He abolished foreign cults, especially the
Egyptian and the Jewish rites, compelling all who
were addicted to such superstitions to burn their
religious vestments and all their paraphernalia. Those
of the Jews who were of military age he assigned
to provinces of less healthy climate, ostensibly
to serve in the army; the others of that same race
or of similar beliefs he banished from the city, on
pain of slavery for life if they did not obey. He
banished the astrologers as well, but pardoned such

reason for his divorcing his wife is problematical. Evidently
his marriage brought him some advantage which no longer
existed after his province was determined.

precantibus ac se artem desituros promittentibus
veniam dedit.

XXXVII. In primis tuendae pacis a grassaturis ac
latrociniis seditionumque licentia curam habuit.
Stationes militum per Italiam solito frequentiores
disposuit. Romae castra constituit, quibus praetorianae cohortes vagae ante id tempus et per hospitia
dispersae continerentur.

2 Populares tumultus et ortos gravissime coercuit et
ne orerentur sedulo cavit. Caede in theatro per
discordiam admissa capita factionum et histriones,
propter quos dissidebatur, relegavit, nec ut revocaret

3 umquam ullis populi precibus potuit evinci. Cum
Pollentina plebs funus cuiusdam primipilaris non
prius ex foro misisset quam extorta pecunia per vim
heredibus ad gladiatorium munus, cohortem ab urbe
et aliam a Cotti regno dissimulata itineris causa
detectis repente armis concinentibusque signis per
diversas portas in oppidum immisit ac partem maiorem
plebei ac decurionum in perpetua vincula coniecit.
Abolevit et ius moremque asylorum, quae usquam
erant. Cyzicenis in cives R. violentius quaedam
ausis publice libertatem ademit, quam Mithridatico
bello meruerant.[1]

4 Hostiles motus nulla postea expeditione suscepta
per legatos compescuit, ne per eos quidem nisi
cunctanter et necessario. Reges infestos suspec-

---

[1] meruerant, ς (Beroaldus); meruerunt, Ω.

[a] That is, the supporters and partisans of the rival actors ;
see Tac Ann. 1. 77.

[b] The members of the local senate.

[c] Taking refuge in temples and holy places, to avoid
punishment for crimes ; for its abuse see Tac. Ann. 3. 60.

TIBERIUS

as begged for indulgence and promised to give up
their art.

XXXVII. He gave special attention to securing
safety from prowling brigands and lawless outbreaks.
He stationed garrisons of soldiers nearer together
than before throughout Italy, while at Rome he
established a camp for the barracks of the praetorian
cohorts, which before that time had been quartered
in isolated groups in divers lodging houses.

He took great pains to prevent outbreaks of the
populace and punished such as occurred with the
utmost severity. When a quarrel in the theatre
ended in bloodshed, he banished the leaders of the
factions,[a] as well as the actors who were the cause of
the dissension; and no entreaties of the people could
ever induce him to recall them. When the populace
of Pollentia would not allow the body of a chief-
centurion to be taken from the forum until their
violence had extorted money from his heirs for a
gladiatorial show, he dispatched one cohort from the
city and another from the kingdom of Cottius, concealing the reason for the move, sent them into the
city by different gates, suddenly revealing their arms
and sounding their trumpets, and consigned the
greater part of the populace and of the decurions[b]
to life imprisonment. He abolished the customary
right of asylum[c] in all parts of the empire. Because
the people of Cyzicus ventured to commit acts of
special lawlessness against Roman citizens, he took
from them the freedom which they had earned in the
war with Mithridates.

He undertook no campaign after his accession, but
quelled outbreaks of the enemy through his generals;
and even this he did only reluctantly and of necessity.

347

tosque comminationibus magis et querelis quam vi
repressit; quosdam per blanditias atque promissa
extractos ad se non remisit, ut Marobodum Ger-
manum, Rhascuporim[1] Thracem, Archelaum Cappa-
docem, cuius etiam regnum in formam provinciae
redegit.

XXXVIII. Biennio continuo post adeptum
imperium pedem porta non extulit; sequenti tempore praeterquam in propinqua oppida et, cum
longissime, Antio tenus nusquam afuit, idque perraro
et paucos dies; quamvis provincias quoque et
exercitus revisurum se saepe pronuntiasset et prope
quotannis profectionem praepararet, vehiculis com-
prehensis, commeatibus per municipia et colonias
dispositis, ad extremum vota pro itu et reditu suo
suscipi passus, ut vulgo iam per iocum " Callippides "[2]
vocaretur, quem cursitare ac ne cubiti quidem
mensuram progredi proverbio Graeco notatum est.

XXXIX. Sed orbatus utroque filio, quorum Germanicus in Syria, Drusus Romae obierat, secessum
Campaniae petit; constanti et opinione et sermone
paene omnium quasi neque rediturus umquam et cito
mortem etiam obiturus. Quod paulo minus utrumque evenit; nam neque Romam amplius rediit et[3]
paucos post dies iuxta Tarracinam in praetorio, cui
Speluncae nomen est, incenante eo complura et
ingentia saxa fortuito superne dilapsa sunt, multisque

---

[1] Rhascuporim, *Ihm*; Thrascipolim, Ω.
[2] Callippides, *Basle ed. of* 1533; Gallipidis (Gallipedes),
mss.   [3] et, *Erasmus*; sed, *MGX'*; sed et, Υ.

[a] The same proverb is mentioned by Cic. *ad Att.* 13. 12.
The reference is to an Athenian actor of mimes, who imitated

Such kings as were disaffected and objects of his suspicion he held in check rather by threats and remonstrances than by force; some he lured to Rome by flattering promises and detained there, such as Marobodus the German, Rhascuporis the Thracian, and Archelaus of Cappadocia, whose realm he also reduced to the form of a province.

XXXVIII. For two whole years after becoming emperor he did not set foot outside the gates; after that he went nowhere except to the neighbouring towns, at farthest to Antium, and even that very seldom and for a few days at a time. Yet he often gave out that he would revisit the provinces too and the armies, and nearly every year he made preparations for a journey by chartering carriages and arranging for supplies in the free towns and colonies. Finally he allowed vows to be put up for his voyage and return, so that at last everybody jokingly gave him the name of Callippides, who was proverbial among the Greeks for running without getting ahead a cubit's length.[a]

XXXIX. But after being bereft of both his sons, —Germanicus had died in Syria and Drusus at Rome,—he retired to Campania, and almost everyone firmly believed and openly declared that he would never come back, but would soon die there. And both predictions were all but fulfilled; for he did not return again to Rome, and it chanced a few days later that as he was dining near Tarracina in a villa called the Grotto, many huge rocks fell from the ceiling and crushed a number of the guests and

the movements of running but remained in the same spot.

convivarum et ministrorum elisis praeter spem evasit.

XL. Peragrata Campania, cum Capuae Capitolium, Nolae templum Augusti, quam causam profectionis praetenderat, dedicasset, Capreas se contulit, praecipue delectatus insula, quod uno parvoque litore adiretur, saepta undique praeruptis immensae altitudinis rupibus et profundo mari.[1] Statimque revocante assidua obtestatione populo propter cladem, qua apud Fidenas supra viginti hominum milia gladiatorio munere amphitheatri ruina perierant, transiit in continentem potestatemque omnibus adeundi sui fecit ; tanto magis, quod urbe egrediens ne quis se interpellaret edixerat ac toto itinere adeuntis submoverat.

XLI. Regressus in insulam rei p. quidem curam usque adeo abiecit, ut postea non decurias equitum umquam supplerit, non tribunos militum praefectosque, non provinciarum praesides ullos mutaverit, Hispaniam et Syriam per aliquot annos sine consularibus legatis habuerit, Armeniam a Parthis occupari, Moesiam a Dacis Sarmatisque, Gallias a Germanis vastari neglexerit ; magno dedecore imperii nec minore discrimine.

XLII. Ceterum secreti licentiam nanctus et quasi civitatis oculis remotis, cuncta simul vitia male diu dissimulata tandem profudit ; de quibus singillatim

---

[1] mari, *Stephanus* ; maris, *mss.*

---

[a] That is, to make some amends for his conduct.
[b] The divisions selected for jury duty.

servants, while the emperor himself had a narrow escape.

XL. After traversing Campania and dedicating the Capitolium at Capua and a temple to Augustus at Nola, which was the pretext he had given for his journey, he went to Capreae, particularly attracted to that island because it was accessible by only one small beach, being everywhere else girt with sheer cliffs of great height and by deep water. But he was at once recalled by the constant entreaties of the people, because of a disaster at Fidenae, where more than twenty thousand spectators had perished through the collapse of the amphitheatre during a gladiatorial show. So he crossed to the mainland and made himself accessible to all, the more willingly because he had given orders on leaving the city that no one was to disturb him, and during the whole trip had repulsed those who tried to approach him.[a]

XLI. Then returning to the island, he utterly neglected the conduct of state affairs, from that time on never filling the vacancies in the decuries[b] of the knights, nor changing the tribunes of the soldiers and prefects or the governors of any of his provinces He left Spain and Syria without consular governors for several years, suffered Armenia to be overrun by the Parthians, Moesia to be laid waste by the Dacians and Sarmatians, and the Gallic provinces by the Germans, to the great dishonour of the empire and no less to its danger.

XLII. Moreover, having gained the licence of privacy, and being as it were out of sight of the citizens, he at last gave free rein at once to all the vices which he had for a long time ill concealed; and of these I shall give a detailed account from the

THE LIVES OF THE CAESARS, BOOK III

ab exordio referam. In castris tiro etiam tum propter
nimiam vini aviditatem pro Tiberio " Biberius," pro
Claudio " Caldius," pro Nerone " Mero " vocabatur.
Postea princeps in ipsa publicorum morum correctione
cum Pomponio Flacco et L. Pisone noctem continuum-
que biduum epulando potandoque consumpsit, quorum
alteri Syriam provinciam, alteri praefecturam urbis
confestim detulit, codicillis quoque iucundissimos et
2 omnium horarum amicos professus. Cestio Gallo,[1]
libidinoso ac prodigo seni, olim ab Augusto ignominia notato et a se ante paucos dies apud
senatum increpito cenam ea lege condixit, ne quid
ex consuetudine immutaret aut demeret, utque nudis
puellis ministrantibus cenaretur. Ignotissimum quae-
sturae candidatum nobilissimis anteposuit ob epotam
in convivio propinante se vini amphoram. Asellio
Sabino sestertia ducenta donavit pro dialogo, in
quo boleti et ficedulae et ostreae et turdi certamen induxerat. Novum denique officium instituit
a voluptatibus, praeposito equite R. T. Caesonio
Prisco.

XLIII. Secessu vero Caprensi etiam sellaria excogitavit, sedem arcanarum libidinum, in quam undique conquisiti puellarum et exoletorum greges
monstrosique concubitus repertores, quos spintrias
appellabat, triplici serie conexi, in vicem incestarent
coram ipso, ut aspectu deficientis libidines excitaret.

---

[1] Cestio, *Roth*; Sestio, Ω. Gallo, *V²* (*Torrentius*).

---

[a] See Index *s.v.* Biberius.

[b] Probably the emperor took a sip from the huge vessel and
passed it to the man, who drained it to the dregs ; cf. Verg.
Aen. 1. 738. Since the amphora as a measure contained
about seven gallons, the word is here probably used of a
large tankard of that shape.

352

beginning. Even at the outset of his military career his excessive love of wine gave him the name of Biberius, instead of Tiberius, Caldius for Claudius, and Mero for Nero.[a] Later, when emperor and at the very time that he was busy correcting the public morals, he spent a night and two whole days feasting and drinking with Pomponius Flaccus and Lucius Piso, immediately afterward making the one governor of the province of Syria and the other prefect of the city, and even declaring in their commissions that they were the most agreeable of friends, who could always be counted on. He had a dinner given him by Cestius Gallus, a lustful and prodigal old man, who had once been degraded by Augustus and whom he had himself rebuked a few days before in the senate, making the condition that Cestius should change or omit none of his usual customs, and that nude girls should wait upon them at table. He gave a very obscure candidate for the quaestorship preference over men of the noblest families, because at the emperor's challenge he had drained an amphora[b] of wine at a banquet. He paid Asellius Sabinus two hundred thousand sesterces for a dialogue, in which he had introduced a contest of a mushroom, a fig-pecker, an oyster and a thrush. He established a new office, master of the imperial pleasures, assigning it to Titus Caesonius Priscus, a Roman knight.

XLIII. On retiring to Capri he devised a pleasance for his secret orgies: teams of wantons of both sexes, selected as experts in deviant intercourse and dubbed analists, copulated before him in triple unions to excite his flagging passions. Its bedrooms were furnished with the most salacious paintings and

2 Cubicula plurifariam disposita tabellis ac sigillis lascivissimarum picturarum et figurarum adornavit librisque Elephantidis instruxit, ne cui in opera edenda exemplar imperatae[1] schemae deesset. In silvis quoque ac nemoribus passim Venerios locos commentus est prostantisque[2] per antra et cavas rupes ex utriusque sexus pube Paniscorum et Nympharum habitu, quae palam[3] iam et vulgo nomine insulae abutentes "Caprineum" dictitabant.

XLIV. Maiore adhuc ac turpiore infamia flagravit, vix ut referri audirive, nedum credi fas sit, quasi pueros primae teneritudinis, quos pisciculos vocabat, institueret, ut natanti sibi inter femina versarentur ac luderent lingua morsuque sensim adpetentes ; atque etiam quasi infantes firmiores, necdum tamen lacte depulsos, inguini ceu papillae admoveret, pronior sane

2 ad id genus libidinis et natura et aetate. Quare Parrasi quoque tabulam, in qua Meleagro Atalanta ore morigeratur, legatam sibi sub condicione, ut si argumento offenderetur decies pro ea sestertium acciperet, non modo praetulit, sed et in cubiculo dedicavit. Fertur etiam in sacrificando quondam captus facie ministri acerram praeferentis nequisse abstinere, quin paene vixdum re divina peracta ibidem statim seductum constupraret simulque fratrem eius tibicinem ; atque utrique mox, quod mutuo flagitium exprobrarant, crura fregisse.

XLV. Feminarum quoque, et quidem illustrium, capitibus quanto opere solitus sit inludere, evidentissime apparuit Malloniae cuiusdam exitu, quam perductam nec quicquam amplius pati constantissime

---

[1] imperatae, ς ; impetratae, Ω.
[2] prostantesque, ΠQ ; *the other mss. have* prostrantesque *or* prostrantisque.   [3] habitu, quae palam] habituque palam, Ω.

sculptures, as well as with an erotic library, in case a performer should need an illustration of what was required. Then in Capri's woods and groves he arranged a number of nooks of venery where boys and girls got up as Pans and nymphs solicited outside bowers and grottoes: people openly called this "the old goat's garden," punning on the island's name.

XLIV. He acquired a reputation for still grosser depravities that one can hardly bear to tell or be told, let alone believe. For example, he trained little boys (whom he termed tiddlers) to crawl between his thighs when he went swimming and tease him with their licks and nibbles; and unweaned babies he would put to his organ as though to the breast, being by both nature and age rather fond of this form of satisfaction. Left a painting of Parrhasius's depicting Atalanta pleasuring Meleager with her lips on condition that if the theme displeased him he was to have a million sesterces instead, he chose to keep it and actually hung it in his bedroom. The story is also told that once at a sacrifice, attracted by the acolyte's beauty, he lost control of himself and, hardly waiting for the ceremony to end, rushed him off and debauched him and his brother, the flute-player, too; and subsequently, when they complained of the assault, he had their legs broken.

XLV. How grossly he was in the habit of abusing women even of high birth is very clearly shown by the death of a certain Mallonia. When she was brought to his bed and refused most vigorously to submit to his lust, he turned her

recusantem delatoribus obiecit ac ne ream quidem
interpellare desiit, " ecquid paeniteret " ; donec ea
relicto iudicio domum se abripuit ferroque transegit,
obscaenitate oris hirsuto atque olido seni clare ex-
probrata. Unde nota[1] in Atellanico exhodio proximis
ludis adsensu maximo excepta percrebruit, " hircum
vetulum capreis naturam ligurire."

XLVI. Pecuniae parcus ac tenax comites peregrina-
tionum expeditionumque numquam salario, cibariis
tantum sustentavit, una modo liberalitate ex indulgentia vitrici prosecutus, cum tribus classibus factis
pro dignitate cuiusque, primae sescenta sestertia,
secundae quadringenta distribuit, ducenta tertiae,
quam non amicorum sed Graecorum[2] appellabat.

XLVII. Princeps neque opera ulla magnifica fecit—
nam et quae sola susceperat, Augusti templum re-
stitutionemque Pompeiani theatri, imperfecta post tot
annos reliquit—neque spectacula omnino edidit ; et
iis, quae ab aliquo ederentur, rarissime interfuit,
ne quid exposceretur, utique postquam comoedum
Actium coactus est manumittere. Paucorum senatorum inopia sustentata, ne pluribus opem ferret,
negavit se aliis subventurum, nisi senatui iustas
necessitatium causas probassent. Quo pacto plerosque modestia et pudore deterruit, in quibus
Hortalum, Quinti Hortensi oratoris nepotem, qui

---

[1] nota, $P^2T\varsigma$; *the other mss. have* mora.
[2] Graecorum] gratorum, *Turnebus.*

---

a See chap. lvi.

over to the informers, and even when she was
on trial he did not cease to call out and ask her
"whether she was sorry"; so that finally she left
the court and went home, where she stabbed
herself, openly upbraiding the ugly old man for
his obscenity. Hence a stigma put upon him at the
next plays in an Atellan farce was received with
great applause and became current, that "the old
goat was licking the does."

XLVI. In money matters he was frugal and
close, never allowing the companions of his foreign
tours and campaigns a salary, but merely their
keep. Only once did he treat them liberally, and
then through the generosity of his stepfather, when
he formed three classes according to each man's
rank and gave to the first six hundred thousand
sesterces, to the second four hundred thousand,
and to the third, which he called one, not of his
friends, but of his Greeks,[a] two hundred thousand.

XLVII. While emperor he constructed no magnificent public works, for the only ones which he
undertook, the temple of Augustus and the restoration of Pompey's theatre, he left unfinished after so
many years. He gave no public shows at all, and
very seldom attended those given by others, for fear
that some request would be made of him, especially
after he was forced to buy the freedom of a comic
actor named Actius. Having relieved the neediness
of a few senators, he avoided the necessity of further
aid by declaring that he would help no others unless
they proved to the senate that there were legitimate
causes for their condition. Therefore diffidence and
a sense of shame kept many from applying, among
them Hortalus, grandson of Quintus Hortensius the

permodica re familiari auctore Augusto quattuor
liberos tulerat.

XLVIII. Publice munificentiam bis omnino exhibuit, proposito milies sestertium gratuito in trienni
tempus et rursus quibusdam dominis insularum, quae
in monte Caelio deflagrarant, pretio restituto.
Quorum alterum magna difficultate nummaria populo
auxilium flagitante coactus est facere, cum per
senatus consultum sanxisset, ut faeneratores duas
patrimonii partes in solo collocarent, debitores totidem aeris alieni statim solverent, nec res expedire-
tur; alterum ad mitigandam temporum atrocitatem.
Quod tamen beneficium tanti aestimavit, ut montem
Caelium appellatione mutata vocari Augustum
iusserit. Militi post duplicata ex Augusti testamento
legata nihil umquam largitus est, praeterquam singula
milia denariorum praetorianis, quod Seiano se non
accommodassent, et quaedam munera Syriacis
legionibus, quod solae nullam Seiani imaginem inter
signa coluissent. Atque etiam missiones veteranorum rarissimas fecit, ex senio mortem, ex morte
compendium captans. Ne provincias quidem liberali-

---

a Cf. *Aug.* xli. 1 ; Tac. *Ann.* 2. 37.

b This occurred twice, in 27 and 36; see Tac. *Ann.* 4. 64
and 6. 45. The second fire was on and near the Aventine.

c The decree is quoted by Tac. *Ann.* 6. 17. The purpose
was to put the money into circulation and at the same time
to allow the debtors to pay in land.

d According to Tacitus (*Ann.* 4. 64) this was done by the
senate, because the statue of Tiberius remained uninjured
in the midst of the burned district.

e The standards had a sacred character; see, for example,

orator, who though of very limited means had begotten four children with the encouragement of Augustus.[a]

XLVIII. He showed generosity to the public in but two instances, once when he offered to lend a hundred million sesterces without interest for a period of three years, and again when he made good the losses of some owners of blocks of houses on the Caelian Mount, which had burned down.[b] The former was forced upon him by the clamour of the people for help in a time of great financial stress, after he had failed to relieve the situation by a decree of the senate,[c] providing that the money-lenders should invest two-thirds of their property in land, and that the debtors should at once pay the same proportion of their indebtedness; and the latter also was to relieve a condition of great hardship. Yet he made so much of his liberality in the latter case, that he had the name of the Caelian changed to the Augustan Mount.[d] After he had doubled the legacies provided for in the will of Augustus, he never gave largess to the soldiers, with the exception of a thousand denarii to each of the praetorians, for not taking sides with Sejanus, and some presents to the legions in Syria, because they alone had consecrated no image of Sejanus among their standards.[e] He also very rarely allowed veteran soldiers their discharge, having an eye to their death from years, and a saving of money through their death.[f] He did not relieve the provinces either by

Tac. *Ann.* 1. 39. 7 ; and the head of the reigning emperor was often placed under the eagle or other emblem.

[f] Since he would save the rewards to be paid on the completion of their term of service.

tate ulla sublevavit, excepta Asia, disiectis terrae
motu civitatibus.

XLIX. Procedente mox tempore etiam ad rapinas
convertit animum. Satis constat, Cn. Lentulum Augu-
rem, cui census maximus fuerit, metu et angore ad
fastidium vitae ab eo actum et ut ne quo nisi ipso
herede moreretur; condemnatam et generosissimam
feminam Lepidam in gratiam Quirini consularis
praedivitis et orbi, qui dimissam eam e matrimonio
post vicensimum annum veneni olim in se com-
2 parati arguebat; praeterea Galliarum et Hispaniarum
Syriaeque et Graeciae principes confiscatos ob tam
leve ac tam impudens calumniarum genus, ut quibusdam non aliud sit obiectum, quam quod partem
rei familiaris in pecunia haberent; plurimis etiam
civitatibus et privatis veteres immunitates et ius
metallorum ac vectigalium adempta; sed et Vononem
regem Parthorum, qui pulsus a suis quasi in fidem
p. R. cum ingenti gaza Antiochiam se receperat,
spoliatum perfidia et occisum.

L. Odium adversus necessitudines in Druso primum
fratre detexit, prodita eius epistula, qua secum de
cogendo ad restituendam libertatem Augusto agebat,
deinde et in reliquis. Iuliae uxori tantum afuit ut
relegatae, quod minimum est, offici aut humanitatis
aliquid impertiret, ut ex constitutione patris uno
oppido clausam domo quoque egredi et commercio

<hr>

[a] Under pretence that they were hoarding money for
revolutionary purposes. Caesar had limited the amount to be
held by any one person in Italy to 60,000 sesterces; cf. Tac.
Ann. 6. 16; Dio, 41. 38.   [b] But cf. chap. xi. 4, above.

any act of liberality, except Asia, when some cities were destroyed by an earthquake.

XLIX. Presently, as time went on, he even resorted to plunder. All the world knows that he drove Gnaeus Lentulus Augur, a man of great wealth, to take his own life through fear and mental anxiety, and to make the emperor his sole heir; that Lepida, too, a woman of very high birth, was condemned to banishment to gratify Quirinius, an opulent and childless ex-consul, who had divorced her, and twenty years later accused her of having attempted to poison him many years before; that besides this the leading men of the Spanish and Gallic provinces, as well as of Syria and Greece, had their property confiscated on trivial and shameless charges, some being accused of nothing more serious than having a part of their property in ready money;[a] that many states and individuals were deprived of immunities of long standing, and of the right of working mines and collecting revenues; that Vonones, king of the Parthians, who on being dethroned by his subjects had taken refuge at Antioch with a vast treasure, in the belief that he was putting himself under the protection of the Roman people, was treacherously despoiled and put to death.

L. He first showed his hatred of his kindred in the case of his brother Drusus, producing a letter of his, in which Drusus discussed with him the question of compelling Augustus to restore the Republic; and then he turned against the rest. So far from showing any courtesy or kindness to his wife Julia, after her banishment, which is the least that one might expect,[b] although her father's order had merely confined her to one town, he would not allow her even to

hominum frui vetuerit; sed et peculio concesso a
patre praebitisque annuis fraudavit, per speciem
publici iuris, quod nihil de his Augustus testamento
2 cavisset. Matrem Liviam gravatus velut partes sibi
aequas potentiae vindicantem, et congressum eius
assiduum vitavit et longiores secretioresque sermones,
ne consiliis, quibus tamen interdum et egere et uti
solebat, regi videretur. Tulit etiam perindigne actum in senatu, ut titulis suis quasi " Augusti," ita et
3 " Liviae filius " adiceretur. Quare non " parentem
patriae " appellari, non ullum insignem honorem
recipere publice passus est; sed et frequenter admonuit, maioribus nec feminae convenientibus
negotiis abstineret, praecipue ut animadvertit
incendio iuxta aedem Vestae et ipsam intervenisse
populumque et milites, quo enixius opem ferrent,
adhortatam, sicut sub marito solita esset.

LI. Dehinc ad simultatem usque processit hac,
ut ferunt, de causa. Instanti saepius, ut civitate
donatum in decurias adlegeret, negavit alia se
condicione adlecturum, quam si patereter ascribi
albo extortum id sibi a matre. At illa commota
veteres quosdam ad se Augusti codicillos de acerbitate et intolerantia morum eius e sacrario protulit
atque recitavit. Hos et custoditos tam diu et

---

  a See note on chap. xv. 2.
  b *Sacrarium* is really a shrine (perhaps to Augustus) in
which the letters had been deposited.

leave her house or enjoy the society of mankind. Nay more, he even deprived her of the allowance[a] granted her by her father and of her yearly income, under colour of observance of the common law, since Augustus had made no provision for these in his will. Vexed at his mother Livia, alleging that she claimed an equal share in the rule, he shunned frequent meetings with her and long and confidential conversations, to avoid the appearance of being guided by her advice; though in point of fact he was wont every now and then to need and to follow it. He was greatly offended too by a decree of the senate, providing that "son of Livia," as well as "son of Augustus" should be written in his honorary inscriptions. For this reason he would not suffer her to be named "Parent of her Country," nor to receive any conspicuous public honour. More than that, he often warned her not to meddle with affairs of importance and unbecoming a woman, especially after he learned that at a fire near the temple of Vesta she had been present in person, and urged the people and soldiers to greater efforts, as had been her way while her husband was alive.

LI. Afterwards he reached the point of open enmity, and the reason, they say, was this. On her urging him again and again to appoint among the jurors a man who had been made a citizen, he declared that he would do it only on condition that she would allow an entry to be made in the official list that it was forced upon him by his mother. Then Livia, in a rage, drew from a secret place[b] and read some old letters written to her by Augustus with regard to the austerity and stubbornness of Tiberius' disposition. He in turn was so put out

exprobratos tam infeste adeo graviter tulit, ut
quidam putent inter causas secessus hanc ei vel
2 praecipuam fuisse.   Toto quidem triennio, quo
vivente matre afuit, semel omnino eam nec amplius
quam uno die paucissimis vidit horis ; ac mox neque
aegrae adesse curavit defunctamque et, dum adventus
sui spem facit, complurium dierum mora corrupto
demum et tabido corpore funeratam prohibuit con-
secrari, quasi id ipsa mandasset.   Testamentum
quoque eius pro irrito habuit omnisque amicitias et
familiaritates, etiam quibus ea funeris sui curam
moriens demandaverat, intra breve tempus afflixit,
uno ex iis, equestris ordinis viro, et in antliam
condemnato.

LII. Filiorum neque naturalem Drusum neque
adoptivum Germanicum patria caritate dilexit,
alterius vitiis infensus.   Nam Drusus fluxioris re-
missiorisque vitae erat.   Itaque ne mortuo quidem
perinde adfectus est, sed tantum non statim a funere
ad negotiorum consuetudinem rediit iustitio longiore
2 inhibito.   Quin et Iliensium legatis paulo serius
consolantibus, quasi obliterata iam doloris memoria,
irridens se quoque respondit vicem eorum dolere,
quod egregium civem Hectorem amisissent.   Germanico usque adeo obtrectavit, ut et praeclara facta
364

that these had been preserved so long and were
thrown up at him in such a spiteful spirit, that some
think that this was the very strongest of the reasons
for his retirement. At all events, during all the three
years that she lived after he left Rome he saw her
but once, and then only one day, for a very few
hours; and when shortly after that she fell ill, he
took no trouble to visit her. When she died, and
after a delay of several days, during which he held
out hope of his coming, had at last been buried
because the condition of the corpse made it necessary,
he forbade her deification, alleging that he was
acting according to her own instructions. He further
disregarded the provisions of her will, and within a
short time caused the downfall of all her friends and
intimates, even of those to whom she had on her
deathbed entrusted the care of her obsequies, actually
condemning one of them, and that a man of equestrian
rank, to the treadmill.

LII. He had a father's affection neither for his
own son Drusus nor his adopted son Germanicus,
being exasperated at the former's vices; and, in fact,
Drusus led a somewhat loose and dissolute life.
Therefore, even when he died, Tiberius was not
greatly affected, but almost immediately after the
funeral returned to his usual routine, forbidding
a longer period of mourning. Nay, more, when a
deputation from Ilium offered him somewhat belated
condolences, he replied with a smile, as if the
memory of his bereavement had faded from his
mind, that they, too, had his sympathy for the loss
of their eminent fellow-citizen Hector. As to
Germanicus, he was so far from appreciating him,
that he made light of his illustrious deeds as un-

eius pro supervacuis elevarit et gloriosissimas victorias ceu damnosas rei p. increparet. Quod vero Alexandream propter immensam et repentinam famem inconsulto se adisset, questus est in senatu. 3 Etiam causa mortis fuisse ei per Cn. Pisonem legatum Syriae creditur, quem mox huius criminis reum putant quidam mandata prolaturum, nisi ea secreto ostentanti auferenda ipsumque iugulandum curasset.[1] Propter quae multifariam inscriptum et per noctes celeberrime adclamatum est : " Redde Germanicum ! " Quam suspicionem confirmavit ipse postea coniuge etiam ac liberis Germanici crudelem in modum afflictis.

LIII. Nurum Agrippinam post mariti mortem liberius quiddam questam manu apprehendit Graecoque versu : " Si non dominaris," inquit, " filiola, iniuriam te accipere existimas " ? Nec ullo mox sermone dignatus est. Quondam vero inter cenam porrecta a se poma gustare non ausam etiam vocare desiit, simulans veneni se crimine accersi ; cum praestructum utrumque consulto esset, ut et ipse temptandi gratia offerret et illa quasi certissimum exitium [2] 2 caveret. Novissime calumniatus modo ad statuam Augusti modo ad exercitus confugere velle, Pandatariam relegavit conviciantique oculum per centurionem verberibus excussit. Rursus mori inedia desti-

---

[1] ostentant(i auferenda ipsumque iugulandum curasset Propter) quae : *the part in parenthesis is supplied by Roth.*

[2] exitium, *GS²; the other mss. have* exitium.

important, and railed at his brilliant victories as ruinous to his country. He even made complaint in the senate when Germanicus, on the occasion of a sudden and terrible famine, went to Alexandria without consulting him. It is even believed that he caused his death at the hands of Gnaeus Piso, governor of Syria, and some think that when Piso was tried on that charge, he would have produced his instructions, had not Tiberius caused them to be taken from him when Piso privately showed them, and the man himself to be put to death. Because of this the words, "Give us back Germanicus," were posted in many places, and shouted at night all over the city. And Tiberius afterwards strengthened this suspicion by cruelly abusing the wife and children of Germanicus as well.

LIII. When his daughter-in-law Agrippina was somewhat outspoken in her complaints after her husband's death, he took her by the hand and quoted a Greek verse, meaning "Do you think a wrong is done you, dear daughter, if you are not empress?" After that he never deigned to hold any conversation with her. Indeed, after she showed fear of tasting an apple which he handed her at dinner, he even ceased to invite her to his table, alleging that he had been charged with an attempt to poison her; but as a matter of fact, the whole affair had been pre-arranged, that he should offer her the fruit to test her, and that she should refuse it as containing certain death. At last, falsely charging her with a desire to take refuge, now at the statue of Augustus and now with the armies, he exiled her to Panda-taria, and when she loaded him with reproaches, he had her beaten by a centurion until one of her eyes

nanti per vim ore diducto infulciri cibum iussit. Sed
et perseverantem atque ita absumptam criminosissime
insectatus, cum diem quoque natalem eius inter ne-
fastos referendum suasisset, imputavit etiam, quod non
laqueo strangulatam in Gemonias abiecerit ; proque
tali clementia interponi decretum passus est, quo sibi
gratiae agerentur et Capitolino Iovi donum ex auro
sacraretur.

LIV. Cum ex Germanico tres nepotes, Neronem
et Drusum et Gaium, ex Druso unum Tiberium
haberet, destitutus morte liberorum maximos natu de
Germanici filiis, Neronem et Drusum, patribus conscriptis commendavit diemque utriusque tirocinii
congiario plebei dato celebravit. Sed ut comperit
ineunte anno pro eorum quoque salute publice vota
suscepta, egit cum senatu, non debere talia praemia
2 tribui nisi expertis et aetate provectis. Atque ex eo
patefacta interiore animi sui nota omnium criminationibus obnoxios reddidit variaque fraude inductos, ut et
concitarentur ad convicia et concitati proderentur,
accusavit per litteras amarissime congestis etiam
probris et iudicatos hostis fame necavit, Neronem in
insula Pontia, Drusum in ima parte Palatii. Putant
Neronem ad voluntariam mortem coactum, cum ei
368

was destroyed. Again, when she resolved to die of starvation, he had her mouth pried open and food crammed into it. Worst of all, when she persisted in her resolution and so perished, he assailed her memory with the basest slanders, persuading the senate to add her birthday to the days of ill omen, and actually taking credit to himself for not having had her strangled and her body cast out on the Stairs of Mourning. He even allowed a decree to be passed in recognition of this remarkable clemency, in which thanks were offered him and a golden gift was consecrated to Jupiter of the Capitol.

LIV. By Germanicus he had three grandsons, Nero, Drusus, and Gaius, and by Drusus one, called Tiberius. Bereft of his own children, he recommended Nero and Drusus, the elder sons of Germanicus, to the senate, and celebrated the day when each of them came to his majority by giving largess to the commons. But as soon as he learned that at the beginning of the year vows were being put up for their safety also, he referred the matter to the senate, saying that such honours ought to be conferred only on those of tried character and mature years. By revealing his true feelings towards them from that time on, he exposed them to accusations from all quarters, and after resorting to various tricks to rouse them to rail at him, and seeing to it that they were betrayed when they did so, he brought most bitter charges against them both in writing; and when they had in consequence been pronounced public enemies, he starved them to death, Nero on the island of Pontia and Drusus in a lower room of the Palace. It is thought that Nero was forced to take his own life, since an executioner,

carnifex quasi ex senatus auctoritate missus laqueos et uncos ostentaret, Druso autem adeo alimenta subducta, ut tomentum e culcita temptaverit mandere ; amborum sic reliquias dispersas, ut vix quandoque colligi possent.

LV. Super veteres amicos ac familiares viginti sibi e numero principum civitatis depoposcerat velut consiliarios in negotiis publicis. Horum omnium vix duos anne tres incolumis praestitit, ceteros alium alia de causa perculit, inter quos cum plurimorum clade Aelium Seianum ; quem ad summam potentiam non tam benivolentia provexerat, quam ut esset cuius ministerio ac fraudibus liberos Germanici circumveniret, nepotemque suum ex Druso filio naturalem ad successionem imperii confirmaret.

LVI. Nihilo lenior in convictores Graeculos, quibus vel maxime adquiescebat, Xenonem quendam exquisitius sermocinantem cum interrogasset, quaenam illa tam molesta dialectos esset, et ille respondisset Doridem, relegavit Cinariam, existimans exprobratum sibi veterem secessum, quod Dorice Rhodii loquantur. Item cum soleret ex lectione cotidiana quaestiones super cenam proponere comperissetque Seleucum grammaticum a ministris suis perquirere, quos quoque tempore tractaret auctores, atque ita praeparatum venire, primum a contubernio removit, deinde etiam ad mortem compulit.

LVII. Saeva ac lenta natura ne in puero quidem latuit ; quam Theodorus Gadareus [1] rhetoricae prae-

---

[1] Gadareus, *editions of* 1472 (?) *and* 1480 ; cadareus, Ω.

---

[a] A sign that he was condemned to death ; the noose was for strangling him and the hooks for dragging his body to the Tiber.

who pretended that he came by authority of the senate, showed him the noose and hooks,[a] but that Drusus was so tortured by hunger that he tried to eat the stuffing of his mattress; while the remains of both were so scattered that it was with difficulty that they could ever be collected.

LV. In addition to his old friends and intimates, he had asked for twenty of the leading men of the State as advisers on public affairs. Of all these he spared hardly two or three; the others he destroyed on one pretext or another, including Aelius Sejanus, whose downfall involved the death of many others. This man he had advanced to the highest power, not so much from regard for him, as that he might through his services and wiles destroy the children of Germanicus and secure the succession for his own grandson, the child of his son Drusus.

LVI. He was not a whit milder towards his Greek companions, in whose society he took special pleasure. When one Xeno was holding forth in somewhat far-fetched phrases, he asked him what dialect that was which was so affected, and on Xeno's replying that it was Doric, he banished him to Cinaria, believing that he was being taunted with his old-time exile, inasmuch as the Rhodians spoke Doric. He had the habit, too, of putting questions at dinner suggested by his daily reading, and learning that the grammarian Seleucus inquired of the imperial attendants what authors Tiberius was reading and so came primed, he at first banished the offender from his society, and later even forced him to commit suicide.

LVII. His cruel and cold-blooded character was not completely hidden even in his boyhood. His teacher of rhetoric, Theodorus of Gadara, seems first

ceptor et perspexisse primus sagaciter et assimilasse
aptissime visus est, subinde in obiurgando appellans
eum πηλὸν αἵματι πεφυραμένον, id est lutum a sanguine
maceratum. Sed aliquanto magis in principe eluxit,
etiam inter initia cum adhuc favorem hominum
2 moderationis simulatione captaret. Scurram, qui
praetereunte funere clare mortuo mandarat, ut
nuntiaret Augusto nondum reddi legata quae plebei
reliquisset, adtractum ad se recipere debitum ducique
ad supplicium imperavit et patri suo verum referre.
Nec multo post in senatu Pompeio cuidam equiti R.
quiddam perneganti, dum vincula minatur, affirmavit
fore ut ex Pompeio Pompeianus fieret, acerba cavil-
latione simul hominis nomen incessens veteremque [1]
partium fortunam.

LVIII. Sub idem tempus consulente praetore an
iudicia maiestatis cogi iuberet, exercendas esse leges
respondit et atrocissime exercuit. Statuae quidam
Augusti caput dempserat, ut alterius imponeret; acta
res in senatu et, quia ambigebatur, per tormenta
quaesita est. Damnato reo paulatim genus calumniae
eo processit, ut haec quoque capitalia essent: circa
Augusti simulacrum servum cecidisse, vestimenta
mutasse, nummo vel anulo effigiem impressam latrinae
aut lupanari intulisse, dictum ullum factumve eius

---

[1] veterumque, *PR* (*Roth*, *Preud'homme*).

[a] With a play on the double meaning of *debitum*.

to have had the insight to detect it, and to have
characterized it very aptly, since in taking him to
task he would now and then call him πηλὸν αἵματι
πεφυραμένον, that is to say, "mud kneaded with
blood." But it grew still more noticeable after he
became emperor, even at the beginning, when he
was still courting popularity by a show of moderation. When a funeral was passing by and a jester
called aloud to the corpse to let Augustus know that
the legacies which he had left to the people were
not yet being paid, Tiberius had the man haled before
him, ordered that he be given his due [a] and put
to death, and bade him go tell the truth to his
father. Shortly afterwards, when a Roman knight
called Pompeius stoutly opposed some action in the
senate, Tiberius threatened him with imprisonment,
declaring that from a Pompeius he would make of
him a Pompeian, punning cruelly on the man's
name and the fate of the old party.

LVIII. It was at about this time that a praetor
asked him whether he should have the courts convened to consider cases of lese-majesty ; to which he
replied that the laws must be enforced, and he did
enforce them most rigorously. One man had removed the head from a statue of Augustus, to substitute that of another; the case was tried in the
senate, and since the evidence was conflicting, the
witnesses were examined by torture. After the
defendant had been condemned, this kind of accusation gradually went so far that even such acts as
these were regarded as capital crimes: to beat a
slave near a statue of Augustus, or to change one's
clothes there ; to carry a ring or coin stamped with
his image into a privy or a brothel, or to criticize any

existimatione aliqua laesisse.   Perit [1] denique et is,
qui honorem in colonia sua eodem die decerni sibi
passus est, quo decreti et Augusto olim erant.

LIX. Multa praeterea specie gravitatis ac morum
corrigendorum, sed et magis naturae optemperans,
ita saeve et atrociter factitavit, ut nonnulli versiculis quoque et praesentia exprobrarent et futura
denuntiarent mala :

" Asper et immitis, breviter vis omnia dicam ?
    Dispeream, si te mater amare potest.

  Non es eques ; quare ? non sunt tibi milia centum ;
    Omnia si quaeras, et Rhodus exilium est.

  Aurea mutasti Saturni saecula, Caesar ;
    Incolumi nam te ferrea semper erunt.

  Fastidit vinum, quia iam sitit iste cruorem ;
    Tam bibit hunc avide, quam bibit ante merum.

2 Aspice felicem sibi, non tibi, Romule, Sullam
    Et Marium, si vis, aspice, sed reducem,
  Nec non Antoni civilia bella moventis
    Non semel infectas aspice caede manus,

---

[1] periit, *X*Υ.

---

[a] A knight must possess four hundred thousand sesterces ;
Tiberius, as the adopted son of Augustus, had no property.
See chap. xv. 2.

[b] That is, not even a Roman citizen, since an exile lost his
citizenship ; still less a knight.

[c] Sulla adopted the surname Felix.

word or act of his. Finally, a man was put to death merely for allowing an honour to be voted him in his native town on the same day that honours had previously been voted to Augustus.

LIX. He did so many other cruel and savage deeds under the guise of strictness and improvement of the public morals, but in reality rather to gratify his natural instincts, that some resorted to verses to express their detestation of the present ills and a warning against those to come:

" Cruel and merciless man, shall I briefly say all I would utter?
Hang me if even your dam for you affection can feel.

You are no knight. Why so? The hundred thousands are lacking; [a]
If you ask the whole tale, you were an exile at Rhodes.[b]

You, O Caesar, have altered the golden ages of Saturn;
For while you are alive, iron they ever will be.

Nothing for wine cares this fellow, since now 'tis for blood he is thirsting;
This he as greedily quaffs as before wine without water.

Look, son of Rome, upon Sulla, for himself not for you blest and happy,[c]
Marius too, if you will, but after capturing Rome;
Hands of an Antony see, rousing the strife of the people,
Hands stained with blood not once, dripping again and again;

375

Et dic : Roma perit ! regnavit sanguine multo,
    Ad regnum quisquis venit ab exsilio."

Quae primo, quasi ab impatientibus remediorum[1] ac
non tam ex animi sententia quam bile et stomacho
fingerentur, volebat accipi dicebatque identidem :
" Oderint, dum probent." Dein vera plane certaque
esse ipse fecit fidem.

LX. In paucis diebus quam Capreas attigit pis-
catori, qui sibi secretum agenti grandem mullum
inopinanter obtulerat, perfricari eodem pisce faciem
iussit, territus quod is a tergo insulae per aspera et
devia erepsisset ad se ; gratulanti autem inter
poenam, quod non et lucustam, quam praegrandem
ceperat, obtulisset, lucusta quoque lacerari os imperavit. Militem praetorianum ob subreptum e
viridiario pavonem capite puniit. In quodam itinere
lectica, qua vehebatur, vepribus impedita explora-
torem viae, primarum[2] cohortium centurionem,
stratum humi paene ad necem verberavit.

LXI. Mox in omne genus crudelitatis erupit numquam deficiente materia, cum primo matris, deinde
nepotum et nurus, postremo Seiani familiares atque
etiam notos persequeretur ; post cuius interitum vel
saevissimus exstitit. Quo maxime apparuit, non tam

---

[1] remediorum, *Graevius* ; remedium, *mss.*
[2] primarum, *mss.* ; praetoriarum, *Lipsius.*

---

[a] Cf. *Calig.* xxx. 1.
[b] If the text is correct, *primae cohortes* would seem to refer
to the praetorians.

Then say : Rome is no more !   He ever has reigned
   with great bloodshed
  Whoso made himself king, coming from banish-
    ment home."

These at first he wished to be taken as the work of
those who were impatient of his reforms, voicing
not so much their real feelings as their anger and
vexation ; and he used to say from time to time :
" Let them hate me, provided they respect my
conduct." [a]   Later he himself proved them only too
true and unerring.

LX. A few days after he reached Capreae and was
by himself, a fisherman appeared unexpectedly and
offered him a huge mullet; whereupon in his alarm
that the man had clambered up to him from the back
of the island over rough and pathless rocks, he had
the poor fellow's face scrubbed with the fish.   And
because in the midst of his torture the man thanked
his stars that he had not given the emperor an
enormous crab that he had caught, Tiberius had his
face torn with the crab also.   He punished a soldier
of the praetorian guard with death for having stolen
a peacock from his preserves.   When the litter in
which he was making a trip was stopped by brambles,
he had the man who went ahead to clear the way, a
centurion of the first cohorts,[b] stretched out on the
ground and flogged half to death.

LXI. Presently he broke out into every form of
cruelty, for which he never lacked occasion, venting
it on the friends and even the acquaintances, first
of his mother, then of his grandsons and daughter-
in-law, and finally of Sejanus.   After the death of
Sejanus he was more cruel than ever, which showed

ipsum ab Seiano concitari solitum, quam Seianum
quaerenti occasiones sumministrasse ; etsi com-
mentario, quem de vita sua summatim breviterque
composuit, ausus est scribere Seianum se punisse,
quod comperisset furere adversus liberos Germanici
filii sui ; quorum ipse alterum suspecto iam, alterum
oppresso demum Seiano interemit.

2   Singillatim crudeliter facta eius exsequi longum
est ; genera, velut exemplaria saevitiae, enumerare
sat erit.   Nullus a poena hominum cessavit dies, ne
religiosus quidem ac sacer ; animadversum in quosdam ineunte anno novo.   Accusati damnatique multi
cum liberis atque etiam a liberis suis.   Interdictum
ne capite damnatos propinqui lugerent.   Decreta
accusatoribus praecipua praemia, nonnumquam et
3 testibus.   Nemini delatorum fides abrogata.   Omne
crimen pro capitali receptum, etiam paucorum sim-
pliciumque verborum.   Obiectum est poetae, quod in
tragoedia Agamemnonem probris lacessisset ; obiectum et historico, quod Brutum Cassiumque ultimos
Romanorum dixisset ; animadversum statim in
auctores scriptaque abolita, quamvis probarentur
ante aliquot annos etiam Augusto audiente recitata.
4 Quibusdam custodiae traditis non modo studendi
solacium ademptum, sed etiam sermonis et conloqui
usus. Citati ad causam dicendam partim se domi
vulneraverunt certi damnationis et ad vexationem

378

that his favourite was not wont to egg him on, but on the contrary gave him the opportunities which he himself desired. Yet in a brief and sketchy autobiography which he composed he had the assurance to write that he had punished Sejanus because he found him venting his hatred on the children of his son Germanicus. Whereas in fact he had himself put one of them to death after he had begun to suspect Sejanus and the other after the latter's downfall.

It is a long story to run through his acts of cruelty in detail; it will be enough to mention the forms which they took, as samples of his barbarity. Not a day passed without an execution, not even those that were sacred and holy; for he put some to death even on New Year's day. Many were accused and condemned with their children and even by their children. The relatives of the victims were forbidden to mourn for them. Special rewards were voted the accusers and sometimes even the witnesses. The word of no informer was doubted. Every crime was treated as capital, even the utterance of a few simple words. A poet was charged with having slandered Agamemnon in a tragedy, and a writer of history of having called Brutus and Cassius the last of the Romans. The writers were at once put to death and their works destroyed, although they had been read with approval in public some years before in the presence of Augustus himself. Some of those who were consigned to prison were denied not only the consolation of reading, but even the privilege of conversing and talking together. Of those who were cited to plead their causes some opened their veins at home, feeling sure of being condemned and wishing to avoid

ignominiamque vitandam, partim in media curia
venenum hauserunt ; et tamen conligatis vulneribus
ac semianimes palpitantesque adhuc in carcerem
rapti. Nemo punitorum non in [1] Gemonias abiectus
uncoque tractus, viginti uno die abiecti tractique,
5 inter eos feminae et pueri. Immaturae puellae, quia
more tradito nefas esset virgines strangulari, vitiatae
prius a carnifice, dein strangulatae. Mori volentibus
vis adhibita vivendi. Nam mortem adeo leve supplicium putabat, ut cum audisset unum e reis,
Carnulum nomine, anticipasse eam, exclamaverit :
" Carnulus me evasit." Et in recognoscendis custodiis
precanti cuidam poenae maturitatem, respondit :
6 " Nondum tecum in gratiam redii." Annalibus suis
vir consularis inseruit, frequenti quodam convivio,
cui et ipse affuerit, interrogatum eum subito et clare
a quodam nano astante mensae inter copreas, cur
Paconius maiestatis reus tam diu viveret, statim
quidem petulantiam linguae obiurgasse, ceterum
post paucos dies scripsisse senatui, ut de poena
Paconi quam primum statueret.

LXII. Auxit intenditque saevitiam exacerbatus
indicio de morte filii sui Drusi. Quem cum morbo et
intemperantia perisse existimaret, ut tandem veneno
interemptum fraude Livillae uxoris atque Seiani
cognovit, neque tormentis neque supplicio cuiusquam

---

[1] in, *M* ; *the other mss. have* et in.

annoyance and humiliation, while others drank poison in full view of the senate; yet the wounds of the former were bandaged and they were hurried half-dead, but still quivering, to the prison. Every one of those who were executed was thrown out upon the Stairs of Mourning and dragged to the Tiber with hooks, as many as twenty being so treated in a single day, including women and children. Since ancient usage made it impious to strangle maidens, young girls were first violated by the executioner and then strangled. Those who wished to die were forced to live; for he thought death so light a punishment that when he heard that one of the accused, Carnulus by name, had anticipated his execution, he cried: "Carnulus has given me the slip"; and when he was inspecting the prisons and a man begged for a speedy death, he replied: "I have not yet become your friend." An ex-consul has recorded in his Annals that once at a large dinner-party, at which the writer himself was present, Tiberius was suddenly asked in a loud voice by one of the dwarfs that stood beside the table among the jesters why Paconius, who was charged with treason, remained so long alive; that the emperor at the time chided him for his saucy tongue, but a few days later wrote to the senate to decide as soon as possible about the execution of Paconius.

LXII. He increased his cruelty and carried it to greater lengths, exasperated by what he learned about the death of his son Drusus. At first supposing that he had died of disease, due to his bad habits, on finally learning that he had been poisoned by the treachery of his wife Livilla and Sejanus, there was no one whom Tiberius spared from torment and death. Indeed, he gave himself up so utterly for

pepercit, soli huic cognitioni adeo per totos dies deditus et intentus, ut Rhodiensem hospitem, quem familiaribus litteris Romam evocarat,[1] advenisse sibi nuntiatum torqueri sine mora iusserit, quasi aliquis ex necessariis quaestioni adesset, deinde errore
2 detecto et occidi, ne vulgaret iniuriam.   Carnificinae eius ostenditur locus Capreis, unde damnatos post longa et exquisita tormenta praecipitari coram se in mare iubebat, excipiente classiariorum manu et contis atque remis elidente cadavera, ne cui residui spiritus quicquam inesset.   Excogitaverat autem inter genera cruciatus etiam, ut larga meri potione per fallaciam oneratos, repente veretris deligatis, fidicularum simul
3 urinaeque tormento distenderet.   Quod nisi eum et mors praevenisset et Thrasyllus consulto, ut aiunt, differre quaedam spe longioris vitae compulisset, plures aliquanto necaturus ac ne reliquis quidem nepotibus parsurus creditur, cum et Gaium suspectum haberet et Tiberium ut ex adulterio conceptum aspernaretur.   Nec abhorret a vero ; namque identidem felicem Priamum vocabat, quod superstes omnium suorum exstitisset.

LXIII. Quam inter haec non modo invisus ac detestabilis, sed praetrepidus quoque atque etiam contumeliis obnoxius vixerit, multa indicia sunt.

[1] evocarat, ς (*Beroaldus*) ; evocabat, Ω.

whole days to this investigation and was so wrapped up in it, that when he was told of the arrival of a host of his from Rhodes, whom he had invited to Rome in a friendly letter, he had him put to the torture at once, supposing that someone had come whose testimony was important for the case. On discovering his mistake, he even had the man put to death, to keep him from giving publicity to the wrong done him.

At Capreae they still point out the scene of his executions, from which he used to order that those who had been condemned after long and exquisite tortures be cast headlong into the sea before his eyes, while a band of marines waited below for the bodies and broke their bones with boathooks and oars, to prevent any breath of life from remaining in them. Among various forms of torture he had devised this one : he would trick men into loading themselves with copious draughts of wine, and then on a sudden tying up their private parts, would torment them at the same time by the torture of the cords and of the stoppage of their water. And had not death prevented him, and Thrasyllus, purposely it is said, induced him to put off some things through hope of a longer life, it is believed that still more would have perished, and that he would not even have spared the rest of his grandsons; for he had his suspicions of Gaius and detested Tiberius as the fruit of adultery. And this is highly probable, for he used at times to call Priam happy, because he had outlived all his kindred.

LXIII. Many things go to show, not only how hated and execrable he was all this time, but also that he lived a life of extreme fear and was even exposed

383

Haruspices secreto ac sine testibus consuli vetuit.
Vicina vero urbi oracula etiam disicere conatus est,
sed maiestate Praenestinarum sortium territus
destitit, cum obsignatas devectasque Romam non
repperisset in arca nisi relata rursus ad templum.
2 Unum et alterum consulares oblatis provinciis non
ausus a se dimittere usque eo detinuit, donec succes-
sores post aliquot annos praesentibus daret, cum
interim manente officii titulo etiam delegaret plurima
assidue, quae illi per legatos et adiutores suos ex-
sequenda curarent.

LXIV. Nurum ac nepotes numquam aliter post
damnationem quam catenatos obsutaque lectica loco
movit, prohibitis per militem obviis ac viatoribus
respicere usquam vel consistere.

LXV. Seianum res novas molientem, quamvis iam
et natalem eius publice celebrari et imagines aureas
coli passim videret, vix tandem et astu magis ac dolo
quam principali auctoritate subvertit. Nam primo,
ut a se per speciem honoris dimitteret, collegam sibi
assumpsit in quinto consulatu, quem longo intervallo
absens ob id ipsum susceperat. Deinde spe affinitatis
ac tribuniciae potestatis deceptum inopinantem
criminatus est pudenda miserandaque oratione, cum
inter alia patres conscriptos precaretur, mitterent

---

to insult. He forbade anyone to consult soothsayers secretly and without witnesses. Indeed, he even attempted to do away with the oracles near the city, but forbore through terror at the divine power of the Praenestine lots; for though he had them sealed up in a chest and brought to Rome, he could not find them until the box was taken back to the temple.[a] He had assigned provinces to one or two ex-consuls, of whom he did not dare to lose sight, but he detained them at Rome and finally appointed their successors several years later without their having left the city. In the meantime they retained their titles, and he even continued to assign them numerous commissions, to execute through their deputies and assistants.

LXIV. After the exile of his daughter-in-law and grandchildren he never moved them anywhere except in fetters and in a tightly closed litter, while a guard of soldiers kept any who met them on the road from looking at them or even from stopping as they went by.

LXV. When Sejanus was plotting revolution, although he saw the man's birthday publicly celebrated and his golden statues honoured everywhere, yet it was with difficulty that he at last overthrew him, rather by craft and deceit than by his imperial authority. First of all, to remove him from his person under colour of showing him honour, he chose him as his colleague in a fifth consulship,[b] which, with **31 A.D.** this very end in view, he assumed after a long interval while absent from the city. Then beguiling him with hope of marriage into the imperial family and of the tribunicial power, he accused him when he least expected it in a shameful and pitiable speech, begging the senators among other things

385

alterum e consulibus, qui se senem et solum in
conspectum eorum cum aliquo militari praesidio
2 perduceret. Sic quoque diffidens tumultumque
metuens Drusum nepotem, quem vinculis adhuc
Romae continebat, solvi, si res posceret, ducemque [1]
constitui praeceperat. Aptatis etiam navibus ad
quascumque legiones meditabatur fugam, specula-
bundus ex altissima rupe identidem signa, quae,
ne nuntii morarentur, tolli procul, ut quidque factum
foret, mandaverat. Verum et oppressa coniuratione
Seiani nihilo securior aut constantior per novem
proximos menses non egressus est villa, quae vocatur
Iovis.[2]

LXVI. Urebant insuper anxiam mentem varia
undique convicia, nullo non damnatorum omne probri
genus coram vel per libellos in orchestra positos
ingerente. Quibus quidem diversissime adficiebatur,
modo ut prae pudore ignota et celata cuncta cuperet,
nonnumquam eadem contemneret et proferret ultro
atque vulgaret. Quin et Artabani Parthorum regis
laceratus est litteris parricidia et caedes et ignaviam
et luxuriam obicientis monentisque, ut voluntaria
morte maximo iustissimoque civium odio quam
primum satis faceret.

---

[1] ducem (*omitting* que), *M*; et ducem, *Salmasius.*
[2] Iovis, *L⸑ and the editors*; Iunonis, *Heinsius.*

---

[a] Since Tiberius and Sejanus were consuls for the year,
the reference is to *consules suffecti*, appointed to succeed to
the honour for a part of the year, probably from July 1st.
[b] A somewhat similar method of telegraphy is mentioned

to send one of the consuls *a* to bring him, a lonely
old man, into their presence under military protection. Even then distrustful and fearful of an outbreak, he had given orders that his grandson Drusus,
whom he still kept imprisoned in Rome, should be
set free, if occasion demanded, and made commander-
in-chief. He even got ships ready and thought of
flight to some of the legions, constantly watching
from a high cliff for the signals which he had
ordered to be raised afar off *b* as each step was
taken, for fear the messengers should be delayed.
But even when the conspiracy of Sejanus was crushed,
he was no whit more confident or courageous, but for
the next nine months he did not leave the villa
which is called Io's.

LXVI. His anxiety of mind became torture
because of reproaches of all kinds from every quarter,
since every single one of those who were condemned
to death heaped all kinds of abuse upon him, either
to his face or by billets placed in the orchestra.*c*
By these, however, he was most diversely affected, now
through a sense of shame desiring that they all be
concealed and kept secret, sometimes scorning them
and producing them of his own accord and giving them
publicity. Why, he was even attacked by Artabanus,
king of the Parthians, who charged him in a letter
with the murder of his kindred,*d* with other bloody
deeds, and with shameless and dissolute living, coun-
selling him to gratify the intense and just hatred of
the citizens as soon as possible by a voluntary death.

at the beginning of the *Agamemnon* of Aeschylus as the
means of sending the news of the fall of Troy to Mycenae.
  c Where the senators sat at the theatre ; cf. *Aug.* lv.
  d For this meaning of *parricidium* see note on *Jul.* xlii. 3.

LXVII. Postremo semet ipse pertaesus, tali [1] epistulae principio tantum non summam malorum suorum professus est: "Quid scribam vobis, p. c., aut quo modo scribam, aut quid omnino non scribam hoc tempore, dii me deaeque peius perdant quam cotidie perire sentio, si scio."

2 Existimant quidam praescisse haec eum peritia futurorum ac multo ante, quanta se quandoque acerbitas et infamia maneret, prospexisse; ideoque, ut imperium inierit, et patris patriae appellationem et ne in acta sua iuraretur obstinatissime recusasse, ne mox maiore dedecore impar tantis honoribus 3 inveniretur. Quod sane ex [2] oratione eius, quam de utraque re habuit, colligi potest; vel cum ait, similem se semper sui futurum nec umquam mutaturum mores suos, quam diu sanae mentis fuisset; sed exempli causa cavendum esse, ne se senatus in acta cuiusquam obligaret, quia aliquo casu mutari posset. Et rursus:

4 "Si quando autem," inquit, "de moribus meis devotoque vobis animo dubitaveritis,—quod prius quam eveniat, opto ut me supremus dies huic mutatae vestrae de me opinioni eripiat—nihil honoris adiciet mihi patria appellatio, vobis autem exprobrabit aut temeritatem delati mihi eius cognominis aut inconstantiam contrarii de me iudicii."

LXVIII. Corpore fuit amplo atque robusto, statura quae iustam excederet; latus ab umeris et pectore,

---

[1] tali, *Muretus*; talis, *mss.*
[2] ex, *MT*; *the other mss. have* et ex.

---

[a] Quoted also by Tac. *Ann.* 6. 6.
[b] That is, the change in his character and its consequences.

LXVII. At last in utter self-disgust he all but admitted the extremity of his wretchedness in a 32 A.D. letter beginning as follows[a]: "If I know what to write to you, Fathers of the Senate, or how to write it, or what to leave unwritten at present, may all gods and goddesses visit me with more utter destruction than I feel that I am daily suffering." Some think that through his knowledge of the future he foresaw this situation,[b] and knew long beforehand what detestation and ill-repute one day awaited him; and that therefore when he became emperor, he positively refused the title of "Father of his Country" and to allow the senate to take oath to support his acts, for fear that he might presently be found undeserving of such honours and thus be the more shamed. In fact, this may be gathered from the speech which he made regarding these two matters; for example, when he says: "I shall always be consistent and never change my ways so long as I am in my senses; but for the sake of precedent the senate should beware of binding itself to support the acts of any man, since he might through some mischance suffer a change." Again: "If you ever come to feel any doubt," he says, "of my character or of my heartfelt devotion to you (and before that happens, I pray that my last day may save me from this altered opinion of me), the title of Father of my Country will give me no additional honour, but will be a reproach to you, either for your hasty action in conferring the appellation upon me, or for your inconsistency in changing your estimate of my character."

LXVIII. He was large and strong of frame, and of a stature above the average; broad of shoulders

ceteris quoque membris usque ad imos pedes aequalis
et congruens; sinistra manu agiliore ac validiore,
articulis ita firmis, ut recens et integrum malum
digito terebraret, caput pueri vel etiam adulescentis
2 talitro vulneraret. Colore erat candido, capillo pone
occipitium summissiore ut cervicem etiam obtegeret,
quod gentile in illo videbatur; facie honesta, in qua
tamen crebri et subiti tumores, cum praegrandibus
oculis et qui, quod mirum esset, noctu etiam et
in tenebris viderent, sed ad breve et cum primum e
somno patuissent; deinde rursum hebescebant.
3 Incedebat cervice rigida et obstipa, adducto fere
vultu, plerumque tacitus, nullo aut rarissimo etiam
cum proximis sermone eoque tardissimo, nec sine
molli quadam digitorum gesticulatione. Quae omnia
ingrata atque arrogantiae plena et animadvertit
Augustus in eo et excusare temptavit saepe apud
senatum ac populum professus naturae vitia esse,
4 non animi. Valitudine prosperrima usus est, tempore quidem principatus paene toto prope inlaesa,
quamvis a tricesimo aetatis anno arbitratu eam suo
rexerit sine adiumento consiliove medicorum.

LXIX. Circa deos ac religiones neglegentior,
quippe addictus mathematicae plenusque persuasionis
cuncta fato agi, tonitrua tamen praeter modum
expavescebat et turbatiore caelo numquam non

---

^a One of the strongest arguments against the truth of the
tales of his debauchery.

and chest; well proportioned and symmetrical from head to foot. His left hand was the more nimble and stronger, and its joints were so powerful that he could bore through a fresh, sound apple with his finger, and break the head of a boy, or even a young man, with a fillip. He was of fair complexion and wore his hair rather long at the back, so much so as even to cover the nape of his neck; which was apparently a family trait. His face was handsome, but would break out on a sudden with many pimples. His eyes were unusually large and, strange to say, had the power of seeing even at night and in the dark, but only for a short time when first opened after sleep; presently they grew dim-sighted again. He strode along with his neck stiff and bent forward, usually with a stern countenance and for the most part in silence, never or very rarely conversing with his companions, and then speaking with great deliberation and with a kind of supple movement of his fingers. All of these mannerisms of his, which were disagreeable and signs of arrogance, were remarked by Augustus, who often tried to excuse them to the senate and people by declaring that they were natural failings, and not intentional. He enjoyed excellent health, which was all but perfect during nearly the whole of his reign,[a] although from the thirtieth year of his age he took care of it according to his own ideas, without the aid or advice of physicians.

LXIX. Although somewhat neglectful of the gods and of religious matters, being addicted to astrology and firmly convinced that everything was in the hands of fate, he was nevertheless immoderately afraid of thunder. Whenever the sky was lowering,

coronam lauream capite gestavit, quod fulmine afflari
negetur id genus frondis.

LXX. Artes liberales utriusque generis studiosissime coluit. In oratione Latina secutus est
Corvinum Messalam, quem senem adulescens
observarat. Sed adfectatione et morositate nimia
obscurabat stilum, ut aliquanto ex tempore quam a
2 cura praestantior haberetur. Composuit et carmen
lyricum, cuius est titulus "Conquestio de morte L.
Caesaris." Fecit et Graeca poemata imitatus
Euphorionem et Rhianum et Parthenium, quibus
poetis admodum delectatus scripta omnium et
imagines publicis bibliothecis inter veteres et praecipuos auctores dedicavit; et ob hoc plerique
eruditorum certatim ad eum multa de his ediderunt.
3 Maxime tamen curavit notitiam historiae fabularis
usque ad ineptias atque derisum; nam et gram-
maticos, quod genus hominum praecipue, ut diximus,
appetebat, eius modi fere quaestionibus experiebatur:
"Quae mater Hecubae, quod Achilli nomen inter
virgines fuisset, quid Sirenes cantare sint solitae."
Et quo primum die post excessum Augusti curiam
intravit, quasi pietati simul ac religioni satis facturus
Minonis exemplo ture quidem ac vino verum sine
tibicine supplicavit, ut ille olim in morte filii.

LXXI. Sermone Graeco quamquam alioqui promptus et facilis, non tamen usque quaque usus est
abstinuitque maxime in senatu; adeo quidem, ut

---

a See note on *Aug.* xc.

b The *grammaticus* was a critic and teacher of literature,
but "grammarian" has become conventional in this sense,
as well as in its more restricted meaning.

392

he always wore a laurel wreath, because it is said that that kind of leaf is not blasted by lightning.[a]

LXX. He was greatly devoted to liberal studies in both languages. In his Latin oratory he followed Messala Corvinus, to whom he had given attention in his youth, when Messala was an old man. But he so obscured his style by excessive mannerisms and pedantry, that he was thought to speak much better off-hand than in a prepared address. He also composed a lyric poem, entitled " A Lament for the Death of Lucius Caesar," and made Greek verses in imitation of Euphorion, Rhianus, and Parthenius, poets of whom he was very fond, placing their busts in the public libraries among those of the eminent writers of old; and on that account many learned men vied with one another in issuing commentaries on their works and dedicating them to the emperor. Yet his special aim was a knowledge of mythology, which he carried to a silly and laughable extreme; for he used to test even the grammarians,[b] a class of men in whom, as I have said, he was especially interested, by questions something like this : " Who was Hecuba's mother?" " What was the name of Achilles among the maidens?" " What were the Sirens in the habit of singing?" Moreover, on the first day that he entered the senate after the death of Augustus, to satisfy at once the demands of filial piety and of religion, he offered sacrifice after the example of Minos with incense and wine, but without a fluteplayer, as Minos had done in ancient times on the death of his son.

LXXI. Though he spoke Greek readily and fluently, yet he would not use it on all occasions, and especially eschewed it in the senate ; so much

monopolium nominaturus veniam prius postularet, quod sibi verbo peregrino utendum esset. Atque etiam cum in quodam decreto patrum ἔμβλημα recitaretur, commutandam censuit vocem et pro peregrina nostratem requirendam aut, si non reperiretur, vel pluribus et per ambitum verborum rem enuntiandam. Militem quoque Graece testimonium interrogatum nisi Latine respondere vetuit.

LXXII. Bis omnino toto secessus tempore Romam redire conatus, semel triremi usque ad proximos naumachiae hortos subvectus est disposita statione per ripas Tiberis, quae obviam prodeuntis submoveret, iterum Appia usque ad septimum lapidem; sed prospectis modo nec aditis urbis moenibus rediit, primo incertum qua de causa, postea ostento territus. Erat ei in oblectamentis serpens draco, quem ex consuetudine manu sua cibaturus cum consumptum a formicis invenisset, monitus est ut vim multitudinis caveret. Rediens ergo propere Campaniam Asturae in languorem incidit, quo paulum levatus Cerceios pertendit. Ac ne quam suspicionem infirmitatis daret, castrensibus ludis non tantum interfuit, sed etiam missum in harenam aprum iaculis desuper petit; statimque latere convulso et, ut exaestuarat, afflatus aura in graviorem recidit morbum. Susten-

2

3

---

^a "Monopoly," a Greek word transliterated into Latin; see note on chap. xxx.

^b The Greek word for inlaid figures of metal riveted or soldered to cups. There is no exact equivalent in Latin, but Cicero twice uses the transliterated form *emblema* (*In Verr.* 4. 49).

^c See *Jul.* xxxix. 4.

so that before using the word "monopolium," [a] he begged pardon for the necessity of employing a foreign term. Again, when the word ἔμβλημα [b] was read in a decree of the senate, he recommended that it be changed and a native word substituted for the foreign one; and if one could not be found, that the idea be expressed by several words, if necessary, and by periphrasis. On another occasion, when a soldier was asked in Greek to give testimony, he forbade him to answer except in Latin.

LXXII. Twice only during the whole period of his retirement did he try to return to Rome, once sailing in a trireme as far as the gardens near the artificial lake,[c] after first posting a guard along the banks of the Tiber to keep off those who came out to meet him; and again coming up the Appian Way as far as the seventh milestone. But he returned after merely having a distant view of the city walls, without approaching them; the first time for some unknown reason, the second through alarm at a portent. He had among his pets a serpent, and when he was going to feed it from his own hand, as his custom was, and discovered that it had been devoured by ants, he was warned to beware of the power of the multitude. So he went back in haste to Campania, fell ill at Astura, but recovering somewhat kept on to Circeii. To avoid giving any suspicion of his weak condition, he not only attended the games of the soldiers, but even threw down darts from his high seat at a boar which was let into the arena. Immediately he was taken with a pain in the side, and then being exposed to a draught when he was overheated, his illness increased. For all that, he kept up for some time, although he con-

tavit tamen aliquamdiu, quamvis Misenum usque
devectus nihil ex ordine cotidiano praetermitteret, ne
convivia quidem aut ceteras voluptates partim intemperantia partim dissimulatione. Nam Chariclen
medicum, quod commeatu afuturus e convivio egrediens manum sibi osculandi causa apprehendisset,
existimans temptatas ab eo venas, remanere ac
recumbere hortatus est cenamque protraxit. Nec
abstinuit consuetudine quin tunc quoque instans in
medio triclinio astante lictore singulos valere dicentis
appellaret.

LXXIII. Interim cum in actis senatus legisset
dimissos ac ne auditos quidem quosdam reos,
de quibus strictim et nihil aliud quam nominatos ab
indice scripserat, pro contempto se habitum fremens
repetere Capreas quoquo modo destinavit, non temere
quicquam nisi ex tuto ausurus. Sed tempestatibus et
ingravescente vi morbi retentus paulo post obiit in
villa Lucullana octavo et septuagesimo aetatis anno,
tertio et vicesimo imperii, XVII. Kal. Ap. Cn.
Acerronio Proculo C. Pontio Nigrino [1] conss.

2 Sunt qui putent venenum ei a Gaio datum lentum
atque tabificum ; alii, in remissione fortuitae febris
cibum desideranti negatum ; nonnulli, pulvinum iniec-
tum, cum extractum sibi deficienti anulum mox

[1] Nigrino, *Torrentius* ; Nigro, Ω.

tinued his journey as far as Misenum and made no change in his usual habits, not even giving up his banquets and other pleasures, partly from lack of self-denial and partly to conceal his condition. Indeed, when the physician Charicles had taken his hand to kiss it as he left the dining-room, since he was going away on leave of absence, Tiberius, thinking that he was trying to feel his pulse, urged him to remain and take his place again, and prolonged the dinner to a late hour. Even then he did not give up his custom of standing in the middle of the dining-room with a lictor by his side and addressing all the guests by name as they said farewell.

LXXIII. Meanwhile, having read in the proceedings of the senate that some of those under accusation, about whom he had written briefly, merely stating that they had been named by an informer, had been discharged without a hearing, he cried out in anger that he was held in contempt, and resolved to return to Capreae at any cost, since he would not risk any step except from his place of refuge. Detained, however, by bad weather and the increasing violence of his illness, he died a little later in the villa of Lucullus, in the seventy-eighth year of his age and the twenty-third of his reign, on the seventeenth day before the Kalends of April, in the consulship of Gnaeus Acerronius Proculus and Gaius Pontius Nigrinus. Mar. 16, 37 A.D.

Some think that Gaius gave him a slow and wasting poison; others that during convalescence from an attack of fever food was refused him when he asked for it. Some say that a pillow was thrown upon his face, when he came to and asked for a ring which had been taken from him during a fainting _Vid. Cal. xii._

resipiscens requisisset. Seneca eum scribit intellecta defectione exemptum anulum quasi alicui traditurum parumper tenuisse, dein rursus aptasse digito et compressa sinistra manu iacuisse diu immobilem ; subito vocatis ministris ac nemine respondente consurrexisse nec procul a lectulo deficientibus viribus concidisse.

LXXIV. Supremo natali suo Apollinem Temenitem *et* amplitudinis et artis eximiae, advectum Syracusis ut in bibliotheca templi novi poneretur, viderat per quietem affirmantem sibi non posse se ab ipso dedicari. Et ante paucos quam obiret dies, turris phari terrae motu Capreis concidit. Ac Miseni cinis e favilla et carbonibus ad calficiendum triclinium inlatis,[1] exstinctus iam et diu frigidus, exarsit repente prima vespera atque in multam noctem pertinaciter luxit.

LXXV. Morte eius ita laetatus est populus, ut ad primum nuntium discurrentes pars : " Tiberium in Tiberim ! " clamitarent, pars Terram matrem deosque Manes orarent, ne mortuo sedem ullam nisi inter impios darent, alii uncum et Gemonias cadaveri minarentur, exacerbati super memoriam pristinae 2 crudelitatis etiam recenti atrocitate. Nam cum senatus consulto cautum esset, ut poena damnatorum in decimum semper diem differretur, forte accidit ut quorundam supplicii dies is esset, quo nuntiatum de Tiberio erat. Hos implorantis hominum fidem, quia

---

[1] illatis, ς ; inlatus (illatus), Ω.

---

[a] This statue, which took its name from Temenos, a suburb of Syracuse, was a celebrated one ; cf. Cic. *In Verr.* 2. 4. 119.

[b] Of Augustus, on the western slope of the Palatine Hill.

[c] *Pharos*, the lighthouse at Alexandria, became a general term. Cf. *euripus, Jul.* xxxix. 2.

fit. Seneca writes that conscious of his approaching end, he took off the ring, as if to give it to someone, but held fast to it for a time; then he put it back on his finger, and clenching his left hand, lay for a long time motionless; suddenly he called for his attendants, and on receiving no response, got up; but his strength failed him and he fell dead near the couch.

LXXIV. On his last birthday he dreamt that the Apollo of Temenos,[a] a statue of remarkable size and beauty, which he had brought from Syracuse to be set up in the library of the new temple,[b] appeared to him in a dream, declaring that it could not be dedicated by Tiberius. A few days before his death the lighthouse[c] at Capreae was wrecked by an earthquake. At Misenum the ashes from the glowing coals and embers which had been brought in to warm his dining-room, after they had died out and been for a long time cold, suddenly blazed up in the early evening and glowed without cessation until late at night.

LXXV. The people were so glad of his death, that at the first news of it some ran about shouting, "Tiberius to the Tiber," while others prayed to Mother Earth and the Manes to allow the dead man no abode except among the damned. Still others threatened his body with the hook and the Stairs of Mourning, especially embittered by a recent outrage, added to the memory of his former cruelty. It had been provided by decree of the senate that the 21 A.D. execution of the condemned should in all cases be put off for ten days, and it chanced that the punishment of some fell due on the day when the news came about Tiberius. The poor wretches

399

absente adhuc Gaio nemo exstabat qui adiri inter-
pellarique posset, custodes, ne quid adversus constitutum facerent, strangulaverunt abieceruntque
3 in Gemonias. Crevit igitur invidia, quasi etiam post
mortem tyranni saevitia permanente. Corpus ut
moveri a Miseno coepit, conclamantibus plerisque
Atellam potius deferendum et in amphitheatro se-
miustilandum, Romam per milites deportatum est
crematumque publico funere.

LXXVI. Testamentum duplex ante biennium
fecerat, alterum sua, alterum liberti manu, sed eodem
exemplo, obsignaveratque etiam humillimorum signis.
Eo testamento heredes aequis partibus reliquit Gaium
ex Germanico et Tiberium ex Druso nepotes sub-
stituitque in vicem; dedit et legata plerisque, inter
quos virginibus Vestalibus, sed et militibus universis
plebeique Romanae viritim atque etiam separatim
vicorum magistris.

The exact point is not clear. Perhaps an amphitheatre
was chosen for the sake of ignominy, as well as to furnish
accommodation for spectators, and that of Atella seems to
have been the one nearest to Misenum. Or it may have been
because of Tiberius's failure to entertain the people with
shows (see chap. xlvii.) that it was proposed to make a farce
of his funeral in Atella, the home of the popular Atellan
farces.

begged the public for protection; but since in the
continued absence of Gaius there was no one who
could be approached and appealed to, the jailers,
fearing to act contrary to the law, strangled them
and cast out their bodies on the Stairs of Mourning.
Therefore hatred of the tyrant waxed greater, since
his cruelty endured even after his death. When the
funeral procession left Misenum, many cried out that
the body ought rather to be carried to Atella,[a] and
half-burned in the amphitheatre; but it was taken
to Rome by the soldiers and reduced to ashes with
public ceremonies.

LXXVI. Two years before his death he had made
two copies of a will, one in his own hand and the
other in that of a freedman, but of the same content,
and had caused them to be signed and sealed by
persons of the very lowest condition. In this will
he named his grandsons, Gaius, son of Germanicus,
and Tiberius, son of Drusus, heirs to equal shares
of his estate, each to be sole heir in case of the
other's death. Besides, he gave legacies to several,
including the Vestal virgins, as well as to each and
every man of the soldiers and the commons of Rome,
with separate ones to the masters of the city wards.

BOOK IV

GAIUS CALIGULA

LIBER IV

C. CALIGULA

I. Germanicus, C. Caesaris pater, Drusi et minoris Antoniae filius, a Tiberio patruo adoptatus, quaesturam quinquennio ante quam per leges liceret et post eam consulatum statim gessit, missusque ad exercitum in Germaniam, excessu Augusti nuntiato, legiones universas imperatorem Tiberium pertinacissime recusantis et sibi summam rei p. deferentis incertum pietate an constantia maiore compescuit atque hoste mox devicto

2 triumphavit. Consul deinde iterum creatus ac prius quam honorem iniret ad componendum Orientis statum expulsus, cum Armeniae regem devicisset, Cappadociam in provinciae formam redegisset, annum agens aetatis quartum et tricensimum diuturno morbo Antiochiae obiit, non sine veneni suspicione. Nam praeter livores, qui toto corpore erant, et spumas, quae per os fluebant, cremati quoque cor inter ossa incorruptum repertum est, cuius ea natura existimatur, ut tinctum veneno igne confici nequeat.

---

^a That is, without holding the intermediate offices ; the interval between his quaestorship and consulship was five years.

^b Cf. *Tib.* xxv. 2.

BOOK IV

GAIUS CALIGULA

I. Germanicus, father of Gaius Caesar, son of Drusus and the younger Antonia, after being adopted by his paternal uncle Tiberius, held the quaestorship five years before the legal age and passed directly to the consulship.^a When the death of Augustus was announced, he was sent to the army in Germany, where it is hard to say whether his filial piety or his courage was more conspicuous; for although all the legions obstinately refused to accept Tiberius as emperor, and offered him the rule of the state,^b he held them to their allegiance. And later he won a victory over the enemy and celebrated a triumph. Then chosen consul for a second time, before he entered on his term he was hurried off to restore order in the Orient, and after vanquishing the king of Armenia and reducing Cappadocia to the form of a province, died of a lingering illness at Antioch, in the thirty-fourth year of his age. There was some suspicion that he was poisoned; for besides the dark spots which appeared all over his body and the froth which flowed from his mouth, after he had been reduced to ashes his heart was found entire among his bones; and it is supposed to be a characteristic of that organ that when steeped in poison it cannot be destroyed by fire.

II. Obiit autem, ut opinio fuit, fraude Tiberi, ministerio et opera Cn. Pisonis, qui sub idem tempus Syriae praepositus, nec dissimulans offendendum sibi aut patrem aut filium, quasi plane ita necesse esset, etiam aegrum Germanicum gravissimis verborum ac rerum acerbitatibus nullo adhibito modo adfecit; propter quae, ut Romam rediit, paene discerptus a populo, a senatu capitis damnatus est.

III. Omnes Germanico corporis animique virtutes, et quantas nemini cuiquam, contigisse satis constat : formam et fortitudinem egregiam, ingenium in utroque eloquentiae doctrinaeque genere praecellens, benivolentiam singularem conciliandaeque hominum gratiae ac promerendi amoris mirum et efficax studium. Formae minus congruebat gracilitas crurum, sed ea quoque paulatim repleta assidua equi vectatione post 2 cibum. Hostem comminus saepe percussit. Oravit causas etiam triumphalis ; atque inter cetera studiorum monimenta reliquit et comoedias Graecas. Domi forisque civilis, libera ac foederata oppida sine lictoribus adibat. Sicubi clarorum virorum sepulcra cognosceret, inferias Manibus dabat. Caesorum clade Variana veteres ac dispersas reliquias uno tumulo humaturus, colligere sua manu et comportare primus 3 adgressus est. Obtrectatoribus etiam, qualescumque et quantacumque de causa nanctus esset, lenis adeo

---

a Cf. *Tib.* lii. 3.
b *See note on Tib.* xxvi. 1.

GAIUS CALIGULA

II. Now the belief was that he met his death through the wiles of Tiberius, aided and abetted by Gnaeus Piso.[a] This man had been made governor of Syria at about that time, and realising that he must give offence either to the father or the son, as if there were no alternative, he never ceased to show the bitterest enmity towards Germanicus in word and deed, even after the latter fell ill. In consequence Piso narrowly escaped being torn to pieces by the people on his return to Rome, and was condemned to death by the senate.

III. It is the general opinion that Germanicus possessed all the highest qualities of body and mind, to a degree never equalled by anyone; a handsome person, unequalled valour, surpassing ability in the oratory and learning of Greece and Rome, unexampled kindliness, and a remarkable desire and capacity for winning men's regard and inspiring their affection. His legs were too slender for the rest of his figure, but he gradually brought them to proper proportions by constant horseback riding after meals. He often slew a foeman in hand-to-hand combat. He pleaded causes even after receiving the triumphal regalia; and among other fruits of his studies he left some Greek comedies. Unassuming [b] at home and abroad, he always entered the free and federate towns without lictors. Wherever he came upon the tombs of distinguished men, he always offered sacrifice to their shades. Planning to bury in one mound the old and scattered relics of those who fell in the overthrow of Varus, he was the first to attempt to collect and assemble them with his own hand. Even towards his detractors, whosoever they were and whatever their motives, he was so

et innoxius, ut Pisoni decreta sua rescindenti, clientelas divexanti[1] non prius suscensere in animum induxerit, quam veneficiis quoque et devotionibus impugnari se comperisset; ac ne tunc quidem ultra progressus, quam ut amicitiam ei more maiorum renuntiaret mandaretque domesticis ultionem, si quid sibi accideret.

IV. Quarum virtutum fructum uberrimum tulit, sic probatus et dilectus a suis, ut Augustus—omitto enim necessitudines reliquas—diu cunctatus an sibi successorem destinaret, adoptandum Tiberio dederit; sic vulgo favorabilis, ut plurimi tradant, quotiens aliquo adveniret vel sicunde discederet, prae turba occurrentium prosequentiumve nonnumquam eum discrimen vitae adisse, e Germania vero post compressam seditionem revertenti praetorianas cohortes universas prodisse obviam, quamvis pronuntiatum esset, ut duae tantum modo exirent, populi autem Romani sexum, aetatem, ordinem omnem usque ad vicesimum lapidem effudisse se.

V. Tamen longe maiora et firmiora de eo iudicia in morte ac post mortem exstiterunt. Quo defunctus est die, lapidata sunt templa, subversae deum arae, Lares a quibusdam familiares in publicum abiecti, partus coniugum expositi. Quin et barbaros ferunt, quibus intestinum quibusque adversus nos bellum esset, velut in domestico communique maerore consensisse ad indutias; regulos quosdam barbam posuisse

---

[1] divexanti, *Torrentius;* diu vexanti, *mss.*

[a] Fuller details are given by Tac. *Ann.* 2. **69**. 5. Such spells were often inscribed on leaden tablets (*defixiones; plumbeis tabulis,* Tac.), specimens of which have come down to us.
[b] See note on *Aug.* ci. 3.   [c] See note on *Tib.* vii. 2.

mïld and lenient, that when Piso was annulling his decrees and maltreating his dependents, he could not make up his mind to break with him, until he found himself assailed also by potions and spells.[a] Even then he went no farther than formally to renounce Piso's friendship in the old-time fashion, and to bid his household avenge him, in case anything should befall him.[b]

IV. He reaped plentiful fruit from these virtues, for he was so respected and beloved by his kindred that Augustus (to say nothing of the rest of his relatives) after hesitating for a long time whether to appoint him his successor, had him adopted by Tiberius. He was so popular with the masses, that, according to many writers, whenever he came to any place or left one, he was sometimes in danger of his life from the crowds that met him or saw him off; in fact, when he returned from Germany after quelling the outbreak, all the cohorts of the praetorian guard went forth to meet him, although orders had been given that only two should go, and the whole populace, regardless of age, sex, or rank, poured out of Rome as far as the twentieth milestone.

V. Yet far greater and stronger tokens of regard were shown at the time of his death and immediately afterwards. On the day when he passed away the temples were stoned and the altars of the gods thrown down, while some flung their household gods into the street and cast out their newly born children.[c] Even barbarian peoples, so they say, who were engaged in war with us or with one another, unanimously consented to a truce, as if all in common had suffered a domestic tragedy. It is said that some princes put off their beards and had their wives' heads shaved, as

et uxorum capita rasisse ad indicium maximi luctus; regum etiam regem et exercitatione venandi et convictu megistanum abstinuisse, quod apud Parthos iustiti[1] instar est.

VI. Romae quidem, cum ad primam famam valitudinis attonita et maesta civitas sequentis nuntios opperiretur, et repente iam vesperi incertis auctoribus convaluisse tandem percrebruisset, passim cum luminibus et victimis in Capitolium concursus est ac paene revolsae templi fores, ne quid gestientis vota reddere moraretur, expergefactus e somno Tiberius gratulantium vocibus atque undique concinentium:

" Salva Roma, salva patria, salvus est Germanicus."

2 Et ut demum fato functum palam factum est, non solaciis ullis, non edictis inhiberi luctus publicus potuit duravitque etiam per festos Decembris mensis dies. Auxit gloriam desideriumque defuncti et atrocitas insequentium temporum, cunctis nec temere opinantibus reverentia eius ac metu repressam Tiberi saevitiam, quae mox eruperit.

VII. Habuit in matrimonio Agrippinam, M. Agrippae et Iuliae filiam, et ex[2] ea novem liberos tulit; quorum duo infantes adhuc rapti, unus iam puerascens insigni festivitate, cuius effigiem habitu Cupidinis in aede Capitolinae Veneris Livia dedicavit,

---

[1] iusticii ΠQ; *the other mss. have* iusti.
[2] et ex ΥT; *the other mss. have* ex *only.*

---

[a] A title originally applied to the king of Persia and transferred to the king of the Parthians.

[b] The Saturnalia, see Index and cf. note on *Aug.* lxxi. 1.

a token of the deepest mourning ; that even the king of kings[a] suspended his exercise at hunting and the banquets with his grandees, which among the Parthians is a sign of public mourning.

VI. At Rome when the community, in grief and consternation at the first report of his illness, was awaiting further news, and suddenly after nightfall a report at last spread abroad, on doubtful authority, that he had recovered, a general rush was made from every side to the Capitol with torches and victims, and the temple gates were all but torn off, that nothing might hinder them in their eagerness to pay their vows. Tiberius was roused from sleep by the cries of the rejoicing throng, who all united in singing :—

" Safe is Rome, safe too our country, for Germanicus is safe."

But when it was at last made known that he was no more, the public grief could be checked neither by any consolation nor edict, and it continued even during the festal days of the month of December.[b]

The fame of the deceased and regret for his loss were increased by the horror of the times which followed, since all believed, and with good reason, that the cruelty of Tiberius, which soon burst forth, had been held in check through his respect and awe for Germanicus.

VII. He had to wife Agrippina, daughter of Marcus Agrippa and Julia, who bore him nine children. Two of these were taken off when they were still in infancy, and one just as he was reaching the age of boyhood, a charming child, whose statue, in the guise of Cupid, Livia dedicated in the temple

Augustus in cubiculo suo positam, quotiensque introiret, exosculabatur ; ceteri superstites patri fuerunt, tres sexus feminini, Agrippina Drusilla Livilla, continuo triennio natae ; totidem mares, Nero et Drusus et C. Caesar. Neronem et Drusum senatus Tiberio criminante hostes iudicavit.

VIII. C. Caesar natus est pridie Kal. Sept. patre suo et C. Fonteio Capitone coss. Ubi natus sit, incertum diversitas tradentium facit. Cn. Lentulus Gaetulicus Tiburi genitum scribit, Plinius Secundus in Treveris vico Ambitarvio supra Confluentes ; addit etiam pro argumento aras ibi ostendi inscriptas OB AGRIPPINAE PVERPERIVM. Versiculi imperante mox eo divulgati apud hibernas legiones procreatum indicant :

> " In castris natus, patriis nutritus in armis,
> Iam designati principis omen erat."

2 Ego in actis Anti editum invenio. Gaetulicum refellit Plinius quasi mentitum per adulationem, ut ad laudes iuvenis gloriosique principis aliquid etiam ex urbe Herculi sacra sumeret, abusumque audentius mendacio, quod ante annum fere natus Germanico filius Tiburi fuerat, appellatus et ipse C. Caesar, de cuius amabili pueritia immaturoque obitu supra diximus.

3 Plinium arguit ratio temporum. Nam qui res Augusti

ᵃ See *Tib.* liv.
ᵇ The *acta publica* or *acta diurna*, an official publication of important events.
ᶜ Chap. vii.

of the Capitoline Venus, while Augustus had another
placed in his bed chamber and used to kiss it fondly
whenever he entered the room. The other children
survived their father, three girls, Agrippina, Drusilla,
and Livilla, born in successive years, and three boys,
Nero, Drusus, and Gaius Caesar. Nero and Drusus
were adjudged public enemies by the senate on the
accusation of Tiberius.[a]

VIII. Gaius Caesar was born the day before the
Kalends of September in the consulship of his father
and Gaius Fonteius Capito. Conflicting testimony
makes his birthplace uncertain. Gnaeus Lentulus
Gaetulicus writes that he was born at Tibur, Plinius
Secundus among the Treveri, in a village called
Ambitarvium above the Confluence. Pliny adds as
proof that altars are shown there, inscribed " For
the Delivery of Agrippina." Verses which were in
circulation soon after he became emperor indicate
that he was begotten in the winter-quarters of the
legions :

> " He who was born in the camp and reared 'mid the
> arms of his country,
>> Gave at the outset a sign that he was fated to
>> rule."

I myself find in the gazette[b] that he first saw the
light at Antium. Gaetulicus is shown to be wrong
by Pliny, who says that he told a flattering lie, to add
some lustre to the fame of a young and vainglorious
prince from the city sacred to Hercules ; and that
he lied with the more assurance because Germanicus
really did have a son born to him at Tibur, also
called Gaius Caesar, of whose lovable disposition and
untimely death I have already spoken.[c] Pliny has

memoriae mandarunt, Germanicum exacto consulatu
in Galliam missum consentiunt iam nato Gaio.   Nec
Plini opinionem inscriptio arae quicquam adiuverit,
cum Agrippina bis in ea regione filias enixa sit, et
qualiscumque partus sine ullo sexus discrimine puerperium vocetur, quod antiqui etiam puellas pueras,
4 sicut et pueros puellos dictitarent.   Exstat et Augusti
epistula, ante paucos quam obiret menses ad Agrippinam neptem ita scripta de Gaio hoc—neque enim
quisquam iam alius infans nomine pari tunc supere-
rat : "Puerum Gaium XV. Kal. Iun. si dii volent,
ut ducerent Talarius et Asillius, heri cum iis constitui.   Mitto praeterea cum eo ex servis meis
medicum, quem scripsi Germanico si vellet ut
retineret.   Valebis, mea Agrippina, et dabis operam
5 ut valens pervenias ad Germanicum tuum."   Abunde
parere arbitror non potuisse ibi nasci Gaium, quo
prope bimulus demum perductus ab urbe sit.   Versi-
culorum quoque fidem eadem haec elevant et eo
facilius, quod ii sine auctore sunt.   Sequenda est
igitur, quae sola[1] restat et publici instrumenti
auctoritas, praesertim cum Gaius Antium omnibus
semper locis atque secessibus praelatum non aliter
quam natale solum dilexerit tradaturque etiam sedem
ac domicilium imperii taedio urbis transferre eo destinasse.

IX. Caligulae cognomen castrensi ioco[2] traxit,
quia manipulario habitu inter milites educabatur.

---

[1] *The mss. have* auctor *after* sola.
[2] ioco, *Beroaldus* ; loco, Ω.

---

[a] "Little Boots" (though really singular number).   The
caliga, or half-boot, was regularly worn by the soldiers.

erred in his chronology; for the historians of
Augustus agree that Germanicus was not sent to
Germany until the close of his consulship, when
Gaius was already born. Moreover, the inscription
on the altar adds no strength to Pliny's view, for
Agrippina twice gave birth to daughters in that
region, and any childbirth, regardless of sex, is called
puerperium, since the men of old called girls *puerae*,
just as they called boys *puelli*. Furthermore, we
have a letter written by Augustus to his granddaughter Agrippina, a few months before he died,
about the Gaius in question (for no other child of the
name was still alive at that time), reading as follows:
" Yesterday I arranged with Talarius and Asillius to
bring your boy Gaius on the fifteenth day before the
Kalends of June, if it be the will of the gods. I
send with him besides one of my slaves who is a
physician, and I have written Germanicus to keep
him if he wishes. Farewell, my own Agrippina,
and take care to come in good health to your
Germanicus." May 18 14 A.D.

I think it is clear enough that Gaius could not have
been born in a place to which he was first taken from
Rome when he was nearly two years old. This letter
also weakens our confidence in the verses, the more
so because they are anonymous. We must then accept the only remaining testimony, that of the public
record, particularly since Gaius loved Antium as if it
were his native soil, always preferring it to all other
places of retreat, and even thinking, it is said, of
transferring thither the seat and abode of the empire
through weariness of Rome.

IX. His surname Caligula[a] he derived from a joke
of the troops, because he was brought up in their

Apud quos quantum praeterea per hanc nutrimentorum consuetudinem amore et gratia valuerit, maxime cognitum est, cum post excessum Augusti tumultuantis et in furorem usque praecipites solus haud dubie ex conspectu suo flexit. Non enim prius destiterunt, quam ablegari[1] eum ob seditionis periculum et in proximam civitatem demandari animadvertissent; tunc demum ad paenitentiam versi reprenso ac retento vehiculo invidiam quae sibi fieret deprecati sunt.

X. Comitatus est patrem et Syriaca expeditione. Unde reversus primum in matris, deinde ea relegata in Liviae Augustae proaviae suae contubernio mansit; quam defunctam praetextatus etiam tunc pro rostris laudavit. Transitque ad Antoniam aviam et undevicensimo aetatis anno accitus Capreas a Tiberio uno atque eodem die togam sumpsit barbamque posuit, sine ullo honore qualis contigerat tirocinio
2 fratrum eius. Hic omnibus insidiis temptatus elicientium[2] cogentiumque se ad querelas nullam umquam occasionem dedit, perinde obliterato suorum casu ac si nihil cuiquam accidisset, quae vero ipse pateretur incredibili dissimulatione transmittens tantique in avum et qui iuxta erant obsequii, ut non immerito sit dictum nec servum meliorem ullum nec deteriorem dominum fuisse.

XI. Naturam tamen saevam atque probrosam ne[3]

---

[1] ablegari, *G*; *the other mss. have* oblegari.
[2] elicientium, *L*³ς; elicentium, *X*π*Q*; *the other mss. have* et licentium.
[3] ne, *G*ς; *the other mss. have* nec.

midst in the dress of a common soldier. To what extent besides he won their love and devotion by being reared in fellowship with them is especially evident from the fact that when they threatened mutiny after the death of Augustus and were ready for any act of madness, the mere sight of Gaius unquestionably calmed them. For they did not become quiet until they saw that he was being spirited away because of the danger from their outbreak and taken for protection to the nearest town. Then at last they became contrite, and laying hold of the carriage and stopping it, begged to be spared the disgrace which was being put upon them.

X. He attended his father also on his expedition to Syria. On his return from there he first lived with his mother and after her banishment, with his great-grandmother Livia; and when Livia died, though he 29 A.D. was not yet of age, he spoke her eulogy from the rostra. Then he fell to the care of his grandmother Antonia and in the nineteenth year of his age he was called to Capreae by Tiberius, on the same day assuming the gown of manhood and shaving his first beard, but without any such ceremony as had attended the coming of age of his brothers. Although at Capreae every kind of wile was resorted to by those who tried to lure him or force him to utter complaints, he never gave them any satisfaction, ignoring the ruin of his kindred as if nothing at all had happened, passing over his own ill-treatment with an incredible pretence of indifference, and so obsequious towards his grandfather and his household, that it was well said of him that no one had ever been a better slave or a worse master.

XI. Yet even at that time he could not control

tunc quidem inhibere poterat, quin et animadversioni-
bus poenisque ad supplicium datorum cupidissime
interesset et ganeas atque adulteria capillamento
celatus et veste longa noctibus obiret ac scaenicas
saltandi canendique artes studiosissime appeteret, facile id sane Tiberio patiente, si per has mansuefieri
posset ferum eius ingenium. Quod sagacissimus senex
ita prorsus perspexerat, ut aliquotiens praedicaret
exitio suo omniumque Gaium vivere et se natricem[1] populo Romano, Phaethontem orbi terrarum
educare.

XII. Non ita multo post Iuniam Claudillam M.
Silani nobilissimi viri filiam duxit uxorem. Deinde
augur in locum fratris sui Drusi destinatus, prius
quam inauguraretur ad pontificatum traductus est
insigni testimonio pietatis atque indolis, cum deserta
desolataque reliquis subsidiis aula, Seiano hoste[2] suspecto mox et oppresso, ad spem successionis paulatim
2 admoveretur. Quam quo magis confirmaret, amissa
Iunia ex partu Enniam Naeviam, Macronis uxorem,
qui tum praetorianis cohortibus praeerat, sollicitavit
ad stuprum, pollicitus et matrimonium suum, si
potitus imperio fuisset; deque ea re et iure iurando
et chirographo cavit. Per hanc insinuatus Macroni
veneno Tiberium adgressus est, ut quidam opinantur, spirantique adhuc detrahi anulum et, quoniam
suspicionem retinentis dabat, pulvinum iussit inici

---

[1] *The mss. have the gloss* serpentis id genus *after* natricem.
[2] hoste, Υ; vete, *M*; vetere, *G*; ve tunc, *LP*¹ς (ne, *L*); hoste
tunc, *OP*²*T*. *Leg.* Seiano ve[l] tc̄ suspecto, mox et oppresso,
e.q.s.

his natural cruelty and viciousness, but he was a most eager witness of the tortures and executions of those who suffered punishment, revelling at night in gluttony and adultery, disguised in a wig and a long robe, passionately devoted besides to the theatrical arts of dancing and singing, in which Tiberius very willingly indulged him, in the hope that through these his savage nature might be softened. This last was so clearly evident to the shrewd old man, that he used to say now and then that to allow Gaius to live would prove the ruin of himself and of all men, and that he was rearing a viper for the Roman people and a Phaethon for the world.

XII. Not so very long afterward Gaius took to wife Junia Claudilla, daughter of Marcus Silanus, a man of noble rank. Then appointed augur in place of his brother Drusus, before he was invested with the office he was advanced to that of pontiff, with strong commendation of his dutiful conduct and general character; for since the court was deserted and deprived of its other supports, after Sejanus had been suspected of hostile designs and presently put out of the way, he was little by little encouraged to look forward to the succession. To have a better chance of realising this, after losing Junia in childbirth, he seduced Ennia Naevia, wife of Macro, who at that time commanded the praetorian guard, even promising to marry her if he became emperor, and guaranteeing this promise by an oath and a written contract. Having through her wormed himself into Macro's favour, he poisoned Tiberius, as some think, and ordered that his ring be taken from him while he still breathed, and then suspecting that he was trying to hold fast to it, that a pillow be put over his face;

atque etiam fauces manu sua oppressit, liberto, qui
ob atrocitatem facinoris exclamaverat, confestim in
3 crucem acto. Nec abhorret a veritate, cum sint
quidam auctores, ipsum postea etsi non de perfecto,
at certe de cogitato quondam parricidio professum ;
gloriatum enim assidue in commemoranda sua pietate,
ad ulciscendam necem matris et fratrum introisse se
cum pugione cubiculum Tiberi dormientis et miseri-
cordia correptum abiecto ferro recessisse ; nec illum,
quanquam sensisset, aut inquirere quicquam aut
exsequi ausum.

XIII. Sic imperium adeptus, populum Romanum,
vel dicam hominum genus, voti compotem fecit,
exoptatissimus princeps maximae parti provincialium
ac militum, quod infantem plerique cognoverant, sed
et universae plebi urbanae ob memoriam Germanici
patris miserationemque prope afflictae domus. Itaque
ut a Miseno movit quamvis lugentis habitu et funus
Tiberi prosequens, tamen inter altaria et victimas
ardentisque taedas densissimo et laetissimo obviorum
agmine incessit, super fausta nomina " sidus " et
" pullum " et " pupum " et " alumnum " appellan-
tium.

XIV. Ingressoque urbem, statim consensu senatus
et irrumpentis in curiam turbae, inrita Tiberi voluntate, qui testamento alterum nepotem suum praetex-

or even strangled the old man with his own hand, immediately ordering the crucifixion of a freedman who cried out at the awful deed. And this is likely enough; for some writers say that Caligula himself later admitted, not it is true that he had committed parricide, but that he had at least meditated it at one time; for they say that he constantly boasted, in speaking of his filial piety, that he had entered the bedchamber of the sleeping Tiberius dagger in hand, to avenge the death of his mother and brothers; but that, seized with pity, he threw down the dagger and went out again; and that though Tiberius knew of this, he had never dared to make any inquiry or take any action.

XIII. By thus gaining the throne he fulfilled the ^{37 A.D.} highest hopes of the Roman people, or I may say of all mankind, since he was the prince most earnestly desired by the great part of the provincials and soldiers, many of whom had known him in his infancy, as well as by the whole body of the city populace, because of the memory of his father Germanicus and pity for a family that was all but extinct. Accordingly, when he set out from Misenum, though he was in mourning garb and escorting the body of Tiberius, yet his progress was marked by altars, victims, and blazing torches, and he was met by a dense and joyful throng, who called him besides other propitious names their "star," their "chick," their "babe," and their "nursling."

XIV. When he entered the city, full and absolute power was at once put into his hands by the unanimous consent of the senate and of the mob, which forced its way into the House, and no attention was paid to the wish of Tiberius, who in his will had

THE LIVES OF THE CAESARS, BOOK IV

tatum adhuc coheredem ei dederat, ius arbitriumque
omnium rerum illi permissum est tanta publica
laetitia, ut tribus proximis mensibus ac ne totis quidem supra centum sexaginta milia victimarum caesa
tradantur.

2   Cum deinde paucos post dies in proximas Campaniae insulas traiecisset, vota pro reditu suscepta
sunt, ne minimam quidem occasionem quoquam
omittente in testificanda sollicitudine et cura de
incolumitate eius. Ut vero in adversam valitudinem
incidit, pernoctantibus cunctis circa Palatium, non
defuerunt qui depugnaturos se armis pro salute aegri
3 quique capita sua titulo proposito voverent. Accessit
ad immensum civium amorem notabilis etiam externorum favor. Namque Artabanus Parthorum rex,
odium semper contemptumque Tiberi prae se ferens,
amicitiam huius ultro petiit venitque ad colloquium
legati consularis et transgressus Euphraten aquilas et
signa Romana Caesarumque imagines adoravit.

   XV. Incendebat et ipse studia hominum omni
genere popularitatis. Tiberio cum plurimis lacrimis
pro contione laudato funeratoque amplissime, confestim Pandateriam et Pontias ad transferendos
matris fratrisque cineres festinavit, tempestate tur-
bida, quo magis pietas emineret, adiitque venera-
bundus ac per semet in urnas condidit; nec minore
scaena Ostiam praefixo in biremis puppe vexillo et
inde Romam Tiberi subvectos per splendidissimum

---

a See *Tib.* lxxvi.
b They were compelled to fulfil their vows; see chap.
xxvii. 2.
c Cf. *Vit.* ii. 4.

named his other grandson, still a boy, joint heir with
Caligula.*a* So great was the public rejoicing, that
within the next three months, or less than that,
more than a hundred and sixty thousand victims are
said to have been slain in sacrifice.

A few days after this, when he crossed to the
islands near Campania, vows were put up for his
safe return, while no one let slip even the slightest
chance of giving testimony to his anxiety and regard
for his safety. But when he fell ill, they all spent
the whole night about the Palace; some even vowed
to fight as gladiators, and others posted placards
offering their lives, if the ailing prince were spared.*b*
To this unbounded love of his citizens was added
marked devotion from foreigners. Artabanus, for Tib. 66
example, king of the Parthians, who was always
outspoken in his hatred and contempt for Tiberius,
voluntarily sought Caligula's friendship and came to
a conference with the consular governor; then
crossing the Euphrates, he paid homage to the
Roman eagles and standards and to the statues of
the Caesars.*c*

XV. Gaius himself tried to rouse men's devotion
by courting popularity in every way. After eulo-
gising Tiberius with many tears before the assembled
people and giving him a magnificent funeral, he
at once posted off to Pandateria and the Pontian
islands, to remove the ashes of his mother and
brother to Rome; and in stormy weather, too, to
make his filial piety the more conspicuous. He
approached them with reverence and placed them in
the urns with his own hands. With no less theatrical
effect he brought them to Ostia in a bireme with a
banner set in the stern, and from there up the Tiber

quemque equestris ordinis medio ac frequenti die
duobus ferculis Mausoleo intulit, inferiasque iis annua
religione publice instituit, et eo amplius matri circenses carpentumque quo in pompa traduceretur.

2 At in memoriam patris Septembrem mensem Germanicum appellavit. Post haec Antoniae aviae,
quidquid umquam Livia Augusta honorum cepisset,
uno senatus consulto congessit; patruum Claudium,
equitem R. ad id tempus, collegam sibi in consulatu
assumpsit; fratrem Tiberium die virilis togae adop-
3 tavit appellavitque principem iuventutis. De sororibus auctor fuit, ut omnibus sacramentis adiceretur [1]:
"Neque me liberosque meos cariores habebo quam
Gaium habeo et sorores eius"; item relationibus
consulum: "Quod bonum felixque sit C. Caesari
sororibusque eius."

4   Pari popularitate damnatos relegatosque restituit;
criminum, si quae residua ex priore tempore mane-
bant, omnium gratiam fecit; commentarios ad
matris fratrumque suorum causas pertinentis, ne cui
postmodum delatori aut testi maneret ullus metus,
convectos in Forum, et ante clare obtestatus deos
neque legisse neque attigisse quicquam, concremavit;
libellum de salute sua oblatum non recepit, conten-

---

[1] adiicerentur, *sixteenth century editions*; afficerentur
(adficerentur) Ω.

---

a Of Augustus; see *Aug.* c. 4.

b Originally the title of the commander of the knights who
were under forty-five and in active service. Conferred on
C. and L. Caesar by Augustus, it became the designation of
the heir to the throne, and was later assumed by the emperors
themselves.

c The consuls in making propositions to the senate began

to Rome, where he had them carried to the Mausoleum[a] on two biers by the most distinguished men of the order of knights, in the middle of the day, when the streets were crowded. He appointed funeral sacrifices, too, to be offered each year with due ceremony, as well as games in the Circus in honour of his mother, providing a carriage to carry her image in the procession. But in memory of his father he gave to the month of September the name of Germanicus. After this, by a single decree of the senate, he heaped upon his grandmother Antonia whatever honours Livia Augusta had ever enjoyed; took his uncle Claudius, who up to that time had been a Roman knight, as his colleague in the consulship; 37 A.D. adopted his brother Tiberius on the day that he assumed the gown of manhood, and gave him the title of Chief of the Youth.[b] He caused the names of his sisters to be included in all oaths: "And I will not hold myself and my children dearer than I do Gaius and his sisters"; as well as in the propositions[c] of the consuls: "Favour and good fortune attend Gaius Caesar and his sisters."

With the same degree of popularity he recalled those who had been condemned to banishment; took no cognizance of any charges that remained untried from an earlier time; had all documents relating to the cases of his mother and brothers carried to the Forum and burned, to give no informer or witness occasion for further fear, having first loudly called the gods to witness that he had neither read nor touched any of them. He refused a note which was offered him regarding his own safety, maintaining that

with a set formula (cf. *Aug.* lviii. 2, *Jul.* lxxx. 2), wishing success to the emperor, or in earlier days to the State.

dens nihil sibi admissum cur cuiquam invisus esset,
negavitque se delatoribus aures habere.

XVI. Spintrias monstrosarum libidinum aegre ne
profundo mergeret exoratus, urbe submovit. Titi
Labieni, Cordi Cremuti, Cassi Severi scripta senatus
consultis abolita requiri et esse in manibus lectitari-
que permisit, quando maxime sua interesset ut
facta quaeque posteris tradantur. Rationes imperii
ab Augusto proponi solitas sed a Tiberio intermissas
2 publicavit. Magistratibus liberam iuris dictionem et
sine sui appellatione concessit. Equites R. severe
curioseque nec sine moderatione recognovit, palam
adempto equo quibus aut probri aliquid aut ignomi-
niae inesset, eorum qui minore culpa tenerentur
nominibus modo in recitatione praeteritis. Ut levior
labor iudicantibus foret, ad quattuor prioris quintam
decuriam addidit. Temptavit et comitiorum more
3 revocato suffragia populo reddere. Legata ex testamento Tiberi quamquam abolito, sed et Iuliae
Augustae, quod Tiberius suppresserat, cum fide
ac sine calumnia repraesentata persolvit. Ducentesimam auctionum Italiae remisit; multis incendiorum
damna supplevit; ac si quibus regna restituit, adiecit [1]
et fructum omnem vectigaliorum et reditum medii
temporis, ut Antiocho Commageno sestertium milies
4 confiscatum. Quoque magis nullius non boni

---

[1] adiecit, ⌐ (*Beroaldus*); affecit (adfecit), Ω.

---

[a] See *Tib.* xliii. 1.
[b] Cf. *Aug.* xxxv. 2.
[c] See *Aug.* xxviii. 1 and ci. 4.
[d] *Ducentesimam* (sc. *partem*), one half of one per cent.

he had done nothing to make anyone hate him, and that he had no ears for informers.

XVI. He banished from the city the sexual perverts called *spintriae*,[a] barely persuaded not to sink them in the sea. The writings of Titus Labienus, Cremutius Cordus,[b] and Cassius Severus, which had been suppressed by decrees of the senate, he allowed to be hunted up, circulated, and read, saying that it was wholly to his interest that everything which happened be handed down to posterity. He published the accounts of the empire, which had regularly been made public by Augustus,[c] a practice discontinued by Tiberius. He allowed the magistrates unrestricted jurisdiction, without appeal to himself. He revised the lists of the Roman knights strictly and scrupulously, yet with due moderation, publicly taking their horses from those guilty of any wicked or scandalous act, but merely omitting to read the names of men convicted of lesser offences. To lighten the labour of the jurors, he added a fifth division to the previous four. He tried also to restore the suffrage to the people by reviving the custom of elections. He at once paid faithfully and without dispute the legacies named in the will of Tiberius, though this had been set aside, as well as in that of Julia Augusta, which Tiberius had suppressed. He remitted the tax of a two-hundredth [d] on auction sales in Italy; made good to many their losses from fires; and whenever he restored kings to their thrones, he allowed them all the arrears of their taxes and their revenue for the meantime; for example, to Antiochus of Commagene, a hundred million sesterces that had accrued to the Treasury. To make it known that he encouraged every kind of

exempli fautor videretur, mulieri libertinae octingenta donavit, quod excruciata gravissimis tormentis de scelere patroni reticuisset. Quas ob res inter reliquos honores decretus est ei clipeus aureus, quem quotannis certo die collegia sacerdotum in Capitolium ferrent, senatu prosequente nobilibusque pueris ac puellis carmine modulato laudes virtutum eius canentibus. Decretum autem ut dies, quo cepisset imperium, Parilia vocaretur, velut argumentum rursus conditae urbis.

XVII. Consulatus quattuor gessit, primum ex Kal. Iul. per duos menses, secundum ex Kal. Ian. per XXX dies, tertium usque in Idus Ian., quartum usque septimum Idus easdem. Ex omnibus duos novissimos coniunxit. Tertium autem Luguduni iniit solus, non ut quidam opinantur superbia neglegentiave, sed quod defunctum sub Kalendarum diem collegam

2 rescisse absens non potuerat. Congiarium populo bis dedit trecenos sestertios, totiens abundantissimum epulum senatui equestrique ordini, etiam coniugibus ac liberis utrorumque ; posteriore epulo forensia insuper viris, feminis ac pueris fascias [1] purpurae atque [2] conchylii distribuit. Et ut laetitiam publicam in perpetuum quoque augeret, adiecit diem Saturnalibus appellavitque Iuvenalem.

XVIII. Munera gladiatoria partim in amphitheatro Tauri partim in Saeptis aliquot edidit, quibus inseruit catervas Afrorum Campanorumque pugilum

---

[1] fascias, ç (*Beroaldus*); fasces, Ω.
[2] atque, *G* ; ac, ΠΧ ; at, *MQR*.

---

[a] An error, since he was consul in 39, 40, and 41.
[b] See *Aug.* xxix. 5.

noble action, he gave eight hundred thousand sesterces to a freedwoman, because she had kept silence
about the guilt of her patron, though subjected to
the utmost torture. Because of these acts, besides
other honours, a golden shield was voted him, which
was to be borne every year to the Capitol on an
appointed day by the colleges of priests, escorted by
the senate, while boys and girls of noble birth sang
the praises of his virtues in a choral ode. It was
further decreed that the day on which he began to
reign should be called the Parilia, as a token that
the city had been founded a second time.

XVII. He held four consulships, one from the
Kalends of July for two months, a second from the
Kalends of January for thirty days, a third up to the
Ides of January, and the fourth until the seventh
day before the Ides of the same month.ᵃ Of all
these only the last two were continuous.ᵃ The third
he assumed at Lugdunum without a colleague, not,
as some think, through arrogance or disregard of
precedent, but because at that distance from Rome
he had been unable to get news of the death of the
other consul just before the day of the Kalends. He
twice gave the people a largess of three hundred sesterces each, and twice a lavish banquet to the senate
and the equestrian order, together with their wives
and children. At the former of these he also distributed togas to the men, and to the women and
children scarves of red and scarlet. Furthermore, to
make a permanent addition to the public gaiety, he
added a day to the Saturnalia, and called it *Juvenalis.*

XVIII. He gave several gladiatorial shows, some
in the amphitheatre of Taurus ᵇ and some in the
Saepta, in which he introduced pairs of African and

July1,37 A.D.
Jan.1,39 ,,
Jan.13,40 ʙ
Jan.7,41 ,,

ex utraque regione electissimorum. Neque spectaculis semper ipse praesedit, sed interdum aut magistratibus aut amicis praesidendi munus iniunxit.

2 Scaenicos ludos et assidue et varii generis ac multifariam fecit, quondam et nocturnos accensis tota urbe luminibus. Sparsit et missilia variarum rerum et panaria cum obsonio viritim divisit; qua epulatione equiti R. contra se hilarius avidiusque vescenti partes suas misit, sed et senatori ob eandem causam codicillos, quibus praetorem eum extra

3 ordinem designabat. Edidit et circenses plurimos a mane ad vesperam interiecta modo Africanarum venatione modo Troiae decursione, et quosdam praecipuos, minio et chrysocolla constrato Circo nec ullis nisi ex senatorio ordine aurigantibus. Commisit et subitos, cum e Gelotiana apparatum Circi prospicientem pauci ex proximis Maenianis postulassent.

XIX. Novum praeterea atque inauditum genus spectaculi excogitavit. Nam Baiarum medium intervallum ad[1] Puteolanas moles, trium milium et sescentorum fere passuum spatium, ponte coniunxit contractis undique onerariis navibus et ordine duplici ad ancoras conlocatis superiectoque aggere[2]

2 terreno ac derecto in Appiae viae formam. Per hunc pontem ultro citro commeavit biduo continenti,

---

[1] ad, *inserted by Torrentius.*
[2] aggere terreno, $\Upsilon' P^2$; *the other mss. omit* aggere.

---

[a] To be scrambled for by the spectators.
[b] *Africanae*, supply *bestiae* and see Index.
[c] On the houses adjoining the Circus; called *Maeniana*

Campanian boxers, the pick of both regions. He did not always preside at the games in person, but sometimes assigned the honour to the magistrates or to friends. He exhibited stage-plays continually, of various kinds and in many different places, sometimes even by night, lighting up the whole city. He also threw about gifts [a] of various kinds, and gave each man a basket of victuals. During the feasting he sent his share to a Roman knight opposite him, who was eating with evident relish and appetite, while to a senator for the same reason he gave a commission naming him praetor out of the regular order. He also gave many games in the Circus, lasting from early morning until evening, introducing between the races now a baiting of panthers [b] and now the manœuvres of the game called Troy; some, too, of special splendour, in which the Circus was strewn with red and green, while the charioteers were all men of senatorial rank. He also started some games off-hand, when a few people called for them from the neighbouring balconies,[c] as he was inspecting the outfit of the Circus from the Gelotian house.

XIX. Besides this, he devised a novel and unheard of kind of pageant; for he bridged the gap between Baiae and the mole at Puteoli, a distance of about thirty-six hundred paces,[d] by bringing together merchant ships from all sides and anchoring them in a double line, after which a mound of earth was heaped upon them and fashioned in the manner of the Appian Way. Over this bridge he rode back and forth for two successive days, the first day on a

after a certain Maenius, who was supposed to have been the first to build such balconies.

[d] Over three and a half Roman miles.

primo die phalerato[1] equo insignisque quercea[2]
corona et caetra et gladio aureaque chlamyde,
postridie quadrigario habitu curriculoque biiugi
famosorum equorum, prae se ferens Dareum puerum
ex Parthorum obsidibus, comitante praetorianorum
3 agmine et in essedis cohorte amicorum.   Scio
plerosque existimasse talem a Gaio pontem excogitatum aemulatione Xerxis, qui non sine admiratione   aliquanto   angustiorem   Hellespontum
contabulaverit; alios, ut Germaniam et Britanniam,
quibus imminebat, alicuius inmensi operis fama
territaret.   Sed avum meum narrantem puer audie-
bam, causam operis ab interioribus aulicis proditam,
quod Thrasyllus mathematicus anxio de successore
Tiberio et in verum nepotem proniori affirmasset
non magis Gaium imperaturum quam per Baianum
sinum equis discursurum.

XX. Edidit et peregre spectacula, in Sicilia
Syracusis asticos ludos et in Gallia Luguduni mis-
cellos; sed hic certamen quoque Graecae Latinaeque
facundiae, quo certamine ferunt victoribus praemia
victos contulisse, eorundem et laudes componere
coactos; eos autem, qui maxime displicuissent,
scripta sua spongia linguave delere iussos, nisi
ferulis obiurgari aut flumine proximo mergi malu-
issent.

XXI. Opera sub Tiberio semiperfecta, templum

¹ falerato, Ω.
² quercea, ς (*Roth*); quiercica, *MG*; quercica, ϒ; insignis
quoque aerea, *X*.

ᵃ See *Tib.* lv.
ᵇ See note on *Tib.* vi. 4.
ᶜ Obviously not a choice, but determined by the degree of
success of the contestants.

caparisoned horse, himself resplendent in a crown of
oak leaves, a buckler, a sword, and a cloak of cloth of
gold ; on the second, in the dress of a charioteer in
a car drawn by a pair of famous horses, carrying
before him a boy named Dareus, one of the hostages
from Parthia, and attended by the entire praetorian
guard and a company of his friends in Gallic
chariots. I know that many have supposed that
Gaius devised this kind of bridge in rivalry of
Xerxes, who excited no little admiration by bridging
the much narrower Hellespont; others, that it was
to inspire fear in Germany and Britain, on which he
had designs, by the fame of some stupendous work.
But when I was a boy, I used to hear my grandfather
say that the reason for the work, as revealed by the
emperor's confidential courtiers, was that Thrasyllus
the astrologer had declared to Tiberius, when he was
worried about his successor and inclined towards his
natural grandson,[a] that Gaius had no more chance of
becoming emperor than of riding about over the gulf
of Baiae with horses.

XX. He also gave shows in foreign lands,
Athenian games[b] at Syracuse in Sicily, and mis-
cellaneous games at Lugdunum in Gaul; at the
latter place also a contest in Greek and Latin
oratory, in which, they say, the losers gave prizes to
the victors and were forced to compose eulogies
upon them, while those who were least successful
were ordered to erase their writings with a sponge
or with their tongue,[c] unless they elected rather
to be beaten with rods or thrown into the neighbouring river.

XXI. He completed the public works which had
been half finished under Tiberius, namely the temple

Augusti theatrumque Pompei, absolvit. Incohavit autem aquae ductum regione Tiburti et amphitheatrum iuxta Saepta, quorum operum a successore eius Claudio alterum peractum, omissum alterum est. Syracusis conlapsa vetustate moenia deorumque aedes refectae. Destinaverat et Sami Polycratis regiam restituere, Mileti Didymeum peragere, in iugo Alpium urbem condere, sed ante omnia Isthmum in Achaia perfodere, miseratque iam ad dimetiendum opus primipilarem.

XXII. Hactenus quasi de principe, reliqua ut de monstro narranda sunt.

Compluribus cognominibus adsumptis—nam et "pius" et "castrorum filius" et "pater exercituum" et "optimus maximus Caesar" vocabatur—cum audiret forte reges, qui officii causa in urbem advenerant, concertantis apud se super cenam de nobilitate generis, exclamavit:

$$\text{Εἷς κοίρανος ἔστω, εἷς βασιλεύς.}$$

Nec multum afuit quin statim diadema sumeret speciemque principatus in regni formam converteret.
2 Verum admonitus et principum et regum se excessisse fastigium, divinam ex eo maiestatem asserere sibi coepit; datoque negotio, ut simulacra numinum religione et arte praeclara, inter quae Olympii Iovis, apportarentur e Graecia,[1] quibus

---

[1] e Graecia, *Venetian ed. of* 1510; egregia, Ω.

---

[a] See *Claud.* xx. 1.
[b] Cf. *Jul.* xliv. 3.   [c] *Iliad* 2. 204.
[d] Under Caligula the so-called "principate" had become an absolute monarchy. Caligula proposed to assume the pomp of a king.

of Augustus and the theatre of Pompey. He likewise began an aqueduct in the region near Tibur and an amphitheatre beside the Saepta, the former finished by his successor Claudius,[a] while the latter was abandoned. At Syracuse he repaired the city walls, which had fallen into ruin through lapse of time, and the temples of the gods. He had planned, besides, to rebuild the palace of Polycrates at Samos, to finish the temple of Didymaean Apollo at Ephesus, to found a city high up in the Alps, but, above all, to dig a canal through the Isthmus in Greece,[b] and he had already sent a chief centurion to survey the work.

XXII. So much for Caligula as emperor; we must now tell of his career as a monster.

After he had assumed various surnames (for he was called "Pious," "Child of the Camp," "Father of the Armies," and "Greatest and Best of Caesars "), chancing to overhear some kings, who had come to Rome to pay their respects to him, disputing at dinner about the nobility of their descent, he cried:

"Let there be one Lord, one King."[c]

And he came near assuming a crown at once and changing the semblance of a principate into the form of a monarchy.[d] But on being reminded that he had risen above the elevation both of princes and kings, he began from that time on to lay claim to divine majesty; for after giving orders that such statues of the gods as were especially famous for their sanctity or their artistic merit, including that of Jupiter of Olympia,[e] should be brought from

[e] The chryselephantine statue of Zeus by Pheidias; see chap. lvii. 1.

capite dempto suum imponeret, partem Palatii ad
Forum usque promovit, atque aede Castoris et
Pollucis in vestibulum transfigurata, consistens saepe
inter fratres deos, medium adorandum se adeuntibus
exhibebat ; et quidam eum Latiarem Iovem con-

3 salutarunt. Templum etiam numini suo proprium
et sacerdotes et excogitatissimas hostias instituit.
In templo simulacrum stabat aureum iconicum
amiciebaturque cotidie veste, quali ipse uteretur.
Magisteria sacerdotii ditissimus quisque et ambitione
et licitatione maxima vicibus comparabant.   Hostiae
erant phoenicopteri, pavones, tetraones, numidicae,
meleagrides, phasianae, quae generatim per singulos

4 dies immolarentur.   Et noctibus quidem plenam
fulgentemque lunam invitabat assidue in amplexus
atque concubitum, interdiu vero cum Capitolino Iove
secreto fabulabatur, modo insusurrans ac praebens
in vicem aurem, modo clarius nec sine iurgiis.   Nam
vox comminantis audita est :

Ἦ μ᾽ ἀνάειρ᾽ ἢ ἐγὼ σέ,

donec exoratus, ut referebat, et in contubernium
ultro invitatus super templum Divi Augusti ponte
transmisso Palatium Capitoliumque coniunxit.   Mox,
quo propior esset, in area Capitolina novae domus
fundamenta iecit.

XXIII. Agrippae se nepotem neque credi neque
dici ob ignobilitatem eius volebat suscensebatque,
si qui vel oratione vel carmine imaginibus eum
Caesarum insererent.   Praedicabat autem matrem

a *numidicae* and *meleagrides* are the same.
b *Iliad*, 23. 724, where after a long and indecisive wrestling
bout Ajax thus challenges Odysseus to settle the contest.
Ἀνάειρε is doubtless used in a double sense, perhaps with
aposiopesis, " Raise me up (to heaven), or thee I'll —."

Greece, in order to remove their heads and put his own in their place, he built out a part of the Palace as far as the Forum, and making the temple of Castor and Pollux its vestibule, he often took his place between the divine brethren, and exhibited himself there to be worshipped by those who presented themselves; and some hailed him as Jupiter Latiaris. He also set up a special temple to his own godhead, with priests and with victims of the choicest kind. In this temple was a life-sized statue of the emperor in gold, which was dressed each day in clothing such as he wore himself. The richest citizens used all their influence to secure the priesthoods of his cult and bid high for the honour. The victims were flamingoes, peacocks, black grouse, guinea-hens [a] and pheasants, offered day by day each after its own kind. At night he used constantly to invite the full and radiant moon to his embraces and his bed, while in the daytime he would talk confidentially with Jupiter Capitolinus, now whispering and then in turn putting his ear to the mouth of the god, now in louder and even angry language; for he was heard to make the threat: " Lift me up, or I'll lift thee." [b] But finally won by entreaties, as he reported, and even invited to live with the god, he built a bridge over the temple of the Deified Augustus, and thus joined his Palace to the Capitol. Presently, to be nearer yet, he laid the foundations of a new house in the court of the Capitol.

XXIII. He did not wish to be thought the grandson of Agrippa, or called so, because of the latter's humble origin; and he grew very angry if anyone in a speech or a song included Agrippa among the ancestors of the Caesars. He even boasted that

suam ex incesto, quod Augustus cum Iulia filia
admisisset, procreatam ; ac non contentus hac
Augusti insectatione Actiacas Siculasque [1] victorias,
ut funestas p. R. et calamitosas, vetuit sollemnibus
2 feriis celebrari. Liviam Augustam proaviam " Ulixem
stolatum " identidem appellans, etiam ignobilitatis
quadam ad senatum epistula arguere ausus est quasi
materno avo decurione Fundano ortam, cum publicis
monumentis certum sit, Aufidium Lurconem [2] Romae
honoribus functum. Aviae Antoniae secretum petenti
denegavit, nisi ut interveniret Macro praefectus,
ac per istius modi indignitates et taedia causa
exstitit mortis, dato tamen, ut quidam putant, et
veneno ; nec defunctae ullum honorem habuit
3 prospexitque e triclinio ardentem rogum. Fratrem
Tiberium inopinantem repente immisso tribuno
militum interemit, Silanum item socerum ad necem
secandasque novacula fauces compulit, causatus in
utroque, quod hic ingressum se turbatius mare non
esset secutus ac spe occupandi urbem, si quid sibi
per tempestates accideret, remansisset, ille antidotum
oboluisset,[3] quasi ad praecavenda venena sua sump-
tum, cum et Silanus impatientiam nauseae vitasset
et molestiam navigandi, et Tiberius propter assiduam
et ingravescentem tussim medicamento usus esset.

---

[1] Siculasque, ς ; singulasque, Ω.
[2] Lurconem, *Stephanus* ; Lyrgonem, Ω.
[3] oboluisset, *Beroaldus* ; obolevisset, *mss.*

---

[a] See *Aug.* xvi. 1.
[b] The *stola* was the characteristic dress of the Roman
matron, as the *toga* was that of the man.
[c] See note on *Tib.* xxxvii. 3.
[d] By adoption ; see chap. xv. 2.

his own mother was born in incest, which Augustus
had committed with his daughter Julia; and not
content with this slur on the memory of Augustus,
he forbade the celebration of his victories at Actium
and off Sicily by annual festivals,[a] on the ground that
they were disastrous and ruinous to the Roman
people. He often called his greatgrandmother Livia
Augusta "a Ulysses in petticoats,"[b] and he had the
audacity to accuse her of low birth in a letter to the
senate, alleging that her maternal grandfather had
been nothing but a decurion[c] of Fundi; whereas it is
proved by public records that Aufidius Lurco held
high offices at Rome. When his grandmother
Antonia asked for a private interview, he refused it
except in the presence of the praefect Macro, and by
such indignities and annoyances he caused her death;
although some think that he also gave her poison.
After she was dead, he paid her no honour, but
viewed her burning pyre from his dining-room. He
had his brother[d] Tiberius put to death without warning, suddenly sending a tribune of the soldiers to do
the deed; besides driving his father-in-law Silanus to
end his life by cutting his throat with a razor. His
charge against the latter was that Silanus had not
followed him when he put to sea in stormy weather,
but had remained behind in the hope of taking
possession of the city in case he should be lost in the
storm; against Tiberius, that his breath smelled
of an antidote, which he had taken to guard against
being poisoned at his hand. Now as a matter of
fact, Silanus was subject to sea-sickness and wished
to avoid the discomforts of the voyage, while
Tiberius had taken medicine for a chronic cough,
which was growing worse. As for his uncle

439

Nam Claudium patruum non nisi in ludibrium reservavit.

XXIV. Cum omnibus sororibus suis consuetudinem stupri fecit plenoque convivio singulas infra se vicissim conlocabat uxore supra cubante. Ex iis Drusillam vitiasse virginem praetextatus adhuc creditur atque etiam in concubitu eius quondam deprehensus ab Antonia avia, apud quam simul educabantur; mox Lucio Cassio Longino consulari conlocatam abduxit et in modum iustae uxoris propalam habuit; heredem quoque bonorum atque

2 imperii aeger instituit. Eadem defuncta iustitium indixit, in quo risisse lavisse cenasse cum parentibus aut coniuge liberisve capital fuit. Ac maeroris impatiens, cum repente noctu profugisset ab urbe transcucurrissetque Campaniam, Syracusas petit, rursusque inde propere rediit barba capilloque promisso; nec umquam postea quantiscumque de rebus, ne pro contione quidem populi aut apud milites, nisi per

3 numen Drusillae deieravit. Reliquas sorores nec cupiditate tanta nec dignatione dilexit, ut quas saepe exoletis suis prostraverit[1]; quo facilius eas in causa Aemili Lepidi condemnavit quasi adulteras et insidiarum adversus se conscias ei. Nec solum chirographa omnium requisita fraude ac stupro divulgavit, sed et tres gladios in necem suam praeparatos Marti Ultori addito elogio consecravit.

[1] prostraverit, ς ; *the earlier mss. have* prostravit.

Claudius, he spared him merely as a laughing-stock.

XXIV. He lived in habitual incest with all his sisters, and at a large banquet he placed each of them in turn below him, while his wife reclined above. Of these he is believed to have violated Drusilla when he was still a minor, and even to have been caught lying with her by his grandmother Antonia, at whose house they were brought up in company. Afterwards, when she was the wife of Lucius Cassius Longinus, an ex-consul, he took her from him and openly treated her as his lawful wife; and when ill, he made her heir to his property and the throne. When she died, he appointed a season of public mourning, during which it was a capital offence to laugh, bathe, or dine in company with one's parents, wife, or children. He was so beside himself with grief that suddenly fleeing the city by night and traversing Campania, he went to Syracuse and hurriedly returned from there without cutting his hair or shaving his beard. And he never afterwards took oath about matters of the highest moment, even before the assembly of the people or in the presence of the soldiers, except by the godhead of Drusilla. The rest of his sisters he did not love with so great affection, nor honour so highly, but often prostituted them to his favourites; so that he was the readier at the trial of Aemilius Lepidus to condemn them, as adulteresses and privy to the conspiracies against him; and he not only made public letters in the handwriting of all of them, procured by fraud and seduction, but also dedicated to Mars the Avenger, with an explanatory inscription, three swords designed to take his life.

441

XXV. Matrimonia contraxerit turpius an dimiserit an tenuerit, non est facile discernere. Liviam Orestillam C. Pisoni nubentem, cum ad officium et ipse venisset, ad se deduci imperavit intraque paucos dies repudiatam biennio post relegavit, quod repetisse usum prioris mariti tempore medio videbatur. Alii tradunt adhibitum cenae nuptiali mandasse ad Pisonem contra accumbentem : "Noli uxorem meam premere," statimque e convivio abduxisse secum ac proximo die edixisse : matrimonium sibi repertum exemplo Romuli

2 et Augusti. Lolliam Paulinam, C.[1] Memmio consulari exercitus regenti nuptam, facta mentione aviae eius ut quondam pulcherrimae, subito ex provincia evocavit ac perductam a marito coniunxit sibi brevique missam fecit interdicto cuiusquam in perpetuum coitu.

3 Caesoniam neque facie insigni neque aetate integra matremque iam ex alio viro trium filiarum, sed luxuriae ac lasciviae perditae, et ardentius et constantius amavit, ut saepe chlamyde peltaque et galea ornatam ac iuxta adequitantem militibus ostenderit, amicis vero etiam nudam. Uxorio nomine non prius[2] dignatus est quam enixam, uno atque eodem die professus et

4 maritum se eius et patrem infantis ex ea natae. Infantem autem, Iuliam Drusillam appellatam, per

---

[1] C., *mss.*; P., *inscriptions.*
[2] non prius, *supplied by Roth.*

XXV. It is not easy to decide whether he acted more basely in contracting his marriages, in annulling them, or as a husband. At the marriage of Livia Orestilla to Gaius Piso, he attended the ceremony himself, gave orders that the bride be taken to his own house, and within a few days divorced her; two years later he banished her, because of a suspicion that in the meantime she had gone back to her former husband. Others write that being invited to the wedding banquet, he sent word to Piso, who reclined opposite to him: " Don't take liberties with my wife," and at once carried her off with him from the table, the next day issuing a proclamation that he had got himself a wife in the manner of Romulus and Augustus. When the statement was made that the grandmother of Lollia Paulina, who was married to Gaius Memmius, an ex-consul commanding armies, had once been a remarkably beautiful woman, he suddenly called Lollia from the province, separated her from her husband, and married her; then in a short time he put her away, with the command never to have intercourse with anyone. Though Caesonia was neither beautiful nor young, and was already mother of three daughters by another, besides being a woman of reckless extravagance and wantonness, he loved her not only more passionately but more faithfully, often exhibiting her to the soldiers riding by his side, decked with cloak, helmet and shield, and to his friends even in a state of nudity. He did not honour her with the title of wife until she had borne him a child, announcing on the selfsame day that he had married her and that he was the father of her babe. This babe, whom he named Julia Drusilla, he carried to the temples of all the goddesses, finally placing

omnium dearum templa circumferens Minervae gremio imposuit alendamque et instituendam commendavit. Nec ullo firmiore indicio sui seminis esse credebat quam feritatis, quae illi quoque tanta iam tunc erat, ut infestis digitis ora et oculos simul ludentium infantium incesseret.

XXVI. Leve ac frigidum sit his addere, quo propinquos amicosque pacto tractaverit, Ptolemaeum regis Iubae filium, consobrinum suum—erat enim et is M. Antoni ex Selene filia nepos—et in primis ipsum Macronem, ipsam Enniam, adiutores imperii; quibus omnibus pro necessitudinis iure proque meritorum gratia cruenta mors persoluta est.

2 Nihilo reverentior leniorve erga senatum, quosdam summis honoribus functos ad essedum sibi currere togatos per aliquot passuum milia et cenanti modo ad pluteum modo ad pedes stare succinctos linteo passus est; alios cum clam interemisset, citare nihilo minus ut vivos perseveravit, paucos post dies voluntaria morte perisse mentitus.[1] Consulibus oblitis

3 de natali suo edicere abrogavit magistratum fuitque per triduum sine summa potestate res p. Quaestorem suum in coniuratione nominatum flagellavit veste detracta subiectaque militum pedibus, quo firme verberaturi insisterent.

4 Simili superbia violentiaque ceteros tractavit ordines. Inquietatus fremitu gratuita in Circo loca de media nocte occupantium, omnis fustibus abegit; elisi

---

[1] ementitus, *Bentley.*

[a] Or perhaps, in short linen tunics.
[b] This remark shows the regard in which the empty title of "consul" was still held.

her in the lap of Minerva and commending to her the child's nurture and training. And no evidence convinced him so positively that she was sprung from his own loins as her savage temper, which was even then so violent that she would try to scratch the faces and eyes of the little children who played with her.

XXVI. It would be trivial and pointless to add to this an account of his treatment of his relatives and friends, Ptolemy, son of king Juba, his cousin (for he was the grandson of Mark Antony by Antony's daughter Selene), and in particular Macro himself and even Ennia, who helped him to the throne; all these were rewarded for their kinship and their faithful services by a bloody death.

He was no whit more respectful or mild towards the senate, allowing some who had held the highest offices to run in their togas for several miles beside his chariot and to wait on him at table, standing napkin in hand [a] either at the head of his couch, or at his feet. Others he secretly put to death, yet continued to send for them as if they were alive, after a few days falsely asserting that they had committed suicide. When the consuls forgot to make proclamation of his birthday, he deposed them, and left the state for three days without its highest magistrates.[b] He flogged his quaestor, who was charged with conspiracy, stripping off the man's clothes and spreading them under the soldiers' feet, to give them a firm footing as they beat him.

He treated the other orders with like insolence and cruelty. Being disturbed by the noise made by those who came in the middle of the night to secure the free seats in the Circus, he drove them all out

445

per eum tumultum viginti amplius equites R., totidem
matronae, super innumeram turbam ceteram. Scaenicis
ludis, inter plebem et equitem causam discordiarum
serens, decimas maturius dabat, ut equestria [1] ab
5 infimo quoque occuparentur. Gladiatorio munere re-
ductis interdum flagrantissimo sole velis emitti quemquam vetabat, remotoque ordinario apparatu tabidas
feras, vilissimos senioque confectos gladiatores, proque [2] paegniariis [3] patres familiarum notos in bonam
partem sed insignis debilitate aliqua corporis subicie-
bat. Ac nonnumquam horreis praeclusis populo
famem indixit.

XXVII. Saevitiam ingenii per haec maxime ostendit. Cum ad saginam ferarum muneri praeparatarum
carius pecudes compararentur, ex noxiis laniandos
adnotavit, et custodiarum seriem recognoscens, nullius
inspecto elogio, stans tantum modo intra porticum
2 mediam, "a calvo ad calvum" duci imperavit. Votum
exegit ab eo, qui pro salute sua gladiatoriam operam
promiserat, spectavitque ferro dimicantem nec dimisit
nisi victorem et post multas preces. Alterum, qui se
periturum ea de causa voverat, cunctantem pueris

[1] equestria, S_5 ; equestri, Ω.
[2] proque, *Bücheler* ; quoque, *mss.*
[3] paegniaris (-iis), *MGX* ; pegmares, ΠQ.

[a] The reason for the term *decimas*, if the reading be correct,
is uncertain ; cf. note on *Aug.* xli. 2. Obviously his purpose
was to lead the rabble to occupy the knights' seats before
the plays began, and thus to start a fight.

[b] The meaning of *paegniarii* is uncertain ; they may have
carried *arma lusoria* or arms incapable of causing death. See
Friedländer, *Roman Life and Manners*, Eng. trans. iv. p. 179.

[c] The *elogium* was the tablet on which the charge against
the prisoner was recorded.

with cudgels; in the confusion more than twenty Roman knights were crushed to death, with as many matrons and a countless number of others. At the plays in the theatre, sowing discord between the commons and the knights, he scattered the gift tickets *a* ahead of time, to induce the rabble to take the seats reserved for the equestrian order. At a gladiatorial show he would sometimes draw back the awnings when the sun was hottest and give orders that no one be allowed to leave; then removing the usual equipment, he would match worthless and decrepit gladiators against mangy wild beasts, and have sham fights *b* between householders who were of good repute, but conspicuous for some bodily infirmity. Sometimes too he would shut up the granaries and condemn the people to hunger.

XXVII. The following are special instances of his innate brutality. When cattle to feed the wild beasts which he had provided for a gladiatorial show were rather costly, he selected criminals to be devoured, and reviewing the line of prisoners without examining the charges,*c* but merely taking his place in the middle of a colonnade, he bade them be led away " from baldhead to baldhead." *d* A man who had made a vow to fight in the arena,*e* if the emperor recovered, he compelled to keep his word, watched him as he fought sword in hand, and would not let him go until he was victorious, and then only after many entreaties. Another who had offered his life for the same reason, but delayed to kill himself, he turned

d It seems probable that there happened to be a bald-headed man at each end of the line; the expression became proverbial.

e See chap. xiv. 2.

tradidit, verbenatum infulatumque votum repos-
centes per vicos agerent, quoad praecipitaretur ex
3 aggere.   Multos honesti ordinis deformatos prius
stigmatum notis ad metalla et munitiones viarum
aut ad bestias condemnavit aut bestiarum more
quadripedes cavea coercuit aut medios serra dissecuit,
nec omnes gravibus ex causis, verum male de munere
suo opinatos, vel quod numquam per genium suum
4 deierassent.   Parentes supplicio filiorum interesse
cogebat : quorum uni valitudinem excusanti lecticam
misit, alium a spectaculo poenae epulis statim adhibuit atque omni comitate ad hilaritatem et iocos
provocavit.   Curatorem munerum ac venationum per
continuos dies in conspectu suo catenis verberatum
non prius occidit quam offensus putrefacti cerebri
odore.   Atellanae poetam ob ambigui ioci versiculum
media amphitheatri harena igni cremavit.   Equitem
R. obiectum feris, cum se innocentem proclamasset,
reduxit abscisaque lingua rursus induxit.

XXVIII. Revocatum quendam a vetere exilio
sciscitatus, quidnam ibi facere consuesset, respondente eo per adulationem : " Deos semper oravi ut,
quod evenit, periret Tiberius et tu imperares,"
opinans sibi quoque exsules suos mortem imprecari,

" See *Aug.* lx.

over to his slaves, with orders to drive him through the streets decked with sacred boughs and fillets, calling for the fulfilment of his vow, and finally hurl him from the embankment. Many men of honourable rank were first disfigured with the marks of branding-irons and then condemned to the mines, to work at building roads, or to be thrown to the wild beasts; or else he shut them up in cages on all fours, like animals, or had them sawn asunder. Not all these punishments were for serious offences, but merely for criticising one of his shows, or for never having sworn by his Genius.[a] He forced parents to attend the executions of their sons, sending a litter for one man who pleaded ill health, and inviting another to dinner immediately after witnessing the death, and trying to rouse him to gaiety and jesting by a great show of affability. He had the manager of his gladiatorial shows and beast-baitings beaten with chains in his presence for several successive days, and would not kill him until he was disgusted at the stench of his putrefied brain. He burned a writer of Atellan farces alive in the middle of the arena of the amphitheatre, because of a humorous line of double meaning. When a Roman knight on being thrown to the wild beasts loudly protested his innocence, he took him out, cut off his tongue, and put him back again.

XXVIII. Having asked a man who had been recalled from an exile of long standing, how in the world he spent his time there, the man replied by way of flattery : "I constantly prayed the gods for what has come to pass, that Tiberius might die and you become emperor." Thereupon Caligula, thinking that his exiles were likewise praying for his death,

misit circum insulas, qui universos contrucidarent.
Cum discerpi senatorem concupisset, subornavit qui
ingredientem curiam repente hostem publicum appell-
antes invaderent, graphiisque confossum lacerandum
ceteris traderent; nec ante satiatus est quam membra
et artus et viscera hominis tracta per vicos atque
ante se congesta vidisset.

XXIX. Immanissima facta augebat atrocitate verborum. Nihil magis in natura sua laudare se ac
probare dicebat quam, ut ipsius verbo utar, ἀδιατρε-
ψίαν, hoc est inverecundiam. Monenti Antoniae aviae
tamquam parum esset non oboedire: "Memento,"
ait, "omnia mihi et in omnis licere." Trucidaturus
fratrem, quem metu venenorum praemuniri medica-
mentis suspicabatur: "Antidotum," inquit, "adversus
Caesarem?" Relegatis sororibus non solum insulas
2 habere se, sed etiam gladios minabatur. Praetorium
virum ex secessu Anticyrae, quam valitudinis causa
petierat, propagari sibi commeatum saepius desideran-
tem cum mandasset interimi, adiecit necessariam
esse sanguinis missionem, cui tam diu non prodesset
elleborum. Decimo quoque die numerum punien-
dorum ex custodia subscribens, rationem se purgare
dicebat. Gallis Graecisque aliquot uno tempore
condemnatis gloriabatur Gallograeciam se subegisse.

XXX. Non temere in quemquam nisi crebris et
minutis ictibus animadverti passus est, perpetuo

---

a "Immobility," a Stoic virtue. Since in Gaius this took
the form of callous indifference to suffering and to public
opinion, it became *inverecundia*.

sent emissaries from island to island to butcher them all. Wishing to have one of the senators torn to pieces, he induced some of the members to assail him suddenly, on his entrance into the House, with the charge of being a public enemy, to stab him with their styles, and turn him over to the rest to be mangled; and his cruelty was not sated until he saw the man's limbs, members, and bowels dragged through the streets and heaped up before him.

XXIX. He added to the enormity of his crimes by the brutality of his language. He used to say that there was nothing in his own character which he admired and approved more highly than what he called his ἀδιατρεψία,ᵃ that is to say, his shameless impudence. When his grandmother Antonia gave him some advice, he was not satisfied merely not to listen but replied: " Remember that I have the right to do anything to anybody." When he was on the point of killing his brother, and suspected that he had taken drugs as a precaution against poison, he cried: "What! an antidote against Caesar?" After banishing his sisters, he made the threat that he not only had islands, but swords as well. An ex-praetor who had retired to Anticyra for his health, sent frequent requests for an extension of his leave, but Caligula had him put to death, adding that a man who had not been helped by so long a course of hellebore needed to be bled. On signing the list of prisoners who were to be put to death later, he said that he was clearing his accounts. Having condemned several Gauls and Greeks to death in a body, he boasted that he had subdued Gallograecia.

XXX. He seldom had anyone put to death except by numerous slight wounds, his constant order, which

451

notoque iam praecepto : " Ita feri ut se mori sentiat."
Punito per errorem nominis alio quam quem destinaverat, ipsum quoque paria meruisse dixit.   Tragicum
illud subinde iactabat :

> " Oderint, dum metuant."

2 Saepe in cunctos pariter senatores ut Seiani clientis,
ut matris ac fratrum suorum delatores, invectus est
prolatis libellis, quos crematos simulaverat, defensa-
que Tiberi saevitia quasi necessaria, cum tot
criminantibus credendum esset.   Equestrem ordinem
ut scaenae harenaeque devotum assidue proscidit.
Infensus turbae faventi adversus studium suum
exclamavit : " Utinam p. R. unam cervicem haberet ! "
cumque Tetrinius latro postularetur, et qui
3 postularent, Tetrinios esse ait.   Retiarii tunicati
quinque numero gregatim dimicantes sine certamine
ullo totidem secutoribus succubuerant ; cum occidi
iuberentur, unus resumpta fuscina omnes victores
interemit ; hanc ut crudelissimam caedem et deflevit
edicto et eos, qui spectare sustinuissent, exsecratus
est.

XXXI. Queri etiam palam de condicione temporum
suorum solebat, quod nullis calamitatibus publicis
insignirentur ; Augusti principatum clade Variana,
Tiberi ruina spectaculorum apud Fidenas memora-

---

[a] Accius, *Trag.*, 203.

[b] See chap. xv. 4.

[c] For punishment, or to fight in the arena.

[d] See Index and Friedländer, *op. cit.* (p. 446, ftn. *b*) iv,
171 ff.

[e] See *Aug.* xxiii. 1.   [f] See *Tib.* xl.

soon became well-known, being: "Strike so that he may feel that he is dying." When a different man than he had intended had been killed, through a mistake in the names, he said that the victim too had deserved the same fate. He often uttered the familiar line of the tragic poet[a]:

"Let them hate me, so they but fear me."

He often inveighed against all the senators alike, as adherents of Sejanus and informers against his mother and brothers, producing the documents which he pretended to have burned,[b] and upholding the cruelty of Tiberius as forced upon him, since he could not but believe so many accusers. He constantly tongue-lashed the equestrian order as devotees of the stage and the arena. Angered at the rabble for applauding a faction which he opposed, he cried: "I wish the Roman people had but a single neck," and when the brigand Tetrinius was demanded,[c] he said that those who asked for him were Tetriniuses also. Once a band of five *retiarii*[d] in tunics, matched against the same number of *secutores*,[d] yielded without a struggle; but when their death was ordered, one of them caught up his trident and slew all the victors. Caligula bewailed this in a public proclamation as a most cruel murder, and expressed his horror of those who had had the heart to witness it.

XXXI. He even used openly to deplore the state of his times, because they had been marked by no public disasters, saying that the rule of Augustus had been made famous by the Varus massacre,[e] and that of Tiberius by the collapse of the amphitheatre at Fidenae,[f] while his own was threatened with

bilem factum, suo oblivionem imminere prosperitate rerum; atque identidem exercituum caedes, famem, pestilentiam, incendia, hiatum aliquem terrae optabat.

XXXII. Animum quoque remittenti ludoque et epulis dedito eadem factorum dictorumque saevitia aderat. Saepe in conspectu prandentis vel comis-antis seriae quaestiones per tormenta habebantur, miles decollandi artifex quibuscumque e custodia capita amputabat. Puteolis dedicatione pontis, quem excogitatum ab eo significavimus, cum multos e litore invitasset ad se, repente omnis praecipitavit, quosdam gubernacula apprehendentes contis remis-

2 que detrusit in mare. Romae publico epulo servum ob detractam lectis argenteam laminam carnifici confestim tradidit, ut manibus abscisis atque ante pectus e collo pendentibus, praecedente titulo qui causam poenae indicaret, per coetus epulantium circumduceretur. Murmillonem e ludo rudibus secum battuentem et sponte prostratum confodit ferrea sica ac more victorum cum palma discucurrit.

3 Admota altaribus victima succinctus poparum habitu elato alte malleo cultrarium mactavit. Lautiore convivio effusus subito in cachinnos consulibus, qui iuxta cubabant, quidnam rideret blande quaerentibus:

---

^a See chap. xix.   ^b See note on chap. xxx. 3.
^c The *popa* knocked down the victim with a mallet or with the back of an axe-head, and the *cultrarius* then cut the animal's throat.

454

oblivion because of its prosperity; and every now and then he wished for the destruction of his armies, for famine, pestilence, fires, or a great earthquake.

XXXII. His acts and words were equally cruel, even when he was indulging in relaxation and given up to amusement and feasting. While he was lunching or revelling capital examinations by torture were often made in his presence, and a soldier who was an adept at decapitation cut off the heads of those who were brought from prison. At Puteoli, at the dedication of the bridge that he contrived,[a] as has been said, after inviting a number to come to him from the shore, on a sudden he had them all thrown overboard; and when some caught hold of the rudders of the ships, he pushed them off into the sea with boathooks and oars. At a public banquet in Rome he immediately handed a slave over to the executioners for stealing a strip of silver from the couches, with orders that his hands be cut off and hung from his neck upon his breast, and that he then be led about among the guests, preceded by a placard giving the reason for his punishment. When a *murmillo* [b] from the gladiatorial school fought with him with wooden swords and fell on purpose, he stabbed him with a real dagger and then ran about with a palm-branch, as victors do. Once when he stood by the altar dressed as a *popa,*[c] and a victim was brought up, he raised his mallet on high and slew the *cultrarius.* At one of his more sumptuous banquets he suddenly burst into a fit of laughter, and when the consuls, who were reclining next him, politely inquired at what he was laughing, he replied: "What do you suppose,

"Quid," inquit, "nisi uno meo nutu iugulari utrumque
vestrum statim posse?"

XXXIII. Inter varios iocos, cum assistens simulacro
Iovis Apellen tragoedum consuluisset uter illi maior
videretur, cunctantem flagellis discidit conlaudans
subinde vocem deprecantis quasi etiam in gemitu
praedulcem. Quotiens uxoris vel amiculae collum
exoscularetur, addebat: "Tam bona cervix simul ac
iussero demetur." Quin et subinde iactabat exquisi-
turum se vel fidiculis de Caesonia sua, cur eam tanto
opere diligeret.

XXXIV. Nec minore livore ac malignitate quam
superbia saevitiaque paene adversus omnis aevi
hominum genus grassatus est. Statuas virorum
inlustrium ab Augusto ex Capitolina area propter
angustias in campum Martium conlatas ita subvertit
atque disiecit ut restitui salvis titulis non potuerint,
vetuitque posthac viventium cuiquam usquam statuam
aut imaginem nisi consulto et auctore se poni.
2 Cogitavit etiam de Homeri carminibus abolendis, cur
enim sibi non licere, dicens, quod Platoni licuisset,
qui eum e civitate quam constituebat eiecerit? Sed
et Vergili ac Titi Livi scripta et imagines paulum afuit
quin ex omnibus bibliothecis amoveret, quorum
alterum ut nullius ingenii minimaeque doctrinae,
alterum ut verbosum in historia neglegentemque
carpebat. De iuris quoque consultis, quasi scientiae

---

[a] Literally, "the cords," as an instrument of torture: cf.
Tib. lxii. 2. On the whole passage cf. *Calig.* xxv. 3 and l. 2.

except that at a single nod of mine both of you could have your throats cut on the spot?"

XXXIII. As a sample of his humour, he took his place beside a statue of Jupiter, and asked the tragic actor Apelles which of the two seemed to him the greater, and when he hesitated, Caligula had him flayed with whips, extolling his voice from time to time, when the wretch begged for mercy, as passing sweet even in his groans. Whenever he kissed the neck of his wife or sweetheart, he would say: "Off comes this beautiful head whenever I give the word." He even used to threaten now and then that he would resort to torture *a* if necessary, to find out from his dear Caesonia why he loved her so passionately.

XXXIV. He assailed mankind of almost every epoch with no less envy and malice than insolence and cruelty. He threw down the statues of famous men, which for lack of room Augustus had moved from the court of the Capitol to the Campus Martius, and so utterly demolished them that they could not be set up again with their inscriptions entire; and thereafter he forbade the erection of the statue of any living man anywhere, without his knowledge and consent. He even thought of destroying the poems of Homer, asking why he should not have the same privilege as Plato, who excluded Homer from his ideal commonwealth. More than that, he all but removed the writings and the busts of Vergil and of Titus Livius from all the libraries, railing at the former as a man of no talent and very little learning, and the latter as a verbose and careless historian. With regard to lawyers too, as if intending to do away with any practice of their profession,

457

eorum omnem usum aboliturus, saepe iactavit se mehercule effecturum ne quid respondere possint praeter eum.

XXXV. Vetera familiarum insignia nobilissimo cuique ademit, Torquato torquem, Cincinnato crinem, Cn. Pompeio stirpis antiquae Magni cognomen. Ptolemaeum, de quo rettuli, et arcessitum e regno et exceptum honorifice, non alia de causa repente percussit, quam quod edente se munus ingressum spectacula convertisse hominum oculos fulgore
2 purpureae abollae animadvertit.   Pulchros et comatos quotiens sibi occurrerent, occipitio raso deturpabat. Erat Aesius[1] Proculus patre primipilari, ob egregiam corporis amplitudinem et speciem Colosseros dictus; hunc spectaculis detractum repente et in harenam deductum Thraeci et mox hoplomacho[2] comparavit bisque victorem constringi sine mora iussit et pannis obsitum vicatim circumduci ac mulieribus ostendi,
3 deinde iugulari.   Nullus denique tam abiectae condicionis tamque extremae sortis fuit, cuius non commodis obtrectaret. Nemorensi[3] regi, quod multos iam annos poteretur sacerdotio, validiorem adversarium subornavit. Cum quodam die muneris essedario Porio post prosperam pugnam servum suum manumittenti

---

[1] Aesius, *Ihm*; Esius, Ω.
[2] hoplomacho, *Sabellicus*; aplomacho, Ω.
[3] Nemorensi, G^3 ⌐; nemoressi, Ω.

---

[a] See chap. xxvi. 1.
[b] He himself was bald; see chap. l. 1.
[c] The "Giant Cupid" from κολοσσός and ἔρως.
[d] The priest of Diana at Nemi, who must be a fugitive slave and obtain his office by slaying his predecessor.
[e] A gladiator who fought from a British chariot; see note on chap. xxx. 3.

he often threatened that he would see to it, by Heaven, that they could give no advice contrary to his wish.

XXXV. He took from all the noblest of the city the ancient devices of their families, from Torquatus his collar, from Cincinnatus his lock of hair, from Gnaeus Pompeius the surname Great belonging to his ancient race. After inviting Ptolemy, whom I have mentioned before,[a] to come from his kingdom and receiving him with honour, he suddenly had him executed for no other reason than that when giving a gladiatorial show, he noticed that Ptolemy on entering the theatre attracted general attention by the splendour of his purple cloak. Whenever he ran across handsome men with fine heads of hair,[b] he disfigured them by having the backs of their heads shaved. There was a certain Aesius Proculus, son of a chief centurion, called Colosseros[c] because of his remarkable size and handsome appearance ; this man Caligula ordered to be suddenly dragged from his seat in the amphitheatre and led into the arena, where he matched him first against a Thracian and then against a heavy-armed gladiator ; when Proculus was victor in both contests, Caligula gave orders that he be bound at once, clad in rags, and then put to death, after first being led about the streets and exhibited to the women. In short, there was no one of such low condition or such abject fortune that he did not envy him such advantages as he possessed. Since the king of Nemi[d] had now held his priesthood for many years, he hired a stronger adversary to attack him. When an *essedarius*[e] called Porius was vigorously applauded on the day of one of the games for setting his slave free after a victory, Caligula

studiosius plausum esset, ita proripuit[1] se spectaculis, ut calcata lacinia togae praeceps per gradus iret, indignabundus et clamitans dominum gentium populum ex re levissima plus honoris gladiatori tribuentem quam consecratis principibus aut praesenti sibi.

XXXVI. Pudicitiae neque suae[2] neque alienae pepercit. M. Lepidum, Mnesterem pantomimum, quosdam obsides dilexisse fertur commercio mutui stupri. Valerius Catullus, consulari familia iuvenis, stupratum a se ac latera sibi contubernio eius defessa etiam vociferatus est. Super sororum incesta et notissimum prostitutae Pyrallidis amorem non temere
2 ulla inlustriore femina abstinuit. Quas plerumque cum maritis ad cenam vocatas praeterque pedes suos transeuntis diligenter ac lente mercantium more considerabat, etiam faciem manu adlevans, si quae pudore submitterent; quotiens deinde libuisset egressus triclinio, cum maxime placitam sevocasset, paulo post recentibus adhuc lasciviae notis reversus vel laudabat palam vel vituperabat, singula enumerans bona malave corporis atque concubitus. Quibusdam absentium maritorum nomine repudium ipse misit iussitque in acta ita referri.

XXXVII. Nepotatus sumptibus omnium prodigorum ingenia superavit, commentus novum balnearum usum, portentosissima genera ciborum atque

[1] proripuit se, *Roth;* proripuit, *ML*[1]*P*; proripuit e, *GR*; se proripuit, *L*[3]*ST*; se proripuit e, ΠQ.
[2] neque suae, *added in* *N*ς; *omitted by the other mss.*

rushed from the amphitheatre in such haste that he trod on the fringe of his toga and went headlong down the steps, fuming and shouting: "The people that rule the world give more honour to a gladiator for a trifling act than to their deified emperors or to the one still present with them."

XXXVI. He respected neither his own chastity nor that of anyone else. He is said to have had unnatural relations with Marcus Lepidus, the pantomimic actor Mnester, and certain hostages. Valerius Catullus, a young man of a consular family, publicly proclaimed that he had violated the emperor and worn himself out in commerce with him. To say nothing of his incest with his sisters and his notorious passion for the concubine Pyrallis, there was scarcely any woman of rank whom he did not approach. These as a rule he invited to dinner with their husbands, and as they passed by the foot of his couch, he would inspect them critically and deliberately, as if buying slaves, even putting out his hand and lifting up the face of anyone who looked down in modesty; then as often as the fancy took him he would leave the room, sending for the one who pleased him best, and returning soon afterward with evident signs of what had occurred, he would openly commend or criticise his partner, recounting her charms or defects and commenting on her conduct. To some he personally sent a bill of divorce in the name of their absent husbands, and had it entered in the public records.

XXXVII. In reckless extravagance he outdid the prodigals of all times in ingenuity, inventing a new sort of baths and unnatural varieties of food

cenarum, ut calidis frigidisque unguentis lavaretur,
pretiosissima margarita aceto liquefacta sorberet, convivis ex auro panes et obsonia apponeret, aut frugi
hominem esse oportere dictitans aut Caesarem.
Quin et nummos non mediocris summae e fastigio
basilicae Iuliae per aliquot dies sparsit in plebem.

2 Fabricavit et deceris Liburnicas gemmatis puppibus,
versicoloribus velis, magna thermarum et porticuum
et tricliniorum laxitate magnaque etiam vitium
et pomiferarum arborum varietate; quibus discumbens
de die inter choros ac symphonias[1] litora Campaniae
peragraret. In extructionibus praetoriorum atque
villarum omni ratione posthabita nihil tam efficere

3 concupiscebat quam quod posse effici negaretur. Et
iactae itaque moles infesto ac profundo mari et excisae
rupes durissimi silicis et campi montibus aggere
aequati et complanata fossuris montium iuga, incredibili quidem celeritate, cum morae culpa capite
lueretur. Ac ne singula enumerem, immensas opes
totumque illud Ti.[2] Caesaris vicies ac septies milies
sestertium non toto vertente anno absumpsit.

XXXVIII. Exhaustus igitur atque egens ad rapinas
convertit animum vario et exquisitissimo calumniarum
et auctionum et vectigalium genere. Negabat iure
civitatem Romanam usurpare eos, quorum maiores
sibi posterisque eam impetrassent, nisi si filii essent,
neque enim intellegi debere "posteros" ultra hunc

---

[1] symphonias, *GSNς*; *the other mss have* symphro *or*
simphro.
[2] Ti., *Roth*; T., Ω.

---

[a] The Liburnian galleys, so-called from a people of Illyricum, were famous for their speed. They commonly had
but one or two banks of oars.

and feasts; for he would bathe in hot or cold perfumed oils, drink pearls of great price dissolved in vinegar, and set before his guests loaves and meats of gold, declaring that a man ought either to be frugal or Caesar. He even scattered large sums of money among the commons from the roof of the basilica Julia for several days in succession. He also built Liburnian galleys *a* with ten banks of oars, with sterns set with gems, particoloured sails, huge spacious baths, colonnades, and banquet-halls, and even a great variety of vines and fruit trees; that on board of them he might recline at table from an early hour, and coast along the shores of Campania amid songs and choruses. He built villas and country houses with utter disregard of expense, caring for nothing so much as to do what men said was impossible. So he built moles out into the deep and stormy sea, tunnelled rocks of hardest flint, built up plains to the height of mountains and razed mountains to the level of the plain; all with incredible dispatch, since the penalty for delay was death. To make a long story short, vast sums of money, including the 2,700,000,000 sesterces which Tiberius Caesar had amassed, were squandered by him in less than the revolution of a year.

XXXVIII. Having thus impoverished himself, from very need he turned his attention to pillage through a complicated and cunningly devised system of false accusations, auction sales, and imposts. He ruled that Roman citizenship could not lawfully be enjoyed by those whose forefathers had obtained it for themselves and their descendants, except in the case of sons, since "descendants"

gradum; prolataque Divorum Iuli et Augusti diplo-
2 mata ut vetera et obsoleta deflabat.[1]   Arguebat et
perperam editos census, quibus postea quacumque de
causa quicquam incrementi accessisset.   Testamenta
primipilarium, qui ab initio Tiberi principatus neque
illum neque se heredem reliquissent, ut ingrata
rescidit; item ceterorum ut irrita et vana quoscumque
quis diceret herede Caesare mori destinasse.   Quo
metu iniecto cum iam et ab ignotis inter familiares et
a parentibus inter liberos palam heres nuncuparetur,
derisores vocabat, quod post nuncupationem vivere
perseverarent, et multis venenatas matteas misit.
3 Cognoscebat autem de talibus causis, taxato prius modo
summae ad quem conficiendum consideret, confecto
demum excitabatur.   Ac ne paululum quidem morae
patiens super quadraginta reos quondam ex diversis
criminibus una sententia condemnavit gloriatus-
que est expergefacta e somno Caesonia quantum
egisset, dum ea meridiaret.
4   Auctione proposita reliquias omnium spectaculorum
subiecit ac vendidit, exquirens per se pretia et usque
eo extendens, ut quidam immenso coacti quaedam
emere ac bonis exuti venas sibi inciderent.   Nota res

---

[1] deflabat, *Lipsius*; deflabat, *corrected to* deflaebat (= de-·
flebat), *M*; deflebat, *X*Υ; delebat, G.

---

[a] That is, if anyone chanced to have received an addition
to his income since the last census, he charged him with
having made a false report to the censors, and of course confiscated his estate.

ought not to be understood as going beyond that degree ; and when certificates of the deified Julius and Augustus were presented to him, he waved them aside as old and out of date. He also charged that those estates had been falsely returned, to which any addition had later been made from any cause whatever.ª If any chief centurions since the beginning of Tiberius' reign had not named that emperor or himself among their heirs, he set aside their wills on the ground of ingratitude ; also the testaments of all others, as null and void, if anyone said that they had intended to make Caesar their heir when they died. When he had roused such fear in this way that he came to be named openly as heir by strangers among their intimates and by parents among their children, he accused them of making game of him by continuing to live after such a declaration, and to many of them he sent poisoned dainties. He used further to conduct the trial of such cases in person, naming in advance the sum which he proposed to raise at each sitting, and not rising until it was made up. Impatient of the slightest delay, he once condemned in a single sentence more than forty who were accused on different counts, boasting to Caesonia, when she woke after a nap, of the great amount of business he had done while she was taking her siesta.

Appointing an auction, he put up and sold what was left from all the shows, personally soliciting bids and running them up so high, that some who were forced to buy articles at an enormous price and were thus stripped of their possessions, opened their veins. A well-known

est, Aponio Saturnino inter subsellia dormitante
monitum a Gaio praeconem ne praetorium virum
crebro capitis motu nutantem síbi praeteriret, nec
licendi finem factum, quoad tredecim gladiatores
sestertium nonagies ignoranti addicerentur.

XXXIX. In Gallia quoque, cum damnatarum
sororum ornamenta et supellectilem et servos atque
etiam libertos immensis pretiis vendidisset, invitatus
lucro, quidquid instrumenti veteris aulae erat ab urbe
repetiit comprensis ad deportandum meritoriis quoque
vehiculis et pistrinensibus iumentis, adeo ut et panis
Romae saepe deficeret et litigatorum plerique, quod
occurrere absentes ad vadimonium non possent, causa
2 caderent.   Cui instrumento distrahendo nihil non
fraudis ac lenocinii adhibuit, modo avaritiae singulos
increpans et quod non puderet eos locupletiores esse
quam se, modo paenitentiam simulans quod princi-
palium rerum privatis copiam faceret.   Compererat
provincialem locupletem ducenta sestertia numerasse
vocatoribus, ut per fallaciam convivio interponeretur,
nec tulerat moleste tam magno aestimari honorem
cenae suae ; huic postero die sedenti in auctione misit,
qui nescio quid frivoli ducentis milibus traderet diceret-
que cenaturum apud Caesarem vocatu ipsius.

XL. Vectigalia nova atque inaudita primum per

---

a The part occupied by Augustus and Tiberius, to which
Caligula had made some additions.

466

incident is that of Aponius Saturninus; he fell
asleep on one of the benches, and as the auc-
tioneer was warned by Gaius not to overlook the
praetorian gentleman who kept nodding to him,
the bidding was not stopped until thirteen gladiators were knocked down to the unconscious sleeper
at nine million sesterces.

XXXIX. When he was in Gaul and had sold
at immense figures the jewels, furniture, slaves,
and even the freedmen of his sisters who had
been condemned to death, finding the business
so profitable, he sent to the city for all the paraphernalia of the old palace,[a] seizing for its trans-
portation even public carriages and animals from
the bakeries; with the result that bread was often
scarce at Rome and many who had cases in court
lost them from inability to appear and meet their
bail. To get rid of this furniture, he resorted to
every kind of trickery and wheedling, now railing at the bidders for avarice and because they
were not ashamed to be richer than he, and
now feigning regret for allowing common men
to acquire the property of princes. Having learned
that a rich provincial had paid those who issued the
emperor's invitations two hundred thousand sesterces,
to be smuggled in among the guests at one of his
dinner-parties, he was not in the least displeased
that the honour of dining with him was rated
so high; but when next day the man appeared
at his auction, he sent a messenger to hand him
some trifle or other at the price of two hundred
thousand sesterces and say that he should dine
with Caesar on his personal invitation.

XL. He levied new and unheard of taxes, at

publicanos, deinde, quia lucrum exuberabat, per
centuriones tribunosque praetorianos exercuit, nullo
rerum aut hominum genere omisso, cui non tributi
aliquid imponeret. Pro edulibus, quae tota urbe
venirent, certum statumque exigebatur ; pro litibus
ac iudiciis ubicumque conceptis quadragesima summae,
de qua litigaretur, nec sine poena, si quis composuisse
vel doñasse negotium convinceretur ; ex gerulorum
diurnis quaestibus pars octava ; ex capturis prostitu-
tarum quantum quaeque uno concubitu mereret ;
additumque ad caput legis, ut tenerentur publico et
quae meretricium quive lenocinium fecissent, nec non
et matrimonia obnoxia essent.

XLI. Eius modi vectigalibus indictis neque propo-
sitis, cum per ignorantiam scripturae multa commissa
fierent, tandem flagitante populo proposuit quidem
legem, sed et minutissimis litteris et angustissimo
loco, uti ne cui describere liceret. Ac ne quod non
manubiarum genus experiretur, lupanar in Palatio
constituit, districtisque et instructis pro loci dignitate
compluribus cellis, in quibus matronae ingenuique
starent, misit circum fora et basilicas nomenculatores
ad invitandos ad libidinem iuvenes senesque ; praebita
advenientibus pecunia faenebris appositique qui
nomina palam subnotarent, quasi adiuvantium
2 Caesaris reditus. Ac ne ex lusu quidem aleae
compendium spernens plus mendacio atque etiam

---

first through the publicans and then, because their
profit was so great, through the centurions and
tribunes of the praetorian guard ; and there was
no class of commodities or men on which he did
not impose some form of tariff. On all eatables
sold in any part of the city he levied a fixed and
definite charge ; on lawsuits and legal processes
begun anywhere, a fortieth part of the sum
involved, providing a penalty in case anyone was
found guilty of compromising or abandoning a
suit : on the daily wages of porters, an eighth ;
on the earnings of prostitutes, as much as each
received for one embrace ; and a clause was added
to this chapter of the law, providing that those who
had ever been prostitutes or acted as panders should
be liable to this public tax, and that even matri-
mony should not be exempt.

XLI. When taxes of this kind had been proclaimed,
but not published in writing, inasmuch as many
offences were committed through ignorance of the
letter of the law, he at last, on the urgent demand of
the people, had the law posted up, but in a very
narrow place and in excessively small letters, to
prevent the making of a copy. To leave no kind of
plunder untried, he opened a brothel in his palace,
setting apart a number of rooms and furnishing them
to suit the grandeur of the place, where matrons
and freeborn youths should stand exposed. Then
he sent his pages [a] about the fora and basilicas,
to invite young men and old to enjoy themselves,
lending money on interest to those who came and
having clerks openly take down their names, as
contributors to Caesar's revenues. He did not
even disdain to make money from play, and to

periurio lucrabatur. Et quondam proximo conlusori demandata vice sua progressus in atrium domus, cum praetereuntis duos equites R. locupletis sine mora corripi confiscarique iussisset, exultans rediit gloriansque numquam se prosperiore alea usum.

XLII. Filia vero nata paupertatem nec iam imperatoria modo sed et patria conquerens onera conlationes in alimonium ac dotem puellae recepit. Edixit et strenas ineunte anno se recepturum stetitque in vestibulo aedium Kal. Ian. ad captandas stipes, quas plenis ante eum manibus ac sinu omnis generis turba fundebat. Novissime contrectandae pecuniae cupidine incensus, saepe super immensos aureorum acervos patentissimo diffusos loco et nudis pedibus spatiatus et toto corpore aliquamdiu volutatus est.

XLIII. Militiam resque bellicas semel attigit neque ex destinato, sed cum ad visendum nemus flumenque Clitumni Mevaniam processisset, admonitus de supplendo numero Batavorum, quos circa se habebat, expeditionis Germanicae impetum cepit ; neque distulit, sed legionibus et auxiliis undique excitis, dilectibus ubique acerbissime actis, contracto et omnis generis commeatu quanto numquam antea,[1] iter ingressus est confecitque modo tam festinanter et rapide, ut praetorianae cohortes contra morem

[1] antea iter, *Gronovius* : ante alter, Ω. Ante iter *R. Steph.* (" duo probatissimi libri " *Tom*).

---

* See *Aug.* lvii. 1.
ᵇ *Sinus* means the bosom of the toga, which was often used as a pocket.
ᶜ Celebrated for its beautiful scenery, described by Pliny, *Epist.* 8. 8.

increase his gains by falsehood and even by perjury. Having on one occasion given up his place to the player next him and gone into the courtyard, he spied two wealthy Roman knights passing by; he ordered them to be seized at once and their property confiscated and came back exultant, boasting that he had never played in better luck.

XLII. But when his daughter was born, complaining of his narrow means, and no longer merely of the burdens of a ruler but of those of a father as well, he took up contributions for the girl's maintenance and dowry. He also made proclamation that he would receive New Year's gifts,[a] and on the Kalends of January took his place in the entrance to the Palace, to clutch the coins which a throng of people of all classes showered on him by handfuls and lapfuls.[b] Finally, seized with a mania for feeling the touch of money, he would often pour out huge piles of goldpieces in some open place, walk over them barefooted, and wallow in them for a long time with his whole body.

XLIII. He had but one experience with military affairs or war, and then on a sudden impulse; for having gone to Mevania to visit the river Clitumnus[c] and its grove, he was reminded of the necessity of recruiting his body-guard of Batavians and was seized with the idea of an expedition to Germany. So without delay he assembled legions and auxiliaries from all quarters, holding levies everywhere with the utmost strictness, and collecting provisions of every kind on an unheard of scale. Then he began his march and made it now so hurriedly and rapidly, that the praetorian cohorts were forced, contrary to all precedent, to lay their

signa iumentis imponere et ita subsequi cogerentur, interdum adeo segniter delicateque, ut octaphoro veheretur atque a propinquarum urbium plebe verri sibi vias et conspergi propter pulverem exigeret.

XLIV. Postquam castra attigit, ut se acrem ac severum ducem ostenderet, legatos, qui auxilia serius ex diversis locis adduxerant, cum ignominia dimisit; at in exercitu recensendo plerisque centurionum maturis iam et nonnullis ante paucissimos quam consummaturi essent dies, primos pilos ademit, causatus senium cuiusque et imbecillitatem; ceterorum increpita cupiditate commoda emeritae militiae ad senum[1] milium summam recidit. Nihil autem amplius quam Adminio Cynobellini Britannorum regis filio, qui pulsus a patre cum exigua manu transfugerat, in deditionem recepto, quasi universa tradita insula, magnificas Romam litteras misit, monitis speculatoribus, ut vehiculo ad Forum usque et curiam pertenderent nec nisi in aede Martis ac frequente senatu consulibus traderent.

XLV. Mox deficiente belli materia paucos de custodia Germanos traici occulique trans Rhenum iussit ac sibi post prandium quam tumultuosissime adesse hostem nuntiari. Quo facto proripuit se cum

---

[1] senum, *Lipsius*; sescentorum, Ω.

---

[a] Half the amount established by Augustus; see Dio, 55. 23.
[b] Ordinarily such vehicles were allowed to pass through the city streets only before sunrise or during the last two hours of the day. See Friedländer, *Roman Life and Manners*, Eng. trans. iv. p. 28.
[c] See *Aug.* xxix. 2.

standards on the pack-animals and thus to follow him; again he was so lazy and luxurious that he was carried in a litter by eight bearers, requiring the inhabitants of the towns through which he passed to sweep the roads for him and sprinkle them to lay the dust.

XLIV. On reaching his camp, to show his vigilance and strictness as a commander, he dismissed in disgrace the generals who were late in bringing in the auxiliaries from various places, and in reviewing his troops he deprived many of the chief centurions who were well on in years of their rank, in some cases only a few days before they would have served their time, giving as a reason their age and infirmity; then railing at the rest for their avarice, he reduced the rewards given on completion of full military service to six thousand sesterces.[a]

All that he accomplished was to receive the surrender of Adminius, son of Cynobellinus king of the Britons, who had been banished by his father and had deserted to the Romans with a small force; yet as if the entire island had submitted to him, he sent a grandiloquent letter to Rome, commanding the couriers who carried it to ride in their post-chaise [b] all the way to the Forum and the House, and not to deliver it to anyone except the consuls, in the temple of Mars the Avenger,[c] before a full meeting of the senate.

XLV. Presently, finding no one to fight with, he had a few Germans of his body-guard taken across the river and concealed there, and word brought him after luncheon with great bustle and confusion that the enemy were close at hand. Upon

amicis et parte equitum praetorianorum in proximam
silvam, truncatisque arboribus et in modum tropae-
orum adornatis ad lumina reversus, eorum quidem qui
secuti non essent timiditatem et ignaviam corripuit,
comites autem et participes victoriae novo genere ac
nomine coronarum donavit, quas distinctas solis ac
lunae siderumque specie exploratorias appellavit.

2 Rursus obsides quosdam abductos e litterario ludo
clamque praemissos, deserto repente convivio, cum
equitatu insecutus veluti profugos ac reprehensos in
catenis reduxit ; in hoc quoque mimo praeter modum
intemperans. Repetita cena renuntiantis coactum
agmen sic ut erant loricatos ad discumbendum
adhortatus est. Monuit etiam notissimo Vergili
versu "durarent secundisque se rebus servarent."

3 Atque inter haec absentem senatum populumque
gravissimo obiurgavit edicto, quod Caesare proeli-
ante et tantis discriminibus obiecto tempestiva
convivia, circum et theatra et amoenos secessus
celebrarent.

XLVI. Postremo quasi perpetraturus bellum, de-
recta acie in litore Oceani ac ballistis machinisque
dispositis, nemine gnaro aut opinante quidnam
coepturus esset, repente ut conchas legerent galeas-
que et sinus replerent imperavit, "spolia Oceani"
vocans "Capitolio Palatioque debita," et in indicium

---

^a From *exploratores*, scouts or rangers.

^b *Aen.* 1. 207.

^c One of the various kinds of "torsion-engines" (*tormenta*)
used by the Romans. The *ballista* cast stones, the *catapulta*
large arrows or darts.

this he rushed out with his friends and a part of the praetorian cavalry to the woods close by, and after cutting the branches from some trees and adorning them like trophies, he returned by torchlight, taunting those who had not followed him as timorous and cowardly, and presenting his companions and the partners in his victory with crowns of a new kind and of a new name, ornamented with figures of the sun, moon and stars, and called *exploratoriae.*[a] Another time some hostages were taken from a common school and secretly sent on ahead of him, when he suddenly left a banquet and pursued them with the cavalry as if they were runaways, caught them, and brought them back in fetters, in this farce too showing immoderate extravagance. On coming back to the table, when some announced that the army was assembled, he urged them to take their places just as they were, in their coats of mail. He also admonished them in the familiar line of Vergil to "bear up and save themselves for better days."[b]

Meanwhile he rebuked the absent senate and people in a stern edict because "while Caesar was fighting and exposed to such dangers they were indulging in revels and frequenting the theatres and their pleasant villas."

XLVI. Finally, as if he intended to bring the war to an end, he drew up a line of battle on the shore of the Ocean, arranging his ballistas[c] and other artillery; and when no one knew or could imagine what he was going to do, he suddenly bade them gather shells and fill their helmets and the folds of their gowns, calling them "spoils from the Ocean, due to the Capitol and Palatine." As a monument

475

victoriae altissimam turrem excitavit, ex qua ut Pharo noctibus ad regendos navium cursus ignes emicarent ; pronuntiatoque militi donativo centenis viritim denariis, quasi omne exemplum liberalitatis supergressus : "Abite," inquit, "laeti, abite locupletes."

XLVII. Conversus hinc ad curam triumphi praeter captivos ac transfugas barbaros Galliarum quoque procerissimum quemque et, ut ipse dicebat, ἀξιοθριάμβευτον, ac nonnullos ex principibus legit ac seposuit ad pompam coegitque non tantum rutilare et summittere comam, sed et sermonem Germanicum addiscere et nomina barbarica ferre.   Praecepit etiam triremis, quibus introierat Oceanum, magna ex parte itinere terrestri Romam devehi.   Scripsit et procuratoribus, triumphum apparrarent quam minima summa, sed quantus numquam alius fuisset, quando in omnium hominum bona ius haberent.

XLVIII.   Prius quam provincia decederet, consilium iniit nefandae atrocitatis legiones, quae post excessum Augusti seditionem olim moverant, contrucidandi, quod et patrem suum Germanicum ducem et se infantem tunc obsedissent, vixque a tam praecipiti cogitatione revocatus, inhiberi nullo modo potuit quin decimare velle perseveraret.   Vocatas itaque ad contionem inermes, atque etiam gladiis depositis, equitatu 2 armato circumdedit.   Sed cum videret suspecta re plerosque dilabi ad resumenda si qua vis fieret arma,

---

^a The lighthouse at Alexandria.
^b To the privy-purse, of course.
^c See chap. ix.
^d See *Aug.* xxiv. 2.

of his victory he erected a lofty tower, from which lights were to shine at night to guide the course of ships, as from the Pharos.[a] Then promising the soldiers a gratuity of a hundred denarii each, as if he had shown unprecedented liberality, he said, " Go your way happy ; go your way rich."

XLVII. Then turning his attention to his triumph, in addition to a few captives and deserters from the barbarians he chose all the tallest of the Gauls, and as he expressed it, those who were "worthy of a triumph," as well as some of the chiefs. These he reserved for his parade, compelling them not only to dye their hair red and to let it grow long, but also to learn the language of the Germans and assume barbarian names. He also had the triremes in which he had entered the Ocean carried overland to Rome for the greater part of the way. He wrote besides to his financial agents to prepare for a triumph at the smallest possible cost,[b] but on a grander scale than had ever before been known, since the goods of all were at their disposal.

XLVIII. Before leaving the province he formed a design of unspeakable cruelty, that of butchering the legions that had begun the mutiny years before just after the death of Augustus,[c] because they had beleagured his father Germanicus, their leader, and himself, at the time an infant ; and though he was with difficulty turned from this mad purpose, he could by no means be prevented from persisting in his desire to decimate [d] them. Accordingly he summoned them to an assembly without their arms, not even wearing their swords, and surrounded them with armed horsemen. But seeing that some of the legionaries, suspecting his purpose, were stealing off

profugit contionem confestimque urbem [1] petit, deflexa omni acerbitate in senatum, cui ad avertendos [2] tantorum dedecorum rumores palam minabatur, querens inter cetera fraudatum se iusto triumpho, cum ipse paulo ante, ne quid de honoribus suis ageretur, etiam sub mortis poena denuntiasset.

XLIX. Aditus ergo in itinere a legatis amplissimi ordinis ut maturaret orantibus, quam maxima voce : " Veniam," inquit, " veniam, et hic mecum," capulum gladii crebro verberans, quo cinctus erat. Edixit et reverti se, sed iis tantum qui optarent, equestri ordini et populo ; nam se neque civem neque 2 principem senatui amplius fore. Vetuit etiam quemquam senatorum sibi occurrere. Atque omisso vel dilato triumpho ovans urbem natali suo ingressus est ; intraque quartum mensem periit, ingentia facinora ausus et aliquanto maiora moliens, siquidem proposuerat Antium, deinde Alexandream commigrare interempto prius utriusque ordinis electissimo quoque. 3 Quod ne cui dubium videatur, in secretis eius reperti sunt duo libelli diverso titulo, alteri " Gladius," alteri " Pugio " index erat ; ambo nomina et notas continebant morti destinatorum. Inventa et arca ingens variorum venenorum plena, quibus mox a

---

[1] urbem, Υ ; urbem omnem, *MGS* ; omnem urbem, *X*.
[2] ad avertendos, *TL*³; animadvertendos, Υ ; *the other mss. have* advertendos.

---

to resume their arms, in case any violence should be offered them, he fled from the assembly and set out for the city in a hurry, turning all his ferocity upon the senate, against which he uttered open threats, in order to divert the gossip about his own dishonour. He complained among other things that he had been cheated of his fairly earned triumph; whereas a short time before he had himself given orders that on pain of death no action should be taken about his honours.

XLIX. Therefore when he was met on the road by envoys from that distinguished body, begging him to hasten his return, he roared, "I will come, and this will be with me," frequently smiting the hilt of the sword which he wore at his side. He also made proclamation that he was returning, but only to those who desired his presence, the equestrian order and the people, for to the senate he would never more be fellow-citizen nor prince. He even forbade anyone of the senators to meet him. Then giving up or postponing his triumph, he entered the city on his birthday in an ovation;[a] and within four months he perished, having dared great crimes and meditating still greater ones. For he had made up his mind to move to Antium, and later to Alexandria, after first slaying the noblest members of the two orders. That no one may doubt this, let me say that among his private papers two notebooks were found with different titles, one called "The Sword" and the other "The Dagger," and both containing the names and marks of identification of those whom he had doomed to death. There was found besides a great chest full of divers kinds of poisons, which they say were later thrown into the sea

Claudio demersis infecta maria traduntur non sine piscium exitio, quos enectos aestus in proxima litora eiecit.

L. Statura fuit eminenti, colore expallido, corpore enormi, gracilitate maxima cervicis et crurum, oculis et temporibus concavis, fronte lata et torva, capillo raro at circa verticem nullo, hirsutus cetera. Quare transeunte eo prospicere ex superiore parte aut omnino quacumque de causa capram nominare, criminosum et exitiale habebatur. Vultum vero natura horridum ac taetrum etiam ex industria efferabat componens ad speculum in omnem terrorem ac formidinem.

2 Valitudo ei neque corporis neque animi constitit. Puer comitiali morbo vexatus, in adulescentia ita patiens laborum erat, ut tamen nonnumquam subita defectione ingredi, stare, colligere semet ac sufferre vix posset. Mentis valitudinem et ipse senserat ac subinde de secessu deque purgando cerebro cogitavit. Creditur potionatus a Caesonia uxore amatorio quidem medicamento, sed quod in furorem verterit. Incita-
3 batur insomnio maxime ; neque enim plus quam tribus nocturnis horis quiescebat ac ne iis quidem placida quiete, sed pavida miris rerum imaginibus, ut qui inter ceteras pelagi quondam speciem conloquentem secum videre visus sit. Ideoque magna parte noctis vigiliae cubandique taedio nunc toro residens,

---

by Claudius and so infected it as to kill the fish, which were thrown up by the tide upon the neighbouring shores.

L. He was very tall and extremely pale, with an unshapely body, but very thin neck and legs.[a] His eyes and temples were hollow, his forehead broad and grim, his hair thin and entirely gone on the top of his head, though his body was hairy. Because of this to look upon him from a higher place as he passed by, or for any reason whatever to mention a goat, was treated as a capital offence. While his face was naturally forbidding and ugly, he purposely made it even more savage, practising all kinds of terrible and fearsome expressions before a mirror.

He was sound neither of body nor mind. As a boy he was troubled with the falling sickness,[b] and while in his youth he had some endurance, yet at times because of sudden faintness he was hardly able to walk, to stand up, to collect his thoughts, or to hold up his head. He himself realised his mental infirmity, and thought at times of going into retirement and clearing his brain. It is thought that his wife Caesonia gave him a drug intended for a love potion, which however had the effect of driving him mad. He was especially tormented with sleeplessness ; for he never rested more than three hours at night, and even for that length of time he did not sleep quietly, but was terrified by strange apparitions, once for example dreaming that the spirit of the Ocean talked with him. Therefore weary of lying in bed wide awake during the greater part of the night, he would now sit upon his couch, and now wander through the long colonnades, crying

nunc per longissimas porticus vagus invocare
identidem atque expectare lucem consuerat.

LI. Non inmerito mentis valitudini attribuerim
diversissima in eodem vitia, summam confidentiam et
contra nimium metum. Nam qui deos tanto opere
contemneret, ad minima tonitrua et fulgura conivere,
caput obvolvere, at vero maiore[1] proripere se e strato
sub lectumque condere solebat. Peregrinatione
quidem Siciliensi irrisis multum locorum miraculis
repente a Messana noctu profugit Aetnaei verticis
2 fumo ac murmure pavefactus. Adversus barbaros
quoque minacissimus, cum trans Rhenum inter
angustias densumque agmen iter essedo faceret,
dicente quodam non mediocrem fore consternationem
sicunde hostis appareat, equum ilico conscendit ac
propere reversus [2]ad pontes, ut eos calonibus et
impedimentis stipatos repperit, impatiens morae per
3 manus ac super capita hominum translatus est. Mox
etiam audita rebellione Germaniae fugam et subsidia
fugae classes apparabat, uno solacio adquiescens
transmarinas certe sibi superfuturas provincias, si
victores Alpium iuga, ut Cimbri, vel etiam urbem, ut
Senones quondam, occuparent; unde credo percussoribus eius postea consilium natum apud tumultuantes
milites ementiendi, ipsum sibi manus intulisse nuntio
malae pugnae perterritum.

---

[1] at vero maiore, *MLP* (ad, *M.*); ad (at) vero maiora,
GTʹO; ad maiora vero *HNϛ*.
[2] reversus, *Bentley, Cannegieter*; versus, Ω.

---

[a] After his murder; probably referring to the praetorians.

out from time to time for daylight and longing for its coming.

LI. I think I may fairly attribute to mental weakness the existence of two exactly opposite faults in the same person, extreme assurance and, on the other hand, excessive timorousness. For this man, who so utterly despised the gods, was wont at the slightest thunder and lightning to shut his eyes, to muffle up his head, and if they increased, to leap from his bed and hide under it. In his journey through Sicily, though he made all manner of fun of the miracles in various places, he suddenly fled from Messana by night, panic-stricken by the smoke and roaring from Aetna's crater. Full of threats as he was also against the barbarians, when he was riding in a chariot through a narrow defile on the far side of the Rhine, and someone said that there would be no slight panic if the enemy should appear anywhere, he immediately mounted a horse and hastily returned to the bridges. Finding them crowded with camp servants and baggage, in his impatience of any delay he was passed along from hand to hand over the men's heads. Soon after, hearing of an uprising in Germany, he made preparations to flee from the city and equipped fleets for the purpose, finding comfort only in the thought that the provinces across the sea would at any rate be left him, in case the enemy should be victorious and take possession of the summits of the Alps, as the Cimbri, or even of the city, as the Senones had once done. And it was this, I think, that later inspired his assassins with the idea of pretending to the riotous soldiers [a] that he had laid hands on himself in terror at the report of a defeat.

LII. Vestitu calciatuque et cetero habitu neque patrio neque civili, ac ne virili quidem ac denique humano semper usus est. Saepe depictas gemmatasque indutus paenulas, manuleatus et armillatus in publicum processit ; aliquando sericatus et cycladatus ; ac modo in crepidis vel coturnis, modo in speculatoria caliga, nonnumquam socco muliebri ; plerumque vero aurea barba, fulmen tenens aut fuscinam aut caduceum deorum insignia, atque etiam Veneris cultu conspectus est. Triumphalem quidem ornatum etiam ante expeditionem assidue gestavit, interdum et Magni Alexandri thoracem repetitum e conditorio eius.

LIII. Ex disciplinis liberalibus minimum eruditioni, eloquentiae plurimum attendit, quamtumvis facundus et promptus, utique si perorandum in aliquem esset. Irato et verba et sententiae suppetebant, pronuntiatio quoque et vox, ut neque eodem loci prae ardore 2 consisteret et exaudiretur a procul stantibus. Peroraturus stricturum se lucubrationis suae telum minabatur, lenius comptiusque scribendi genus adeo contemnens, ut Senecam tum maxime placentem "commissiones meras" componere et "harenam esse sine calce" diceret. Solebat etiam prosperis oratorum actionibus rescribere et magnorum in senatu reorum accusationes defensionesque meditari ac, prout stilus

---

a Men were forbidden to wear silk garments ; see Tac. *Ann.* 2. 33, *ne vestis serica viros* foedaret.
b The *cyclas* was a kind of robe worn by women and embroidered with gold and purple.
c Cf. *Aug.* xviii. 1.

LII. In his clothing, his shoes, and the rest of his attire he did not follow the usage of his country and his fellow-citizens; not always even that of his sex; or in fact, that of an ordinary mortal. He often appeared in public in embroidered cloaks covered with precious stones, with a long-sleeved tunic and bracelets; sometimes in silk *a* and in a woman's robe *b*; now in slippers or buskins, again in boots, such as the emperor's body-guard wear, and at times in the low shoes which are used by females. But oftentimes he exhibited himself with a golden beard, holding in his hand a thunderbolt, a trident, or a caduceus, emblems of the gods, and even in the garb of Venus. He frequently wore the dress of a triumphing general, even before his campaign, and sometimes the breastplate of Alexander the Great, which he had taken from his sarcophagus.*c*

LIII. As regards liberal studies, he gave little attention to literature but a great deal to oratory, and he was as ready of speech and eloquent as you please, especially if he had occasion to make a charge against anyone. For when he was angry, he had an abundant flow of words and thoughts, and his voice and delivery were such that for very excitement he could not stand still and he was clearly heard by those at a distance. When about to begin an harangue, he threatened to draw the sword of his nightly labours, and he had such scorn of a polished and elegant style that he used to say that Seneca, who was very popular just then, composed "mere school exercises," and that he was "sand without lime." He had the habit too of writing replies to the successful pleas of orators and composing accusations and defences of important personages

cesserat, vel onerare sententia sua quemque vel
sublevare, equestri quoque ordine ad audiendum
invitato per edicta.

LIV. Sed et aliorum generum artes studiosissime
et diversissimas exercuit. Thraex [1] et auriga, idem
cantor atque saltator, battuebat pugnatoriis armis,
aurigabat exstructo plurifariam circo; canendi ac
saltandi voluptate ita efferebatur, ut ne publicis
quidem spectaculis temperaret quo minus et tragoedo
pronuntianti concineret et gestum histrionis quasi
2 laudans vel corrigens palam effingeret. Nec alia de
causa videtur eo die, quo periit, pervigilium indixisse
quam ut initium in scaenam prodeundi licentia temporis
auspicaretur. Saltabat autem nonnumquam etiam
noctu; et quondam tres consulares secunda vigilia in
Palatium accitos multaque et extrema metuentis super
pulpitum conlocavit, deinde [2] repente magno tibiarum
et scabellorum crepitu cum palla tunicaque talari
prosiluit ac desaltato cantico abiit. Atque hic tam
docilis ad cetera natare nesciit.

LV. Quorum vero studio teneretur, omnibus ad
insaniam favit. Mnesterem pantomimum etiam inter
spectacula osculabatur, ac si qui saltante eo vel leviter

---

[1] Thrax, Ω.
[2] deinde, *MT*; *the other mss. have* dein.

---

[a] That is, if he succeeded better in his accusation, he took
sides against the defendant, and *vice versa*, regardless of
justice.

[b] Cf. chap. xxxii. 2.

[c] A festival in honour of some god or goddess, celebrated
with feasting, dancing, and plays of all kinds.

[d] About midnight, since the night was divided into four
vigiliae.

who were brought to trial before the senate; and according as his pen had run most easily, he brought ruin or relief to each of them by his speech,[a] while he would also invite the equestrian order by proclamation to come in and hear him.

LIV. Moreover he devoted himself with much enthusiasm to arts of other kinds and of great variety, appearing as a Thracian gladiator, as a charioteer, and even as a singer and dancer, fighting with the weapons of actual warfare,[b] and driving in circuses built in various places; so carried away by his interest in singing and dancing that even at the public performances he could not refrain from singing with the tragic actor as he delivered his lines, or from openly imitating his gestures by way of praise or correction. Indeed, on the day when he was slain he seems to have ordered an all-night vigil[c] for the sole purpose of taking advantage of the licence of the occasion to make his first appearance on the stage. Sometimes he danced even at night, and once he summoned three consulars to the Palace at the close of the second watch,[d] and when they arrived in great and deathly fear, he seated them on a stage and then on a sudden burst out with a great din of flutes and clogs,[e] dressed in a cloak and a tunic reaching to his heels, and after dancing a number went off again. And yet varied as were his accomplishments, the man could not swim.

LV. Toward those to whom he was devoted his partiality became madness. He used to kiss Mnester, an actor of pantomimes, even in the theatre, and if anyone made even the slightest sound while his

[e] The *scabellum* was attached to the feet of dancers and sounded an accompaniment to their movements.

obstreperet, detrahi iussum manu sua flagellabat.
Equiti R. tumultuanti per centurionem denuntiavit,
abiret sine mora Ostiam perferretque ad Ptolemaeum
regem in Mauretaniam[1] codicillos suos; quorum
exemplum erat: "Ei quem istoc misi, neque boni
2 quicquam neque mali feceris." Thracces quosdam
Germanis corporis custodibus praeposuit. Murmil-
lonum armaturas recidit. Columbo victori, leviter
tamen saucio, venenum in plagam addidit, quod ex
eo Columbinum appellavit; sic certe inter alia
venena scriptum ab eo repertum est. Prasinae
factioni ita addictus et deditus, ut cenaret in stabulo
assidue et maneret, agitatori Eutycho comisatione
quadam in apophoretis vicies sestertium contulit.
3 Incitato equo, cuius causa pridie circenses, ne inquie-
taretur, viciniae silentium per milites indicere solebat,
praeter equile marmoreum et praesaepe eburneum
praeterque purpurea tegumenta ac monilia e gemmis
domum etiam et familiam et supellectilem dedit,
quo lautius nomine eius invitati acciperentur; consulatum quoque traditur destinasse.

LVI. Ita bacchantem atque grassantem non defuit
plerisque animus adoriri. Sed una atque altera[2]
conspiratione detecta, aliis per inopiam occasionis

---

[1] Mauritaniam, Ω.
[2] atque altera, *Ihm*; altera, *M*; et altera, *G*π*Q*; alteraque
XR.

---

a See note on chap. xxx. 3. He disliked the *murmillones*,
as the opponents of his favourites, the Thracians.

b The charioteers in the Circus were divided into four
parties, distinguished by their colours, which were red, white,
blue, and green. Domitian added two more; see Dom. vii. 1.

c The "stable" was in reality a kind of club, containing
the quarters of the drivers as well as the stalls of the horses.

d The host at a dinner party often gave gifts to his guests

favourite was dancing, he had him dragged from
his seat and scourged him with his own hand.
When a Roman knight created a disturbance, he
sent a centurion to bid him go without delay
to Ostia and carry a message for him to king
Ptolemy in Mauretania; and its purport was this:
"Do neither good nor ill to the man whom I have
sent you." He gave some Thracian gladiators command of his German body-guard. He reduced the
amount of armour of the *murmillones.*[a] When one
Columbus had won a victory, but had suffered a
slight wound, he had the place rubbed with a poison
which he henceforth called "Columbinum"; at least
that name was found included in his list of poisons.
He was so passionately devoted to the green faction [b]
that he constantly dined and spent the night in their
stable,[c] and in one of his revels with them he gave
the driver Eutychus two million sesterces in gifts.[d]
He used to send his soldiers on the day before the
games and order silence in the neighbourhood, to
prevent the horse Incitatus [e] from being disturbed.
Besides a stall of marble, a manger of ivory, purple
blankets and a collar of precious stones, he even gave
this horse a house, a troop of slaves and furniture,
for the more elegant entertainment of the guests
invited in his name; and it is also said that he
planned to make him consul.

LVI. During this frantic and riotous career several
thought of attempting his life. But when one or
two conspiracies had been detected and the rest were
waiting for a favourable opportunity, two men made

to take away with them (hence called by the Greek name
apophoreta); cf. *Aug.* lxxv.
[e] Swift, "Flyer."

cunctantibus, duo consilium communicaverunt perfeceruntque, non sine conscientia potentissimorum libertorum praefectorumque praetori; quod ipsi quoque etsi falso in quadam coniuratione quasi participes nominati, suspectos tamen se et invisos sentiebant. Nam et statim seductis magnam fecit invidiam districto gladio affirmans sponte se periturum, si et illis morte dignus videretur, nec cessavit ex eo criminari alterum alteri atque inter se omnis committere

2   Cum placuisset Palatinis ludis spectaculo egressum meridie adgredi, primas sibi partes Cassius Chaerea tribunus cohortis praetoriae depoposcit, quem Gaius seniorem iam et mollem et effeminatum denotare omni probro consuerat et modo signum petenti " Priapum " aut "Venerem " dare, modo ex aliqua causa agenti gratias osculandam manum offerre formatam commotamque in obscaenum modum.

LVII. Futurae caedis multa prodigia exstiterunt. Olympiae simulacrum Iovis, quod dissolvi transferrique Romam placuerat, tantum cachinnum repente edidit, ut machinis labefactis opifices diffugerint; supervenitque ilico quidam Cassius nomine, iussum se somnio

2   affirmans immolare taurum Iovi. Capitolium Capuae Id. Mart. de caelo tactum est, item Romae cella Palatini atriensis. Nec defuerunt qui coniectarent altero ostento periculum a custodibus domino

---

common cause and succeeded, with the connivance of his most influential freedmen and the officers of the praetorian guard; for although the charge that these last were privy to one of the former conspiracies was false, they realised that Caligula hated and feared them. In fact, he exposed them to great odium by at once taking them aside and declaring, drawn sword in hand, that he would kill himself, if they too thought he deserved death; and from that time on he never ceased accusing them one to the other and setting them all at odds.

When they had decided to attempt his life at the exhibition of the Palatine games, as he went out at noon, Cassius Chaerea, tribune of a cohort of the praetorian guard, claimed for himself the principal part; for Gaius used to taunt him, a man already well on in years, with voluptuousness and effeminacy by every form of insult. When he asked for the watchword Gaius would give him "Priapus" or "Venus," and when Chaerea had occasion to thank him for anything, he would hold out his hand to kiss, forming and moving it in an obscene fashion.[a]

LVII. His approaching murder was foretold by many prodigies. The statue of Jupiter at Olympia, which he had ordered to be taken to pieces and moved to Rome, suddenly uttered such a peal of laughter that the scaffoldings collapsed and the workmen took to their heels; and at once a man called Cassius turned up, who declared that he had been bidden in a dream to sacrifice a bull to Jupiter. The Capitol at Capua was struck by lightning on the Ides of March, and also the room of the doorkeeper of the Palace at Rome. Some inferred from the latter omen that danger was threatened to the owner at the hands of   Mar. 15.

portendi, altero caedem rursus insignem, qualis
eodem die facta quondam fuisset. Consulenti quoque
de genitura sua Sulla mathematicus certissimam
3 necem appropinquare affirmavit. Monuerunt et
Fortunae Antiatinae, ut a Cassio caveret; qua causa
ille Cassium Longinum Asiae tum proconsulem
occidendum delegaverat, inmemor Chaeream Cassium
nominari. Pridie quam periret, somniavit consistere
se in caelo iuxta solium Iovis impulsumque ab eo
dextri pedis pollice et in terras praecipitatum.
Prodigiorum loco habita sunt etiam, quae forte illo
4 ipso die paulo prius acciderant. Sacrificans respersus
est phoenicopteri sanguine ; et pantomimus Mnester
tragoediam saltavit, quam olim Neoptolemus tragoedus ludis, quibus rex Macedonum Philippus occisus
est, egerat ; et cum in Laureolo mimo, in quo actor [1]
proripiens se ruina sanguinem vomit, plures secundarum certatim experimentum artis darent, cruore
scaena abundavit. Parabatur et in noctem spectaculum, quo argumenta inferorum per Aegyptios et
Aethiopas explicarentur.

LVIII. VIIII. Kal. Febr. hora fere septima cunctatus an ad prandium surgeret marcente adhuc
stomacho pridiani cibi onere, tandem suadentibus
amicis egressus est. Cum in crypta, per quam trans-

---

[1] auctor, ϛ ; actor, Ω.

---

[a] Referring of course to the assassination of Julius Caesar.

[b] See chap. xxii. 3.

[c] It was called Cinyras, and its story is told by Ovid,
Metam. 10. 298 ff.

[d] Its name was derived from a famous highwayman ; cf.
Juv. 8. 186.

[e] The actors *secundarum partium* entertained the spectators
after a play by imitating the actions of the star.

his guards; and from the former, the murder of a
second distinguished personage, such as had taken
place long before on that same day.[a] The soothsayer Sulla too, when Gaius consulted him about his
horoscope, declared that inevitable death was close
at hand. The lots of Fortune at Antium warned
him to beware of Cassius, and he accordingly ordered
the death of Cassius Longinus, who was at the time
proconsul of Asia, forgetting that the family name
of Chaerea was Cassius. The day before he was
killed he dreamt that he stood in heaven beside the
throne of Jupiter and that the god struck him with
the toe of his right foot and hurled him to earth.
Some things which had happened on that very day
shortly before he was killed were also regarded as
portents. As he was sacrificing, he was sprinkled
with the blood of a flamingo,[b] and the pantomimic
actor Mnester danced a tragedy[c] which the tragedian
Neoptolemus had acted years before during the
games at which Philip king of the Macedonians was
assassinated. In a farce called "Laureolus,"[d] in
which the chief actor falls as he is making his escape
and vomits blood, several understudies[e] so vied with
one another in giving evidence of their proficiency
that the stage swam in blood. A nocturnal performance besides was rehearsing, in which scenes from
the lower world were represented by Egyptians and
Aethiopians.

LVIII. On the ninth day before the Kalends of
February at about the seventh hour he hesitated
whether or not to get up for luncheon, since his
stomach was still disordered from excess of food
on the day before, but at length he came out at the
persuasion of his friends. In the covered passage

Jan. 24,
41 A.D.

eundum erat, pueri nobiles ex Asia ad edendas in
scaena operas evocati praepararentur, ut eos inspiceret
hortareturque restitit, ac nisi princeps gregis algere
se diceret, redire ac repraesentare spectaculum voluit.

2 Duplex dehinc fama est : alii tradunt adloquenti
pueros a tergo Chaeream cervicem gladio caesim
graviter percussisse praemissa voce : " Hoc age ! "
dehinc Cornelium Sabinum, alterum e coniuratis,
tribunum ex adverso traiecisse pectus ; alii Sabinum
summota per conscios centuriones turba signum more
militiae petisse et Gaio " Iovem " dante Chaeream
exclamasse : " Accipe ratum ! " respicientique maxillam

3 ictu discidisse.   Iacentem contractisque membris
clamitantem se vivere ceteri vulneribus triginta
confecerunt ; nam signum erat omnium : " Repete ! "
Quidam etiam per obscaena ferrum adegerunt.   Ad
primum tumultum lecticarii cum asseribus in auxilium
accucurrerunt, mox Germani corporis custodes, ac nonnullos ex percussoribus, quosdam etiam senatores in-
noxios interemerunt.

LIX. Vixit annis viginti novem, imperavit triennio
et decem mensibus diebusque octo.[1]   Cadaver eius
clam in hortos Lamianos asportatum et tumultuario
rogo semiambustum levi caespite obrutum est, postea
per sorores ab exsilio reversas erutum et crematum

---

[1] viii, **ΧΥ** ; vii, *G*.

---

[a] Part of the ritual at a sacrifice.   The slayer raised his
axe with the question " *Agone?* "   " Shall I do the deed (*i.e.*,
strike) ? "   To which the priest replied " *Hoc age.*"   Cf. *Galba*,
xx. 1, *ut hoc agerent ac ferirent*.   Chaerea addressed himself.

[b] Another formula " Receive the fulfilment of your omen ",
i.e., in naming Jupiter, the god of the thunderbolt and sudden
death.   " Qui legendum vidit *iratum*, verum vidit : hoc est
aliquid Latine dicere, cum alterum nihil sit," Gronovius.

[c] With which they carried his litter.

through which he had to pass, some boys of good birth, who had been summoned from Asia to appear on the stage, were rehearsing their parts, and he stopped to watch and encourage them; and had not the leader of the troop complained that he had a chill, he would have returned and had the performance given at once. From this point there are two versions of the story : some say that as he was talking with the boys, Chaerea came up behind, and gave him a deep cut in the neck, having first cried, "Take that," and that then the tribune Cornelius Sabinus, who was the other conspirator and faced Gaius, stabbed him in the breast. Others say that Sabinus, after getting rid of the crowd through centurions who were in the plot, asked for the watchword, as soldiers do, and that when Gaius gave him "Jupiter," he cried "So be it," [b] and as Gaius looked around, he split his jawbone with a blow of his sword. As he lay upon the ground and with writhing limbs called out that he still lived, the others dispatched him with thirty wounds; for the general signal was "Strike again." Some even thrust their swords through his privates. At the beginning of the disturbance his bearers ran to his aid with their poles, [c] and presently the Germans of his body-guard, and they slew several of his assassins, as well as some inoffensive senators.

LIX. He lived twenty-nine years and ruled three years, ten months and eight days. His body was conveyed secretly to the gardens of the Lamian family, where it was partly consumed on a hastily erected pyre and buried beneath a light covering of turf ; later his sisters on their return from exile dug it up, cremated it, and consigned it to

sepultumque. Satis constat, prius quam id fieret, hortorum custodes umbris inquietatos; in ea quoque domo, in qua occubuerit, nullam noctem sine aliquo terrore transactam, donec ipsa domus incendio consumpta sit. Periit una et uxor Caesonia gladio a centurione confossa et filia parieti inlisa.

LX. Condicionem temporum illorum etiam per haec aestimare quivis possit. Nam neque caede vulgata statim creditum est, fuitque suspicio ab ipso Gaio famam caedis simulatam et emissam, ut eo pacto hominum erga se mentes deprehenderet; neque coniurati cuiquam imperium destinaverunt; et senatus in asserenda libertate adeo consensit, ut consules primo non in curiam, quia Iulia vocabatur, sed in Capitolium convocarent, quidam vero sententiae loco abolendam Caesarum memoriam ac diruenda templa censuerint. Observatum autem notatumque est in primis Caesares omnes, quibus Gai praenomen fuerit, ferro perisse, iam inde ab eo, qui Cinnanis temporibus sit occisus.

---

^a Gaius Julius Caesar Strabo, slain in 87 B.C. But the Dictator's father died a natural death, as did also Gaius Caesar, grandson of Augustus; see *Aug.* lxv. 1.

the tomb. Before this was done, it is well known that the caretakers of the gardens were disturbed by ghosts, and that in the house where he was slain not a night passed without some fearsome apparition, until at last the house itself was destroyed by fire. With him died his wife Caesonia, stabbed with a sword by a centurion, while his daughter's brains were dashed out against a wall.

LX. One may form an idea of the state of those times by what followed. Not even after the murder was made known was it at once believed that he was dead, but it was suspected that Gaius himself had made up and circulated the report, to find out by that means how men felt towards him. The conspirators too had not agreed on a successor, and the senate was so unanimously in favour of re-establishing the republic that the consuls called the first meeting, not in the senate house, because it had the name Julia, but in the Capitol; while some in expressing their views proposed that the memory of the Caesars be done away with and their temples destroyed. Men further observed and commented on the fact that all the Caesars whose forename was Gaius perished by the sword, beginning with the one who was slain in the times of Cinna.[a]

STEMMA OF THE JULIO-CLAUDIAN FAMILY

A

C. Iulius Caesar = Aurelia

Cornelia = DIVUS IULIUS
Iulia (3) = Cn. Pompeius Magnus

Iulia (1) = M. Atius Balbus
Atia = C. Octavius = Ancharia
Octavia maior

Iulia (2)

DIVUS AUGUSTUS = Scribonia — Livia Drusilla (see B)
Iulia (4) = M. Agrippa

Octavia minor = C. Marcellus and M. Antonius

Antonia maior = L. Domitius

Antonia minor = Drusus (1) (see B)

M. Marcellus

Marcella maior = M. Agrippa and Iullus Antonius

Marcella minor

Domitia Lepida = M. Valerius
Valeria Messalina = Divus Claudius (see B)

Domitia

C. Caesar

L. Caesar

Iulia (5) = L. Aemilius Paulus

Agrippina (2) = Germanicus (see B)

Agrippa Postumus

Agrippina (3) = Cn. Domitius, dau. of Germanicus

Poppaea Sabina = NERO (2)

Claudia Augusta

Drusilla, dau. of Germanicus = M. Aemilius Lepidus

Aemilia Lepida = Appius Iunius Silanus

M. Iunius Silanus

L. Iunius Silanus

Iunia Calvina

B

Divus Augustus = Livia Drusilla = Tib. Claudius Nero
(*Tib.* iv. 3)

Drusus (1) = Antonia minor

DIVUS CLAUDIUS

Agrippina (2) = Germanicus

Livilla
Drusus (2)

Nero (1) = Iulia (6)

Drusus = Aemilia Lepida

C. CAESAR CALIGULA

Agrippina (3) = Cn. Domitius

NERO (2)

Drusilla = L. Cassius Longinus and
M. Aemilius Lepidus

Iulia Livilla = M. Vinicius

Agrippina * (1) = TIBERIUS

Livilla = Drusus (2)

Tiberius

Iulia (6) = Nero (1)
and C. Rubellius
Blandus

Rubellius Plautus

* Vipsania Agrippina, daughter of M. Agrippa by his first wife Pomponia: divorced by Tiberius at the order of Augustus,
who desired him to marry Julia.

Printed in Great Britain by
Fletcher & Son Ltd, Norwich

THE LOEB CLASSICAL LIBRARY

VOLUMES ALREADY PUBLISHED

Latin Authors

AMMIANUS MARCELLINUS. Translated by J. C. Rolfe. 3 Vols.

APULEIUS: THE GOLDEN ASS (METAMORPHOSES). W. Adlington (1566). Revised by S. Gaselee.

ST. AUGUSTINE: CITY OF GOD. 7 Vols. Vol. I. G. E. McCracken. Vol. II. and VII. W. M. Green. Vol. III. D. Wiesen. Vol. IV. P. Levine. Vol. V. E. M. Sanford and W. M. Green. Vol. VI. W. C. Greene.

ST. AUGUSTINE, CONFESSIONS OF. W. Watts (1631). 2 Vols.

ST. AUGUSTINE, SELECT LETTERS. J. H. Baxter.

AUSONIUS. H. G. Evelyn White. 2 Vols.

BEDE. J. E. King. 2 Vols.

BOETHIUS: TRACTS and DE CONSOLATIONE PHILOSOPHIAE. REV. H. F. Stewart and E. K. Rand. Revised by S. J. Tester.

CAESER: ALEXANDRIAN, AFRICAN and SPANISH WARS. A. G. Way.

CAESER: CIVIL WARS. A. G. Peskett.

CAESER: GALLIC WAR. H. J. Edwards.

CATO: DE RE RUSTICA; VARRO: DE RE RUSTICA. H. B. Ash and W. D. Hooper.

CATULLUS. F. W. Cornish; TIBULLUS. J. B. Postgate; PERVIGILIUM VENERIS. J. W. Mackail.

CELSUS: DE MEDICINA. W. G. Spencer. 3 Vols.

CICERO: BRUTUS, and ORATOR. G. L. Hendrickson and H. M. Hubbell.

[CICERO]: AD HERENNIUM. H. Caplan.

CICERO: DE ORATORE, etc. 2 Vols. Vol. I. DE ORATORE, BOOKS I. and II. E. W. Sutton and H. Rackham. Vol. II. DE ORATORE, Book III. De Fato; Paradoxa Stoicorum; De Partitione Oratoria. H. Rackham.

CICERO: DE FINIBUS. H. Rackham.

CICERO: DE INVENTIONE, etc. H. M. Hubbell.

CICERO: DE NATURA DEORUM and ACADEMICA. H. Rackham.

CICERO: DE OFFICIIS. Walter Miller.

CICERO: DE REPUBLICA and DE LEGIBUS: SOMNIUM SCIPIONIS. Clinton W. Keyes.

1

CICERO: DE SENECTUTE, DE AMICITIA, DE DIVINATIONE. W. A. Falconer.

CICERO: IN CATILINAM, PRO FLACCO, PRO MURENA, PRO SULLA. New version by C. Macdonald.

CICERO: LETTERS TO ATTICUS. E. O. Winstedt. 3 Vols.

CICERO: LETTERS TO HIS FRIENDS. W. Glynn Williams, M. Cary, M. Henderson. 4 Vols.

CICERO: PHILIPPICS. W. C. A. Ker.

CICERO: PRO ARCHIA POST REDITUM, DE DOMO, DE HARUSPICUM RESPONSIS, PRO PLANCIO. N. H. Watts.

CICERO: PRO CAECINA, PRO LEGE MANILIA, PRO CLUENTIO, PRO RABIRIO. H. Grose Hodge.

CICERO: PRO CAELIO, DE PROVINCIIS CONSULARIBUS, PRO BALBO. R. Gardner.

CICERO: PRO MILONE, IN PISONEM, PRO SCAURO, PRO FONTEIO, PRO RABIRIO POSTUMO, PRO MARCELLO, PRO LIGARIO, PRO REGE DEIOTARO. N. H. Watts.

CICERO: PRO QUINCTIO, PRO ROSCIO AMERINO, PRO ROSCIO COMOEDO, CONTRA RULLUM. J. H. Freese.

CICERO: PRO SESTIO, IN VATINIUM. R. Gardner.

CICERO: TUSCULAN DISPUTATIONS. J. E. King.

CICERO: VERRINE ORATIONS. L. H. G. Greenwood. 2 Vols.

CLAUDIAN. M. Platnauer. 2 Vols.

COLUMELLA: DE RE RUSTICA. DE ARBORIBUS. H. B. Ash, E. S. Forster and E. Heffner. 3 Vols.

CURTIUS, Q.: HISTORY OF ALEXANDER. J. C. Rolfe. 2 Vols.

FLORUS. E. S. Forster; and CORNELIUS NEPOS. J. C. Rolfe.

FRONTINUS: STRATAGEMS and AQUEDUCTS. C. E. Bennett and M. B. McElwain.

FRONTO: CORRESPONDENCE. C. R. Haines. 2 Vols.

GELLIUS, J. C. Rolfe. 3 Vols.

HORACE: ODES AND EPODES. C. E. Bennett.

HORACE: SATIRES, EPISTLES, ARS POETICA. H. R. Fairclough.

JEROME: SELECTED LETTERS. F. A. Wright.

JUVENAL and PERSIUS. G. G. Ramsay.

LIVY. B. O. Foster, F. G. Moore, Evan T. Sage, and A. C. Schlesinger and R. M. Geer (General Index). 14 Vols.

LUCAN. J. D. Duff.

LUCRETIUS. W. H. D. Rouse. Revised by M. F. Smith.

MANILIUS. G. P. Goold.

MARTIAL. W. C. A. Ker. 2 Vols.

MINOR LATIN POETS: from PUBLILIUS SYRUS TO RUTILIUS NAMATIANUS, including GRATTIUS, CALPURNIUS SICULUS, NEMESIANUS, AVIANUS, and others with "Aetna" and the "Phoenix." J. Wight Duff and Arnold M. Duff.

OVID: THE ART OF LOVE and OTHER POEMS. J. H. Mosley. Revised by G. P. Goold.

OVID: FASTI. Sir James G. Frazer.

OVID: HEROIDES and AMORES. Grant Showerman. Revised by G. P. Goold

OVID: METAMORPHOSES. F. J. Miller. 2 Vols. Vol. 1 revised by G. P. Goold.

OVID: TRISTIA and EX PONTO. A. L. Wheeler.

PERSIUS. Cf. JUVENAL.

PETRONIUS. M. Heseltine; SENECA; APOCOLOCYNTOSIS. W. H. D. Rouse.

PHAEDRUS AND BABRIUS (Greek). B. E. Perry.

PLAUTUS. Paul Nixon. 5 Vols.

PLINY: LETTERS, PANEGYRICUS. Betty Radice. 2 Vols.

PLINY: NATURAL HISTORY. Vols. I.–V. and IX. H. Rackham. VI.–VIII. W. H. S. Jones. X. D. E. Eichholz. 10 Vols.

PROPERTIUS. H. E. Butler.

PRUDENTIUS. H. J. Thomson. 2 Vols.

QUINTILIAN. H. E. Butler. 4 Vols.

REMAINS OF OLD LATIN. E. H. Warmington. 4 Vols. Vol. I. (ENNIUS AND CAECILIUS.) Vol. II. (LIVIUS, NAEVIUS, PACUVIUS, ACCIUS.) Vol. III. (LUCILIUS and LAWS OF XII TABLES.) Vol. IV. (ARCHAIC INSCRIPTIONS.)

SALLUST. J. C. Rolfe.

SCRIPTORES HISTORIAE AUGUSTAE. D. Magie. 3 Vols.

SENECA, THE ELDER: CONTROVERSIAE, SUASORIAE. M. Winterbottom. 2 Vols.

SENECA: APOCOLOCYNTOSIS. Cf. PETRONIUS.

SENECA: EPISTULAE MORALES. R. M. Gummere. 3 Vols.

SENECA: MORAL ESSAYS. J. W. Basore. 3 Vols.

SENECA: TRAGEDIES. F. J. Miller. 2 Vols.

SENECA: NATURALES QUAESTIONES. T. H. Corcoran. 2 Vols.

SIDONIUS: POEMS and LETTERS. W. B. Anderson. 2 Vols.

SILIUS ITALICUS. J. D. Duff. 2 Vols.

STATIUS. J. H. Mozley. 2 Vols.

SUETONIUS. J. C. Rolfe. 2 Vols.

TACITUS: DIALOGUS. Sir Wm. Peterson. AGRICOLA and GERMANIA. Maurice Hutton. Revised by M. Winterbottom, R. M. Ogilvie, E. H. Warmington.

TACITUS: HISTORIES AND ANNALS. C. H. Moore and J. Jackson. 4 Vols.

TERENCE. John Sargeaunt. 2 Vols.

TERTULLIAN: APOLOGIA and DE SPECTACULIS. T. R. Glover. MINUCIUS FELIX. G. H. Rendall.

VALERIUS FLACCUS. J. H. Mozley.

VARRO: DE LINGUA LATINA. R. G. Kent. 2 Vols.

VELLEIUS PATERCULUS and RES GESTAE DIVI AUGUSTI. F. W. Shipley.

VIRGIL. H. R. Fairclough. 2 Vols.

VITRUVIUS: DE ARCHITECTURA. F. Granger. 2 Vols.

Greek Authors

ACHILLES TATIUS. S. Gaselee.

AELIAN: ON THE NATURE OF ANIMALS. A. F. Scholfield. 3 Vols.

AENEAS TACTICUS, ASCLEPIODOTUS and ONASANDER. The Illinois Greek Club.

AESCHINES. C. D. Adams.

AESCHYLUS. H. Weir Smyth. 2 Vols.

ALCIPHRON, AELIAN, PHILOSTRATUS: LETTERS. A. R. Benner and F. H. Fobes.

ANDOCIDES, ANTIPHON, Cf. MINOR ATTIC ORATORS.

APOLLODORUS. Sir James G. Frazer. 2 Vols.

APOLLONIUS RHODIUS. R. C. Seaton.

THE APOSTOLIC FATHERS. Kirsopp Lake. 2 Vols.

APPIAN: ROMAN HISTORY. Horace White. 4 Vols.

ARATUS. Cf. CALLIMACHUS.

ARISTIDES: ORATIONS. C. A. Behr. Vol. I.

ARISTOPHANES. Benjamin Bickley Rogers. 3 Vols. Verse trans.

ARISTOTLE: ART OF RHETORIC. J. H. Freese.

ARISTOTLE: ATHENIAN CONSTITUTION, EUDEMIAN ETHICS, VICES AND VIRTUES. H. Rackham.

ARISTOTLE: GENERATION OF ANIMALS. A. L. Peck.

ARISTOTLE: HISTORIA ANIMALIUM. A. L. Peck. Vols I.–II.

ARISTOTLE: METAPHYSICS. H. Tredennick. 2 Vols.

ARISTOTLE: METEOROLOGICA. H. D. P. Lee.

ARISTOTLE: MINOR WORKS. W. S. Hett. On Colours, On Things Heard, On Physiognomies, On Plants, On Marvellous Things Heard, Mechanical Problems, On Indivisible Lines, On Situations and Names of Winds, On Melissus, Xenophanes, and Gorgias.

ARISTOTLE: NICOMACHEAN ETHICS. H. Rackham.

ARISTOTLE: OECONOMICA and MAGNA MORALIA. G. C. Armstrong; (with METAPHYSICS, Vol. II.).

ARISTOTLE: ON THE HEAVENS. W. K. C. Guthrie.

ARISTOTLE: ON THE SOUL. PARVA NATURALIA. ON BREATH. W. S. Hett.

ARISTOTLE: CATEGORIES, ON INTERPRETATION, PRIOR ANALYTICS. H. P. Cooke and H. Tredennick.

ARISTOTLE: POSTERIOR ANALYTICS, TOPICS. H. Tredennick and E. S. Forster.

ARISTOTLE: ON SOPHISTICAL REFUTATIONS.
On Coming to be and Passing Away, On the Cosmos. E. S. Forster and D. J. Furley.

ARISTOTLE: PARTS OF ANIMALS. A. L. Peck; MOTION AND PROGRESSION OF ANIMALS. E. S. Forster.

Aristotle: Physics. Rev. P. Wicksteed and F. M. Cornford. 2 Vols.
Aristotle: Poetics and Longinus. W. Hamilton Fyfe; Demetrius on Style. W. Rhys Roberts.
Aristotle: Politics. H. Rackham.
Aristotle: Problems. W. S. Hett. 2 Vols.
Aristotle: Rhetorica Ad Alexandrum (with Problems. Vol. II). H. Rackham.
Arrian: History of Alexander and Indica. 2 Vols. Vol. I. P. Brunt. Vol. II. Rev. E. Iliffe Robson.
Athenaeus: Deipnosophistae. C. B. Gulick. 7 Vols.
Babrius and Phaedrus (Latin). B. E. Perry.
St. Basil: Letters. R. J. Deferrair. 4 Vols.
Callimachus: Fragments. C. A. Trypanis. Musaeus: Hero and Leander. T. Gelzer and C. Whitman.
Callimachus, Hymns and Epigrams, and Lycophron. A. W. Mair; Aratus. G. R. Mair.
Clement of Alexandria. Rev. G. W. Butterworth.
Colluthus. Cf. Oppian.
Daphnis and Chloe. Thornley's Translation revised by J. M. Edmonds: and Parthenius. S. Gaselee.
Demosthenes I.: Olynthiacs, Philippics and Minor Orations. I.–XVII. and XX. J. H. Vince.
Demosthenes II.: De Corona and De Falsa Legatione. C. A. Vince and J. H. Vince.
Demosthenes III.: Meidias, Androtion, Aristocrates, Timocrates and Aristogeiton, I. and II. J. H. Vince.
Demosthenes IV.–VI.: Private Orations and In Neaeram. A. T. Murray.
Demosthenes VII: Funeral Speech, Erotic Essay, Exordia and Letters. N. W. and N. J. DeWitt.
Dio Cassius: Roman History. E. Cary. 9 Vols.
Dio Chrysostom. J. W. Cohoon and H. Lamar Crosby. 5 Vols.
Diodorus Siculus. 12 Vols. Vols. I.–VI. C. H. Oldfather. Vol. VII. C. L. Sherman. Vol. VIII. C. B. Welles. Vols. IX. and X. R. M. Geer. Vol. XI. F. Walton. Vol. XII. F. Walton. General Index. R. M. Geer.
Diogenes Laertius. R. D. Hicks. 2 Vols. New Introduction by H. S. Long.
Dionysius of Halicarnassus: Roman Antiquities. Spelman's translation revised by E. Cary. 7 Vols.
Dionysius of Halicarnassus: Critical Essays. S. Usher. 2 Vols.
Epictetus. W. A. Oldfather. 2 Vols.
Euripides. A. S. Way. 4 Vols. Verse trans.
Eusebius: Ecclesiastical History. Kirsopp Lake and J. E. L. Oulton. 2 Vols.

GALEN: ON THE NATURAL FACULTIES. A. J. Brock.

THE GREEK ANTHOLOGY. W. R. Paton. 5 Vols.

GREEK ELEGY AND IAMBUS with the ANACREONTEA. J. M. Edmonds. 2 Vols.

THE GREEK BUCOLIC POETS (THEOCRITUS, BION, MOSCHUS). J. M. Edmonds.

GREEK MATHEMATICAL WORKS. Ivor Thomas. 2 Vols.

HERODES. Cf. THEOPHRASTUS: CHARACTERS.

HERODIAN. C. R. Whittaker. 2 Vols.

HERODOTUS. A. D. Godley. 4 Vols.

HESIOD AND THE HOMERIC HYMNS. H. G. Evelyn White.

HIPPOCRATES and the FRAGMENTS OF HERACLEITUS. W. H. S. Jones and E. T. Withington. 4 Vols.

HOMER: ILIAD. A. T. Murray. 2 Vols.

HOMER: ODYSSEY. A. T. Murray. 2 Vols.

ISAEUS. E. W. Forster.

ISOCRATES. George Norlin and LaRue Van Hook. 3 Vols.

[ST. JOHN DAMASCENE]: BARLAAM AND IOASAPH. Rev. G. R. Woodward, Harold Mattingly and D. M. Lang.

JOSEPHUS. 9 Vols. Vols. I.–IV. H. Thackeray. Vol. V. H. Thackeray and R. Marcus. Vols. VI.–VII. R. Marcus. Vol. VIII. R. Marcus and Allen Wikgren. Vol. IX. L. H. Feldman.

JULIAN. Wilmer Cave Wright. 3 Vols.

LIBANIUS. A. F. Norman. Vols. I.–II.

LUCIAN. 8 Vols. Vols. I.–V. A. M. Harmon. Vol. VI. K. Kilburn. Vols. VII.–VIII. M. D. Macleod.

LYCOPHRON. Cf. CALLIMACHUS.

LYRA GRAECA. J. M. Edmonds. 3 Vols.

LYSIAS. W. R. M. Lamb.

MANETHO. W. G. Waddell: PTOLEMY: TETRABIBLOS. F. E. Robbins.

MARCUS AURELIUS. C. R. Haines.

MENANDER. F. G. Allison.

MINOR ATTIC ORATORS (ANTIPHON, ANDOCIDES, LYCURGUS, DEMADES, DINARCHUS, HYPERIDES). K. J. Maidment and J. O. Burtt. 2 Vols.

MUSAEUS: HEOR AND LEANDER. Cf. CALLIMACHUS.

NONNOS: DIONYSIACA. W. H. D. Rouse. 3 Vols.

OPPIAN, COLLUTHUS, TRYPHIODORUS. A. W. Mair.

PAPYRI. NON-LITERARY SELECTIONS. A. S. Hunt and C. C. Edgar. 2 Vols. LITERARY SELECTIONS (Poetry). D. L. Page.

PARTHENIUS. Cf. DAPHNIS and CHLOE.

PAUSANIAS: DESCRIPTION OF GREECE. W. H. S. Jones. 4 Vols. and Companion Vol. arranged by R. E. Wycherley.

PHILO. 10 Vols. Vols. I.–V. F. H. Colson and Rev. G. H. Whitaker. Vols. VI.–IX. F. H. Colson. Vol. X. F. H. Colson and the Rev. J. W. Earp.

PHILO: two supplementary Vols. (*Translation only.*) Ralph Marcus.

PHILOSTRATUS: THE LIFE OF APOLLONIUS OF TYANA. F. C. Conybeare. 2 Vols.

PHILOSTRATUS: IMAGINES; CALLISTRATUS: DESCRIPTIONS. A. Fairbanks.

PHILOSTRATUS and EUNAPIUS: LIVES OF THE SOPHISTS. Wilmer Cave Wright.

PINDAR. Sir J. E. Sandys.

PLATO: CHARMIDES, ALCIBIADES, HIPPARCHUS, THE LOVERS, THEAGES, MINOS and EPINOMIS. W. R. M. Lamb.

PLATO: CRATYLUS, PARMENIDES, GREATER HIPPIAS, LESSER HIPPIAS. H. N. Fowler.

PLATO: EUTHYPHRO, APOLOGY, CRITO, PHAEDO, PHAEDRUS, H. N. Fowler.

PLATO: LACHES, PROTAGORAS, MENO, EUTHYDEMUS. W. R. M. Lamb.

PLATO: LAWS. Rev. R. G. Bury. 2 Vols.

PLATO: LYSIS, SYMPOSIUM, GORGIAS. W. R. M. Lamb.

PLATO: Republic. Paul Shorey. 2 Vols.

PLATO: STATESMAN, PHILEBUS. H. N. Fowler; Ion. W. R. M. Lamb.

PLATO: THEAETETUS and SOPHIST. H. N. Fowler.

PLATO: TIMAEUS, CRITIAS, CLITOPHO, MENEXENUS, EPISTULAE. Rev. R. G. Bury.

PLOTINUS: A. H. Armstrong. Vols. I.–III.

PLUTARCH: MORALIA. 17 Vols. Vols. I.–V. F. C. Babbitt. Vol. VI. W. C. Helmbold. Vols. VII. and XIV. P. H. De Lacy and B. Einarson. Vol. VIII. P. A. Clement and H. B. Hoffleit. Vol. IX. E. L. Minar, Jr., F. H. Sandbach, W. C. Helmbold. Vol. X. H. N. Fowler. Vol. XI. L. Pearson and F. H. Sandbach. Vol. XII. H. Cherniss and W. C. Helmbold. Vol. XIII 1–2. H. Cherniss. Vol. XV. F. H. Sandbach.

PLUTARCH: THE PARALLEL LIVES. B. Perrin. 11 Vols.

POLYBIUS. W. R. Paton. 6 Vols.

PROCOPIUS: HISTORY OF THE WARS. H. B. Dewing. 7 Vols.

PTOLEMY: TETRABIBLOS. Cf. MANETHO.

QUINTUS SMYRNAEUS. A. S. Way. Verse trans.

SEXTUS EMPIRICUS. Rev. R. G. Bury. 4 Vols.

SOPHOCLES. F. Storr. 2 Vols. Verse trans.

STRABO: GEOGRAPHY. Horace L. Jones. 8 Vols.

THEOPHRASTUS: CHARACTERS. J. M. Edmonds. HERODES, etc. A. D. Knox.

THEOPHRASTUS: ENQUIRY INTO PLANTS. Sir Arthur Hort, Bart. 2 Vols.

THEOPHRASTUS: DE CAUSIS PLANTARUM. G. K. K. Link and B. Einarson. 3 Vols. Vol. I.

THUCYDIDES. C. F. Smith. 4 Vols.

TRYPHIODORUS. Cf. OPPIAN.

XENOPHON: CYROPAEDIA. Walter Miller. 2 Vols.

XENOPHON: HELLENICA. C. L. Brownson. 2 Vols.

XENOPHON: ANABASIS. C. L. Brownson.

XENOPHON: MEMORABILIA AND OECONOMICUS. E. C. Marchant. SYMPOSIUM AND APOLOGY. O. J. Todd.

XENOPHON: SCRIPTA MINORA. E. C. Marchant. CONSTITUTION OF THE ATHENIANS (Athenians.) G. W. Bowersock